Instructor's Manual

An Introduction to

Critical Reading

SIXTH EDITION

LEAH McCRANEY
University of Alabama at Birmingham

THOMSON ™

WADSWORTH

Australia·Brazil·Canada·Mexico·Singapore·Spain·UnitedKingdom·United States

Instructor's Manual
An Introduction to Critical Reading, Sixth Edition
Leah McCraney

Publisher: *Michael Rosenberg*
Acquisitions Editor: *Stephen Dalphin*
Development Editor: *Cathy Richard Dodson*
Editorial Assistant: *Cheryl Forman*
Technology Project Manager: *Joe Gallagher*
Managing Marketing Manager: *Mandee Eckersley*
Senior Marketing Assistant: *Dawn Giovanniello*

Associate Marketing Communications Manager: *Patrick Rooney*
Associate Project Manager, Editorial Production: *Sarah Sherman*
Print Buyer: *Betsy Donaghey*
Production Service/Compositor: *International Typesetting and Compositie*
Cover Designer: *Gina Petti*
Printer: *P.A. Hutchison*

Cover art: *Summer Garden,* 1989 by Larusdottir, Karolina (b.1944)
Private Collection © Noel Oddy Fine Art, Bridgeman Art Library.

Thomson Higher Education
25 Thomson Place
Boston, MA 02210-1202
USA

For more information about our products, contact us at:
Thomson Learning Academic Resource Center
1-800-423-0563

For permission to use material from this text or product, submit
a request online at **http://www.thomsonrights.com**
Any additional questions about permissions can be submitted
by e-mail to **thomsonrights@thomson.com**

Printed in the United States of America.
1 2 3 4 5 6 7 09 08 07 06

ISBN 1-4130-1622-7

Instructor's Manual

An Introduction to

Critical Reading

Contents

An Invitation to
Teach Critical Reading

An Introduction to Critical Reading and this instructor's manual recommend a unique and exciting system for teaching developmental reading to college students. This system is based on three fundamental principals:

1. Reading programs should have as their primary goal the teaching of *critical* reading.
2. A holistic, interactive approach is the most effective method of teaching students to read critically.
3. Critical reading is best learned by working with college-level materials from several genres.

While many teachers of reading share these principles, textbooks rarely reflect them. Developmental reading textbooks tend to approach reading as a series of individually developed skills (building vocabulary, identifying main points, locating supporting details, etc.). Typically, the majority of their pages are devoted to isolating and explaining various skills. These discussions are often followed by a short essay or two and some questions designed to help students practice the skills that were presented in the chapter. While the discussions present useful information, they also encourage students to see reading as a set of separate (albeit related) skills. They may even teach students to view the skills taught as applicable primarily to their academic reading. The method of teaching developmental reading reflected in *An Introduction to Critical Reading* inverts the traditional approach. Students do not study the *skills*. Instead, with the guidance of the instructor, they learn and develop the skills they need to read critically while they read college-level material from four genres: poetry, fiction, essays, and textbook chapters.

Literature is rarely included in traditional developmental reading textbooks. This omission may be the result of a perception that having students read and analyze literature means one must "teach literature." Certainly, this is not the case. In literature courses, students read texts to learn about specific aspects of literature; in developmental courses, students read literature to improve their critical reading skills. Reading students do analyze and interpret literature, but their analysis and interpretation is not nearly as detailed or "literary" as would be expected in a literature class. While literature students study a wide variety of literary elements, reading students do not. They are taught a few literary terms, but the majority of these terms denote elements that are common in nonliterary writing as well as everyday speech (metaphor, simile, paradox, irony, etc.). The pieces studied in a literature course are chosen based on their usefulness in furthering students' understanding of devices, styles, periods, movements, themes, or authors. The texts in a developmental course are chosen based on their accessibility and their ability to stimulate critical thinking (the same criteria used in the selection of nonliterary pieces).

Developmental reading textbooks may have excluded literature because of the assumption that students need to master "practical" reading before they attempt literary reading. Actually, developmental students need to read and analyze literature *before* they move on to nonliterary texts. This approach helps counter the resistance that some students feel toward taking a developmental reading course. Their resistance usually stems from anger and/or fear. Students who are hostile often believe that the course will be a waste of their time, energy, and money; students who are afraid usually fear that they lack the ability to develop the skills they need. A developmental reading course that begins with literature immediately challenges their suppositions. Literature encourages the reader's personal involvement in a way that nonliterary pieces often do not.

While essays and textbooks communicate information, literature is designed to tell readers about an experience *and* to have them participate in it. To achieve this end, literature appeals to readers' senses, emotions, and imagination as well as their intellect. This multifaceted appeal generally makes literature accessible to a broad population of readers:

- *Intellect.* The ideas presented in literature reflect the human experience and are usually within the intellectual grasp of adult readers.

- *Imagination.* All readers have some degree of imagination, and it is frequently stimulated (and enhanced) by literature.

- *Emotions.* Readers, having experienced feelings similar to the ones evoked by a piece of literature, are able to relate to most pieces of literature on an emotional level. (Human emotions can be classified in five categories: gladness, sadness, shame, anger, and fear. Table 1 in Appendix 2 of this manual is a "Categories of Feelings" chart that illustrates this system of classification.)

- *Senses.* Because readers have faculties that permit them to receive and respond to at least some external and internal stimuli, they can connect their own sensory experiences with those described in literature.

Able to relate to a literary piece on a variety of levels, readers are usually engaged by literary pieces much more readily than they are by nonliterary pieces. As teachers are well aware, people who are personally engaged in what they are doing learn more easily and quickly than people who are not.

The recommendation that a developmental reading course begin with literature—specifically, with poetry—admittedly flies in the face of convention. After all, poetry is elliptical, abstract, figurative. True. Yet, these are the very qualities that make poetry not only appropriate for inclusion in a developmental course but the ideal genre with which to begin the course. Poetry, more than any other genre, requires that it be read slowly and thoughtfully. Readers must pay close attention to the semantic and syntactic meanings of words. Instructors establish the importance of this scrutiny by explaining to students that any interpretation of a text is acceptable provided it is textually grounded. This means not only that students must defend their interpretations with details from the poem, but also that their interpretations cannot be invalidated with details they have overlooked or ignored. Learning to carefully examine a text is an essential part of learning to read critically. (In fact, the importance that students themselves attach to their work with poetry has been repeatedly revealed in their evaluations of the developmental reading course that I teach. On the evaluations I have collected during the past fifteen years, 96 percent of students identified poetry as the genre that most helped them improve their ability to read critically.)

Beginning with poetry serves a number of important psychological functions as well. Most students will have had little experience with poetry and will have considered it a form of writing well beyond their ken. In fact, they are likely to feel some anxiety when they realize that they are going to be reading poetry. This anxiety helps them realize that the course is substantive and requires commitment. By the time they take their first exam, they have learned that they do have the ability to read and understand poetry. Having been challenged and having met that challenge, students experience success and a consequent boost in self-esteem.

Like poetry, fiction appeals to readers' senses, emotions, and imagination as well as their intellect. This helps students continue their engagement with the text and encourages them to continue their practice of close reading. Just as they did with poetry, students look for and examine the issues, themes, and questions raised by the text. Fiction also presents students with the opportunity to analyze a few literary elements such as plot, setting, and character. Analyzing these elements compels students to continue their examination of language, details, development, organization, and so forth. Students are also likely to see characters in the short stories that remind them of themselves or someone they know. This type of identification can prompt students to consider that reading might have some personal value to them.

The critical reading of essays—texts that present and support a central idea—requires that students perform a number of cognitive tasks. Students who have studied literature have already developed most of the skills they will need. They have a good deal of experience analyzing language and structure. They also have a significant amount of practice locating details and examining the ways in which details are used to develop an idea, a theme, a character, and so forth. This experience enables them to understand concepts with relative ease such as thesis, main points, supporting detail, and organization. They are able to develop the skills they learned through their study of literature and to acquire the skills necessary to analyze evidence offered in support of an argument.

Textbook chapters follow essays because a traditional textbook chapter is essentially a series of related essays. When presented as such, students are not likely to be overwhelmed by the amount of material they are expected to learn. In addition, students who have studied poetry, fiction, and essays have come to realize that reading critically involves a wide range of cognitive activities, all of which are contingent on the reader's being actively engaged in the text. With this knowledge and the skills they have developed, students are less inclined to approach textbook chapters as an exercise in academic tedium and are more receptive to accepting responsibility for finding ways to engage themselves in the material. Various approaches students might use to interest themselves in a textbook chapter are presented in the instructor's manual (p. 171).

Critical Thinking/Critical Reading

Definitions of "critical thinking" and "critical reading" vary greatly, depending on one's philosophy, profession, and training. In the approach presented here, "critical thinking" is used to denote a process that involves analysis, synthesis, and application; "critical reading" is simply the incorporation of this process in reading.

Analysis The process by which one identifies and analyzes the important details of a piece of writing. Initially, this process involves identifying and understanding the "who," "what," "when," and "where." Beyond that, it can involve any number of tasks:

arranging	identifying	paraphrasing	repeating
categorizing	illustrating	prioritizing	restating
citing	labeling	ranking	retelling
classifying	listing	rearranging	reviewing
comparing	locating	recalling	selecting
contrasting	matching	recognizing	separating
defining	naming	reconstructing	showing
describing	ordering	recording	specifying
examining	organizing	relating	stating

Synthesis The process by which one fits parts of a piece together and reaches accurate conclusions about the whole. Synthesis involves such performances as deduction, induction, and inference.

Application The process by which one relates the piece to one's prior knowledge or experience and to later pieces of writing or ideas that one encounters.

Obviously, a wide variety of cognitive tasks are involved in analysis, synthesis, and application.

A consideration of Robinson's "Richard Cory" helps to illustrate the types of questions a reader would answer in performing these tasks:

Whenever Richard Cory went down town,
We people on the pavement looked at him;
He was a gentleman from sole to crown,
Clean favored, and imperially slim.

And he was always quietly arrayed,
And he was always human when he talked;
But still he fluttered pulses when he said,
"Good-morning," and he glittered when he walked.

And he was rich—yes, richer than a king—
And admirably schooled in every grace:
In fine, we thought that he was everything
To make us wish that we were in his place.

So on we worked, and waited for the light,
And went without the meat, and cursed the bread;
And Richard Cory, one calm summer night,
Went home and put a bullet through his head.

Analysis

1. Identifying problems and issues
   • What social classes are represented in this poem?
2. Defining, describing
   • What does the poet mean by Richard's being "human" when he talked?
   • What effects does Richard have on the townspeople?
3. Identifying point of view
   • Who is telling the story?
4. Identifying values
   • What attitude toward wealth does the speaker have?
5. Comparing
   • Compare the public life of Richard to the lives of the townspeople.
6. Classifying
   • Which details about Richard are impressions of the speaker?
   • Which details are verifiable facts?
7. Establishing logical relationships (e.g., cause and effect)
   • Why do the townspeople wish they were in Richard's place?

Synthesis

1. Inferring meanings, interpreting
   • What points does this poem make about human nature or human experience?

2. Generalizing from details (inductive logic)
   - Consider all the descriptions of Richard Cory. What do these descriptions, taken as a whole, indicate about the speaker's values?
3. Predicting from generalizations (deductive logic)
   - Consider your conclusions about the speaker's values. Is Richard's death likely to change those values? Explain.
4. Summarizing
   - Summarize in your own words all that we learn about Richard Cory's life and death.

Application

1. Relating information to already acquired knowledge, experience, values
   - Define "envy" as you understand that term.
   - What criteria do you use to evaluate someone you have just met?
   - Is this story realistic—could this have happened?
   - Is the point made by the poet true to human nature? Do people behave as do the townspeople? As does Richard Cory?
   - What do you especially like about this poem?
   - Consider the expression "people on the pavement." What words would you have used to describe such people?
2. Relating information to later readings or later experiences
   - After reading "Barbie Doll" (p. 20), contrast the life of Richard Cory with that of the "girlchild," and compare the reasons they committed suicide.

Suggestions for Developing Critical Reading

That some students enter college with poorly developed thinking skills is not surprising. After all, critical thinking is often actively discouraged by authority figures (parents, educators, supervisors, clerics, etc.) who prefer that their ideas, opinions, beliefs, and judgments not be questioned. People usually respond to this discouragement with varying degrees of compliance. While some continue to question, regardless of the consequences, others either anesthetize their desire to know or limit their interest to that which is immediate in their lives. Curiosity is necessary if students are to become actively involved in reading, thinking, and, ultimately, living. Thus, the following suggestions are intended not only to help students learn to question and consider, but, as necessary, to reawaken and expand their curiosity.

1. **The Teacher** This method of teaching developmental reading requires that the teacher adopt the role of an enlightened listener, an informed moderator, and a purposeful questioner. A teacher who suggests and directs instead of informing and dictating helps students learn to find their own way, the main purpose of learning to think critically.

2. **Classroom Environment** Learning involves all aspects of a person: intellectual, physical, emotional, and spiritual. The intellectual development of students is a teacher's main concern but the part cannot be divorced from the whole. Consequently, it is necessary for teachers to keep in mind that not all obstacles to learning are intellectual. Fear is one of the greatest impediments to learning because it makes people reluctant to take risks. Most people fear not being correct or not being thought adequate.

   Teachers can encourage students to become aware of this fear and to take risks in spite of it by directly addressing the issue and by taking risks themselves. A simple, straightforward discussion of the fear helps students realize that they are not the only ones who feel anxious about asking questions and sharing ideas. It also provides teachers with the opportunity to reassure students that they are significant and that they will not be belittled or ridiculed. This approach usually decreases students' fear and increases their willingness to connect with their teacher as well as their classmates.

Teachers should also consistently model risk-taking by explicitly acknowledging when they are confused, mistaken, or unknowing. Hearing their instructor say, with no hesitation or embarrassment, "I don't know" teaches students a valuable lesson: There is no shame in not knowing, and there is no dishonor in admitting it. Once students believe that the teacher respects them and values their efforts, students will feel safer and will be more inclined to participate actively and honestly. Their participation and engagement is essential if they are to develop their ability to think critically.

Some teachers of developmental reading courses hypothesize that a significant number of their students have undiagnosed learning disabilities. To assist teachers who are unfamiliar with learning disabilities, two essays are included in this manual. One discusses attention disorders (p. 179); the other, dyslexia (p. 186). Teachers who suspect that a student might have a learning disability can contact their institution's disability support services office for more information and recommendations.

3. **Incorporation of Students' Knowledge, Experience, and Values**   Critical readers are aware that their knowledge, experience, and values have an impact on their understanding and interpretation of a text. Specific exercises can be designed to help students develop this awareness.

Pre-reading exercises.   Answering questions for which there are no right or wrong answers frequently helps students become aware of their personal views, perceptions, and feelings about an issue or situation. They can be asked to offer their own definitions of concepts (e.g., "sin" or "prejudice") that are important in the pieces they will be reading. They might be presented with a hypothetical situation that in some way is analogous to the situation presented in the assigned text and asked how they would respond. Pre-reading exercises should be geared toward eliciting from students ideas, attitudes, and emotions that parallel those raised by the piece.

Post-reading exercises.   The study of a particular piece can be closed by inviting students to share their personal opinions about an issue raised in the text and to examine how their own values, experience, and knowledge affected their reading of the text.

4. **Assignments**

Number of texts per meeting.   The number of texts assigned depends in large measure on the objectives of the instructor, the complexity of the pieces, the abilities of the students, and the time allotted for the class meeting. Generally, a text such as "Richard Cory" can be adequately examined in about an hour; a piece like "When Is It Rape" may take longer to analyze.

Comparison of perspectives.   The teaming of two or more pieces that have similar themes or subjects frequently facilitates critical reading. Students are able to examine the content of each piece and compare the ways in which each addresses a similar idea. Comparison often reveals the universal nature of certain thoughts and feelings, the complexity of certain issues, and the lack of simple solutions for certain problems.

5. **Exercises**   The more closely students work with a text, the more they will come to understand it and think critically about it. This can be encouraged in several ways.

Student-generated criteria.   Each student can formulate two or three questions about the assigned text that he or she would like to have answered. These questions might be about details or about the interpretation of details, as long as the questions deal with some element of the piece about which the student is genuinely uncertain. The entire series of questions can be assigned to students, individually or collectively. Another approach is for students to divide into groups and try to answer all of the questions. After a specified period of time, each group selects the one question it would most like to have addressed by the class. These questions almost invariably deal with the critical elements of a piece and become the focus of class discussion. The process involved in formulating questions, trying to resolve them, and deciding on the most crucial questions forces students not only to consider the text carefully but also to think about what it is they do not know and would most like to know.

Teacher-generated criteria. This manual includes a discussion and series of exercises for each piece in the anthology. Teachers are likely to develop additional exercises to meet the specific needs of their specific class. Whatever form these assignments take, they should require that students carefully examine the text or lead them to discuss what is truly important in the piece.

6. **Student Involvement** People learn best when they are personally involved and actively participating in discussion, but a class dialogue is liable to be limited to the teacher and four or five especially vocal (or self-confident) students. Students must be actively engaged in both their reading and the course work in order to develop their critical reading and thinking skills. Teachers need to vary their class activities to accommodate all of the learning styles of their students. Teachers should also assist students in identifying and understanding their individual learning styles. This information can help them succeed in the course, in college, and in the workplace.

    Individual responses.   Students should be required to respond individually and in writing to the pieces they have read. These responses can take any number of forms from the personal to the academic to the creative. For example, students can keep reading journals (recording their thoughts and feelings as they read), produce paragraphs or essays (exploring an issue raised in class discussion), write editorials (supporting or opposing the views expressed in a text), or compose letters to a writer or a character (challenging his or her ideas). Whatever the form, students should keep their responses focused on the text.

    Group work.   Group work can involve any activity that will encourage critical thinking and critical reading. The most common assignments involve discussion based on assigned questions. However, the possibilities of group work are by no means limited to that. Groups can compose character sketches, illustrate scenes, create diagrams, stage debates, conduct trials, and so forth.

    Class discussion.   Ideally, plenary discussion follows individual and group work. The teacher directs this discussion, affirming, questioning, and challenging the ideas that the groups present. By reading aloud portions of the text and having students explain the meaning of each line or sentence, teachers demonstrate and reinforce the importance of close textual examination. Of course, the teacher should end the discussion with a summary of the essential points.

7. **Time Limits** Limiting the amount of time allowed for certain exercises or group discussions helps maintain focus, creates a slight tension, and reinforces the teacher's expectations.

8. **Quizzes** Short quizzes given at the beginning of each meeting accomplish two objectives: they encourage students to come to class having read and thought about the assigned text(s); they communicate to the students the instructor's belief that they are intelligent people who are capable of mastering much of the text on their own. These quizzes should avoid interpretation as much as possible and focus on details that a fairly conscientious reader would not miss.

9. **Examinations** An examination after each of the three units should provide instructors with a sufficient means of assessment. Each exam should consist of two parts. The first part (worth 60–70 percent of the entire exam) should be designed to test students on the pieces that have been discussed in class. The second part (worth 30–40 percent of the entire exam) should test students on a text that has been assigned beforehand but has not been discussed in class. Testing students on material that has not been discussed in class assures that they apply their own principles of

analysis, synthesis, and application. When taking the second part of the test, students should be permitted to refer to the text. For textbook chapters, the first part of the exam might consist of questions on the facts and theories contained in the chapters, and the second part might ask students to apply the facts and theories to hypothetical situations invented by the teacher.

Suggested Course Outline

While no single course outline is appropriate for every class, every teacher, or every school, the following schedule would be typical for a course lasting ten weeks with four hours of class time per week:

Weeks 1–3	Poetry (12–15 poems)
Weeks 4–6	Fiction (6–8 short stories)
Weeks 7–10	Essays (6–8 essays) and Textbook Chapters (1–2 chapters)

1
Poetry
Discussions and Suggestions

Lot's Wife

Kristine Batey

and

Genesis 19:1.2–26

"Lot's Wife" is an excellent poem to use early in the course. It is, first, a powerful poem that raises such issues as obedience, established sex roles, and natural human curiosity about and human love of the things of this world. Second, because it is grounded in a story from the Bible, it presents an excellent opportunity for examining what an artist can do with another piece of writing. In fact, the many things that can be done with the poem make it an excellent model for demonstrating the processes of critical thinking—analysis, synthesis, and application.

The issues raised by the poem itself are not at all as remote as might be the ancient subject of Lot, his wife, and the destruction of Sodom and Gomorrah. The poet humanizes Lot's wife, making her an understandable and sympathetic character, and raises issues that concern many people. (This accomplishment is an example of what great writers have done many times—expand upon, develop, and find a new metaphor in a well-known story or myth.) One of the issues raised, obedience, is likely to disturb some students once they carefully study the biblical passage. Students have shown concern about the lack of emphasis the messenger places on the matter of not looking back. They have also questioned the severity of the punishment received by Lot's wife, since the biblical passage provides no evidence that she is inherently wicked. Another issue, the subservience of Lot's wife to her husband, is also rich for discussion, especially in light of the continuing struggle for equality between the sexes. Finally, the concern that Lot's wife has with the things of this world (a concern that is only natural, considering her responsibility for the everyday tasks of life) invites discussion of man's love for and service to God.

Suggestions

Pre-Reading Exercise: Before students read the poem, have them respond in writing to a hypothetical situation such as the following:

> Imagine that you live on the Atlantic seaboard. A deadly hurricane is approaching, and officials recommend that everyone living in your area evacuate. You decide to leave your home, but many people you know decide to stay behind. As you gather a few personal items to take with you, what thoughts and feelings might you have?

Such a beginning exercise invites students to apply their own experiences and feelings to the situation in the biblical passage and the poem. After students read the biblical passage, have them write a brief summary (perhaps no more than three sentences). This exercise enables students to gain the proper background for appreciating what the poet does with the biblical story.

1. After students read the poem and the biblical passage, have them respond in writing to the following:

   a. What details about the story of Lot and his wife are contained in the poem but not in the biblical passage?

   b. What details are contained in the biblical passage but not in the poem?

   c. Compare the characterization of Lot and his wife in the two pieces.

   d. What is the primary concern of each writer?

   After each student has responded to these four questions, divide the class into groups of three or four to discuss their responses. Have each group come to a consensus in their responses; then choose one group to report on each question. Groups not chosen to respond to a particular question should be encouraged to give additional comments.

2. Provide an opportunity for a focused class discussion of issues raised by the biblical passage and the poem. Asking students to apply their own values to these pieces will provide a good focal point:

   a. What would you have thought if you had received, from a messenger, the exact instructions that Lot's wife receives in the biblical passage?

   b. What would you have done if you had been in Lot's wife's position, as that position is described in the poem?

   c. Are the social/family roles of Lot and his wife typical of the roles of husband and wife today? Explain.

   d. Comment on the "fairness" of what happens to Lot's wife.

   By addressing such questions, students are given a further opportunity for meaningful application of the issues raised by the poem and the biblical passage.

3. "Lot's Wife" could be teamed with "Barbie Doll" (p. 20), "Hills Like White Elephants" (p. 50), "The Fat Girl" (p. 120), and/or "The Chrysanthemums" (p. 202) for an extended study of the roles of women.

4. For an examination of the ways in which people respond to loss, this poem might be studied with "The Vacuum" (p. 22), "Power" (p. 23), "The Gilded Six-Bits" (p. 63), "Life after High School" (p. 132), "Islands on the Moon" (p. 144), and/or "Shame" (p. 213).

Richard Cory

E. A. Robinson

"Richard Cory" is an excellent poem to use early in the study of poetry. Its simple language makes it immediately accessible, yet a closer examination reveals subtleties that are rich in commentary about human nature. The poem easily can be used as a springboard for discussion of important textual elements: figurative language, connotation versus denotation, form (such as narrative), speaker, tone, and theme. The power and simplicity of the basic story make some themes quickly apparent to students (students see readily the notions that "money can't buy happiness," "people are not always what they appear to be," etc.), and this important foothold makes students more agreeable to exploring the subtleties of the poem. The subtlety of language is a valuable lesson that can come from a study of this particular poem.

The subtlety of the speaker's attitude toward Richard Cory is evident in his use of language. Some of the words—"crown," "imperially," and "grace"—are directly related to royalty (the word "king" is also used as are other words like "arrayed" and "glittered," which suggest a royal nature). That the speaker uses "human" to compliment Richard's way of talking to the townspeople suggests that, to the speaker, Richard is far above "human." The phrase "people on the pavement" suggests lowliness as well as commonness. The enormous gulf between the king-like, god-like Richard Cory and the townspeople is revealed by a close examination of these poetic phrases, and Richard's suicide can be seen as a result of human isolation caused by the wealth and power the townspeople envy so much. It could also be said that the great gulf is more a result of the townspeople's being intimidated by wealth and power rather than a result of wealth and power per se: Richard, it seems, is more able to "come down" than the towns people are able to "come up." Inherent in this conclusion is the passivity of the townspeople as opposed to the activity of Richard Cory (after all, he does go downtown, say "Good Morning," and attempt to carry on a conversation).

Suggestions

Pre-Reading Exercise: Sometimes students focus so intently on Richard Cory's wealth that they overlook his other assets: He is handsome, genteel, friendly, and gregarious as well as liked, admired, and respected. To prepare students to see that there is more to Richard than his money, ask them to list the qualities their ideal mate would have. After they have examined the poem, have them identify and discuss which of those qualities Richard possesses.

1. Have students divide up into groups and analyze the details in the poem:
   a. What social classes are represented in this poem?
   b. What does the poet mean by Richard's being "human" when he talked?
   c. What effects does Richard have on the townspeople?
   d. Who is the speaker?
   e. What attitude toward wealth does the speaker have?
   f. Compare the public life of Richard to the lives of the townspeople.
   g. Which details about Richard are impressions of the speaker? Which details are facts?
   h. Why do the townspeople wish they were in Richard's place?

2. Pose questions that will encourage students to synthesize the details:
   a. What points does this poem make about human nature or human experience?
   b. Consider all the descriptions of Richard Cory. What do these descriptions, taken as a whole, indicate about the speaker's values?
   c. Consider your conclusions about the speaker's values. Is Richard's death likely to change those values? Explain.
   d. Summarize in your own words all that we learn about Richard Cory's life and death.

3. To help students consider the suggestiveness of figurative language, have them rewrite certain figurative phrases:
   - "people of the pavement"
   - "sole to crown"
   - "clean favored"
   - "imperially slim"
   - "quietly arrayed"
   - "human when he talked"
   - "fluttered pulses"
   - "glittered when he walked"
   - "admirably schooled in every grace"
   - "waited for the light"

   Ask students to put the "new" phrases back into the poem and decide whether the new wording covers both the denotative and connotative meaning of the poetic expressions. In addition to helping students understand the speaker's attitude toward Richard, this exercise also leads them to see isolation as a more specific reason for Richard's suicide than general "unhappiness." An overwhelming sense of isolation, of course, is the primary reason for suicide. Thus, Robinson subtly makes a psychologically sound statement about suicide as well as more obvious statements about wealth and happiness, appearance and reality.

4. Pose questions that will encourage students to relate the poem to their knowledge, experience, and values:

    a. Define "envy" as you understand that term.

    b. What criteria do you use to evaluate someone you have just met?

    c. Is the point made by the poet true to human nature? Do people behave as do the townspeople? As does Richard Cory? Explain.

5. To start students thinking in terms of why a piece of writing is effective, ask them to write a paragraph explaining what they thought was especially good (or bad) about the poem. Ask for volunteers to read their paragraphs aloud. After each volunteer reads, initiate a discussion of the way in which his or her assertions are (or could have been) supported with evidence from the text.

6. Many people believe that their problems would magically vanish if they simply had plenty of money. Have students use InfoTrac to explore the validity of that premise (Subject: Wealth; Subdivision: Psychological Aspects).

7. "Richard Cory" could be teamed with "Barbie Doll" (p. 20) and/or "Life after High School" (p. 132). Have students contrast the lives of Richard Cory, the "girlchild," and Zachary and compare the reasons they commit suicide.

8. To explore the idea of success and the various ways in which people define it, "Richard Cory" can be studied with "Warren Pryor" (p. 5), "Everyday Use," (p. 88), and/or "Starved Out" (p. 246).

9. To examine the ways in which writers create a surprise ending, "Richard Cory" could be assigned with "The Lottery" (p. 43), "Life after High School" (p. 132), and/or "A Rose for Emily" (p. 193).

Warren Pryor

Alden Nowlan

Dreams are something that human beings need to have and pursue in order to thrive. Often, though, people pursue not their own dreams but the dreams of others. These pursuits may appear to be successful, but, in reality, they are not. Such is the case in "Warren Pryor."

Warren's parents have had a difficult life and have apparently felt powerless and trapped. Life on the farm has obviously been difficult. The land is "stony," "barren," and "thistle-strewn"; the work is "brutal" and "lonely." The parents want their son to live a life that is different—and presumably easier—than their own. Hoping to spare their son the hardships they have experienced, they decide that Warren will have an education and an occupation that does not involve manual labor. Having made this decision, they devote themselves to seeing that their dreams for their son are realized. They "sacrifice" and "slav[e]" so that he can live and be educated in town and ultimately be "free." They are proud when he graduates and exuberant when he begins work at the bank: Warren has accomplished *their* dream.

The life Warren leads at the bank is different from the life his parents lead, but only superficially. True, his labor is not as physically arduous as theirs, and his attire (white shirts for work; jeans for relaxation) is the converse of theirs. Nonetheless, in leaving the "barren hole" (his prior warren) for the "teller's cage" (his present warren), he has simply exchanged one form of bondage for another.[1] Ironically, Warren experiences the same frustration and misery at the bank as his parents do on the farm. Despite his parents' attempts to "hew" or shape his hands for the handling of "paper bills," he has too

---

[1]The main character's name, Warren Pryor, is significant. *Pryor,* of course, is a homophone for *prior. Warren* denotes an area where small game animals are kept, a network of rabbit burrows, a colony of rabbits, a densely populated area (such as a slum), and a labyrinth of narrow passages (such as halls and alleys).

much energy, too much strength to be content doing sedentary work in a confined area. Trapped "like a young bear," Warren aches "with empty strength and throttled rage."

In keeping with the complexity of human relationships, there is no "villain." All involved are doing what they believe to be best. The parents want their child to have a life better than the one they had, and they believe they know how he can achieve that goal. From the parents' perspective, Warren would be better off not working on the farm. The son apparently wants to please his parents and fulfill their expectations. Perhaps it is his reluctance to disappoint them that motivates him not to share with them his desires and dreams. Nonetheless, he is ultimately responsible for his own life, and "he [says] nothing."

Suggestions

Pre-Reading Exercise: Divide the class into two or three groups, and either assign each group a different scenario or assign all groups the same scenario:

- X's parents did not graduate from high school and see no value in X's getting an education. They think that X should get a job, earn money, and contribute to the family's income. X, who really wants an education, decides to go to college anyway.

- Y's parents have planned for Y to go to college, major in business, and eventually take over the family's company. Y, who has no interest in business, decides to go to college but to major in a field that is in no way related to the family's enterprise.

- Z's parents regret not having gone to college and have spent years saving the money for Z to have the opportunity that they did not. Z, who thinks that higher education for him is a waste of time and money, decides to become an apprentice electrician instead of a college student.

Give each group ten to twenty minutes to develop a short skit or write a brief story in which the parents learn of and react to their child's decision. After the groups are done, the skits can be performed or the stories read aloud. When the presentations are finished, ask the students to identify the similarities and differences between the groups' representations of the parents, the child, and the conflict. Usually, students will portray the parents as trying to direct their child's life; on occasion, some groups will portray the parents as very supportive of their child's decision. It matters little which angle students take. The discussion invariably leads to issues such as the pursuit of one's dreams, control of one's life, responsibility for one's decisions, and so forth.

1. Have students answer questions that will prompt them to analyze as well as synthesize the text:
   a. List details that illustrate the difficulty of Warren's parents' life on the farm.
   b. Describe the type of life they want for their son.
   c. What steps do they take to assure that Warren will have the kind of life they want for him?
   d. In what ways is Warren's life at the bank different from his parents' life?
   e. Are any of Warren's feelings about his work similar to his parents' feelings about their work? Explain.
   f. We are told that Warren says "nothing." What might he have liked to say? To whom? Why did he not say it?
   g. Why are the first three stanzas told from the parents' point of view and the last stanza, from Warren's?

2. Pose questions that will lead students to consider the significance of Warren Pryor's name:
   a. Look up the word *warren* in a dictionary and consider each of its meanings.
   b. In what ways might the word *warren* be applied to life on the farm?

c. In what ways might it be applied to life in town? At the bank?

d. "Pryor" is a homophone for *prior*. Keeping this in mind, explain the significance of the son's name.

3. Team "Warren Pryor" with "A Red Palm" (p. 9) and/or "The Fat Girl" (p. 120) to consider parents' desires for their children.

4. To explore the idea of success and the various ways in which people define it, "Warren Pryor" can be studied with "Richard Cory" (p. 4), "Everyday Use" (p. 88), and/or "Starved Out" (p. 246).

The Road Not Taken

Robert Frost

"The Road Not Taken" is a good poem to use early in the course. Its language is simple, and the metaphor involved is easily grasped by students—at least the basic metaphor of "the road of life." It is also a good poem to use to impress upon students the need to look carefully at *all* parts of a poem. The powerful ending—"I took the road less traveled by / And that has made all the difference"—is likely to be "read" out of its context. That the two roads are actually very much alike is seen in such remarks as "Then took the other, as *just as fair*"; "the passing there / Had worn them *really about the same* / And both that morning *equally lay* / In leaves no step had trodden black" [emphasis added]. To extrapolate only from the ending, a reader might conclude that the speaker has chosen to be "different," a nonconformist. But when this remark is placed in its closest context (what the speaker will be saying in the future, "ages and ages hence") and in the context of the descriptions of the two roads, one could conclude that the ending remark is probably the kind of justification the speaker will offer in the future for his decision. By saying that he took the "one less traveled," the speaker prepares for both success and failure: If he succeeds, he can boast about his accomplishments, whereas if he fails, he can excuse his failure by saying that, after all, he chose *the hard way*.

The speaker seems to contradict himself, and part of his confusion is due to the dilemma of decision making: The choices are likely to be very much alike, and one must find or invent a justification for one's decision. A consideration of the title reveals the greatest dilemma of decision making, the common human torment of always wondering, "what would have happened *if*?"

Suggestions

Pre-Reading Exercise: Generally, people like to have specific reasons for the important decisions they make in life. Have students consider this idea by presenting them with the following situation:

> A person shows you two stones that look exactly alike. One of the stones is a diamond worth $100,000; the other is a cubic zirconia worth $29.95. The person tells you that you cannot touch the stones or have them appraised, but that you can have either one of them. How would you decide which one to take?

As students discuss their approaches, they will ordinarily come to the conclusion that their choice would be arbitrary. After the poem has been discussed, return to this exercise and ask students what thoughts might be going through their minds as they race to the nearest jeweler with the stone they chose clasped firmly in their increasingly sweaty palm. Some students will acknowledge that they would likely convince themselves that they had specific reasons for choosing their stone.

1. Have students write a summary of the poem, including a statement of what they believe to be its main point or central issue. After the summary is completed, have students compose two questions they would most like to have answered about this poem. Frequently, these questions will come

closer to addressing Frost's central concern than the students' summaries. Students often have problems resolving the conflict between the ending and the rest of the poem. Most students want to interpret the last two lines as a statement of the central issue but find that other details (about which they typically ask questions) are contradictory. After students have formulated questions, divide them into groups (three to four per group) and have them try to resolve these questions. After a period of time, ask each group to provide a question the class can address as a whole. These questions become the focus for class discussion.

2. The speaker's uncertainty about his choice is reflected in the ambiguous words "sigh" and "difference." The ambiguity of these words might, in fact, become a suitable focus to begin the discussion of the entire poem. Have each student write down three different common contexts for the word "sigh" ("a sigh of joy," "a sigh of anguish," "a sigh of regret," "a sigh of relief," "a sigh of dismay," "a sigh of despair," "a sigh of contentment," etc.). Then ask each student to decide if the word difference normally has positive or negative connotations. The speaker's ambiguous words are understandable only if one closely considers the rest of the poem. Such a consideration reveals the similarity of the choices and the speaker's inability to know what kind of "sigh" or "difference" will result from his choice. Students may be divided into groups to examine the rest of the poem, with the task of trying to explain the use of these ambiguous words.

3. Another focus for discussion is the title. Have each student write a response to the questions, "Is the title appropriate for the poem? Why or why not?" Then divide the students into groups to compare responses and arrive at a group consensus. Have each group report to the class. The primary aim of this approach is, of course, to bring students closer to Frost's central issue: Decision making involves a rejection, and one usually wonders about what has been rejected.

4. Teaming "The Road Not Taken" with "Hills Like White Elephants" (p. 50) and/or "The Chrysanthemums" (p. 202) invites a discussion of symbolism as well as the dilemma of choices.

5. Because it shows the difficulty of finding a truly untraveled path to take, "The Road Not Taken" serves as an interesting counterpoint to the idea in " The Unknown Citizen" (p. 35) and "Curiosity" (p. 36) that one should be "different."

I, Too
and
Harlem

Langston Hughes

"I, Too" and "Harlem" provide an opportunity for students to compare the way in which the same poet uses a number of elements (theme, tone, figurative language) in different poems. "I, Too" develops a simple but powerful metaphor centered around the speaker's wish to move from the "kitchen" to the "table"; such a movement represents a hope for changing his subservient position to one of equality. In "Harlem," Hughes discusses what happens to such a hope, a dream, when it is "deferred." Again, Hughes uses figurative language to make his point, but the figurative language is more complex and potentially baffling. Though the similes and the metaphor ("Or does it explode?") clearly refer to the question "What happens to a dream deferred?"; there is still a problem of understanding what is meant by the figurative expressions. It is necessary to *translate* these figurative expressions in order to appreciate how encompassing Hughes' statement is.

The poems work well together to illustrate the poet's varying attitudes: "I, Too" is an optimistic statement about a dream that could come true; "Harlem" is a pessimistic (though realistic) statement about the possible results of a dream's not being realized. (The simple metaphor of "I, Too" fits its simple, almost innocent, attitude; the complex similes of "Harlem" suit the difficult task of explaining the abstract results of a "dream deferred.") Used together, the poems can show students that the "difficulty" of a poem is not as important a criterion for judging effectiveness as how well the poet's language fits his or her subject matter and attitude.

Suggestions

1. Ask students to write down which of these poems they like best and to explain their choices. After later examination of the poems, ask them which poem is more effective or powerful and to give reasons for their choices.

2. One focus for discussion is the figurative language of these poems. Start with "I, Too," and have students explicate its metaphor. One interesting way to engage students in this metaphor is to have them examine closely the first and last lines of the poem and decide the difference between the first line (a respect for America) and the last line (a belief in one's right to realize the promises of America). These are philosophical statements that are illustrated by the concrete metaphor contained between them. After students have worked on "I, Too," have them examine the figurative language of "Harlem." Ask each student to rewrite the similes and the metaphor "does it explode?" in equivalent *common* language. For example:

POETIC EXPRESSION	EQUIVALENT
"Does it dry up like a raisin in the sun?"	Does it shrink in importance?
"Does it fester like a sore, and then run?"	Does it become painful and then is it relieved?

It is perhaps impossible to provide an exact equivalent for the sense of Hughes' poetic expressions, but, as noted earlier, it is important for students to translate them in order to understand that one might respond to a "dream deferred" either passively or actively. If the metaphor of "I, Too" has already been examined, then its dream of equality can serve as the concrete example of a "dream deferred."

3. Another approach is to have students decide what these two poems say about the poet: What conclusions could one draw about the poet, based on just these two poems? Have each student put in writing a response to this question, then divide students into groups to discuss and consolidate their responses. If the group responses reveal certain differences (e.g., that in "I, Too" the poet seems more "hopeful" than in "Harlem"), further fruitful discussion might follow. Consider the publication dates of the poems ("I, Too," 1932; "Harlem," 1951). Why might the poet's attitude have changed in the course of twenty years from a generally optimistic attitude to a more pessimistic attitude? Do people usually become more pessimistic as they grow older? In terms of the hope for racial equality, what could account for this change in attitude? What progress had been made by 1951 in the quest for racial equality?

4. Study "I, Too" and "Harlem" along with "The Chimney Sweeper" poems (pp. 24–25) to further examine the difference between innocent and experienced states of being

5. For a discussion of metaphor, "Harlem" would be teamed with works such as "Mother to Son" (p. 7) and/or "Digging" (p. 19).

6. Students might be asked to use InfoTrac to find out more about Langston Hughes and/or the Harlem Renaissance (Subject: Harlem Renaissance; Keyword: "harlem renaissance: Subject: Langston Hughes). Once they have completed their research, ask them to explain what effect (if any) their newfound knowledge has on their understanding of the poems.

Poems on Family Relationships

Mother to Son

Langston Hughes

Those Winter Sundays

Robert Hayden

Austere

Roland Flint

A Red Palm

Gary Soto

Daystar

Rita Dove

Once a Lady Told Me

Nikki Giovanni

These poems all center on family relationships, a subject of interest to most students, no matter their ages. Whether they are struggling to be independent adults, good parents, and/or responsible children, students realize that family relationships play an important role in shaping who they were, who they are, and who they will become. As these poems are discussed in class, encourage students to share their experiences and insights. The poems illustrate a range of problems and attitudes involved in family relationships.

"Mother to Son" is the statement of a mother to her son, made in the present tense, admonishing him not to give up. The poem's theme—determination in the face of life's challenges and hardships—is developed through a simple metaphor. The mother compares her life to a staircase, a reasonable and common comparison. Hughes' staircase vehicle, however, is deceptively subtle, suggesting more specifics about the mother's life than would first seem evident. The poem is therefore an excellent one to introduce students to the concept of metaphor (see suggestion 4).

"Those Winter Sundays" is the statement of a son who looks back upon some of the sacrifices made for him by his father and regrets not having appreciated at the time what his father did for him. His remembrance reveals an absence of communication, perhaps the most common shortcoming in a parent–child relationship. The "chronic angers of that house" are not identified, which both suggests a vagueness in the speaker's childhood understanding and leads the reader to suppose they are the typical angers found in many houses. The focus of the poem is more on the speaker and his adult sense of guilt than on the father and his hard life. In so focusing his poem, Hayden broadens his application to most of us: What child can fully appreciate the sacrifices made by a parent?

Indeed, this sentiment is echoed in "Austere," a poem that takes its title and its epigraph from "Those Winter Sundays." In describing his mother's weekly bathing of the children, the narrator reveals his own retrospective understanding of her work, her self-deprivation, her love. The mother's ritual—heating of the water in kettles on the stove; filling of the corrugated tub; warming of the tub water before washing each child; bathing herself in water that has lost its heat—shows the tenderness and love of the mother for her children and her willingness to deprive herself so that they may have comfort.

In "A Red Palm," we see another hard-working father, but in this case from the father's point of view. His labor is menial and monotonous, and the only way he manages to carry on with it is to imagine its concrete benefits: "fish . . . milk, bread, meat." We get a hint in stanza three of some regret as the father is reminded of his failure to get an education, a failure that has doomed him to menial labor, to being only "a giant among cotton plants." But the last stanza puts his menial labor into a broader perspective. His son is getting an education. The poem offers what surely must be the stimulus that keeps many parents from giving up: One's labor can mean a better life for one's children.

Unlike the father in "A Red Palm," who views his labor in terms of its benefit to his family, the mother in "Daystar" sees only drudgery in her duties. Unlike the mother in "Mother to Son," she does not see life as a staircase that one must climb if one is to become better. She is oppressed rather than challenged by the responsibilities of raising a family. Her life is not her own, except for the brief moments when she can escape from her labors and be "pure nothing, in the middle of the day." The poem points out the very human need for parents to maintain identity in the context of raising a family, a need that most of us, whether young or old, have difficulty attributing to our own parents. Being a parent does not negate the desire to build "a palace" for oneself.

The mother in "Once a Lady Told Me" could be, many years later, the same narrator as in "Daystar." There is an edge of resentment in having given her life to her children, who now "want [her] death." Despite the concerns of her children and the censure of her grandchildren, she will not relinquish her freedom. The tenacity with which she clings to her independence negates the frequently held notion that aging parents are lonely and unhappy and that they want to be taken care of by their children.

Suggestions

Pre-Reading Exercise: Have students make a list of the qualities they consider most important in being a good parent. After the poems are discussed in class, have students apply their lists of qualities to the parents in the poems.

1. Have students examine all six poems, posing questions that will make them take a close look at the text and understand the specific focus of each poem:
    a. What attitude does the parent in each poem seem to have toward her/his obligations as a parent?
    b. Summarize the apparent relationship between parent and child in each piece.
    c. About whom do we learn more in each of these poems, the parent or the child?
    d. Is the attitude of the mother in "Once a Lady Told Me" likely to be the attitude held in later life by any of the other five parents? Explain.

2. Have students compare "Austere" and "Those Winter Sundays" in order to determine the appropriateness of Flint's title and epigraph, both of which are taken from the final two lines of Hayden's poem:
    a. Are the lives of the parents in these poems "easy" or "difficult"? Explain.
    b. Compare and contrast the weekly rituals (events) described in the poems.
    c. Identify the images of cold and warmth in each poem. What do these images suggest about each parent?
    d. What seems to have been the childhood attitude of each speaker toward his parent? Explain.
    e. Describe the current attitude of each speaker toward his parent.
    f. Explain why each speaker's attitude most likely changed.

3. Encourage students to relate their opinions to the ideas in the poems. Ask them to write a brief statement about the greatest problem they find in their relationship with their parents. Have them get into groups and decide on and rank the three greatest problems; make a list on the board of the problems cited by the groups. Which of the problems named are evident in the poems?

4. "Mother to Son" is an excellent poem to use in introducing students to metaphor. The vehicle of the metaphor is a staircase; the tenor is the mother's life. From a cursory reading of the poem, one will certainly draw the correct—but highly general—conclusion that the poet, through metaphor, is pointing out that the mother has had a hard life. A close look at the various parts of the basic staircase vehicle—tacks, splinters, landings, and so on—reveals that the poet is being much more specific. Emphasize to students that they must consider the vehicle carefully before they interpret its tenor: What do tacks and splinters cause? What is a landing? Where are we headed when we turn a corner?

and so on. List the various parts of the vehicle on the board and have the class, as a whole, determine the ideas suggested by each part. The aim is not to come up with just one word or phrase, but rather two or three words or phrases with slightly different connotations. Indeed, several parts of the vehicle lend themselves to widely varying interpretations ("reaching landin's," for example, might refer to achieving goals, periods of rest, transitional periods, or milestones in life).

    For further discussion of metaphor, "Mother to Son" could be studied with works such as "Digging" (p. 19) and "Harlem" (p. 7).

5.   "Mother to Son" could be teamed with "'Indignation' Jones," (p. 17), "A Rose for Emily" (p. 193), "Shame" (p. 213), and/or "Daddy Tucked the Blanket" (p. 215) for an examination of the differing ways in which people respond to the indignities of life.

6.   Studying "Those Winter Sundays" and "Islands on the Moon" (p. 144) together allows students to explore two different treatments of a similar theme: the correction of youthful misperception.

7.   Further explore the ways in which experience alters perspective by teaming "Those Winter Sundays" with "I, Too" (p. 6) and "Harlem" (p. 7) as well as "The Chimney Sweeper" poems (pp. 24–25).

8.   To examine father-son relationships, "Those Winter Sundays" and/or "A Red Palm" can be studied with "My Father's Song" (p. 11), "Elegy for My Father, Who Is Not Dead" (p. 12), and/or "Digging" (p. 19), and/or "Persimmons" (p. 30).

9.   "A Red Palm" can be teamed with "Warren Pryor" (p. 5) and/or "The Fat Girl" (p. 120) to consider parents' desires for their children.

My Father's Song

Simon Ortiz

and

Elegy for My Father, Who Is Not Dead

Andrew Hudgins

"My Father's Song" and "Elegy for My Father, Who Is Not Dead" are both poems that grapple with the difficulty of parental death. Although each poem opens with expressions of melancholy over the loss, the respective speakers use metaphor to explore the possibility that such inevitable earthly partings are only part of the natural and spiritual cycles of the universe. Language serves to heal the speakers, causing the poems to end on a more hopeful note than they begin.

    At the beginning of "My Father's Song," the speaker longs to communicate, but he cannot because his father is not present. Unable to speak with his father, the speaker recalls his father's "voice, the slight catch, / the depth from his thin chest, / the tremble of emotion" as his father told him about an incident when he was planting corn with his own father (the speaker's grandfather). Although they "planted several times," the speaker's father remembers one particular spring when his father found a nest of baby mice. The speaker's grandfather stopped his labor to show the mice to his son and move them to the edge of the field, a gesture that illustrated the grandfather's regard for the natural world and served as a lesson for his son. The speaker's father understood the lesson, vividly remembering the planting ("the very softness of cool and warm sand") and the rescue ("tiny alive mice"), but ultimately, he remembered "[his] father saying things." Even though Ortiz initially feels frustration because of his inability "to say things," he takes comfort in the natural, generational cycle that links him to his father and to his grandfather. Through his father's "song," the speaker's relatives, even if departed, continue "saying things" to him.

Although the father of the speaker in "Elegy for My Father" has not yet died, the speaker feels a similar frustration over the inevitability of grief and loss. The speaker knows that he will play a passive role in his father's death, saying "One day I'll lift the telephone/ and be told my father's dead." His father, like many of the elderly, is "ready." In fact, the speaker thinks "he wants to go" to see "the world beyond this world." Hudgins uses the metaphor of a journey—a voyage—for the passage between the earthly world and the spiritual world. The father has "a new desire/ to travel building up, an itch to see fresh worlds. Or older ones." The father sees death as part of a spiritual cycle of rebirth: "He thinks that when I follow him/ he'll wrap me in his arms and laugh,/ the way he did when I arrived/ on earth." In spite of these reassurances from his father, the speaker is not "ready" to accept his death "cheerfully/ as if he were embarking on a trip." The speaker is afraid that he will approach death with the conviction that his father's "ship's gone down," but the poem ends with his father's more hopeful scenario, that "I'll see him standing on the dock/ and waving, shouting, Welcome back." Hudgins chooses to end the poem with a greeting, perhaps revealing his desire to believe his father's vision of the spiritual cycle of rebirth in spite of himself.

Suggestions

My Father's Song

Pre-Reading Exercise: Most students will have been told stories by their parents of their own experiences growing up. Have students start thinking about the significance of these types of stories by first having them summarize in writing one of the stories they have been told. Once they have finished, ask them to explain in writing why they think the story is important to their parent and what the story means to them.

1. Pose questions that will encourage students to closely analyze the text and interpret its details:

   a. What desire prompts the speaker to miss his father on this specific occasion?

   b. In lines 3–7, what characteristics of his father does the speaker recall? What do those characteristics describe? How does this relate to the following stanzas?

   c. What is indicated by the fact that the speaker's father and grandfather "planted [corn] several times"?

   d. Why does the grandfather have his son touch the baby mice?

   e. Why do they put the mice "in the shade / of a sand moist clod"?

   f. What lesson was the grandfather teaching his son?

   g. Explain how the sand can be both "cool and warm."

   h. Explain the poem's closing stanza:

      I remember the very softness
      of cool and warm sand and tiny alive mice
      and my father saying things.

2. For an examination of Ortiz's use of imagery, have students divide into groups and ask each group to list the images that are used in the poem and categorize them. When all the groups are finished, have the class reassemble, share their findings, and discuss how Ortiz uses the images.

3. Another poem that deals with a son's learning about the value of animal life from his father is "Weakness" (p. 22).

4. To explore the poem in light of Ortiz's background, students can using InfoTrac to research information on the Acoma Pueblo in general (Subjects: Acoma Pueblo and/or pueblos) or Ortiz in particular (Keyword: "Simon Ortiz").

Elegy for My Father, Who Is Not Dead

1. Students generally understand this poem without much difficulty. Their understanding can be assured and deepened by posing questions that require analysis as well as synthesis:

   a. For what is his father ready? For what is the speaker not ready?

   b. Describe and explain the father's attitude toward death.

   c. Show that speaker understands his father's religious beliefs.

   d. What is the speaker's attitude toward his father's faith? Does he share that faith?

   e. What impact does the faith of each have on his attitude toward death?

   f. What is revealed by the speaker's assumption that he will be told of his father's death via the telephone.

   g. Characterize the relationship between the father and son.

   h. Explain how this poem is an elegy.

2. To examine the poet's use of travel imagery, have students make a list of the words in the poem that have to do with travel, denotatively or connotatively. Once they have completed their lists, ask students to explain the significance of the images and the conclusions that can be drawn from them. If needed, specific questions can be posed:

   a. What is portrayed as a trip? Living? Dying? Both? Explain.

   b. What is portrayed as a destination? Birth? Death? After life? All three? Explain.

3. To explore the poem in light of Hudgins' personal history, have students read Hudgins' essay, "Half-Answered Prayers" (*American Scholar,* Spring 1999 v68 i2 p10.1). Students can find the essay using InfoTrac (Keyword: "andrew hudgins" AND essay).

My Father's Song and Elegy for My Father, Who Is Not Dead

1. Ask students to identify and discuss the similarities and differences between the poems. Students may initially focus solely on the most obvious similarities (both speakers are sons talking about their fathers) and differences (one of the fathers is dead; the other is not). Encourage them to delve further by having them compare and contrast the speakers' feelings toward their fathers, their relationships with them, and their acceptance of their father's values.

2. For an extended discussion of father-son relationships, "My Father's Song" and "Elegy for My Father, Who Is Not Dead" can be studied along with "Those Winter Sundays" (p. 8), "A Red Palm" (p. 9), "Digging" (p. 19), and/or "Persimmons" (p. 30)

3. "My Father's Song" and "Elegy for My Father, Who Is Not Dead" could be teamed with "The Vacuum" (p. 22) for a study of grief.

A Martian Sends a Postcard Home

Craig Raine

and

Bedtime Story

George Macbeth

"A Martian Sends a Postcard Home" and "Bedtime Story" are both told from the point of view of a nonhuman. The observations of the speakers reveal as much about the speakers themselves as they do about humanity.

The Martian is preoccupied with the physical, fascinated by the mechanical, and oblivious to the emotional. He mentions the automobile, incorrectly concluding that the car "free(s) the world / for movement" and that the rearview mirror is "a film / to watch for anything missed." He does not understand the telephone, thinking it a "haunted apparatus" that "snores" (the drone of the dial tone) and "cries" (the clamor of the ringer). He seems unable to understand how books, mechanical birds, can "cause the eyes to melt / or the body to shriek without pain." Physical pain is something familiar to the Martian, but the elimination of bodily waste is not: he mistakes the bathroom for a "punishment room." He understands exhaustion and rest ("Mist is when the sky is tired of flight / and rests its soft machine on ground"), but concludes that people are "hiding" when they sleep in a private place with their mate. The Martian understands as little about humanity as he does about their inventions.

The narrator of "Bedtime Story," reflecting on humanity from a historical perspective, has a better understanding than the Martian of human beings, at least in terms of their propensity for violence. The narrator knows that people kill for "pleasure" (an activity that led to the extinction of many creatures), that they wage war (an activity that led to the destruction of cities and the virtual annihilation of humanity), and that they respond to the unfamiliar with fear and aggression (an act that costs the last grey man his life). The narrator is apparently a mammoth termite-like insect with "fine teeth," strong jaws, round eyes, and forked arms. The society in which she lives is highly organized (labor is divided between workers and soldiers) and ruled by a queen who has instructed the soldiers in the Mission Brigade to find surviving humans and feed them. This kindness stands in stark contrast to humankind's apocalyptic aggression.

Suggestions

A Martian Sends a Postcard Home

1. Divide the class into groups and ask each group to look carefully at the Martian's descriptions and to identify each object, phenomenon, or activity that he describes. Once students have finished their identifications, ask them to examine the Martian's descriptions and explain what his descriptions reveal about his perceptions.

2. Have students consider how they and their college campus might be viewed by the Martian: "Taking the point of view of the Martian, write a postcard home about your visit to this college campus."

3. Most students will have been somewhere that is very different from their own community. Encourage them to consider their own reactions to surroundings or behaviors that are out of their norm:

   a. Identify a family, a place of worship, a city, or a country that you have visited that is very different from your own.

   b. When did you go? How old were you? Why did you go? How long were you there?

   c. Describe the place and the people.

   d. How did the place differ from your home and community? How did the people differ from family and friends?

   e. Were you surprised or confused by any of the facilities, furniture, appliances, machinery, etc.? By any of the rituals, customs, behaviors, etc.? Explain.

Bedtime Story

Pre-Reading Exercise: Ask students to explain what types of stories children are read or told at bedtime and what they believe the purpose(s) of those stories to be. After they have read and examined "Bedtime Story," use their answers as a springboard to discuss the significance of the poem's title.

1. Divide students into groups and pose questions that will prompt them to engage in analysis and synthesis:

    a. At what point in time does the story take place?

    b. Who is the speaker? To whom is he or she speaking?

    c. List the details we are given about the physical appearance of the beings in the Mission Brigade. What type of beings do they appear to be?

    d. List the details we are given about the society of the beings. What conclusions can you draw from these details?

    e. Why is the "grey man" the last of his race? What happened to the others?

    f. What is the grey man doing when he is approached by the Mission Brigade?

    g. How does the grey man respond to the soldiers? Why?

    h. What point is the writer trying to make by comparing the bones of the last grey man to those of the dodo?

    i. What is the significance of the poem's title?

2. To examine the ways in which interspecies clashes can be used to illuminate man's follies and foibles, "Bedtime Story" might be examined in conjunction with a film such as *Planet of the Apes* (1968).

A Martian Sends a Postcard Home and Bedtime Story

1. Invite students to consider the encounter between civilizations depicted in the two poems:

    a. How does the world depicted in "Bedtime Story" compare to that in "A Martian Sends a Postcard Home"?

    b. In which of the two stories does the encounter between the civilizations turn out better?

    c. Who is responsible for the happier outcome?

2. "A Martian Sends A Postcard Home" and/or "Bedtime Story" (p. 14) could be studied with "The Veldt" (p. 77) and/or "Harrison Bergeron" (p. 53), stories which present unrealistic situations, but develop realistic statements about human nature.

Counting the Mad

Donald Justice

and

Much Madness Is Divinest Sense

Emily Dickinson

In these poems, Justice and Dickinson both deal with the issue of madness and with society's response to it. Dickinson directly questions society's definition of madness, pointing out that those who contradict the opinions of the majority are far more likely to be called insane than those who affirm them. Those who are deemed "mad" frequently have more "sense" than those who are thought "sane." Indeed, many great leaders, such as Jesus, Gandhi, and Socrates, openly clashed with the leaders of the day and paid the ultimate price for their rebellion, only to be vindicated by the judgments of history.

In "Counting the Mad," a deceptively simple poem with the easy rhymes and familiar cadence of a nursery rhyme, the mad behave in ways that are traditionally thought insane (one stares blankly at a window, one thinks himself a bird, and so forth), and they receive the traditional treatment: confinement in a mental ward or asylum. The speaker is never identified, but he is familiar with some of the patients. He describes the behavior of past patients and prefaces each description with "this one," suggesting that he is working his way through some sort of patient-related list or series and that he is gesturing to the listener to indicate which patient he is talking about. The speaker's repeated use of "this one" may also indicate that he thinks of the patients not as human beings, as men and women, but as mere manifestations of their illness. This makes all the more telling the final stanza of the poem: "And this one thought himself a man, / An ordinary man, / And cried and cried No No No No / All day long."

Suggestions

Pre-Reading Exercise: To prepare students to think about mental illness and mental hospitals as well as the way people who are mentally ill are perceived and treated, have them watch and discuss the film, *One Flew Over the Cuckoo's Nest* (1975).

Counting the Mad

1. One approach is to have students work in groups to answer questions that will ensure their literal understanding of Justice's poem and begin to grapple its meaning:

    a. Who are the "ones" described in the poem?

    b. What is the setting of the poem? In other words, where are "the ones" located when the described action takes place?

    c. In line one, what type of jacket is "this one" put into? What is the purpose of this type of jacket?

    d. In line two, why is "this one" most likely sent home?

    e. In line three, by whom is "this one" most likely given bread and meat?

    f. Explain the following lines: "This one looked at the window / As though it were a wall."

    g. Why might the speaker have concluded that "this one thought himself a bird"? That "this one [thought himself] a dog"? That "this one thought himself a man"?

    h. Who is the speaker?

    i. Why does the speaker refer to those he describes only as "this one"?

    j. Look up the verb *count* in a dictionary. Explain the significance of the poem's title, "Counting the Mad."

2. Most students will readily identify and be curious about the similarities between "This Little Piggy" and Justice's poem. Write the nursery rhyme "This Little Piggy Went to Market" on the board and ask students to explain it. The rhyme, of course, is relatively nonsensical and is one of many counting games that adults play with children.

    a. One approach is to construct a table so that the first six lines of Justice's poem are adjacent to the parallel lines of the nursery rhyme:

This little piggy went	This one was put in
to market	a jacket,
This little piggy	This one was sent
stayed home	home,

This little piggy had roast beef	This one was given bread and meat
This little piggy had none	But would eat none,
This little piggy said wee wee wee	And this one cried No No No No
All the way home	All day long.

Have students compare the lines, identifying changes that have been made and explaining the effect of those changes. In their discussion, students should address such questions as the following:

How does going to market contrast with being put in a jacket?

What is the difference between staying home and being sent home?

What is suggested by a meal of "roast beef"? By a meal of "bread and meat"?

How does having no roast beef differ from refusing to eat?

How does the verb "to say" differ in meaning from the verb "to cry"?

What feelings might be expressed by "wee wee wee"? By "No No No No"? (Students who are familiar with French will note that "wee" is a homophone of *oui,* the French word for "yes," the antonym of "no.")

b. Another approach is to present students with a table containing the nursery rhyme and Justice's entire poem, and have them underscore or highlight all of the verbs (the verbs are bolded in the table below):

| "This Little Piggy" | "Counting the Mad" | | |
	Lines 1–6	Lines 7–11	Lines 12–17
This little piggy **went** to market	This one **was put** in a jacket,	This one **looked** at the window	This one **thought** himself a bird,
This little piggy **stayed** home	This one **was sent** home,	As though it **were** a wall,	This one [**thought** himself] a dog,
This little piggy **had** roast beef	This one **was given** bread and meat	This one **saw** things that were not there,	And this one **thought** himself a man,
This little piggy **had** none	But **would eat** none,		An ordinary man,
This little piggy **said** wee wee wee	And this one **cried** No No No No	And this one **cried No No No**	And **cried** and **cried** No No No No
All the way home	All day long.	All day long.	All day long.

After students have identified the verbs, ask them to answer the following questions:

Who performs the actions in "This Little Piggy"? Explain.

Who performs the actions in lines 1–3 of "Counting the Mad"? Explain.

Who performs the actions in the remainder of "Counting the Mad"? Explain.

Next, have students look closely at specific lines from Justice's poem:

How is the one described in lines 7–8 the opposite of the one described in line 9?

What do the ones described in lines 12 and 13 have in common?

Is the one described in line 14 similar to the ones described in lines 12 and 13? Explain.

Finally, have students look carefully at how Justice organizes the poem and consider how the division of the poem into stanzas contributes to their understanding:

While the lines of "Counting the Mad" clearly parallel the lines of the nursery rhyme, the poem's stanzas do not. Explain the difference.

The lines "And this one cried No No No No / All day long" occur twice: once, at the beginning of the second stanza and again at the beginning of the third. What is the reader's interpretation the first time the line appears? The second time? A variation of the lines occurs in the fourth and final stanza. What is the significance of the variation and of its placement?

Much Madness Is Divinest Sense

1. Students sometimes have some difficulty understanding Dickinson's poem because of its syntax and punctuation. One approach is to have them work through the poem, rephrasing each line. This process not only helps them understand what Dickinson is saying, it also helps them see that a poem cannot effectively be rewritten in prose. Another approach is to present students with questions that help them unravel the syntax and focus on the meaning:

    a. In the first and third lines, the word *madness* is contrasted with the word *sense*. Define each word as it is used in these lines.

    b. What is meant by "divinest *sense*"? By "starkest *madness*"?

    c. The speaker asserts that "the Majority / In this, as All, prevail." What does she mean?

    d. What does the speaker mean when she says "Assent—and you are sane"? "Demur—you're straight away dangerous"?

    e. What does it mean to be "handled with a Chain"?

    f. Do the majority of people have "a discerning Eye"? Explain.

2. Have the class identify some current controversial topics. Write their topics on the board. Once a list has been compiled, ask students which of the topics they believe to be the most controversial. Have students locate, read, and bring in a newspaper or magazine article about that topic. Begin the next class by asking students to use their articles to respond in writing to the following questions:

    a. Summarize the controversy.

    b. What seems to be the view of the majority? Of the minority?

    c. Compare and contrast the treatment being received by the majority with the treatment being received by the minority.

    d. How are those who hold the minority view being treated by the public, their opponents, and/or government officials?

    e. Does the author of the article appear to agree with the majority or the minority? Explain.

3. Have students research a famous historical figure who was executed or assassinated because his or her views were considered heretical or delusional. Students should answer the following questions:

   a. What did this person believe that caused him/her to appear so dangerous at that time?

   b. Prior to the person's death, what actions were taken to silence him or her? To what degree were these measures effective? Explain.

   c. By whom was the person executed or assassinated?

   d. What judgment has history passed on this individual?

   After students have discussed their research and their answers, ask them to discuss whether or not our society treats those who argue against the status quo in a similar fashion.

Counting the Mad and Much Madness Is Divinest Sense

1. Both poets invite the reader to think about society's definitions of insanity and its response to those it considers mad. Ask students to compare and contrast the two poems.

2. Once students have studied both poems, give them a short research project that will focus their attention on historical attitudes toward insanity. To this end, students could be directed to read a historical overview of the treatment of mental disorders in an encyclopedia such as *Encyclopedia Britannica,* choose one aspect that particularly interests them, further research that aspect, and write a short paper on it.

3. Invite students to explore their own attitudes about mental illness:

   a. Is there a difference between being mentally ill and being insane? Explain.

   b. If a person is truly insane, how should that person be treated?

   c. Can mental illnesses be cured? Explain.

4. To further explore the issue of mental illness, these poems might be studied in conjunction with the film, *A Beautiful Mind* (2001), the true story of John Nash, a mathematical genius, a Nobel Prize winner, and a victim of schizophrenia. (Nash's summary of his life can be found on the Nobel Organization's Web site at http://www.nobel.se/economics/laureates/1994/nash-autobio.html.)

5. Have students consider the social stigma associated with mental illness and the effects of that stigma. Numerous articles can be located using InfotTrac (Keyword: stigma of mental illness).

6. For a broader discussion of how people respond to "difference," team these poems with "A Very Old Man with Enormous Wings" (p. 72), "Gimpel the Fool" (p. 95), and/or "What Means Switch" (p. 179).

Four Poems from Spoon River Anthology

Edgar Lee Masters

Minerva Jones
"Indignation" Jones
Doctor Meyers
Mrs. Meyers

These four poems, epitaphs for four citizens of Spoon River, form a rich narrative about related people and events. They are excellent for analyzing a character's nature and motivation. Also, they provide a skeleton framework for what would be a highly interesting play, novel, or movie. The epitaphs reveal the story of

Minerva's background, violation, and death. Her family background is delineated by the epitaph of her father, "Indignation" Jones, whose life had turned "into a cancer," and who had "a slattern for a wife." Out of this life of poverty and disgrace came Minerva, whose sensitive poetic nature made her appear mad to the people of the village. Minerva tells of her violation ("'Butch' Weldy/Captured me after a brutal hunt") as does Doctor Meyers, who performed the abortion. Her death, Doctor Meyers acknowledges, resulted from his attempt to help her out of her dilemma, an act of charity that backfired and was misinterpreted by the rest of the village. The violation of Minerva results in three deaths: her own, Doctor Meyers', and Mrs. Meyers' (who "perished of a broken heart" as a result of the shame of her husband's actions).

Suggestions

This rich, dramatic story can be discerned only by having students first piece together the details from the four poems—what happens to Minerva and what the consequences are. But the real richness of these poems is in the wealth they offer for character study. Several techniques will work to enable students to tap into this wealth:

1. One approach is to divide the class into four groups, one group responsible for each of the poems. Have each member of the group write a brief analysis of the character; then have the members of the group discuss their individual summaries and compose a group description of the character.

2. Another technique is to have students compose a story about Minerva Jones that includes details about her family background, her violation, her death, and the consequences of her death (this will likely be an out-of-class assignment). Students should be free to invent any detail, as long as that detail is consistent with what is stated in or what could be reasonably inferred from the poems (e.g., students could reasonably infer that Minerva's home would be a dilapidated shack; it would be reasonable to picture Mrs. Meyers sitting in her parlor reading the Bible; etc.).

3. A more limited focus would be to divide the class into four groups, assigning one character to each group and having the group compose a story entitled "One Day in the Life of Minerva Jones" (or one of the other characters). Again students are free to invent any detail as long as the detail is consistent with the ideas of the poem. Have the group leader read this story to the rest of the class, who may critique it for its consistency with the ideas of the poems.

4. Another limited focus would be to have students, working together in groups, compose a story called "The Last Day of Minerva Jones." They should bring all four characters into their story, making sure that the details they invent fit the poems' characterizations. Suggest students use third-person omniscient point of view so that the thoughts of the characters can be revealed (Minerva, for example, might think about her treatment by the townspeople as she makes her trip to Dr. Meyers' office). After each group has read its story, have the other groups critique the story for its thoroughness and adherence to the characterizations of the poems.

5. A totally different approach would be to have students look up a definition of the word "indignation." When students understand that indignation is a kind of anger arising from something that is unjust or unfair, have them determine why "indignation" is quite rightly what each of these characters should feel.

6. These pieces could be teamed with "Mother to Son" (p. 7) and/or "A Rose for Emily" (p. 193). "Mother to Son" presents a character struggling against poverty and other problems of life. The attitude of this character, however, is quite different from the bitter attitude of "Indignation" Jones, and a worthwhile discussion is possible about the different responses that people make toward the indignities of life. "A Rose for Emily" also presents a character struggling against forces over which she has little control. In that story, however, great pride causes bizarre responses to the indignities of life.

7. To consider the issue of forgiveness, these poems could be studied with "The Gilded Six-Bits" (p. 63).

Digging

Seamus Heaney

In "Digging," the speaker recalls the back-breaking work of his father and grandfather and tries to find a connection between his work and theirs. The speaker is in the house, attempting to write, when he notices the sound of his father digging and looks out the window. Seeing his father's "straining rump among the flowerbeds," he recalls how his father and grandfather worked when he was a child. The speaker vividly describes his father's expert handling of the shovel as he dug potatoes to feed his family. Equally vivid is his description of his grandfather's masterful "Nicking and slicing" of the turf he cut to provide his family with fuel for heat and cooking. The work done by his father and grandfather was the work they were meant to do: "By God, the old man could handle a spade. / Just like his old man." The speaker clearly respects and admires the work of his forefathers, but he has "no spade to follow men like them." Indeed, he has been called to a different task: he must write. While he cannot continue the tradition of digging with a shovel, he can dig with his pen.

Suggestions

1. One approach is to present students with several conclusions and have them locate the details that support each one:

   a. The speaker's father and grandfather were extraordinarily good at what they did;

   b. The speaker admires and respects the work done by his father and grandfather;

   c. Family history and connection is important to the speaker;

   d. The speaker cannot do the same works as his father and grandfather;

   e. The speaker comes to understand there is a connection between his work and the work of his forebears.

2. Another approach is to present students with questions that ask them to closely examine the text:

   a. What does the poet mean when he says that his father digs down and comes back up "twenty years away"?

   b. When the speaker was a boy, his father dug for potatoes and his grandfather dug for turf. What similarities are there between potatoes and turf (in terms of purpose as well as physical properties)?

   c. Compare and contrast the attitudes of the father and the grandfather toward their work.

   d. What is the speaker's attitude toward the work of his father and grandfather? Explain.

   e. Discuss the multiple meanings of "living roots," as the phrase is used by the speaker in line 27.

   f. What does the speaker mean when he says that he has "no spade to follow men" like his father and grandfather?

   g. Compare the first two lines of the poem with the last three lines. Identify how the final lines differ from the opening lines, and explain what the changes reveal about the change that has taken place within the speaker.

   h. Explain the significance of the poem's title. (Be sure to consider the many meanings of the word *dig*.)

3. To examine father-son relationships, this poem could be coupled with "Those Winter Sundays" (p. 8) and/or "A Red Palm" (p. 9).

4. For discussion of metaphor, "Digging" could be studied with works such as "Mother to Son" (p. 7) and "Harlem" (p. 7).

Barbie Doll

Marge Piercy

and

Mr. Z

M.` Carl Holman

These two poems are powerful statements about the potentially destructive effects of conformity. "Barbie Doll" revolves around expectations based on gender while "Mr. Z" revolves around expectations based on race. The lives of the characters in both poems are shaped by the same forces: childhood training and pressure to conform to "acceptable" patterns of appearance and behavior.

Throughout her short life, the girl in "Barbie Doll" is bombarded with messages regarding the behavior and appearance acceptable for women. As a young child, she is given toys that teach her to be a mother and a housekeeper; she is also given play cosmetics that teach her the importance of feminine beauty. As she grows, the pressure to conform to societal expectations continues: "diet, smile, and wheedle." The many admirable traits of this "girlchild" are small in comparison to her "fat nose on thick legs." Her appearance does not fit the acceptable standard of feminine beauty. She finally despairs of ever fitting it and commits suicide. Ironically, only after killing herself does the girl receive affirmation of her beauty: "Doesn't she look pretty?"

Like the "girlchild," Mr. Z learns society's opinions and expectations at a young age. He is "taught early that his mother's skin [is] the sign of error." Perceiving that his blackness will be a disadvantage in a society dominated by whites, Mr. Z eschews qualities of his black heritage and adopts patterns of behavior that he believes to be more socially advantageous. While the girl in "Barbie Doll" literally kills herself, Mr. Z figuratively kills a part of himself. Holman's tone, like Piercy's, is bitter, mocking. He is bitter toward both a society that discriminates against blacks and blacks who forego their racial heritage and attempt to behave according to their notion of how respectable whites behave. The bitterness toward both these conditions is brought together with great irony in the conclusion of the poem, the obituary reads, "One of the most distinguished members of his race." This statement points out the bigotry of white society, which will not go beyond the fact that Mr. Z is black. It also shows the uselessness of rejecting one's heritage in an effort to facilitate upward mobility. After all, regardless of what Mr. Z has accomplished, white society considers his race the most important fact about him.

Suggestions

Barbie Doll

Pre-Reading Exercise: Have students consider the pressure society puts on girls to fit a certain pattern by asking them to examine the advertisements and articles in a magazine such as *Seventeen*. What messages are sent by these ads and articles? How are they reinforced by other media (television, film, etc.)?

1. Have students construct a "causal chain" that answers the question, "Why did this girl kill herself?" The answer involves despair (the end of the causal chain), stemming from an inability to fit a standard explicitly communicated in adolescence and implicitly communicated in early childhood (the beginning of the causal chain).

2. After students have read and discussed the poem, ask them to discuss how society expects men to look and act and to explain how those expectations are communicated.

3. To explore the relationship between isolation and suicide, the poem could be analyzed in conjunction with "Richard Cory" (p. 4) and/or "Life after High School" (p. 132).

4. "Barbie Doll" could be teamed with "Lot's Wife" (p. 3), "Hills Like White Elephants" (p. 50), "The Fat Girl" (p. 120), and/or "The Chrysanthemums" (p. 202) for an extended study of the roles of women.

5. For an extended discussion of the effects of nurturing, "Barbie Doll" could be teamed with "The Veldt" (p. 77), "I Stand Here Ironing" (p. 114), and/or "The Fat Girl" (p. 120).

6. The notion of what constitutes "acceptable" physical beauty could be examined by studying the poem with "The Fat Girl" (p. 120), "Heavy Judgment" (p. 252), and/or "Starved Out" (p. 246).

Mr. Z

Pre-Reading Exercise: To involve students in the ideas of the poem, have them put in writing their definition of the term "heritage." Then divide them into groups to compile a list of those elements that compose "heritage" (some of the elements are likely to be connected with family, race, country, section of the country, and religion).

1. Have students make a list of the specific things that Mr. Z rejects. (This list would include things such as jazz, pork, certain ethnic restaurants, and so on.) Once students have reported their lists, the question should be asked, "How important are these things in defining what or who one is?" Such an approach should lead students to see that Mr. Z and his wife value many superficial things as indicators of heritage—certainly different from those elements of heritage that the students listed for themselves earlier.

2. For a broader examination of retaining and/or changing ethnic identity, study "Mr. Z" (p. 20) along with "Lost Sister" (p. 28), "Persimmons" (p. 30), "Everyday Use" (p. 88), "What Means Switch" (p. 179), "Mother Tongue" (p. 227), and/or "The Myth of the Latin Woman" (p. 232)

3. To examine the notion of identity in a non-ethnic context, "The Fat Girl" (p. 120) and/or "Life after High School" (p. 132) could be assigned along with "Mr. Z."

Barbie Doll and Mr. Z

1. Provide students with the following sentence: "Both the girl in Barbie Doll and Mr. Z try to change themselves so they will fit the patterns society says they should fit." Have students divide up into groups and describe the pattern each attempts to fit, discuss how each changes to fit it, and explain what each loses and/or gains in the process. Once students have discussed their responses, ask them to describe the attitudes of the poets toward the society in which these characters live.

2. The influence of childhood training can be examined by studying the poems in conjunction with "The Veldt" (p. 77) and/or "The Fat Girl" (p. 120).

3. The influence of social pressure can be explored by teaming "Barbie Doll" and "Mr. Z" with "Life after High School" (p. 132) and/or "Heavy Judgment" (p. 252).

4. For further discussion of the issue of conformity, "Barbie Doll" and "Mr. Z" could be studied with "The Unknown Citizen" (p. 35), "Curiosity" (p. 36), "The Lottery" (p. 43), "Harrison Bergeron" (p. 53), and/or "Life After High School" (p. 132).

The Vacuum

Howard Nemerov

In "The Vacuum," the speaker's wife has died, and he is grieving. Initially, the speaker appears to avoid the vacuum cleaner because he closely associates it with his wife. She was the one who used the machine, crawling under stairs and in corners to vacuum away all vestiges of dirt. His statement that his wife's "soul / Went into that vacuum cleaner" reveals the strength of his association. It also suggests that the speaker is reluctant to acknowledge completely that his wife's death has permanently separated the two of them from each other. The speaker projects onto the vacuum his own thoughts and feelings, projections that reveal the depth of his depression.

The speaker is sullen, withdrawn, and judgmental, and he projects these attributes onto the vacuum cleaner. The vacuum (like the house) is still and silent. The speaker imagines it "sulk[ing]" in the closet and "grinning" at his slovenliness and age. Obviously, the machine is not sentient: It is not brooding about its banishment and smirking at the speaker's consequent inability to maintain a clean home. The speaker feels guilty about the state of the house, believing that he deserves condemnation for being unable to clean it. He imagines that the vacuum's mechanical drone would be a plaintive, remorseful "howl," condemning his filth, his life, him. In fact, he has judged his "life"—not just his house—to be "slovenly" and his youth to be "dog-dead." By using the phrase "dog-dead," the speaker indicates not only that his youth is long past, but also that he has deemed his youthful self to have been worthless. (A dead dog symbolizes something of no value. See, for example, 1 Sam 24:14 and 2 Sam 9:18.)

The speaker is disenchanted with life. His assertion that he has "lived this way long enough" initially seems to mean that he has lived in filth long enough. Yet, the statement also hints at a deeper sense of futility, suggesting that he has lived in misery long enough, that he has lived alone long enough, that he has simply lived long enough. Indeed, this point is reinforced by his preference for inertia. One of the reasons the speaker does not want to engage the vacuum has to do with his avoidance of animation. He does not want to see the vacuum's "bag swell like a belly, eating the dust"; he prefers that the bag remain "limp as a stopped lung." Engaged, the vacuum would seem to the speaker to be alive. And living is something that the speaker, in his depressed state, cannot truly imagine.

Anger is the only feeling that the speaker comes close to acknowledging as his own, noting that his heart is "angry." That the anger stems from his having been separated from his wife is obvious, but it is emphasized and made more pitiable by his description of his heart as "howl[ing]." A howl is a mournful, penetrating sound. It is a sound made by human beings who are feeling profound pain, sorrow, or anger. It is also the sound made by wolves to locate the ones from whom they have been separated. He cannot be reunited with his wife, a woman who apparently kept his life in order and filled. He feels empty and alone: He feels like he is in a vacuum. Unlike the vacuum cleaner, that can fill its void by "eating the dust / And the woolen mice," the speaker cannot fill his "hungry" heart: He is unable to grab hold of anything, "biting" only at "air." In his anger and his anguish, the speaker concludes that life is meaningless, "cheap as dirt." His understanding does not release him from life: "still the . . . heart / Hangs on."

Suggestions

Pre-Reading Exercise: Have students identify something (an object, a place, a scent, etc.) that causes them to think of a specific person. Ask them to explain why they associate the two and to describe how they feel when they come in contact with the thing they identified and are reminded of that person.

1.   To help students understand the speaker's emotional state, have them answer the following:
   a. Why is the house quiet?
   b. Where does he keep the vacuum? Why?

    c. Why, according to the speaker, will he not use the vacuum?

    d. Identify the human qualities that the speaker attributes to the vacuum.

    e. Which of the feelings that the speaker attributes to the vacuum cleaner seem actually to be his own feelings? Explain.

2. Once students have an understanding of the literal meaning of the poem, pose questions that will encourage them to synthesize the details:

    a. Describe the life the speaker appears to have had before his wife died.

    b. Explain how the speaker's life has changed since his wife's death.

    c. The speaker says that life is "cheap as dirt." What does he mean?

    d. For what does the speaker "hunger"?

    e. Why is the speaker "angry"?

    f. To what is the speaker "hang[ing] on"?

    g. Why does his heart "howl"?

    h. In what way is the speaker biting at "air"?

    i. Look up the word *vacuum* in a dictionary. Consider all of the word's meanings, and then explain the significance of the title.

3. Discuss with students Elisabeth Kubler-Ross's stages of grief (see the following essay) and then ask them to determine which stages are manifest in the speaker: denial/isolation, anger, bargaining, depression, and/or acceptance.

4. To explore the issue of grief further, team "The Vacuum" with "Elegy for My Father, Who Is Not Dead" (p. 12) and "My Father's Song" (p. 11).

5. For a broader consideration of the ways in which people respond to loss, this poem might be studied with "Lot's Wife" (p. 3), "Power" (p. 23), "The Gilded Six-Bits" (p. 63), "Life after High School" (p. 132), "Islands on the Moon" (p. 144), and/or "Shame" (p. 213).

Kubler-Ross's Stages of Grief

Loss—the separation of an individual from someone or something of significance—is a fundamental part of the human experience. Various attempts have been made to understand the process that people go through in adjusting to loss. Perhaps the most widely accepted model is the one developed by Elisabeth Kubler-Ross, a psychiatrist who worked extensively with terminally ill patients. In *Death and Dying* (1969), Kubler-Ross identified five stages through which people move when faced with the news that their death is imminent: denial, anger, bargaining, depression, and acceptance. The stages are not necessarily experienced singly or sequentially: People move into, out of, and back into stages according to their individual needs. In fact, people may simultaneously experience two or more stages. Although developed to classify the responses of the terminally ill, the five stages have been found to identify the natural processes involved in working through the various forms of grief, regardless of the specific catalyst. When coming to terms with the loss of a loved one, people do not usually go through the bargaining stage: The loss has occurred and is irreversible. They do, however, usually experience denial, anger, and depression before arriving at acceptance.

    Upon hearing that a loved one has died, many people become numb and deny the veracity of what they have been told. Even after they acknowledge the reality of the death, some form of denial may linger. For example, some people who have lost a spouse may think they see or hear the deceased in the house. These transitory hallucinations are usually manifestations of their denial: They are unable to accept the irreversibility of their loss.

In addition to denial, people in grief often experience anger. Any one of the emotions that survivors feel—hurt, frustration, disappointment, and fear—can, by itself, facilitate anger. It is not surprising, then, that someone who feels all of them becomes angry. Having been permanently separated from a loved one, survivors often feel intense pain as well as absolute powerlessness: There is nothing they can do to control or alter what has happened. On a different level, they may be deeply disappointed and frustrated that they will not be able to complete the plans, achieve the goals, and realize the dreams they had shared with the deceased. Depending on their degree of dependency, they may feel frightened, questioning their own ability to live without the deceased. Feeling victimized, survivors may search for someone to hold responsible. They often direct their anger toward doctors, the hospital, family, God, even the deceased.

People who have lost a loved one usually experience depression. For some, this state consists primarily of profound but manageable sadness. For others, the depression can be overwhelming. They may lose hope that their anguish will ever diminish, that they will ever feel whole, and that they will ever be happy. In their misery, survivors frequently focus on the merits of the deceased, forgetting the flaws, and condemn themselves for all that they did or did not do. By idealizing the deceased and demonizing themselves, survivors exacerbate their pain and their own sense of worthlessness, sometimes concluding that they, not their loved one, should have died and that life in general has no real significance. Survivors who are overcome by despair often isolate themselves, minimizing as much as possible their contact with other human beings.

Weakness

Alden Nowlan

"Weakness" is extremely accessible: Its language and syntax are simple, and the plot is straightforward. With little difficulty, students are able to identify the point of view and summarize the action. Determining the multidimensional significance of the title may prove somewhat more challenging.

All of the primary denotations of the word *weakness*—a lack of strength, a failing or fault, a special fondness—are at work in this poem. Certainly the mare lacks strength. She is, after all, not only "old" but quite ill, "drool[ing] blood into her mash" and "shiver[ing] in her jute blanket." In fact, some readers initially conclude that the father is going to shoot the horse because she is no longer of utilitarian use on the farm. Those who have reached this conclusion will often defend it by pointing out that the father "hates weakness worse than hail" and that he "curs[es] [the horse] for a bad bargain." These readers have failed to consider the father's conduct.

A close look at his actions reveals that he has a good deal of affection for the mare and that he is not particularly eager to be rid of her. Though he will kill her the next morning, he checks on, feeds, and tends to her that night. Even as he is "cursing" her, he tries to make her more comfortable: He takes his own coat and spreads it "*carefully* over her sick shoulders" (emphasis added). He will end her suffering himself, and he will end it efficiently ("shoot[ing] her in the ear, once"), but he will do it reluctantly, "without haste."

The father's decision to shoot the mare, despite his probable preference not to do so, reveals the strength of the father's character: Not to end the mare's suffering—even when doing so means ending her life—would be selfish and cruel. In short, it would be "weak." And the father "hates weakness."

Suggestions

Pre-Reading Exercise: Have students define and give examples of "weakness." Usually, students will provide a variety of meanings, most of which they will later be able to relate to the poem.

1. One method of prompting students to consider the issue of "weakness" is to have them answer the following questions:
   a. Who is the speaker?
   b. Describe the setting.
   c. Why does the father hate hail?
   d. Explain why the father will shoot the mare.
   e. Identify details in the poem that reveal the father's feelings about the mare.
   f. Explain why the poem is entitled "Weakness."

2. Another approach is to discuss briefly with students the fact that most people mentally talk to themselves. Some people have one "voice" in their head; others have a committee of "voices." Ask students to examine the details in the poem and determine what the father might be thinking that night. Then, have students get into groups and write a dialogue between two or three of the father's mental voices that reveals his thoughts and feelings.

3. Ask students to consider an instance in which they had to choose between doing what was "right" or "difficult" and doing what was "less right" or "less difficult." When all students have thought of a time when they faced this choice, have them write a paragraph explaining why they made the choice they made and how they felt after they had taken their chosen course of action. Then, ask for volunteers to read their paragraphs aloud.

4. Pair "Weakness" with "My Father's Song" (p. 11) to compare how the sons learn about the value of animal life.

5. "Weakness" can be studied with "Crusader Rabbit" (p. 58) to examine what a person's treatment of a "weak" being reveals about his or her character. Have students start by comparing and contasting the attitude of the father toward the horse with the attitude of Raglan toward Jeremy.

Power

Adrienne Rich

"Power" focuses, ultimately, on the ways in which our personal strengths and weaknesses often stem from the same source. Students are sometimes confused by the multiple meanings of "power" that are at work in the poem: power as energy, strength, ability, action, and influence. In the first two stanzas of the poem, Rich focuses primarily on impersonal power, but her use of the phrase "our history" suggests that, ultimately, her focus will shift.

The second stanza's image of a backhoe unearthing a bottle subtly displays the breadth of meanings encompassed by the word "power." The backhoe, a machine that can dig more than a foot deep and lift more than five thousand pounds with its bucket, is unquestionably strong, able, and active. Powered by fossil fuel, it is also implicitly symbolic of humanity's dependence on "earth-deposits" for the energy necessary to accomplish its goals. These goals frequently involve the reduction of manual labor (the backhoe certainly does that) and the relief of physical and emotional discomfort. The tonic—"a hundred-year-old / cure for fever or melancholy"—serves as a reminder that people also rely on planetary provisions (organic and inorganic) to influence and ease their maladies. The bottle containing the tonic is amber. Literally, of course, this means that the bottle is brownish-yellow. But, the word "amber" also brings to mind the fossil resin of prehistoric coniferous trees, an "earth-deposit" once widely believed to have healing power. (In fact, Hippocrates recommended its use in the treatment of various aliments.) Using the deceptively simple images of the amber bottle of tonic and the working backhoe, Rich illustrates not only multiple types of power, but also humanity's continuation of the ancient quest to garner power from the planet.

In the third and fourth stanzas of the poem, Rich narrows and then widens her focus on power. Initially, she becomes very specific, examining Marie Curie's "power." Curie was fascinated by radiation and firmly believed that it could play a significant role in combating cancer and relieving human suffering. Her fascination and conviction, combined with her intelligence and education, led her to devote her life to learning as much as she could about radium, "the element / she had purified." Her work gave her intellectual pleasure and earned her worldwide acclaim and influence, but it also caused a number of maladies that were painful, disabling, and, ultimately, fatal. Curie could acknowledge that her work had been beneficial to humanity and that she gained a certain amount of power as a result. She could not admit that it had also been detrimental to her health. For Curie, the truth—that her body had been gravely injured by radiation—was apparently too painful to contemplate, too difficult to accept. Just as her vision was impaired by cataracts so, too, was her perspicacity impeded by denial. She died "denying / her wounds came from the same source as her power."

"Power" has at its core a central paradox of the human experience: One's strengths and one's weaknesses often stem from the same source. This is a truth that many people accept in theory but deny in reality. For example, adults who grew up with an alcoholic parent may acknowledge that their early experiences had a direct impact on their development, but they may have difficulty acknowledging that the characteristics they developed are both empowering (sensitivity, tenacity, etc.) and impairing (distrust, anger, etc.). Indeed, Curie's refusal to acknowledge the damaging effects of her work is illustrative of human behavior: People often deny truths that are too painful or frightening for them to accept.

Suggestions

Pre-Reading Exercise: Have students, working individually, write down as many different examples of power as they can. Then, ask them to divide into groups, classify their examples, and make a list of their categories. You can write the students' lists on the board and use them to generate a discussion of power. Or, you can take up the lists, merge them, and create one list of alphabetized, nonduplicated categories. This list can be used later as a tool to help students in their examination of the poem (see suggestion two).

1. One approach is to pose questions that will prompt students to look closely at the details of the text, determining not only the meanings of individual words and ideas, but connecting the ideas to each other. Have students get into groups and answer the following questions:

    a. What two events does the speaker say happened "Today"?

    b. Explain what the speaker means by an "earth-deposit."

    c. What is contained in the "amber" bottle unearthed by the backhoe? For what purpose was the "tonic" produced?

    d. The "element" that Curie "purified" is radium (ll. 8–9). Look up radium in a dictionary or encyclopedia and answer the following questions in your own words:

    -   For what medical purpose is it used?
    -   Identify a source of radium.
    -   Where is this source found?
    -   What methods might be used to collect this source so the radium can be extracted?

    e. Describe in your own words the effects of radiation sickness on Curie.

    f. Explain how the effects of the radiation sickness might have affected Curie's ability to perform her scientific work.

    g. What type(s) of "power" did Curie have?

    h. In what way(s) did Curie's "wounds" come from "the same source as her power"?

    i. Why did she deny "her wounds came from the same source as her power"?

2. Another approach is to focus on the concept of power. Ask students to go through the poem and mark all the words that in any way relate to any form of power. Then, distribute the list of categories they created as a pre-reading exercise. Have them classify the words according to their categories and make a list of words that do not fit into any of the categories they had previously identified. Ask them to go back through the initial stanzas and see if they overlooked any words that could be categorized. When they are through, students will likely have identified and classified most of the words in the first two stanzas: *living, earth-deposit, earth, deposit, backhoe, divulged, crumbling, flank, amber, perfect, cure, fever, melancholy, tonic, winter,* and *climate.* Have the class discuss their categories (using words from the poem to illustrate their points) and their concepts of power. Then, ask them to reread the last two stanzas, mark any words they might have neglected, and classify all the words they marked. Subsequent discussion of their categories should enable them not only to understand individual stanzas of the poem but also the relationship between the first two and the last two stanzas.

3. After "Power" has been discussed in class, students might be asked to read a biographical article on Marie Curie. They can be asked to locate one themselves (InfoTrac Keyword: marie curie) or they can be given a specific article to read (an excellent article that is available online is Nanny Fröman, "Marie and Pierre Curie and the Discovery of Polonium and Radium," Lecture at the Royal Academy of Sciences, Stockholm, Sweden, 28 February 1996. <www.nobel.se/physics/articles/curie/>). Students can then analyze the way in which their having more knowledge about Curie influenced their reading of the poem.

4. To further explore one of Rich's points—our power and our pain often stem from the same source—this poem can be studied with "I Stand Here Ironing" (p. 114), "The Fat Girl" (p. 120), "Life after High School" (p. 132), "Islands on the Moon" (p. 144), "Shame" (p. 213), and/or "Daddy Tucked the Blanket" (p. 215).

5. For an examination of the ways in which people respond to loss, "Power" might be studied with "Lot's Wife" (p. 3), "Power" (p. 23), "The Gilded Six-Bits" (p. 63), "Life after High School" (p. 132), "Islands on the Moon" (p. 144), and/or "Shame" (p. 213).

The Chimney Sweeper, from
Songs of Innocence

and

The Chimney Sweeper, from
Songs of Experience

William Blake

The perspective from which we view events and people is shaped by our own experience, and our perspective often changes as we gain experience. An adult may recall a childhood event and perceive it quite differently than he or she did as a youngster. Studied together, "The Chimney Sweeper" poems provide the opportunity for students to examine similar situations from differing perspectives, one innocent and one experienced. These differing perspectives were referred to by Blake as "two contrary states of the human soul." These poems are also excellent to use in the study of imagery.

The speakers in both poems are children who have been apprenticed to be chimney sweepers, yet they perceive their plights quite differently. The innocent sweeper is naive, unable to recognize the horror of his situation. He thinks it better that Tom's head be shaved than his hair be "spoil[ed]" by the soot, and he believes that goodness is invariably rewarded: "if all do their duty, they need not fear harm." Tom is also an innocent, and his dream is no doubt comforting wish fulfillment; his present life is horrific, but his next life will be pleasant.

The experienced sweeper understands quite clearly the horror of his plight, the imminence of his death, and the hypocrisy of his parents, who, having turned his life into one of misery, have gone "to the church to pray." (It might be argued that this chimney sweeper's parents are innocents because they "think they have done [him] no injury." If the parents are, indeed, innocents, then the poem clearly illustrates the potentially destructive consequences of adult innocence.) Further, the experienced sweeper perceives that the priest, the king, and their God "make up a heaven of our misery," revealing an attitude toward religion that is quite different from Tom's attitude. Tom dreams that the sweepers will be freed by an angel and "have God for a father and never want joy." The experienced chimney sweeper is bitter and accusatory while the innocent chimney sweeper, oblivious to the true horror of his situation, is naive and accepting.

The poems are also excellent to use to explore imagery in poetry. "The Chimney Sweeper" from *Songs of Innocence* is filled with contrasting images. The boys' lives are described in terms of confinement, darkness, cold, drudgery, and filth. The life dreamed of by Tom is one of freedom, light, warmth, play, and cleanliness. In this dream, the boys are not confined, even by clothing; they are able to "run" and "sport." They are able to attend to their own needs, cleaning themselves rather than chimneys. The coffins from which the sweepers are released in the dream parallel the chimneys in which they spend much of their lives and suggest the sweepers will suffer premature death. The life of the speaker in "The Chimney Sweeper" from *Songs of Experience* also contrasts with Tom's dream. While the children in Tom's dream are "naked," this chimney sweeper perceives that he has been "clothed . . . in the clothes of death." Indeed, he knows that he will soon be placed in a coffin like the one in Tom's dream.

Suggestions

Pre-Reading Exercise: Have students examine the way in which experience alters perspective by having them respond in writing to the following: What event or person do you view differently now than you did as a child? What accounts for the difference?

1. To help students focus on the speakers' differing perspectives, ask them to look up the definitions of *innocence* and *experience,* and, using these definitions, to answer the following questions:

    a. Explain why the sweeper in "The Chimney Sweeper" from *Songs of Innocence* would be considered "innocent."

    b. Explain why the sweeper in "The Chimney Sweeper" from *Songs of Experience* would be considered "experienced."

    c. Would the parents mentioned in "The Chimney Sweeper" from *Songs of Experience* be considered "innocent" or "experienced"? Explain.

2. To examine the imagery in the poems, have students first read the definition of *imagery* in the Glossary. After they have done this, one approach would be to ask them to describe in writing the life Tom has and the life he would like to have. After they have completed their descriptions, have them return to the poem and pick out the words and phrases that led them to their conclusions. Another approach would be to give students two summary words, *confinement* and *freedom,* and have them pick out words and phrases from the poems that indicate these two conditions.

3. To examine further the contrast between innocent and experienced states of being, "The Chimney Sweeper" poems could be studied with "The Gilded Six-Bits" (p. 63), "Gimpel the Fool" (p. 95), and/or "Crusader Rabbit" (p. 58).

4. Have students consider the ways in which experience alters perspective, especially with regard to one's parents, by teaming these poems with "Those Winter Sundays" (p. 8) and/or "Islands on the Moon" (p. 144).

5. "The Chimney Sweeper" poems work well with Hughes' "I, Too" (p. 6) and "Harlem" (p. 7), poems that reflect an innocent and experienced perspective, respectively.

6. Child labor is not a thing of the distant past. Have students use InfoTrac to research contemporary child labor (Subject: Child Labor Practices).

Dulce et Decorum Est

Wilfred Owen

"Dulce et Decorum Est" is a horrifying, graphically realistic depiction of the sufferings of war. Owen's content comes, no doubt, from firsthand experience: He saw much action in World War I and, ironically, was killed one week before the armistice treaty was signed. No doubt he witnessed the terrible death caused by poisonous gas, a newly invented weapon that helped man make, in the words of Hardy, "red war yet redder." The grotesque descriptions of the effects of gas bitterly point out the irony of the attitude that it is "sweet and fitting to die for one's country."

Suggestions

1. Because the poem is obviously antiwar, invite into students' thinking the following considerations:
   a. For what reasons do countries engage in war?
   b. Under what conditions is war justifiable?

   Ask for responses to these questions, and make a list on the board of all distinct responses. The list for the first question is likely to be longer than the list for the second.

2. To focus on the attitude of the poet, divide students into groups and have them discuss and then prepare a group response to the following questions:
   a. Summarize the conditions of battle as shown in "Dulce et Decorum Est."
   b. Summarize the effects upon the body of one who is "gassed."
   c. How does the poet prove that this is a lie: Dulce et decorum est pro patriamori?

3. Students might be asked to explore the use of biological and chemical weapons in general (InfoTrac Keyword: "biological and chemical weapons" or mustard gas in particular (InfoTrac Keyword: "mustard gas"). For a more focused approach, have all students read the same article. One article thought-proviking article that is accessible through InfoTrac is Keith Suter's "The Troubled History of Chemical and Biological Warfare." *Contemporary Review*, Sept 2003: 161-5.

Mending Wall

Robert Frost

"Mending Wall" demonstrates one of Frost's typical patterns of theme development: A common event occurring in a natural setting is used as a springboard for developing statements about human experience and human nature. The wall becomes a symbol for those barriers that people set up to keep others from getting too close or to conceal that which is within. Since most of the observations about the wall are made by the speaker, who says he does not want it, one could conclude that the poet believes we should break down walls between people rather than mend them. The attitude of the neighbor, "Good fences make good neighbors," is also compelling, especially if one has suffered as a result of opening up to someone else. Although it certainly is reasonable to avoid pain, the poem suggests, overall, that walls make one miss the opportunity to become more knowledgeable of others as well as oneself. By choosing to retain the walls, the neighbor remains in "darkness," the darkness of ignorance, both of the speaker and of his own feelings.

Important to the defense of the speaker's point of view is the "Something . . . that doesn't love a wall." The "Something" has to be nature, implying that the walls we construct between ourselves and others are "unnatural" or artificial. The speaker's point of view is also supported by blind adherence to tradition demonstrated by the neighbor. The neighbor's attitude toward barriers is based on his father's beliefs, and he has not asked himself why "Good fences make good neighbors."

One should not ignore, however, the speaker's own unwitting contribution to maintaining the wall. Although he professes disapproval of the wall, he makes little serious attempt to show his disapproval to his neighbor. Further, the speaker announces to his neighbor that it is spring and time to mend the wall, has "gone behind" hunters and repaired the wall without any help from his neighbor, and he keeps to his side of the wall when he gets together with his neighbor to make repairs. These subtle touches indicate the pervasiveness of "walls": We all keep and maintain some barriers, even if we might feel the desire to remove them.

Suggestions

1. Many students have a difficult time getting the facts of the poem straight; often they simply get lost in Frost's complicated poetic sentences. To help students understand the literal meaning of the poem, divide them into groups and have them answer the following questions:

    a. What does the "Something" do to the wall? What, evidently, is the "Something"?

    b. Why do hunters tear down parts of the wall?

    c. Who repairs the damage done to the wall by the hunters?

    d. Who notifies whom about the wall's needing repair?

    e. Describe the process of repairing the wall.

    f. Why, according to the speaker, is the wall not needed "where it is"?

    g. From whom does the neighbor get the idea that "Good fences make good neighbors"?

2. Once students have a good grasp of the literal meaning of the poem, ask them questions that will help them see the issues raised:

    a. What, besides property and animals, could be walled in or out?

    b. The speaker questions the need for the wall, but his actions seem to contradict his words. What actions does the speaker perform to help maintain both the literal and the figurative walls between himself and his neighbor? What does he not do that maintains the wall?

    c. The speaker thinks his neighbor "moves in darkness . . . / Not of woods only and the shade of trees." In what ways is the neighbor in "darkness"?

    d. For what is the wall a symbol?

3.   The issue of unquestioned tradition could be examined by studying "The Lottery" (p. 43) along with "Mending Wall."

Lost Sister

Cathy Song

"Lost Sister" tells the story of a Chinese woman who travels far from her ancestral home in China to the Pacific shores of America. In the process, she escapes the constraints of the culturally subscribed woman's role and finds that she can "stride along with men" in this country.

The tone of the poem changes in the second section and what looked to be a poem about escaping from the prison of her birth into the freedom of the new world is suddenly a poem about confronting the realities of life in a strange new country where fellow immigrants swarm like locusts and the young girl finds herself in "another wilderness." Here, in place of the restrictions of her birth where women learn to "walk in shoes / the size of teacups," she must learn to deal with "Dough-faced landlords" and the dirty realities of city life, such as presumably cramped apartment life near elevated train tracks ("A giant snake rattles above"). Now the traditions of her Chinese culture that once seemed so restrictive have become a link with her homeland, and she seeks tangible connections to her past in community (the communication system of laundry lines and Chinese restaurants) and artifacts (the "jade link / handcuffed to your wrist").

This emotionally complex poem mirrors the journey many immigrants have made. They flee their homeland to escape restrictions of gender, religion, or caste only to find themselves in a new land yearning for roots.

Suggestions

1.   Students usually have very specific questions about this poem. Have each student write down 2–3 questions, then collect their questions. Divide the class into groups, randomly distribute their questions, and ask each group to answer the questions they have been given. When the groups have finished, discuss their questions and answers.

2.   Another method is to provide students with questions that will encourage them to both analyze and synthesize the text.

    a. What value did Jade hold in the traditional Chinese society described in the first section?

    b. Why is it significant that "In China / even the peasants / named their first daughters / Jade"?

    c. Literally and figuratively, why were the daughters unable to move freely?

    d. In what sense did the daughters "travel far"?

    e. Who is the subject of the poem's second section?

    f. What advantages has she found in America?

    g. Explain how, for her, America is also a "wilderness."

    h. What is the "giant snake" that "rattles above"?

    i. Who are the "Dough-faced landlords"?

    j. Why are laundries and restaurants her "communication systems"?

    k. Explain why she "need[s] China."

    l. Like her "mother / who walked for centuries, / footless," she has "left no footprints." Why not?

    m. What is the significance of the poem's title, "Lost Sister"?

3. Still another approach is to have students think about how the sister's experiences in America differ from the experiences of the daughters in China. First, have students underline all the nouns the speaker uses to describe the daughter's experiences in China and the sister's experiences in America. Then, ask them to compare and contrast the daughter's experiences in China with the sister's experiences in America. Finally, challenge them to decide where they think the sister would rather "live."

4. Invite one group of students to list all the complaints the immigrant has against her country of origin. Have the other group list all the complaints she has against her new country. Bring the two groups together and discuss the complaints.

5. Have students relate their experiences to that of the sister. Ask them to think of a time they escaped from one situation to another only to find that the situation they escaped to presented its own set of problems and issues:

    a. What was the original situation?
    b. How did you think the new situation would improve upon the original situation?
    c. What turned out to be the case?
    d. What did you do about it?

6. For a discussion of immigration, study "Lost Sister" in conjunction with "Persimmons (p. 30), "What Means Switch" (p. 179), "Mother Tongue"(p. 227), and/or "The Myth of the Latin Woman" (p. 232).

7. For a broader examination of retaining and/or changing ethnic identity, study "Lost Sister" along with "Mr. Z" (p. 20), "Persimmons" (p. 30), "Everyday Use" (p. 88), "What Means Switch" (p. 179), and/or "Mother Tongue" (p. 227).

Persimmons

Li-Young Lee

In "Persimmons," the speaker moved from China to the United States with his parents when he was young. Now an adult, he reflects on various episodes from his life, episodes that reveal the sense of alienation experienced by many immigrants. As a child, he felt isolated from his classmates because of his cultural background; as an adult, he feels alienated from his Chinese heritage because of his assimilation into American culture. The poem captures the speaker's profound longing for unification. The possibilities for this unification through the symbol of the persimmon, a fruit that is bitter and astringent when unripe, but sweet and soft when ripe. The speaker perhaps hopes that he, like the persimmon, will leave behind the bitter experiences of his childhood and mature into the mellow wisdom exemplified by his father.

The poem begins with a description of an incident between the speaker and his sixth grade teacher, Mrs. Walker, who "slapped the back of [his] head / and made [him] stand in the corner / for not knowing the difference / between *persimmon* and *precision*." The binary between these two words exemplifies the distance between the speaker's home life and the American world. In Mrs. Walker's classroom, precision is of the utmost importance. At home, the speaker's parents, who are artists, teach him about sensual nature of persimmons. The speaker initially tries to connect these two concepts: "How to choose / persimmons. This is precision." However, he immediately contradicts his statement by showing that choosing and eating a ripe persimmon is an inexact science: you must touch and smell, "put the knife away" and "peel the skin tenderly." In fact, Mrs. Walker, the embodiment of precision, does not understand how to choose persimmons. Incorrectly terming the fruit a "Chinese apple," she uses a knife to cut up her unripe persimmon. The speaker does not eat it, but he does watch the faces of the other children as they do.

As a child, the speaker seems more attentive to precision than to persimmons, more interested in assimilating American culture than in preserving his heritage. In the third stanza, he demonstrates his mastery over "Other words / that got [him] into trouble" like "*fight* and *fright*, *wren* and *yarn*." However, this precision in the English language seems to come at a cost. In the second stanza, as the adult speaker tries to unite past and present by teaching Donna, his white lover, Chinese words, but he has "forgotten" many of them. Even though the distance between his sixth grade experiences and his encounter with Donna is marked by a shift from past to present tense, Mrs. Walker's demand for precision continues to haunt the speaker. He is careful to be precise in his seduction and to "remember to tell [Donna] / she is beautiful as the moon."

Ironically, the speaker portrays his seduction of Donna in a way that is not nearly as sensual as the passage that immediately precedes it – the passage about how to eat persimmons. Whereas he compares Donna to the moon, his mother once told him that "every persimmon has a sun / inside, something golden, glowing, / warm as my face." The speaker associates such warmth with his childhood home, where he remembers watching his mother tie soft yarn into animals. He also recalls finding some unripe persimmons in the cellar of his childhood home, which he puts in the sun to ripen. When he gives them to his father, who is slowly losing his eyesight, the speaker describes the fruits as "heavy as sadness, and sweet as love." Here the persimmons embody the speaker's feelings about his father and his father's impending blindness.

It is perhaps the memory of those persimmons that drives the speaker back into his parents' cellar in the last stanzas. His father, now completely blind, sits on the cellar stairs, "so happy that [the speaker has] come home." Digging through the cellar "looking for something that [he] lost," the speaker finds three paintings by his father, one of which is a still-life of persimmons. In talking about painting the picture, his father unites persimmons and precision for the speaker. He recalls the tactile sensuality of painting—"the feel of the wolftail on the silk"—as well as "the tense / precision of the wrist." The father painted the persimmons after he was blind. He was able to do this because "Some things never leave a person." Through the painting of the persimmons, the speaker begins to come to peace with his feelings of alienation. It does not matter what he has "lost" or "forgotten" because he still has, like a persimmon, "a sun inside." Although the speaker was put "in the corner" by Mrs. Walker, like the "forgotten" persimmons in the cellar, he can ripen under the warm influence of his father's insight.

Suggestions

Pre-Reading Exercise: Some students will have had the experience of moving to a new place and entering a new school when they were in primary or secondary school. Those who have not will likely have had the experience of a new student joining their class. Have them discuss what it was like for the new student (Was the new student introduced to the class? How was he or she treated by the teacher? By other students? How did the new student go about trying to fit in?)

1. One approach is to pose questions that will help students examine the two cultures the speaker is struggling to coalesce:

    a. Identify which paragraphs are in the present tense and which ones are in the past tense.

    b. Where was the speaker apparently born?

    c. Characterize Mrs. Walker.

    d. How might Mrs. Walker's treatment of the speaker have affected the way he viewed school? The way he was viewed by his classmates?

    e. Describe the speaker's relationships with his mother and his father.

    f. What about the father is revealed by the fact that he is blind, yet able to paint?

    g. What does the speaker find the first time he goes into the cellar? Discuss the significance of what he finds.

    h. The second time the speaker goes into the cellar, he says he is trying to find something he has lost. What has he lost? What does he find?

    i. According to the speaker's father, "Some things never leave a person." What things have never left the speaker?

    j. What do persimmons symbolize?

2.   Another approach is to have students examine the two cultures by focusing on the poem's contrasts. Either have students make a list of contrasts that occur in the poem or provide them with a list of contrasts and ask them to find examples. (Some of the contrasts evident in the poem include comfort-discomfort; concealment-exposure; freedom-restriction; light-dark; open-closed; pleasant-unpleasant; remembered-forgotten; seeing-not seeing; superficial-essential; thoughtfulness-thoughtlessness; and warm-cool.) Ask student to discuss the contrasts in the poem in terms of their use and their significance.

3.   Show students a film on the Chinese immigrant experience and have them discuss it in light of the poem. An excellent resource for films and videos is PBS's *Becoming an American* series: The Chinese Experience: Resources <http://www.pbs.org/becomingamerican/ce_resources3.html>

4.   To further examine the immigrant experience, study "Persimmons" along with "Lost Sister" (p. 28), "What Means Switch" (p. 179), "Mother Tongue" (p. 227), and/or "The Myth of the Latin Woman" (p. 232).

5.   For a broader examination of retaining and/or changing ethnic identity, "Persimmons" could be studied with "Mr. Z" (p. 20), "Lost Sister" (p. 28), "Everyday Use" (p. 88), "What Means Switch" (p. 179), and/or "Mother Tongue" (p. 227).

6.   For an extended discussion of father-son relationships, "Persimmons" can be studied along with "Those Winter Sundays" (p. 8), "My Father's Song" (p. 11), Elegy for My Father, Who Is Not Dead" (p. 12), and/or "Digging" (p. 19).

7.   Students can be encouraged to further explore the issue of assimilation using InfoTrac (Subject: Assimilation (Sociology); Subdivision: Social Aspects).

"Parsley"

Rita Dove

Rita Dove's poem "Parsley" is loosely based on events that occurred in the Dominican Republic in 1937. The Dominican Republic is located on the eastern two-thirds of the Island of Hispaniola; Haiti, a much smaller country, is located on the western portion. Haitians had crossed into the Dominican Republic in the mid 1920s to work on the sugar plantations. In 1929, the Haitian and the Dominican Republic governments agreed upon a specific border between the two countries. Some Haitians who had been living in Haiti were suddenly living in the Dominican Republic. With the Great Depression of the 1930s, the price of sugar plummeted, and the country was in economic straits. The sugar plantation owners sought the cheap labor of Haitians, a fact that repelled the Dominican dictator, Rafael Trujillo, who loathed the dark-skinned foreigners. (Haitians, primarily descendents of African slaves, tend to be darker-skinned than Dominicans, predominately mulatto descendents of Spanish colonizers and African slaves.) Finally, on October 2, 1937, Trujillo ordered that any Haitian found outside of a sugar plantation be executed. Soldiers would approach darker people, hold up a sprig of parsley, and ask, "*Como se llama esto?*" ("What is this thing called?"). Because Haitians, whose native language is a French-based Creole, have difficulty pronouncing the trilled "*r* "in the Spanish word *perejil* ("parsley"), the soldiers were easily able to distinguish Haitians from Dominicans. Trujillo's soldiers massacred between 15,000 – 35,000 Haitians.[1] In "Parsley," Rita Dove uses vivid visual imagery as a way to connect with the fear, anxiety, and injustice generated by the Haitian massacre.

The first section of the poem, "The Cane Fields," is told in first person from the point of view of the Haitian workers, and the images in it are fragmentary and nightmarish. The first stanza introduces two images that are repeated throughout the section: "a parrot imitating spring" and "out of the swamp the cane appears." The cyclical repetition of these images lines serves to establish a tone of relentless anxiety and fear. The second refrain, "out of the swamp, the cane appears," is particularly important. On one level, the image is realistic: the Haitians' job is to cut down the sugar cane. But the line can also be seen metaphorically. The Dominican soldiers appear out of the swamp to "haunt" the workers. Indeed, the swamp is a place to be feared. It is a place of stormy violence (the "rain punches" and the wind "lash[es]"), of danger (the general "laughs" menacingly with his "teeth shining"), and of death (the workers are "haunted" and "blood" is spilled). In a sense, the Haitians become the cane, cut down by the soldiers. The images convey the fear and the panic of the Haitians as they try to cope with this indiscriminate genocide.

The second section of the poem shifts to "The Palace" and is told from the third person perspective of El General, the man who has condemned so many people to die. The images in this section of the poem are more concrete, but still fragmentary and confusing, shifting quickly between the past and the present. These images are the key to the general's thoughts, which "turn to love and death." In the following stanzas it becomes clear that he is confused about both. Through the mind's eye of the general, the reader sees, in rapid succession, the "four-star blossoms" at his mother's grave and the "parrot in a brass ring" who "traveled all the way from Australia in an ivory / cage" and now lives in "[his mother's] room in the palace, the one without / curtains." Next the reader sees the general's mother "collapsed in the kitchen / while baking skull-shaped candies / for the Day of the Dead," immediately followed by the "pastries . . . dusted with sugar on bed of lace" which he feeds to the parrot. These paired images reveal that the general closely associates the parsley green parrot with his mother, a connection that is made clear near the end of the poem when the parrot "calls out his name in a voice / so like his mother's."

He displaces his affection for his dead mother by spoiling the parrot with sweet treats, a displacement of love that foretells a displacement of death. The general can only calm the "knot of screams" in his throat by thinking about death. When the "knot in his throat starts to twitch," he thinks about his "first day in battle" when he saw a soldier die at his feet. This prompts the general to think of the "fields of sugar / cane, lashed by rain and streaming. / He sees his mother's smile, the teeth / gnawed to arrowheads. He hears the Haitians sing without R's." Ever since his mother's death, "the general / has hated sweets" because they remind him of her passing. The Haitians, of course, chop and gather the cane that is used to produce sugar. He is pained by the sight of the Haitian children, who also "gnaw their teeth to arrowheads." He hates the sound the Haitians singing "without R's" while they work as well as the song the sing, a song whose words include "my mother, my love in death." In trying to excise the pain of his mother's death, in order to still the "knot of screams," the general orders the Haitians executed.

Suggestions

1. One approach is to have students compose their own questions about the poem and then divide into groups to answer them. Once the groups have answered the questions, reassemble to class and use the groups' findings to discuss the poem.

---

[1]Michele Wucker, *Why the Cocks Fight: Dominicans, Haitians and the Struggle for Hispaniola*. New York: Hill & Wang, 1999.

2. Another method is to provide students with questions that will encourage them understand the story and sort out the imagery by analyzing and synthesizing textual details:

    a. From whose point of view is the first section told? The second section?
    b. How is the swamp portrayed as a place to be feared?
    c. Why do the Haitians in the swamp "whisper" the word *Katalina*?
    d. Identify the lines that are repeated in the first section and explain the significance.
    e. Explain the following line: "[El General] is all the world / there is."
    f. Look up the word *appear*. What are the denotations of the word as it is used in lines 3, 9, 15, and 19.
    g. How did the general feel about his mother?
    h. What effect did his mother's death have on the General?
    i. What evidence is there that the general closely associates the parrot with his mother?
    j. How does the General treat the parrot? Why?
    k. In what ways do the Haitians remind the general of his mother?
    l. How does the general calm "the little knot of screams" that is "in his throat"?
    m. Is the general capable of love and tenderness? Explain.

3. For an examination of the ways in which people respond to grief, "Parsley" might be studied with "My Father's Song" (p. 11), "Elegy for My Father Who Is Not Dead" (p. 12), and/or "The Vacuum" (p. 22).

4. To discuss the impact that one's use of language has on the way one is perceived, "Parsley" could be paired with "Mother Tongue" (p. 227).

5. To explore Dove's writing of "Parsley," direct students to Modern American Poetry's Rita Dove page <http://www.english.uiuc.edu/maps/poets/a_f/dove/dove.htm>. There they will find links to "An Interview with Dove: On the Genesis of 'Parsley'" and "On the Origins of 'Parsley.'" They might also be directed to Everypoet's posting of "Rita Dove on the Composition of 'Parsley'" from *Introspections: Contemporary American Poets on One of Their Own Poems* <http://www.everypoet.org/pffa/showthread.php?s=&threadid=27432>

6. To further explore the 1937 Haitian massacre, have students research historical perspectives using InfoTrac (Keyword: "Rafael Trujillo" AND Haitians) and/or read Edwidge Danticat's excellent novel, *The Farming of Bones*.

7. Students might investigate more recent examples of genocide (such as Rwanda or Sudan) using InfoTrac (Subject: genocide; by subdivision).

The Unknown Citizen

W. H. Auden

and

Curiosity

Alastair Reid

"The Unknown Citizen" raises many provocative issues and has many possibilities for critical thinking exercises. The title brings to mind the monument erected to unidentified soldiers who died in battle. Unlike the unknown soldier, the unknown citizen is identified, but *by number,* a very important clue to one of Auden's themes in the poem: The state's concern for its citizens is impersonal. If this citizen is just a number, as the epigraph indicates, the rest of the poem points out how he became such. First, information gathering organizations are not concerned with the inner person, but only with those qualities that can be empirically or scientifically verified and statistically expressed. Second—and this is another of Auden's themes—this citizen has never done anything outside the norm, nothing to make himself known, and thus has no identity other than the identity that statistics can provide. The question is whether the citizen is forced to conform by societal pressures or whether he is by nature a follower. Certainly, it could be that the state encourages him to be a follower; after all, the state has rewarded him with a monument for being a model citizen.

The widely known warning "curiosity killed the cat" is turned on its head in Alastair Reid's delightfully funny (though deadly serious) "Curiosity." Curiosity is not a vice but a virtue. Being curious involves avoiding conformity, trying new things, questioning the norm. In short, curiosity is an interest in the new and different. But more important, it is the foundation for being truly alive. Without curiosity we may as well be dead, for life is not worth living if everything is "predictable." Being incurious is certainly safer and more comfortable. Curiosity leads to rejection by the "doggy circles" involved in status quo lives, in which there is familiarity ("well-smelt baskets"), acceptability ("suitable wives"), comfort ("good lunches"), and agreement. "To change" involves great risks and great pain, but to be fully alive one must take these risks.

The poems work well together, for it is evident that the unknown citizen is a member of the "doggy circles." *He* would never ask an "odd question." And "Curiosity" offers a resounding "no" to the questions about the unknown citizen: "Was he free? Was he happy?"

Suggestions

The Unknown Citizen

1. One approach that helps to bring together both major themes of "The Unknown Citizen" is to have students address this question: In what ways is this citizen "unknown"? This question draws at least three answers: he is unknown by name because he is only a number in everyone's statistics; he is unknown personally because information gatherers are not concerned with the inner person, do not care if he was "free" or "happy"; he is unknown because he never did anything unusual that would have made him "known."

2. Another approach that helps students see Auden's themes is to teach the poem as an example of satire. Have students read the definition of satire in the Glossary of the anthology. Then ask them to address the following question: What is Auden ridiculing or making fun of in the poem? This question should also draw comments about the impersonal concerns of the state and about the conformity of the citizen.

The Unknown Citizen and Curiosity

1. Students might more accurately determine the themes of "The Unknown Citizen" by first working with "Curiosity." Pick out some words and phrases from "Curiosity" and have students decide which ones apply to the unknown citizen (e.g., "incurious," "contradictory," "well-smelt baskets," "to distrust what seems," "predictably").

2. "The Unknown Citizen" and "Curiosity" work well with "Mr. Z" (p. 20), "Barbie Doll" (p. 20), "The Lottery" (p. 43), "Harrison Bergeron" (p. 53), and "Life after High School" (p. 132) in an extended study of social conformity.

3. Because it shows the difficulty of finding a truly untraveled path to take, "The Road Not Taken" serves as an interesting counterpoint to the idea in " The Unknown Citizen" (p. 35) and "Curiosity" (p. 36) that one should be "different."

What Would Freud Say?

Bob Hicok

Hicok's "What Would Freud Say?" is a humorous piece in which the speaker tells of his attempt to atone for his infidelity by building a bookcase for his wife. Along the way, he makes ample use of Freudian techniques and theories. One need not understand all of Freud's theories to understand and enjoy the poem, but some knowledge of them brings more coherence to the poem and heightens its humorous effect. The poem is an excellent way to introduce students to the ways in which attention to allusion can increase our understanding and enjoyment of a piece of writing.

On the first reading, many readers may only notice the explicit allusions to Freudian psychology, which are clustered in the beginning of the poem and center around the sexual dream of the speaker's friend. However, according to Freud, dreams are only one way in which the unconscious mind informs and influences our thoughts. Freud believed that the unconscious mind, which is bent on the realization of pleasure, is the source of all emotional conflict and neuroses. He believed that with the help of a psychiatrist, such conflict could be brought from the unconscious into the conscious mind and be resolved. One method he used to achieve this was "free association," a psychoanalytic technique in which the subject is encouraged to speak freely, allowing one thought to suggest another, until the true motivations of the unconscious mind become clear. On one level, the poem "What Would Freud Say?" constitutes a sort of free association on the part of the speaker. The fragmented, unclear images in the beginning of the poem gain focus once the speaker finally reveals what is truly bothering him: his infidelity to his wife. Thus, the structure of the poem itself is an allusion.

So, too, are the poem's themes, themes that relate to what Freud calls the "pleasure principle." When reading the poem in light of the specific question "what would Freud say?" it becomes clear that the speaker is trying to justify his morally repugnant acts by blaming his error on the pleasure seeking elements of his unconscious. He identifies himself with Judas and Pope Urban VIII, both men who committed acts of betrayal because they, like the speaker, "wanted to be loved" (see suggestion 4 below for an explanation). A more enviable comparison is Dagwood, whom the speaker believes gains his pleasurable love from Blondie through the pursuit of another kind of pleasurable act – the act of eating. Dagwood is loved by Blondie not just in spite of, but because of the fact that he "gets nothing right / except the hallucinogenic/ architecture of sandwiches." The speaker hopes that by remodeling his problematic relationship with his wife after the example of Dagwood and Blondie, he too can enjoy the pleasure saturated life of Dagwood rather than the gnawing guilt of Judas, who eventually hung himself out of remorse. He decides to build his wife a bookcase, something that he thinks Dagwood would have done for Blondie.

Building the bookcase is not, however, "the extent of [the speaker's] apology." The other elements of his apology also play with Freudian concepts, and they demonstrate a less optimistic or playful view of psychological justifications than the previous passages. The speaker was "beaten up" for mispronouncing *huevos rancheros*, in a bar. He may have asked for *huevos de rancheros*—"rancher's testicles"— instead of *huevos rancheros*. Sexual mispronunciations are referred to as "Freudian Slips," examples of the sexual drive of the unconscious slipping into our conversation. Apparently, the patrons in the bar were not sympathetic to the speaker's Freudian explanation. The speaker also "lost his job" for "lying face down on the couch" when he was supposed to be working from his home. In Freudian psychoanalysis, the subject often lies down on a couch while talking to his analyst. Of course, the subject lies face up, not face down, a posture that suggests contrition as well as depression. His boss, like the bar patrons, was unimpressed by the speaker's explanation. Perhaps the speaker is afraid that his wife will not believe his Freudian justifications either. He wanted to build her a bookcase to bring her pleasure, perhaps in order to negate the pain that she felt when he betrayed her. He wants her to "be impressed / that it didn't lean / or wobble even though / [he has] only leaned and often / wobbled." The speaker recognizes, however, that even though the bookcase is "only half / done" it is "certainly / a better gift with its map / of [his] unfaithful blood." The speaker claims at the outset that it "Wasn't on purpose" that he drilled through his finger, but Freud would contend that everything we do is "on purpose," dictated by our unconscious desires if not our conscious mind. Perhaps the speaker unconsciously thought that the physical pain would serve as the most appropriate atonement for the illicit physical pleasure that he took in his infidelity.

Suggestions

1. To make sure that students understand the poem's basic story, first have them summarize it in writing. Then, break the class into groups and have each group write a character analysis of the speaker. When the groups are finished, use their analyses as the basis for discussing the speaker's actions and attitudes.

2. Another approach is to have students work with specific details in the poem:

   a. Identify the men who the speaker claims have done something to be loved. What did each do in order to be loved?

   b. Identify the ways in which the speaker has "apologized."

   c. Identify the "dumb" things the speaker has done.

   d. Why does the speaker choose to apologize to his wife by building a bookcase?

   e. What types of books will be kept in the bookcase the speaker is building? Why is this ironic?

   f. What does the speaker mean when he says he has "only leaned and often / wobbled"?

   g. Explain why the bookcase is a "better gift" now that is has a "map of [the speaker's] unfaithful blood."

3. To examine Hicok's use of allusion, students need to have some knowledge of Freud's theories. One approach is to have students use InfoTrac to research some pertinent Freudian theories (dream symbolism, free association, Freudian slip, pleasure principle, reality principle, theory of the unconscious, and so forth) and explain how they are manifest in the poem.

   Alternatively, students might be pointed to specific articles that discuss Freud's theories and asked to discuss the theories that are incorporated in the poem:

   > Gardner, Martin. "Waking Up from Freud's Theory of Dreams." *Skeptical Inquirer* 19.6 (1995): 10-14.

   > Peter, Gay. "Sigmund Freud: He Opened a Window on the Unconscious—Where, He Said, Lust, Rage and Repression Battle for Supremacy—and Changed the Way We View Ourselves." *Time* 29 March 1999: 66-67.

   Another method is to provide students with the following statement and ask them to explain how Freud's ideas are used by the poet:

   > According to Freud, people have specific instinctual impulses: "their self-preservative instinct, their love of aggression, their need for love and their impulse to attain pleasure and avoid pain." (Lecture XXXV, A Philosophy of Life, New Introductory Lectures on Psycho-analysis (1933) publ. Hogarth Press.)

   How might this statement be illustrated by the poem?

4. To examine the issue of betrayal, students need to understand the allusions to Judas and to Urban VIII.

First, focus their attention on Judas. Have them read about Judas' betrayal of Jesus and his death (the relevant biblical verses are noted in the anthology) and identify the similarities between the speaker's actions those of Judas (both betrayed people whom they loved with a kiss and subsequently felt great remorse about the pain they had caused). Ask students to explain the literal and figurative significance of the following lines: "I woke with a sense/of what nails in the palms/might do to a spirit/temporarily confined to flesh." They should be able to see that the speaker is understanding the pain—spiritual and physical—that is felt by someone who has been betrayed.

Then, have students consider the speaker's assertion that Jesus' crucifixion "was an accident / if you believe Judas / merely wanted to be loved." Having just read the biblical version of events, these lines are likely to startle and confuse most students. Students need to know about the arguments of some modern scholars that Judas, believing that Jesus was the Messiah (and, as such, could not be harmed), handed him over to the authorities so that he would exercise his power, liberate the Jews from the Romans, and take his rightful place as King of the Jews. Students can locate this material using InfoTrac. They can search for material (Keyword: Judas Iscariot) or be pointed to a specific article: Hogan-Albach, Susan. "Was Judas a Good Guy or Bad? Scholars Disagree." *The Dallas Morning News* 15 April 2003, 2nd ed.: G1. Once students have the necessary information, ask them to explain the lines.

Next, have students consider Urban VIII's betrayal of Galileo, his longtime friend. Students can use InfoTrac to search for material (Subject: Galileo; Subdivision: Religious Aspects) or locate a specific article: Owens, Virginia Stem. "Galileo and the Powers Above: The Convoluted Tale of a Faithful Catholic Caught in a Web of Theological Inflexibility, Papal Power, and His Own Political Naiveté." *Christian History* 21.4 (2002): 10-18.

5.   For another look at the consequences of infidelity, "What Would Freud Say" could be paired with "The Gilded Six Bits" (p. 63).

6.   Teaming "What Would Freud Say" with "Time for a Change on Drugs" (p. 264) allows for a study of tone.

The Naked and the Nude

Robert Graves

This is an excellent poem to use to study the subtleties of language and meaning. In the first stanza, the speaker notes that for him there are distinct differences between nakedness and nudity, even though dictionary definitions of the terms may be synonymous. This may lead students to conclude that the poem's focus is solely on the differing connotations of the words *naked* and *nude,* but close examination of the poem reveals that Graves's interest is in the differing attitudes and motives of two types of people: the naked and the nude.

To the speaker, the naked are honest and truthful. For lovers, doctors, and gods, the unclothed body is natural. Lovers gaze on each other's bodies with reciprocal honesty and passion. Doctors examine the bodies of their patients in order to diagnose their ills. And the Goddess, bound by neither flesh nor time, completely exposes the truth of who and what she is. Unlike the naked, the nude are deceptive and artificial, revealing some parts of their unclothed body but concealing others. Exotic dancers and strip tease artists, for example, use "showman's trick[s]" such as boas, fans, and pasties in order to arouse prurient interest. Because they do not reveal their entire body, the nude may claim to be morally superior to the naked. The nude (those who are manipulative and deceptive) may even "defeat" the naked (those who are honest and forthright) in direct competition. Nonetheless, the naked have the comfort of knowing that the nude will get what they deserve in the afterlife: Chased by whip-wielding Gorgons, the nude will be naked (unprotected).

Suggestions

1. This is a poem that challenges and intrigues students. Pose questions that will help them look carefully at the details and the way those details are used:

    a. Why do "lexicographers" consider *naked* and *nude* to be synonymous?

    b. In the second stanza, the speaker presents three situations, each of which illustrates the attitude of the naked toward the unclothed human body. Describe each situation and the attitude(s) it illustrates.

    c. Why do the naked make no attempt to drape or conceal their bodies?

    d. Why are the nude "bold" and "sly"?

    e. What does it mean to "hold someone's eye"? (Think about what it means to "catch someone's eye.")

    f. Why is the eye that the nude want to hold "treasonable"?

    g. The speaker says that the nude use "a showman's trick." How? Why?

    h. Why do the nude express "scorn" for the naked? Is their scorn justified? Explain.

    i. Why might the naked by "defeat[ed]" by the nude if they were to compete?

    j. Explain the last four lines of the poem, paying special attention to the final line: "How naked go the sometimes nude!"

    k. In the opening stanza, the speaker says that the naked and the nude "stand as wide apart / As love from lies, or truth from art." He spends the rest of the poem illustrating his point. Does he succeed?

2. Ask students to think of other situations in which people are unclothed, and decide whether Graves would describe them as naked or nude. (Students sometimes need a few examples to get started: a toddler playing in a sprinkler; MTV dancers; athletes showering after a game; etc.)

3. To further explore Graves's distinctions, divide the class into groups A and B, and present them with the following scenarios:

    <u>Situation One:</u> A husband comes home and finds his wife standing without clothing in the living room talking to a male neighbor.

    <u>Situation Two:</u> A husband comes home and finds his wife standing without clothing in the living room while students from a local art studio sit sketching her.

    Have group A prepare to argue there is no difference between the two situations and group B prepare to argue the two situations are totally different. When students have had sufficient time to prepare their arguments, bring the class back together and have them debate.

2

Fiction

Discussions and Suggestions

Birthday Party

Katharine Brush

"Birthday Party" is an excellent introduction to the study of character, detail, and point of view. The details of this story must be examined closely in order to understand the complexity of the two main characters. Students often overlook the details and, following the narrator's lead, come to false conclusions about the characters. They assume that narrators express the views of writers; of course, narrators often lack knowledge, judgment, objectivity, and so on. Only when students carefully examine the details do they realize that the narrator's assessment of the situation is biased and that their first impressions were probably inaccurate.

Most readers will initially share the narrator's interpretations of the events and sympathize with the woman. But the details, viewed objectively, direct the reader to another interpretation. The husband has chosen a "little narrow restaurant" in which to celebrate his birthday. This detail, coupled with the facts that he is "hotly embarrassed" by the public attention and that he waits until "attention [has] shifted" to say anything to his wife, indicates that he is a shy man. The wife, on the other hand, likes attention: She wears "a big hat," arranges for the celebration, "beam[s] with shy pride over her little surprise," and, instead of excusing herself, "crie[s] at the table quite a long time." She must know that her husband dislikes being the center of attention. As "a couple in their late thirties" that looks "unmistakably married," they should know each other fairly well. In what is likely a genuine attempt to please her husband, she gives a gift that *she* would like to receive. In fact, there is little question about whom the attention is really for: The cake has "one pink candle" on it.

Apparently, the narrator, a patron in the restaurant who witnesses the event, sympathizes with the woman. Nonetheless, the husband seems to deserve our sympathy as much as his wife. In this story, as sometimes in others, the narrator incorrectly assesses the situation.

Suggestions

Pre-Reading Exercise: Ask students to explain in writing the meaning of the Golden Rule: "Do unto others what you would have them do unto you." After they have examined the text, have students discuss the rule in light of the events in the story. Likely, they will conclude that there is wisdom in treating others as others would like to be treated.

1. Ask students to record their first impression about the man, the woman, and the events. Once they have done this, present them with the following list. Have students explain what could be reasonably inferred from each detail. For example, the first detail listed indicates that the man and woman have been married for quite a long time (and, thus, should know each other well).

   - They are "a couple in their late thirties" and look "unmistakably married."
   - They are eating in "a little narrow restaurant."
   - The man has "a round, self-satisfied face, with glasses on it."
   - The woman is "fadingly pretty."
   - The woman wears "a big hat."
   - The "small but glossy birthday cake" has "one pink candle."
   - The woman "beam[s] with shy pride over her little surprise."
   - The man waits until "the general attention ha[s] shifted" before he says anything to his wife.
   - The man says, "under his breath," "some punishing thing."
   - The man is "hotly embarrassed" and "indignant."
   - The woman sits at the table "crying" for "quite a long time."

2. To examine the story's point of view, ask students to characterize the narrator and to note those instances in which the narrator seems to be interpreting the events rather than reporting them.

3. Ask students if they would react as the husband does and to explain why or why not. (Most students will admit that they would be a little embarrassed, but they will likely say that they would not react as the husband does.) Once they have done this, have them explain why the husband reacts as he does, pointing out that such responses as "he's mean" are too simple.

4. "Birthday Party" can be studied in conjunction with "I Stand Here Ironing" (p. 114) and/or "What You Pawn I Will Redeem" (p. 163) to examine the notion of narrator reliability.

The Lottery

Shirley Jackson

"The Lottery" is a good story to introduce early in the study of fiction, not only because its language is simple, but also because it illustrates the way in which theme can be developed almost exclusively through plot as opposed to character. (There is, in fact, little need for character analysis because the characters are simply "types.") The plot is simple: The townspeople gather, draw lots, and select a "winner." But the actual outcome of the lottery is radically different from the expected outcome, presenting a conflict that must be resolved in order to understand the story's theme.

The setting, an important element of plot, does not prepare the reader for the brutality to come. It is summer and the flowers are in bloom. This pleasant setting is reinforced by the seeming innocence of the characters: The children are racing about, happy to be out of school; the adults seem excited about the lottery and greet each other amicably. The many nationalities of the people who live there (Delacroix, Warner, Graves, Dunbar, Adams, Hutchinson) and the mention of such things as "tractors," "house dresses," and "teenage clubs" suggest that the setting is a twentieth-century American town.

The conflict between the innocuous modern-day setting and the violence that occurs reveals the theme: Normal, everyday people do not question the traditions they follow. The people in this village are not evil; instead, they are simply carrying on a tradition they no longer understand. Old Man Warner provides the main clue to the lottery's origin: "Used to be a saying, 'Lottery in June, corn be heavy soon.'" Apparently, the lottery has its roots in the pagan tradition of "scapegoat" sacrifice: One member of a community was sacrificed in an effort to cleanse the community and ensure a good harvest. The villagers do not know exactly why they conduct the lottery and have lost many elements of the ritual (the greeting, the chant, etc.), but they continue the annual event because "'There's always been a lottery.'"

Students find it irrational that the villagers continue the lottery simply because "there's *always* been a lottery." Only when they realize that many traditions (trick-or-treating, shaking hands, folding hands in prayer, etc.) are carried on with little understanding of their origins or significance do they begin to see that we all do things simply because they have "always" been done. Of course, many of the traditions that we unquestioningly follow are harmless by comparison. Nonetheless, although the traditions in which we actively participate may not be destructive, some injustices (e.g., segregation) have been, at different times in history, passively accepted on the grounds that they had always existed and were unchangeable. The story points out that we should question our traditions so we know which are harmful and which are not.

Suggestions

Pre-Reading Exercise: Have students begin to think about the potential danger of social conformity by researching McCarthyism. They can be use InfoTrac to conduct research (Keyword: "joseph mccarthy"; Keyword: "unamerican activities" AND mccarthy; Keyword: mccarthyism). After students have examined "The Lottery," ask them to relate the issues raised in the short story to McCarthyism.

1. One way to approach this story is to ask students to compose at least two questions they would like to have answered about it. (Their questions are likely to focus on the conflict between what they expected to happen in the story and what actually happens.) Then have them break up into groups and answer their questions. Any they cannot answer should be presented to the class for discussion.

2. Discuss setting with the students (refer to the Glossary), including the fact that setting encompasses country, region, century, and so on. Ask students to describe as fully as possible the setting of the story. After they have each written a description, ask them to explain why the setting does or does not seem appropriate to the action. This approach will lead to a discussion of the conflict between the setting and the plot, a discussion which is crucial in directing the reader to the theme.

3. Because the lottery would be more understandable had so much of the ritual and its trappings not been lost or changed, it is important for students to examine these lost parts. Ask students to identify those parts of the ritual that have been lost, those that have been altered, and those that remain the same. Once students have made their lists, break the class up into groups and have each group explain what is significant about the parts that have been lost, the parts that have been altered, and the parts that remain the same.

4. Give students two examples of common things teenagers do. (The list might include such activities as "rolling" someone's yard with toilet paper; "egging" someone's house or car; pulling up the goal post after a team win; "hazing" fraternity and sorority initiates.) Ask students to add to the list. Have them identify which of these activities are potentially destructive and explain why teenagers participate in them. Then ask students why they think the villagers participate in the lottery.

5. Have students examine Stanley Milgram findings about obedience to authority and relate those findings to the short story as well as their own experience. To learn about Milgram's research, students can view Milgram's 1963 film, *Obedience* (available from Pennsylvania State University Audio Visual Services http://www.medianet.libraries.psu.edu/htbin/wwform/175?text=r42864942-42869253-/ca/wwi770.htm>), or they can conduct their own research using InfoTrac (Keyword: milgram AND obedience; Subject: Milgram, Stanley)

6. For an extended study of social conformity, "The Lottery" can be teamed with "Barbie Doll" (p. 20 "Mr. Z" (p. 20), "The Unknown Citizen" (p. 35), "Curiosity" (p. 36), "Harrison Bergeron" (p. 53), and/or "Life After High School" (p. 132).

7. The importance of setting could be further explored by pairing "The Lottery" can be paired with "Hills Like White Elephants" (p. 50).

8. To examine the ways in which writers create a surprise ending, "The Lottery" can be assigned with "Richard Cory" (p. 4), "A Rose for Emily" (p. 193), and/or "Life after High School" (p. 132).

9. The issue of unquestioned tradition could be examined by studying "Mending Wall" (p. 26) with "The Lottery."

Hills Like White Elephants

Ernest Hemingway

When approaching a piece of short fiction, a reader has certain expectations. Typically, a short story begins with exposition about the main characters, information that allows the reader to understand the conflict which will drive the plot of the story. The end of the story is reached when the conflict is resolved. Because "Hills Like White Elephants" does not conform to this criterion, readers might be initially confused by the story. Rather than providing detailed information about the characters in the opening paragraphs of the story, Hemingway gives only a bare description of the couple and the setting. The story is developed primarily through dialogue. The dialogue reveals to the reader that there is a definite conflict between the two main characters, it but does not reveal the exact nature of the conflict: the topic of conversation is never explicitly identified. By the end of the story, the couple has stopped bickering and is preparing to board a train together, seeming indications that they have settled their disagreement. The reader, however, is left wondering exactly how (or even if) the conflict has been resolved.

The sparsity of detail in the story can frustrate readers because they are forced to pay incredibly close attention to the information that *is* provided. In the opening paragraph, for instance, the narrator refers to the main characters as "The American and the girl with him." These details provide insight into the nature of their relationship: the man is dominant and knowledgeable while Jig, "the girl," is dependent and naive. Indeed, the man negotiates all the interaction with the waitress, translating her Spanish for the English-speaking Jig. Through a combination of description and dialogue, the reader begins to get a sense of the hedonistic lifestyle that the couple has been leading: they travel and stay in hotels (their bags are covered with "labels . . . from all the hotels where they had spent nights"); they "look at things and try new drinks." The difference in their commitment to this lifestyle is at the core of their conflict.

The man enjoys their lifestyle and wants it to continue. He pressures Jig to have an abortion so they can be "just like [they] were before" she became pregnant. He knows that Jig is reluctant to have the abortion, and he assumes she is concerned about the operation itself. Were that Jig's sole concern, it would certainly be understandable: after all, abortion was not legalized in Spain until 1985, and illegal abortions were neither safe nor painless. Nevertheless, the man assures her that the procedure is "awfully simple" and that she "won't really mind it… it's not really an operation at all…it's all perfectly natural." Jig is reticent about having an abortion, not because she fears the operation, but because she wants the child (perhaps one of the things that "[she has] waited so long for") and because she knows that "once they take it away, you never get it back." Despite her desire to have the child and her belief that "[they] could get along," Jig does not want the man to be unhappy, and she does not want to lose his affection: "And if I do it you'll be happy and things will be like they were and you'll love me?" Each character expresses a desire to please the other by doing "anything" the other wants. Even so, the characters' preferences for handling the situation are diametrically opposed.

The setting exemplifies the couple's situation. The railway station where they are waiting is between two lines of rails at a junction, a place where different rail lines meet and converge. The rail lines on each side of the station lead in different directions. The options from which Jig must choose—bring her pregnancy to an end or to term—lead to drastically different futures. The station is situated in the middle of a valley: on one side of the station, the valley is hot and sunny, and "the country [is] brown and dry"; on the other side, the land is fertile and inviting. Jig is drawn to the fertile side of the valley, repeatedly looking at it and eventually moving towards it:

The girl stood up and walked to the end of the station. Across, on the other side, were fields of grain and trees along the banks of the Ebro. Far away, beyond the river, were mountains. The shadow of a cloud moved across the field of grain and she saw the river through the trees.

Still staring at "the other side," Jig tells the man that "[they] could have all this" but "every day [they] make it more impossible." The man does not feel the same attraction to the fertile side of the valley, and, though he walked over to her so he could hear what she was saying, he wants her to move away from her vantage point and "Come on back in the shade."

Back at their table, the couple seems to have come to some sort of consensus in regards to the abortion: the man moves their bags to be loaded onto the approaching train. The couple is leaving together, but in which direction are they going? Some elements of the ending suggest that the man has given in to Jig's wish to keep the baby. Most notably, she seems happier: she smiles at the waitress and at the man when he gets up to tend the bags. The man moves their bags "to the other side of the station," suggesting, perhaps, that they will be taking a different train than the one they had planned. (Bag security does not seem to have been of concern: the man moves them to the other side of the tracks and leaves them there.) When he returns, the man asks her if she "feels better," suggesting that he has done something to make her "feel better." Jig smiles at him again and says that "There's nothing wrong with me. I feel fine," indicating that there is "nothing wrong" with pregnancy. On the other hand, the ending might also be interpreted to mean that Jig has agreed to the man's opinion that the pregnancy is "the only thing that bothers us." Perhaps she says there is "nothing wrong" because she has resigned herself to complying with the man's wish to terminate the pregnancy and have "nothing wrong" with their relationship. Then again, perhaps the couple has reached a temporary truce, not a final resolution.

Although close reading of the story can illuminate many of the elements of the narrative that seem obscured at first, the ending remains elusively beyond the grasp of the reader. Perhaps this ambiguity reveals something about the theme of the story itself. Despite what the couple decides about the "operation," the conflict will never be fully resolved: "once they take it away, you never get it back."

Suggestions

1. The story's heavy reliance on dialogue and minimal use of description may leave students confused. To clear up their confusion, they need to carefully consider and analyze the setting, the dialogue, and the action. To encourage this scrutiny, have students "produce" the story as a play. Ask for 3 students (1 male; 2 females) to volunteer to act. Divide the remaining students into 3 groups, explain that they are responsible for preparing and setting the stage, and assign each group a task:

    Group 1: Scenery—the decorated backdrops and painted structures that are meant to represent a particular place.

    Group 2: Props—the furnishings and objects that are on the stage

    Group 3: Hand props—the objects that are handled by the actors

The scenery, props, and hand props do not need to be elaborate or exact, but they do need to accurately represent the scene, location, and props described in the story.

Allow the groups about 10 minutes to review the story, identify what they need to do, and develop a plan; then give them another 10 minutes or so to implement their plans and prepare the stage. While the groups are working on their assignments, the actors should be discussing the characters and preparing to perform. The actors should be reminded to use the narration as stage directions. After the groups have finished setting the stage, the group members become the audience, and the actors present their interpretation of the characters.

Following the performance, have students discuss the story in light of the production. (In addition to helping students make sense of the dialogue, the production should have helped them think about the significance of the setting and the relationship between the couple.)

2.   Another approach is to pose questions that will focus students on Jig, the American, and their relationship:

    a.   The male character is referred to as "the American" and "the man" by the narrator; the main female character is referred to as "the girl" by the narrator and as "Jig" by the American. What does this imply about the characters and their relationship?

    b.   Neither character mentions the topic of their conflict until paragraph 42, almost half-way through the story. Why does it take so long for the subject to be brought up? Are the characters thinking about it before it is actually mentioned? Explain.

    c.   Locate and analyze all references to the operation. What type of operation is it? Why is the operation not referred to by name?

    d.   Compare and contrast Jig's reasons for and against the operation with the American's reasons for and against it.

    e.   To Jig, the setting becomes symbolic of the decision she must make. Explain the symbolism.

    f.   Characterize the American and Jig, as individuals and as a couple.

    g.   Does Jig have the operation?

    h.   Will the couple's relationship survive? Explain.

    i.   How does the title relate to the story?

3.   The importance of setting can be further explored by pairing "Hills Like White Elephants" with "The Lottery" (p. 43).

4.   Teaming "Hills Like White Elephants" with "The Road Not Taken" (p. 6) and/or "The Chrysanthemums" (p. 202) invites a discussion of symbolism as well as the dilemma of choices.

5.   "Hills Like White Elephants" can be assigned in conjunction with "Lot's Wife" (p. 3), "Barbie Doll" (p. 20), "The Fat Girl" (p. 120), and/or "The Chrysanthemums" (p. 202) for an extended study of the roles of women.

6.   To examine the ways in which the movie version of a short story may differ from the original story, students could view the film "Hills Like White Elephants," the third short film in HBO's *Women and Men: Stories of Seduction (1990)*.

Harrison Bergeron

Kurt Vonnegut, Jr.

"The year was 2081, and everybody was finally equal." At first we assume Vonnegut Jr. is describing the ideal universe, a world in which the belief that "all men are created equal" has become a reality. This assumption quickly gives way as we realize that the people in Harrison Bergeron's United States are forced to be equal in every way possible: no one person can be cleverer than another, no one stronger, no one handsomer. The theory is that equalization does away with competition and feelings of inferiority. The reality is that those who are not naturally gifted are praised for "[trying] to do the best [they] [can] with what God gave [them]," while those who are naturally talented are fettered so that they cannot "become what [they] can become."

Suggestions

Pre-Reading Exercise: Ask students to explain the meaning of this sentence from the *Declaration of Independence:* "We hold these truths to be self-evident, that all men are created equal, that they are endowed by their Creator with certain unalienable Rights, that among these are Life, Liberty and the pursuit of Happiness." Direct their attention to the phrase "all men are created equal," and ask to explain what the statement means.

1. To help students consider the causes as well as the effects of equalization, pose the following questions:

    a. Taking the whole story into consideration, explain what the Bergeron's society considers "perfectly average intelligence."

    b. Locate each reference to the ear radio sounding in George's head. For each reference, explain what George is thinking or doing just before it sounds and describe the effect it has on him.

    c. The HG's office uses a number of handicaps other than the ear radio worn by people such as George. Identify the other handicaps and explain what each one is supposed to do.

    d. What can be inferred from the fact that all announcers have "a serious speech impediment" and that the police photograph of Harrison is "flashed on the screen—upside down, then sideways, upside down again, then right side up"?

    e. Has equalization altered people's awareness and/or appreciation of intelligence, talent, strength, beauty, grace, and so forth? Explain.

    f. What goals are supposed to be achieved by equalization? Are these goals achieved? Explain.

    g. Is the state imposing its will on the people or carrying out the will of the people? Explain.

2. "Fairness" seems to be of great concern to those who live in the Bergeron's society. Divide students into groups, assigning half the groups the task of arguing that the equalization is "fair" and the other half the task of arguing that it is not. Give the groups 10–15 minutes to prepare their points, and then have the class debate the issue.

3. After students have read and discussed the short story, have them view the film, *Harrison Bergeron* (1995); identify the elements of the short story that it retains, deletes, or alters; and discuss what effect these changes have on the meaning of the story.

4. "Harrison Bergeron" can be paired with the essay "Making the Grade" (p. 237) to compare/contrast the importance of effort with the importance of achievement.

5. For a discussion of the issue of conformity, "Harrison Bergeron" can be studied with "Barbie Doll" (p. 20), "Mr. Z" (p. 20), "The Unknown Citizen" (p. 35), "Curiosity" (p. 36), "The Lottery" (p. 43), and/or "Life After High School" (p. 132).

6. For a study of the ways in which science fiction raises important human issues, "Harrison Bergeron" can be paired with "The Veldt" (p. 77).

Crusader Rabbit

Jess Mowry

This story takes its title from a cartoon series[1] that revolves around the adventures of the idealistic and aggressive Crusader Rabbit and his pragmatic but timid sidekick, Ragland ("Rags") T. Tiger. Crusader is modeled after Don Quixote,[2] an association that is underscored in the cartoon's original title sequence: Crusader, wearing armor and carrying a lance and shield, thunders toward the screen atop a properly barded horse. In some ways, the characters in the story parallel those in the cartoon. Crusader and Jeremy are both naive but moral, and both are dismissed by society not because of *who* they are, but because of *what* they are: a rabbit and a thirteen-year-old, drug-addicted homeless boy, respectively. Like Rags, who

---

[1] *Crusader Rabbit* was the first animated series made for television. The original series ran from 1949–1951; a new series ran in 1957.
[2] Personal correspondence with Alex Anderson, cocreator of *Crusader Rabbit*, 24 Feb. 1999.

assists Crusader and bails him out of trouble, Raglan—experienced, pragmatic, and compassionate—supports and protects Jeremy.

A veteran of street life and a recovering heroin addict, Raglan knows how to survive and how to help Jeremy survive. In fact, he assures that Jeremy's needs are met. According to psychologist Abraham Maslow, human beings have a hierarchy of needs: physiological needs; safety needs; love and belongingness needs; esteem needs; and self-actualization needs. Raglan provides for Jeremy's physiological needs (food, water, and shelter). He also provides Jeremy with physical safety, being fully capable of protecting him from assault (as indicated by the scar on his chest and the pistol in his truck). He and Jeremy provide each other with love, affection, and a sense of belonging. In effect, they become family, a point made by Jeremy's references to Raglan's being his father. Raglan also meets Jeremy's esteem needs by treating him as a valuable human being. The depth of Raglan's consideration is revealed by his asking Jeremy what he wants to do about the baby. This type of treatment—actions that demonstrate Raglan's regard and respect—communicates to Jeremy that he is significant. Having the first four levels of his needs met, Jeremy is able to "'decide there's somethin else [he] want[s] more'" than escape.

Jeremy's life on the streets, a life alone, unloved and unwanted, is understandably one from which he wished to escape. For a while, heroin probably provided him with a temporary freedom, but it has become his jailer and is destroying him. The toll that drugs have taken on Jeremy's body is evident. Unlike Raglan, who is twice his age, Jeremy sweats and pants; he has "bruise-like marks" beneath his eyes; his hands shake. The single dose of heroin relaxes Jeremy (his face becomes "almost peaceful") and transforms his "stiff and awkward movements" into "smooth [ones,] like a kid's once more." The heroin no longer produces euphoria; it "only makes [him] normal." Jeremy is fearful of the pain he will experience while he is weaning himself off of the drugs. Raglan, who "could have been a larger copy of the boy," does not lie to him about the pain, but he does reassure him that he will be there with him. He knows what Jeremy is going through and what he will experience, not only in breaking his heroin addiction but also in living on the streets.

Raglan seems to struggle with his awareness that Jeremy must confront the inequities and cruelties of life and his desire to protect him from them. Raglan has not become inured to cruelty nor has he come to understand it. When he confronts something painful or disturbing, his eyes become "distant." This happens after he "studies" Jeremy in the dumpster, helps him inject the heroin into his vein, and sees the dead, discarded baby (pars. 7, 11, 15, and 33). The only time his eyes become "hard" is when he thinks of the smirking cops (par. 35). If Jeremy is going to survive on the streets, he has to confront its harsh realities. Raglan's struggle is revealed by his body language. This is perhaps most clearly demonstrated by his behavior after discovering the dead infant in the dumpster. Initially, he "clamp[s] his hand on Jeremy's shoulder, holding the boy back." Jeremy sees the baby's body despite Raglan's efforts and "press[es] suddenly close to Raglan, and Raglan's arm [goes] around him." Raglan "[takes] his hand off the boy" before he tersely tells him that the baby's body will be burned or hauled to the dump. Raglan responds to Jeremy's emotional outburst by "stay[ing] quiet a moment" and then "gripp[ing] Jeremy's shoulder once more." Perhaps Raglan's body language simply reflects his own limitations: He cannot shield Jeremy from life's bitter truths, but he can offer him some measure of support and comfort.

Their choice not only to survive but to live without escape is not a simple one given the realities of living on the street. Every aspect of their daily existence is a reminder of their condition and of the callousness of society. The water Raglan and Jeremy drink tastes like the rubber hoses they use to fill the jug, a plastic container that once held "fresh spring water from clear mountain streams." They have to wade through garbage to pick out recyclable cans. In the alley, the sounds of traffic, the exhaust fumes, and the "tar-and-rot" smells are as omnipresent as the rats that scuttle on the asphalt and the flies that swarm "in clouds over the dumpsters." The brick walls of the buildings are covered in soot. And, Raglan has seen, "too many times," discarded babies and dying children. The horrific nature of their surroundings and their plight is dramatically underscored and emphasized by the milieu of the coast. The clean, fresh ocean air is "scented with things that lived and grew." Grass and wildflowers cover the fields and hills. A small stream runs "sparkling over smooth rocks." On the cliffs, the "waves boom and echo" and "silver streamers of spray drift up." The grass on the cliffs "feel[s] good underfoot." The fertility of the cliffs contrasts starkly with the decay of the alley. For Jeremy, the trip to the cliffs is a revelation: He is amazed to discover that beautiful, lush, peaceful, uninhabited places exist in reality, not just fantasy. Raglan, who is more experienced, has known this.

Despite his exposure to callousness and cruelty, Raglan has retained his compassion, his humanity. He can no more explain why he cares than he can explain why no one else seems to: "who in hell knows." Unable or unwilling to articulate what motivates him to care for Jeremy, he tells the boy to "'figure it out'" and "'let him know.'" Why was Jeremy behind the dumpster? Why was he dying? "Who in hell knew." Perhaps Raglan has learned "never ask questions if you don't want the answers." In this case, the answers would have revealed the awful nature of man's inhumanity to man. Jeremy has been seemingly unaware that people can be cruel. Seeing the baby in the dumpster and hearing what will happen to her begin Jeremy's initiation into the world of experience. During the trip to the coast, Jeremy does not talk or listen to music. He occasionally glances back to look at "the little bundle in the bed," but mainly he stares, "his own eyes a lot like Raglan's now." Jeremy is no longer oblivious to humanity's potential for cruelty, injustice, and callousness.

Jeremy and Raglan both demonstrate the ability to retain their humanity in the face of overwhelming inhumanity. Raglan, twenty-six, saves the life of and assumes responsibility for the thirteen-year-old, drug-addicted Jeremy. No doubt Raglan's daily search for ways to attain the necessities of survival would have been less complicated without Jeremy. Still, he chooses to care for him. He also chooses to take the baby's body for a proper burial. He is aware that burying the baby will prevent them from going to the recycle center, getting money, buying food, and seeing to "Jeremy's need," but he chooses to make those sacrifices. Jeremy, less mature and experienced than Raglan, does not think of the consequences of burying the baby. Nonetheless, after the baby is buried and he realizes that they have no money, too little gas to return to the city, and no heroin to allay the pain of his withdrawals, he does not regret their decision: "I still glad we come, Raglan." They struggle daily to survive, but they both make ethical, compassionate choices that entail significant self-sacrifice. The circumstances of their life might be pitiable, but the quality of their character is admirable.

Suggestions

Pre-Reading Exercise: Ask students to list the qualities or characteristics of a good father–son relationship. After they have read and examined the story, ask them which of the qualities they identified are evident in the relationship between Jeremy and Raglan.

1. To examine the characters of Jeremy and Raglan as well as the relationship they have, pose the following questions:

    a. How do Jeremy and Raglan come to be together?

    b. Why does Jeremy frequently refer to the possibility of Raglan's being his father (pars. 1, 26, and 64)?

    c. Look carefully at the physical descriptions of Jeremy and Raglan contained in paragraphs 1 through 29. Describe the physical toll that heroin has taken on Jeremy's body. How does Jeremy change after he has taken his dose of heroin? What does Jeremy mean when he says that the heroin "only makes [him] normal now"?

    d. Raglan tells Jeremy that he will stop wanting the heroin "When [he] decide[s] there's somethin else [he] want[s] more." Explain what he means.

    e. Examine the references to Raglans' eyes in paragraphs 7, 11, 15, 33, and 35. What does each of these references reveal about Raglan?

    f. Compare and contrast Jeremy's reaction to seeing the baby in the dumpster with Ralgan's reaction. Explain why each reacts as he does.

    g. Examine the interaction between Jeremy and Raglan in paragraphs 30 through 42. What does this interaction reveal about Raglan's feelings toward Jeremy? About Jeremy's feelings toward Raglan?

    h. Why does Raglan, knowing that the recycling center will close shortly, ask Jeremy what he wants to do about the baby?

    i. Describe the life that Jeremy knows. Contrast that with what he experiences on the cliffs. What effect does this experience have on Jeremy?

    j. Consider the references to Jeremy's eyes in paragraphs 44 and 53. What does each of these references reveal about Jeremy?

2. "Crusader Rabbit" is filled with contrasts (life and death; compassion and cruelty; concern and indifference; respect and disrespect; living and existing; loving and hating; nurturing and destroying; etc.). Have students, working in groups, identify and list as many contrasts as they can. When all the groups are through, write their lists on the board and have students discuss the significance of each contrast.

3. Present and discuss with students Maslow's hierarchy of needs: physiological needs; safety needs; love, affection, and belonging needs; esteem needs; self-actualization needs. Ask students to identify which of these needs Raglan meets for Jeremy and to explain how he meets them.

4. To examine the contrast between innocent and experienced states of being, "Crusader Rabbit" can be studied with "I, Too" (p. 6) and "Harlem" (p. 7), "The Chimney Sweeper" poems (pp. 24–25), "The Gilded Six-Bits" (p. 63), and/or "Gimpel the Fool" (p. 95).

5. To focus on the healing power of love, "Crusader Rabbit" can be studied with "The Gilded Six-Bits" (p. 63).

6. "Weakness" (p. 22) can be assigned with "Crusader Rabbit" to examine the issue of "weakness." Comparing and contrasting the attitudes of the father toward the horse and Raglan toward Jeremy leads students to consider what a person's treatment of a "weak" being reveals about his or her true character.

7. "A Worn Path" (p. 107) is a good companion piece for "Crusader Rabbit" because both stories revolve around characters who are unexpected heroes.

8. "Crusader Rabbit" can be used in conjunction with "Time for a Change on Drugs" (p. 264) and/or "Legalization of Narcotics" (p. 267).

9. "What Means Switch" (p. 179) can be teamed with "Crusader Rabbit" for a study of initiation stories (stories in which the main character comes to understand something about himself, another person, human nature, or society that permanently alters his view of the world).

The Gilded Six-Bits

Zora Neale Hurston

This story may initially be a bit difficult for students to read because the dialogue is written in dialect. When the story is assigned, it may be helpful to explain that some words are spelled as they would be pronounced by the characters. For example, "I" would be pronounced "Ah," so it is spelled "Ah"; the "r" in "here" would not be pronounced, so it is spelled "heah"; and the "th" in "the" and "that" would be pronounced as a "d" so "the" is spelled "de" and "that" is spelled "dat." You might have students look at some of the dialogue and show them how the spelling reflects the pronunciation. Assure them that understanding the dialect will become progressively easier as they read.

The story focuses on Missie May and Joe Banks, a couple who has been married over a year and has an idyllic marriage. Their relationship is clearly founded on love and mutual respect. The sincerity and playfulness of their love is illustrated by their games—Joe's tossing money on the porch, Missie May's "fighting" to discover the treasures in Joe's pockets, their bantering at the dinner table. Joe is a hard worker and a good provider: He has a steady job, and he and Missie May live in their own home, have plenty of food, and have money saved. Missie May's efficiency as a homemaker is emphasized by the repeated references to the cleanness and neatness of the house and yard. The Edenic world of Joe and Missie May is corrupted, causing the young couple to lose their innocence and to come to terms with that loss.

Having had little, if any, personal experience with pretentious, deceptive, manipulative men, Missie May and Joe are easily duped by Slemmons. Joe's naïveté is emphasized by his unabashed admiration of the allegedly well-traveled and well-heeled Slemmons. Initially, Missie May seems to be more worldly wise than Joe. She is annoyed with him for being so easily impressed by Slemmons and reminds him that Slemmons can lie just like anyone else. Missie May's veneer of skepticism vanishes when she actually sees Slemmons' gold. While she professes to be unimpressed with the man, she is dazzled by his "gold money," the first she has ever seen. Missie May wants Joe to have gold to wear and invents a "wishful" scenario to explain how they might find some. Aware that Missie May is as gullible as the others in the village, Slemmons plays on her weakness, her desire for gold, and begins to relentlessly pursue her, promising to give her some "gold money." Missie May, made vulnerable by her lack of experience, yields to Slemmons, a decision that ultimately destroys the purity and simplicity of her marriage.

Joe's reaction to his wife's infidelity is one of restraint. He hits Slemmons, but he raises neither hand nor voice to Missie May. The love that Joe has for Missie May is real. He does not leave her, he does not throw her out, and he does not tell anyone, even his mother, of her infidelity. This is not to say he does not punish her. He keeps the coin in his pocket as a constant reminder of her betrayal and he withdraws emotionally, becoming "aloof." Most likely, he withdraws not only to punish Missie May but also to come to terms with what has happened and to heal his hurt. Despite his pain, Joe's love for Missie May remains evident. He is "polite, even kind at times," and, when he realizes she is pregnant, he prevents her from endangering herself or the child by chopping wood. Not knowing for sure that he is the father of the child troubles Joe a great deal. His mother's unsolicited assurance that the child is his completes Joe's healing process, enabling him to forgive Missie May.

The ungilded love that Joe and Missie May have for each other enables them to survive their loss of innocence and their marriage to survive its transformation. Joe rids himself of the gilded coin by buying Missie May candy kisses, transforming the symbol of her infidelity into a symbol of his love. Joe's tossing of the silver coins on the front porch is a signal to Missie May that her punishment is over, that he has forgiven her, and that their marriage will no longer be one of appearance but of substance.

Suggestions

1. Students are often less forgiving of Missie May than is Joe. One approach to helping them understand Missie May's action and Joe's response is to pose questions that focus on the initial relationship between Missie May and Joe, their relationship after Joe discovers her with Slemmons, and their relationship after the baby is born:

    a. List details that illustrate Joe is a good provider and Missie May is a good homemaker.

    b. Describe the relationship between Missie May and Joe before Joe catches her with Slemmons.

    c. Why is Joe impressed with Slemmons? Why is he so easily impressed?

    d. What does Missie May think about Slemmons before she goes to the ice cream parlor?

    e. How does her opinion change once she has met him? Why does her opinion change?

    f. Why does Missie May agree to Slemmons' proposition?

    g. Why does Joe not leave her after he discovers her with Slemmons? Why does she not leave Joe?

    h. How does Missie May's behavior change after Joe catches her with Slemmons?

    i. How does Joe's behavior change?

    j. Why does Joe keep the gilded coin in his pocket?

    k. Why does Joe use the fifty-cent piece to buy candy kisses?

    l. What is the significance of Joe's throwing the money on the porch at the end of the story?

2. Another approach is to have students define and discuss innocence and experience. Their discussion should lead them to realize that being innocent means not only being free of wrongdoing but also being simple, naive, and ignorant. It should also lead them to conclude that innocence is destroyed by experience. Once students have a firm grasp on the meanings of the words, divide them into groups, and ask them to do the following:

    a. Show that Missie May and Joe are, initially, living in a state of innocence.

    b. Explain how and why their innocence is destroyed.

    c. Describe how the characters respond to the loss.

    d. Explain how each adjusts to living in a state of experience.

3. To consider the issue of forgiveness, "The Gilded Six-Bits" can be studied with the poems from "Spoon River Anthology" (p. 16).

4. For another look at the consequences of infidelity, "The Gilded Six Bits" can be paired with "What Would Freud Say" (p. 37)?

5. The contrast between an innocent and an experienced state of being can be examined in more depth by teaming "The Gilded Six Bits" with "I, Too" (p. 6) and "Harlem" (p. 7), "The Chimney Sweeper" poems (pp. 24–25), "Gimpel the Fool" (p. 95), and/or "Crusader Rabbit" (p. 58).

6. "The Gilded Six Bits" can be paired with "Crusader Rabbit" (p. 58) for an examination of the healing power of love.

7. For an examination of the ways in which people respond to loss, "The Gilded Six-Bits" might be studied with "Lot's Wife" (p. 3), "The Vacuum" (p. 22), "Power" (p. 23), "Life after High School" (p. 132), "Islands on the Moon" (p. 144), and/or "Shame" (p. 213).

8. The contrast between an innocent and an experienced state of being could be examined in more depth by teaming this story with "The Chimney Sweeper" poems (pp. 24–25), "Gimpel the Fool" (p. 95), and/or "Crusader Rabbit" (p. 58).

A Very Old Man with Enormous Wings

Gabriel Garcia Marquez

From the opening sentence, many elements combine to paint an unfamiliar world. As the story progresses, it becomes clear that we have moved from the familiar into the phantasmagoria. This story of peasants and poverty, superstitions and fantasy, has been variously interpreted as a satire, a parable, and an allegory. By far the most fascinating aspect of the story is the way in which the other characters react to and treat the angel.

Father Gonzaga, expecting that a true angel would behave according to the precepts of the Church, decides that the old man is not an angel. For one thing, the old man does not understand Latin, "the language of God." For another, the old man looks far too human and far too squalid: "he [has] an unbearable smell of the outdoors, the back side of his wings [is] strewn with parasites . . . and nothing about him measure[s] up to the proud dignity of angels." The priest is oblivious to the comparison that might be drawn between the creature lying in the chicken coop and a child that was born humbly in a manger. Nonetheless, he contacts the Church, informing them of the events and requesting a ruling. In typical bureaucratic fashion, the Church officials respond with neither interest nor excitement and never quite get around to making a decision about whether or not the old man is an angel.

Elisenda has the idea to charge a visitation fee and make some money off the unexpected visitor. In less than a week their house is full of fee-paying guests, and Elisenda and her husband, Pelayo, are "happy with fatigue." The only person not taking part in the carnival is the angel whose "only supernatural virtue seem[s] to be patience." The only time he rouses himself is when the spectators accidentally burn him; some among them think his reaction is one of pain but others think it one of anger. The crowd disperses when a "spider woman" comes to town. Her story inspires the villagers and the visitors, and they find her of greater account than the angel, in whom they have now lost interest.

With all the money they make promoting the angel, Elisenda and Pelayo build a fine new house and buy themselves fancy new things. They neglect the chicken coop and leave the angel alone in filth. When the chicken coop collapses and the child of the family starts school, the angel drags himself to the house and appears in so many rooms almost simultaneously that "the exasperated and unhinged Elisenda shout[s] that it [is] awful living in that hell full of angels." Rather than feed him or tend to his damaged feathers, they throw a blanket over him and extend him "only the charity of letting him sleep in the shed." Running a fever, he becomes "delirious with the tongue twisters of an old Norwegian." He survives the winter, his feathers grow back stiffly, and he begins singing sea chanteys in secret under the stars. One day he attempts flight and finally takes off. Elisenda watches him fly away, "no longer an annoyance in her life but an imaginary dot on the horizon of the sea."

Suggestions

Pre-Reading Exercise: Before students read the story, have them describe in writing what they think an angel would look like. Explain that for the purposes of this activity, their personal belief about the (non)existence of angels is irrelevant. The class can then discuss their descriptions, identifying any elements they have in common. After students have read the story, ask them to compare/contrast their concept of an angel with the depiction of the very old man with enormous wings.

1. Ask students to address the following:
    a. Pelayo's and Elisenda's reactions to the old man change throughout the story. Trace these changes, describing and explaining their different reactions.
    b. How do their reactions to and treatment of the old man compare with their reactions to and treatment of their livestock? Their child?

c. What leads the priest to conclude that the old man is not an angel? What does this indicate about the priest? What other explanation could there be for a man with wings?

d. Why does the doctor find it strange that everyone does not have wings?

e. Compare and contrast the old man with the spider woman.

f. How do the reactions of the people to the spider woman differ from their reactions to the old man? Why?

g. Why is Elisenda relieved when the old man finally goes away?

h. What role does compassion play in this story?

2. Once students have considered what happens in the story, encourage them to think about how they would feel if the events in the story had happened to them:

a. What might the reactions of your family or roommates be if you found an old man with wings lying outside your front door tonight?

b. Would you tell other people about him? If so, who would you tell?

c. Would you contact the media, go on a talk show, sell your story to a news magazine? Why or why not?

d. Would you invite your priest, minister, rabbi, or imam to see the angel? Why or why not?

e. Who would you trust to determine whether the man was a man or an angel? Explain.

3. Have students compare the film version, *Un Señor muy viejo con unas alas enormes / A Very Old Man with Enormous Wings* (1988), to the original story. Which did they like better? Why?

4. To examine the various ways in which people respond to difference, "A Very Old Man with Enormous Wings" can be studied with "Counting the Mad" (p. 15), "Much Madness Is Divinest Sense" (p. 16), and/or "Life after High School" (p. 132).

5. Society's response to difference is at the heart of the 1990 movie *Edward Scissorhands*. At first, the people of Suburbia treat Edward as a curiosity, but their wonder is eventually overwhelmed by their prejudice. Have students view this film and compare/contrast the behavior of the characters in it with the behavior of the characters in "A Very Old Man with Enormous Wings."

6. To further explore the ways in which people with physical abnormalities have been exploited, have students do a short research project on the fairground "freak shows" of the not too distant past. They might write a brief report on such well-known and well-documented personalities as "The Mule-Faced Woman," "The Lobster Boy," "The Living Torso," and "The Gorilla Girl."

The Veldt

Ray Bradbury

"The Veldt" allows students the opportunity to discuss science fiction, a genre with which many of them will be familiar, though perhaps through media such as television and film rather than short stories or novels. Science fiction can be deceptively simple, often raising more issues and containing more nuances than non-science fiction. Technology that exceeds any in current use is usually an element of science fiction. Sometimes the promise of technology is emphasized, sometimes the perils. "The Veldt" points out that technology can backfire if the human element is lost and can actually limit our development as humans. Depending too much on technology to do our work for us can cause us to lose touch with our humanity. Without some connection with the reality of our humanness, we become like nonthinking animals. We become interested in physical comfort and pleasure and unconcerned with love, compassion, and personal responsibility. Whether or not a science fiction story deals with the potential impact of futuristic technology, to be a good story it must have characters and conflicts that have existed or could exist in reality. In "The Veldt, " the Hadleys' house and nursery are far beyond the technology that now exists, but their motivation for having them—a desire for comfort and convenience—is entirely realistic.

The Hadley house defies nature, both in its creation of an artificial scene and in its enabling the parents and the children to act in an "unnatural" fashion—that is, unlike children and parents. The children are cared for and nurtured not by their biological parents but by the house. In addition to taking care of them, the house allows them to do whatever they like. Consequently, they begin to feel allegiance to the house, not to George and Lydia. Like Peter Pan and Wendy, who escape adult restrictions in Never-Never Land, Peter and Wendy Hadley escape parental restrictions in the nursery. They resent any attempts by their biological parents to restrict their activities. After all, their parents are not really their caretakers.

In addition to creating a distance between children and parents, the "Happylife Home" has made the lives of the Hadleys too simple, and when lives become too simple, there is a void. Ultimately, the house so efficiently cares for everyone and everything that George and Lydia are left with nothing to do, and the children learn to do nothing. Peter does not want to learn to paint for himself. He wants a machine to do it. In fact, he wants to be a passive observer of life, not an active participant: "I don't want to do anything but look, listen, and smell." In trying to provide the best for themselves and their children, George and Lydia make themselves miserable, and they make themselves unnecessary in the lives of their children. They also unwittingly teach their children to exist rather than to live.

Ultimately, George and Lydia lose control of their house and their children. In an effort to regain control, George and Lydia want the family to go on vacation, an occasion we associate with lazing about but which they associate with doing for themselves. Lydia longs to "fry eggs," "darn socks," and "sweep the floor." They long to perform the menial tasks that make them human. "The Veldt" points out that part of being human is toil, work, taking care of the business of living. It further points out that involvement in reality, with the chores of the real world, is essential if we are to maintain our sense of kinship and humanity.

Suggestions

Pre-Reading Exercise: Have students describe in writing the characteristics of a good parent. After the story has been discussed, ask them which of the characteristics they named are displayed by George and Lydia and which are not.

1. Since the narrative is relatively simple, pose questions to students that will call for them to synthesize details and draw conclusions:
    a. Compare what the house does for Peter and Wendy with what George and Lydia do.
    b. What do George and Lydia gain with the Happylife Home? What do they lose?
    c. What does Lydia want to do on vacation? What does this indicate about her and George's life?
    d. Why do Peter and Wendy arrange for their parents to be killed? Why are their actions understandable?
    e. Explain fully why the Happylife Home does not give the Hadleys a "happy home."

2. To help students see that the conflict in the story hinges not on futuristic technology but on human nature, have them identify which elements in the story are actually very realistic. This exercise will point out the essential requisite of good science fiction.

3. For an extended discussion of the effects of nurturing, "The Veldt" can be teamed with "Barbie Doll" (p. 20), "I Stand Here Ironing" (p. 114), and/or "The Fat Girl" (p. 120).

4.   Team "The Veldt" with "A Martian Sends A Postcard Home" (p. 13), "Bedtime Story" (p. 14), and/or "Harrison Bergeron" (p. 53), pieces that present highly unrealistic situations, but develop realistic statements about human nature.

Everyday Use

Alice Walker

"Everyday Use" revolves, at least in the mind of Mama, the narrator, around the sibling rivalry between her daughters, Dee and Maggie. Within the framework of this sibling rivalry, the issue of heritage is raised, and a distinction is drawn between ancestral heritage and familial heritage. Our ancestors are relatives who were born at least a generation before our grandparents and are not usually well know to us. Because ancestral heritage is remote, it may seem more exotic and intriguing than familial heritage. After all, we grow up in our families and are familiar with their values, traditions, legacies, and way of life. In this story, Maggie is content with her familial heritage while Dee rejects it and embraces her ancestral heritage.

The difference in Maggie's and Dee's perceptions of heritage is emphasized by the careful presentation of the two sisters as opposites. Maggie is "homely," "not bright," ill-educated, and unsure of herself; Dee is pretty, intelligent, well-educated, and self-confident. Maggie has remained at home and seems content to live the type of life her family has lived. Dee, hating life in rural Georgia, has moved to the city where she has come to feel pride in her ancestral heritage.

Dee's pride is relatively new. When she was going away to college, she refused a quilt her mother had offered her, saying quilts were "old-fashioned, out of style." Because of the growing pride in black heritage, quilts, as well as other hand-crafted utilitarian pieces, are now in style, and Dee, who always "knew what style was." wants the older ones her mother has. Dee wants the quilts because they are "priceless." But Maggie wants them as a remembrance of Grandma Dee. To Dee, the quilts as well as the churn top and dasher are artifacts that should be displayed. To Maggie, who uses the churn to make butter and who would cover her bed with the quilts, they are utilitarian objects intended for everyday use. The difference in their attitudes toward these objects point to a difference in their attitudes toward heritage.

The heritage Dee is interested in is that of her ancestors, not her family. She rejects her name, ignoring the fact that she was named after her grandmother, and gives herself an African name, "Wangero." She dresses in clothes and jewelry that are based on African designs and wears her hair in an African manner. She embraces her African heritage because is it fashionable; she embraces only the parts of her familial heritage that are "in style" and can be displayed. Maggie, on the other hand, is proud of her family and its heritage. She knows the family names and nicknames; she knows how to quilt; she knows which family members made which objects, and, unlike Dee, she will make daily use of these objects. In short, Maggie seems content to live a life similar to the life her mother has lived.

Maggie and Dee are both concerned with their heritage, but heritage means something different to each one of them. The major question raised by the story is what role heritage should play in our daily lives. Is heritage a matter of pride, of artifacts to display, or is it an essential part of self, something that is retained only by putting it to "everyday use"?

Suggestions

1.   Ask students to define in writing the word "heritage.": Discuss their definition and arrive at some agreement on the different types of heritage: familial, ancestral, racial, cultural, and so on. Ask students to consider what their own personal heritage is and have them summarize it in writing.

Do they, for instance, consider their primary heritage to be familial, racial, religious, national, and so on. Ask students then to decide how Dee and Maggie would define "heritage."

2. Have students list the ways in which Dee and Maggie are opposites. When they have completed their lists, ask them to identify which of the two sisters they like better and to explain their choice. If they do not mention the notion of heritage, ask them to explain how each sister views her heritage.

3. Discuss the notion of heritage and how it can be based on a number of elements. Have students break up into groups and compare Dee's perception of heritage with Maggie's. After students have discussed their comparison, the story's point of view might be examined by posing the following question: Why do you think Mama sympathizes more with Maggie than with Dee?

4. After they have read and discussed the short story, have students view the Bruce Schwartz/Wadsworth video production of "Everyday Use." Divide the class into groups and pose questions that will help them to identify the ways in which the film differs from the short story and to explore the impact of those differences: How does the house shown in the film differ from the house described in the story?

   a. In the film, does Mama look like the character described in the short story? Explain.

   b. Does Mama's attitude toward Dee's approaching visit seem to be the same in the film as it is in the short story? Explain.

   c. The film presents the conversation at the kitchen table differently than it is presented in the short story. What are the differences?

   d. What details about Dee's past are included in the short story but not in the film?

   e. Consider all of the differences that you have found. Would these differences cause someone who has only watched the film to see Mama, Maggie, Dee, and/or Hakim a Barber differently than someone who has only read the story? Explain.

   Once the groups have completed their work, reassemble the class and discuss their findings.

5. Pair "Everyday Use" with "What You Pawn I Will Redeem" (p. 163) to focus on the issue of heritage.

6. To explore the idea of success and the various ways in which people define it, "Everyday Use" can be studied with "Richard Cory" (p. 4), "Warren Pryor" (p. 5), and/or "Starved Out" (p. 246).

Gimpel the Fool

Issac Bashevis Singer

The world described in this story is that of the shetl (a small Jewish village in Eastern Europe), where the rabbinical council (council of religious elders) rules absolutely and everyone knows everyone else's business.

In the opening paragraph Gimpel tells us he was always called names by his schoolmates but the name "fool" was the one that stuck. His foolishness contains within itself some wisdom, however; he avoids getting bitten by dogs, presumably because of rabies. He doesn't stare at a woman's belly and is thus easily misled into thinking her with child. This is not foolishness but perhaps innocence or modesty. He grows up an orphan and an easy dupe for the rest of the townsfolk, who seem to take perverse pleasure in being cruel to him. Much of the time their fantastic tales do not fool him, but he pursues the wild stories anyway: "What did I stand to lose by looking?"

The rabbi thinks he is not foolish, rather the townsfolk are cruel; however, even his daughter tries to fool him. The cruelest trick of all is when the townsfolk conspire to marry him off to Elka, a woman they tell him is a virgin though she has a child.

From the outset it is obvious that Elka is a tough woman with an acerbic tongue and a clear desire to look after herself. She calls him "a drip" and demands a dowry of her husband, even though it is her place to give him one. When, during the wedding ceremony, he finds out this "virgin" is actually "a widow and divorced," he marries her anyway for, as he puts it, "What was I to do, run away from under the marriage canopy?"

After the wedding, she will not lie with him. He sees through her deceit but waits until she is ready. Four months later she delivers a child. Everyone congratulates him and even though he is humiliated, he arranges a bris and entertains the whole town. He argues with his wife, but she swears the child is his. Eventually, he accepts what she says because "who really knows how such things are?" As time goes by he comes to love the child and Elka, too, although she treats him badly. He feeds her and spoils her, and she "became fat and handsome."

Elka betrays Gimpel. The rabbi allows Gimpel to support her but forbids him to go near her. Nine months later, after the rabbis have finished arguing the case, Elka gives birth to another child. Gimpel names the child for his mother-in-law. The town busybodies mock and jeer him, but he ignores them, resolving to "always believe what [he] [is] told. What's the good of *not* believing?" The rabbis find an obscure passage that allows him to stay with his wife. He returns home only to find his apprentice in the bed with her. Through some additional trickery, she persuades him it was all his imagination. He spends the next twenty years with his wife, and she bears him six children, four boys and two girls. Eventually, Elka grows quite ill. On her deathbed, she confesses to Gimpel that none of the children are his and begs his forgiveness. Gimpel is shocked.

After the period of mourning is done, the "Spirit of Evil" comes to him and tells him he should deceive the world just as the world has deceived him. At first, Gimpel decides to "revenge [him]self on them for all the shame they've put on [him]." He urinates in the dough, sets the loaves to bake, and dozes. But Elka comes to him in a dream and admonishes him, "You fool! Because I was false is everything false too?" Sensing that "everything hung in the balance," Gimpel buries the loaves in the yard. When he returns home, he divides his hoard among the children and tells them to "forget that such a one as Gimpel ever existed."

He leaves his home and wanders the world, deciding there is no difference in this world between lies and truth and nothing really matters much at all because the true world is the world to come. He sees Elka once in a dream, clearly she is paying for her sins in the world to come, so in this sense, it all works out in the end. Or this is his conclusion. "God be praised," he says. In the world to come "even Gimpel cannot be deceived."

Suggestions

1. One approach to the material might be to have students analyze the material in terms of the following questions:

    a. In what ways is Gimpel foolish?

    b. Describe the attitudes and behavior of the townspeople.

    c. Describe Elka's character and behavior.

    d. What is Gimpel's opinion of Elka? Does it change? Explain.

    e. Describe Gimpel's treatment of Elka and the children.

    f. What is the reader to make of the fact that Gimpel becomes a wealthy man? Of the fact that he almost forgets to share that information with the reader?

g. What happens to Gimpel after his wife dies?

h. Why does he leave his children and wander through the world?

i. Do any of the characters in this story behave honorably?

2. Have students consider the importance of this story being told from Gimpel's point of view:

a. At what points in the story does Gimpel know he is being fooled?

b. Describe Gimpel's reaction each time he is made a fool of.

c. When he goes to his spiritual advisor (rabbi) for advice, what does the rabbi tell him? Does the rabbi's response make Gimpel seem more or less a fool? Explain.

d. How might your reaction to the story have been different if it had not been told from Gimpel's point of view?

3. Have students consider how their experiences may have influenced their reading of the story:

a. Have you ever seen another person be "made a fool of"? What happened? How did you react?

b. Have you ever been "made a fool of"? What happened? How did you react?

c. How might these experiences have affected your reading of "Gimpel the Fool"?

4. To examine innocent and experienced states of being, "Gimpel the Fool" can be studied with "I, Too" (p. 6) and "Harlem" (p. 7), "The Chimney Sweeper" poems (pp. 24–25), "The Gilded Six-Bits" (p. 63), and/or "Crusader Rabbit" (p. 58).

5. For a discussion of how people respond to "difference," team "Gimpel the Fool" with "Counting the Mad" (p. 15), "Much Madness Is Divinest Sense" (p. 16), "A Very Old Man with Enormous Wings" (p. 72), and/or "What Means Switch" (p. 179).

6. The world that Gimpel inhabits is likely to be unfamiliar to students. Students might be asked to use InfoTrac to find out more about Polish Jewry (Subject: "Jews, Polish") and/or the life of Singer (Subject: "Singer, Isaac Bashevis").

A Worn Path

Eudora Welty

Set in Mississippi during the 1930s, "A Worn Path" tells of an old black woman's arduous journey from her home "away back off the Old Natchez Trace" to the town of Natchez. The story opens with the woman, Phoenix Jackson, taking a path through woods that she knows well. Not until the end of the story is the purpose of her journey—to get life-sustaining medicine for her grandson—revealed. Because this is a "slice of life story" (one presenting a particular segment of life), no explicit conflict is introduced, developed, and resolved. To understand the story's significance, the details of the story, particularly those concerning Phoenix, the setting, and the other, seemingly minor characters, must be carefully considered.

From the outset, Phoenix's comments and attitude reveal her courage and her nobility. A "very old woman" whose skin has a "pattern . . . of numberless branching wrinkles," she carefully makes her way through the woods, talking to herself and to the animals. She remains in good humor no matter what obstacle she encounters. She excuses the thorn bush in which she becomes entangled and tells herself that she cannot afford to have a limb amputated if she gets caught in the barbed-wire fence. Dancing with the scarecrow she mistook for a ghost, she laughs at herself and the effects age has had on her. Phoenix recalls her past trips along this path. Approaching a hill, she notes, "Seem like there is chains about my feet, time I get this far." In the field of dead corn, she recalls having seen a "two-headed snake" there "back in the summer." She refers to the wagon track leading into Natchez as "the easy place." In town,

Phoenix "depend[s] on her feet to know where to take her" and, climbing flight after flight of stairs, to know where to stop. Despite her age, Phoenix will continue to make this trip as long as she needs to.

Phoenix's qualities contrast sharply with the qualities of the hunter, making her kindness and gentleness more apparent. The hunter, callous, arrogant, selfish, and racist, is her antithesis. Although he picks Phoenix up after she has fallen, he swings her around, without regard for her age or her possible injuries. He assumes that the purpose of her journey is trivial, simply because she is inconsequential in his eyes. He assures her that he would not travel as far as she without getting "something for [his] trouble." He never suspects that she is motivated by pure altruism, because he would not be. Finally, he tries intimidation by pointing his rifle at her, an action he surely would not have performed had Phoenix been white. In fact, the hunter functions as a foil, a character who makes the qualities of another character more vivid by contrast. He is a predator of animals: The bag he carries is filled with quail he has killed. Phoenix respects the animals and talks to them as she walks, urging those in the thickets to stay "Out of [her] way," the quail to "Walk pretty," and the alligators to "sleep on." The hunter's purpose is to cause death; Phoenix travels to prolong life. The hunter lies, professing that he would be charitable if he had some money with him. Phoenix does not talk about being charitable: She herself is Charity. Appropriately, when they part, they go "in different directions."

Despite the distance and difficulty of the journey, Phoenix is revitalized rather than exhausted by it. That she will be renewed by her journey is indicated by her name. A phoenix is a mythological bird that lived for five hundred years and then flew into the altar fire, was consumed by it, and arose from the ashes regenerated. Images associated with Phoenix that suggest burning run throughout the story. Her skin is wrinkled, "but a golden color ran underneath and the two knobs of her cheeks were illuminated by a yellow burning under the dark." Her face is described as "light[ing]" when she recognizes the scarecrow as such. After seeing the nickel fall from the hunter's pocket, "The deep lines in her face went into a fierce and different radiation." In the doctor's office, while Phoenix stands silently before the attendant, "the wrinkles in her skin [shine] like a bright net." Birds are associated with her: The tapping of her cane on the frozen earth "seemed meditative like the chirping of a solitary little bird," and her beloved grandson holds his mouth open for the medicine "like a little bird." Phoenix appears to the nurse to be dead when she does not speak in the doctor's office; but then, "a flicker and then a flame of comprehension across her face," and "Phoenix rose. . . ." She is revitalized.

Because the phoenix is resurrected from its ashes, it is an often-used symbol for Christ. A number of references in the story reinforce Phoenix's association with Christ, emphasizing her heroism and charity. The story is set at Christmas time. Phoenix walks with a "thin, small cane," becomes caught in a thorn bush, rests beneath a tree with mistletoe growing in its branches, and buys her grandson a windmill. Christ had a thin reed placed in his hand and a crown of thorns placed on his head when he was condemned to death. Legend holds that the crown of thorns was made of mistletoe. The windmill, too, is a symbol for Christ because it brings life-giving water in the same way that Christians believe Jesus brings life-giving salvation to all. Christ's gift was the ultimate act of charity: He died in agony so that others could have eternal life. Phoenix risks her own life in order to bring life to her grandson. It is the ultimate heroic act.

Suggestions

Pre-Reading Exercise: Have students identify people who seem to be considered heroes by young people. A discussion can follow about the types of people whom society makes into heroes—rock stars and athletes—and about the role the media play in shaping these individuals.

1. Have students divide into groups and answer questions that will prepare them to see that Phoenix is heroic:

a. List the various difficulties the journey presents for Phoenix and summarize Phoenix's reaction to each difficulty.

b. Identify the minor characters and rank them in order of their "likability."

c. Identify the ways in which Phoenix and the hunter are opposites.

When the groups have completed their task, have the class reassemble and share their responses. This should lead to an analysis of Phoenix's qualities, a discussion of the characteristics of a hero, and a realization that Phoenix is heroic.

2. To help students understand the significance of charity in the story, ask them to fully define the word. Once they realize that "charity" means both "the provision of help or relief to the poor" and "an act or feeling of benevolence or goodwill," have students locate the word in the story (par. 95). Then, ask them to explain how the word applies to the various characters in the doctor's office as well as the other characters in the tale. Finally, ask them how the word applies to Phoenix. They should conclude that Phoenix's journey is the purest form of charity because she is motivated to make it out of love for another human being, with no thought for herself.

3. Have students view the Bruce Schwartz/Harcourt video production of "A Worn Path," stopping the video before the interview with Eudora Welty begins. Divide the class into groups and pose questions that will help them to consider the faithfulness of the film to the story and, ultimately, to realize that the Phoenix Jackson of the short story is likely to be admired while the Phoenix Jackson of the film is likely to be pitied:

a. Was the setting of the film like that of the story? Explain.

b. Did Phoenix look like you envisioned her as you read the short story? Explain.

c. Did Phoenix's behavior in the film correspond to her behavior in the story? Explain.

d. Were the other characters (the hunter, the lady who ties her shoe, the attendant, the nurse) portrayed in the film in the same way that they were in the short story? Explain.

Have the class reassemble and discuss their findings. If students are able to point out differences in the film and the short story, skip to question e. Otherwise, have them reread paragraphs 35 through 60 of the short story, instructing them to pay careful attention to the behavior of the characters. Then, have students look again at the corresponding film sequence. Ask them to explain how the film version differs from the short story. (For instance, in the short story, Phoenix does not seem afraid of the dog. She "hit[s] him a little with her cane" and describes the dog as "smiling" at her. After she sees the nickel fall from the hunter's pocket, she gives "a little cry," tries to shoo the dog away, and "laugh[s] as if in admiration," observing "He ain't scared of nobody. He a big black dog." Phoenix's "whispered 'Sic him!'" is not clearly addressed to the hunter and may have been directed at the dog. In the video, on the other hand, Phoenix is truly afraid of the dog, both before and after the hunter appears.)

e. Does your perception of the short story's Phoenix Jackson differ from your perception of the film's Phoenix Jackson? Explain.

4. Show students the interview with Eudora Welty that follows the production of "A Worn Path." Have them work individually to answer the following questions:

a. Do Welty's perceptions about the story differ from yours? Explain.

b. Do her comments answer some questions you had about the story? Explain.

c. What does Welty mean when she says it does not matter whether the grandson is alive or dead?

5. For an extended study the unexpected hero, "A Worn Path" might be teamed with "Crusader Rabbit" (p. 58).

I Stand Here Ironing

Tillie Olsen

"I Stand Here Ironing" allows students the perfect opportunity for an in-depth study of character. It is a monologue in which the narrator, by telling her daughter's story, reveals a great deal about herself. Unlike some other narrators who are involved in the stories they tell, the mother here seems to be reliable; at least she attempts to be as honest as possible about events as she perceives them. Her monologue is in response to someone who has called wanting to know more about Emily in order to help her; given this fact, it is remarkable that the mother attempts neither to justify her actions nor to blame herself totally for their effect on Emily. She avoids these self-indulgences, fearing "[she] will become engulfed with all [she] did or did not do, with what should have been and what cannot be helped." Indeed, much of what happened to Emily as well as her mother could not be helped; however, their reaction to this lack of choice is different.

As a child, Emily had little control over her life and had to endure apparent rejections. Twice she is sent to live with her grandparents; she is put in a nursery school she dislikes; she is left alone at much too young an age. These experiences, no doubt, make Emily feel unwanted, a feeling that is intensified when Susan is born. Her mother, who will get up to take care of Susan, will not go to Emily and comfort her during the night. The emotional rejection she must have felt is exacerbated when she is sent to the convalescent home where affection is discouraged. When she returns home, her sister Susan, a pretty, bright, robust, and gregarious child gets far more attention than Emily, who is none of these things. Given her history, it is miraculous that as a teenager she risks even more rejection by going on stage. By taking control of her life, Emily finally feels what it is like to be accepted, appreciated, and wanted.

The mother's actions have been determined mainly by necessity. Deserted during the Depression by her husband and with no social welfare programs to help her support herself and eight-month-old Emily, she soon must send Emily to live with her ex-husband's family. When she is finally able to get Emily back, she has to put her in a nursery school: "It was the only place there was. It was the only way we could be together, the only way I could hold a job." Tired and worried, she is unable to show Emily much joy, and she eventually has to send her back to her ex-husband's family. After she remarries and Emily returns, she has other children who demand her attention. Juggling their needs, her household responsibilities, and her job, she is too exhausted to give Emily the attention she needs. When the war starts and her husband goes to fight, she is solely responsible for her five children and depends on Emily to help her. The circumstances of her life—a broken marriage, the Depression, children, war—left her with few choices, especially when Emily was young. Although her actions have been determined by necessity, she reacts to her lack of choice by feeling defeated and guilty.

The issue of helplessness, lack of choice, is manifested in the metaphor of the iron. The mother tries to explain to the caller how she has "wrinkled" Emily's life. But the mother, who has felt helpless, knows that Emily "is more than [a] dress on the ironing board, helpless before the iron."

Suggestions

1. To direct the students' focus to the major details that illustrate Emily's lack of control over the forces that beset her, ask the following questions:
    a. Why does Emily's father desert his family?
    b. Why is Emily sent to live with her grandparents?
    c. Why is Emily put into nursery school?
    d. Why does Emily's mother not comfort her when she wakes up during the night?
    e. Why is Emily put into the convalescent home?
    f. At the convalescent home, why are Emily and her friend separated?

g. Why does Emily have to "help be a mother, and housekeeper, and shopper"?

After students have reported their answers to these questions, you might ask them which of the mother's actions were the result of her own helplessness and which were the result of youthful ignorance.

2. Have students review the major events of Emily's childhood and make a list of her emotional needs. After they have reported on their lists, ask them to address this question: How does Emily fulfill these needs by becoming a comedienne?

3. Ask students to examine the metaphor of the iron by first locating the references to ironing and then answering the following questions:

   a. Why could it be said that Emily has in some ways been as helpless as the dress on the ironing board?

   b. Why could it be said that Emily is more than a dress, "helpless before the iron"?

   c. Why could it be said that Emily's mother has been "helpless before the iron"?

   d. Why is it appropriate that Emily's mother is ironing as she tells her story?

4. Have students view the Bruce Schwartz/Harcourt video production of "I Stand Here Ironing." Ask them to answer the following question individually and in writing: How does the mother in the film differ from the mother in the short story?

   After the first viewing, students will likely find the mother in the story to be a more reflective, resigned character than the mother in the film. What they may not realize is that the differences in their perceptions are in large part the result of the changes the screenwriter and director made in the short story. Scenes and dialogue have been added (for example, the scenes of Emily's being left with and picked up from her paternal grandparents as well as the mother's dialouge about authority). A great deal of text has been omitted (most obviously the majority of paragraphs 34–45). And scenes have been dramatically altered (for instance, the film's portrayal of Emily's reactions to being left alone (pars. 21–22) and to winning the amateur contest (par. 46) differ greatly from those described in the story).

   Have students watch the film again, this time reading along in their book. They will quickly notice additions, deletions, and alterations. When the story's text and the film are remarkably different, pause the film and ask students to discuss how the changes affect their view of the characters.

5. "I Stand Here Ironing" can be paired with "The Fat Girl" (p. 120) and/or "Islands on the Moon" (p. 144), other stories that deal with the effects of childhood experiences.

6. "Birthday Party" (p. 43) and/or "What You Pawn I Will Redeem" (p. 163) can be studied in conjunction with "I Stand Here Ironing" to examine further the notion of narrator reliability.

7. In "Power" (p. 23), Rich makes the point that our power and our pain often stem from the same source. Have students explore this idea by studying "I Stand Here Ironing" along with "Power" and any of the following: "The Fat Girl" (p. 120), "Life after High School" (p. 132), "Islands on the Moon" (p. 144), "Shame" (p. 213), and/or "Daddy Tucked the Blanket" (p. 215).

8. To explore further the consequences of living in the past, "Islands on the Moon" might be studied with "A Rose for Emily" (p. 193).

9. For an examination of the ways in which people respond to loss, "Islands on the Moon" might be studied with "Lot's Wife" (p. 3), "Power" (p. 23), "The Gilded Six-Bits" (p. 63), "Life after High School" (p. 132), and/or "Shame" (p. 213).

10. The correction of youthful misperceptions could be further examined by studying "Islands on the Moon" with "Those Winter Sundays" (p. 8).

The Fat Girl

Andre Dubus

"The Fat Girl" is both an obvious and a subtle story. It is told simply in third person, and in strict chronological order, yet Dubus drops along the way some compelling insinuations about the nature of identity and the values of society. The story is an indictment against the superficial values of American society, specifically the priority we give to physical beauty.

The value that American society gives to physical beauty has far-reaching effects in the life of Louise. At an early age she is made self-conscious about her weight, the effect of which is to make her eat secretly, a practice described by Dubus as "insular and destructive." In high school, she eats very little in the cafeteria, preferring instead to gorge herself after school in the privacy of her room. She does not eat at all in the college cafeteria, thinking that everyone will notice what she eats. At this point her self-consciousness has made her almost paranoid. She chooses thin friends in high school and college because she "was always thinking about what people saw when they looked at" her and she "didn't want them to see two fat girls."

The story further shows that, for women, being thin is necessary in order to be attractive to many men, and that much of a woman's life can be controlled by this superficial attitude. Louise's mother instructs her to avoid eating because if she is fat, boys won't be interested in her. Louise chooses a college at which there will be no boys; this will eliminate the problem entirely. Her decision to diet is prompted by her friend Carrie, after Carrie has fallen in love with a young man. Carrie makes a very strange remark to Louise, the aim of which is to encourage Louise to lose weight: "I want you to be loved the way I love you." This remark seems to mean that Louise will have to shed weight in order for a man to love her. When Louise becomes thin, she wins a husband, but her life is completely controlled by the obsession to remain thin in order to please Richard. Richard's discontent when Louise begins to gain weight reminds us of her mother's belief that women are acceptable to men only if they fulfill men's notions of feminine beauty. Richard's stated worry is that Louise will not be able to fit into a bathing suit. This trivial concern reveals a deeper truth: Women are but extensions of the egos of men like Richard.

The value that American society places on physical beauty causes a confusion in Louise's personal value system and, ultimately, a confusion in her sense of identity. In high school, Louise knew "the truth," that God had made her "that way." This is a truth, however, that Louise will not be allowed to live by. Neither does she find any fulfillment in the self-realization she has soon after she goes to college: "Her brown eyes . . . were not shallow eyes, she thought; they were indeed windows of a tender soul, a good heart." During her diet, she feels at one point that "she had lost herself too," and at another point "that her soul, like her body aboard the plane, was in some rootless flight." When Louise finally reaches the weight deemed acceptable, she is at first pleased with the result. Her relatives congratulate her and "the applause in their eyes lasted the entire summer, and she loved their eyes." After she marries Richard, she has a moment when she considers all she has and feels that "she had bought into the pleasures of the nation." She has, temporarily, gained the acceptance of others, but what is being accepted is not the real Louise, not Louise's values, not "the truth." She has moments when she realizes this: "There were times when she was suddenly assaulted by the feeling that she had taken the wrong train and arrived at a place where no one knew her, and where she ought not to be."

Louise fails to stay thin not because she is weak, but because she must be who she is. The opinions of others and the values of the society that created those opinions cannot sustain us. What does sustain us is love and acceptance, especially acceptance. Feeling good about oneself is the key to not being a victim of superficial and arbitrary social values. The story implies that by nature we are what we are: we can change, but at a great cost to personal integrity.

Suggestions

1. One approach that will bring out both the issue of social values and the issue of identity is to have students focus on the title. Does the title indicate the identity that others have given Louise? Does the title indicate how Louise defines herself? A good defense can be made for both points of view. Certainly, Louise's mother, Richard, and some of Louise's other relatives evaluate Louise only in terms of her appearance. However, Louise attributes to other people a concern with her weight that does not exist. She is surprised, for example, that not one person notices when she loads her tray up with food the one time she eats in the college cafeteria. She is surprised and disappointed that not one teacher or student at college mentions her weight loss. Louise does not choose friends who are fat because she doesn't want anyone to "see two fat girls." Thus, it seems that Louise has come to identify herself as "the fat girl."

2. To help students to see some of the subtleties of Dubus' story and some of the issues it raises, have them work on questions that call for synthesis of details:

   a. Why is Louise's mother so concerned with Louise's weight?

   b. In what ways is Louise's secret eating "destructive"?

   c. Is thinness the only quality that all of Louise's best friends have in common? Explain. What does Louise's choice of friends tell us about her?

   d. What prompts Carrie's offer to help Louise go on a diet?

   e. What is Richard's primary concern when Louise begins to gain weight?

   f. What does Louise finally see as the real problem in her relationship with Richard?

   g. Explain why Louise feels "vindication" at the end of the story?

3. "Barbie Doll" (p. 20), "Heavy Judgment" (p. 252), and/or "Starved Out" (p. 246) can be assigned along with "The Fat Girl" in order to explore further the value American society places on physical beauty.

4. "The Fat Girl" can be teamed with "Warren Pryor" (p. 5) and/or "A Red Palm" to consider parents' desires for their children.

5. For an extended discussion of the effects of nurturing, "The Fat Girl" can be studied with "Barbie Doll" (p. 20), "The Veldt" (p. 77), and/or "I Stand Here Ironing" (p. 114).

6. To examine further the notion of identity, "Mr. Z" (p. 20), "Everyday Use" (p. 88), and/or "Life after High School" (p. 132) can be assigned along with "The Fat Girl".

7. In "Power" (p. 23), Rich makes the point that our power and our pain often stem from the same source. Have students explore this idea by studying "The Fat Girl" along with "Power" and any of the following: "I Stand Here Ironing" (p. 114), "Life after High School" (p. 132), "Islands on the Moon" (p. 144), "Shame" (p. 213), and/or "Daddy Tucked the Blanket" (p. 215).

8. "The Fat Girl" can be teamed with "Lot's Wife" (p. 3), "Barbie Doll" (p. 20), "The Fat Girl" (p. 120), and/or "The Chrysanthemums" (p. 202) for an extended study of the roles of women.

Life after High School

Joyce Carol Oates

Adolescence is a time when teenagers struggle with their sense of identity and autonomy, examining and defining their own beliefs, values, and goals. They begin to separate from their parents and rely heavily on their peers for approval and affirmation. As teenagers become more self-aware and begin to analyze their feelings, some conclude that certain feelings are unacceptable or inappropriate. Fearful that the feelings they have judged "wrong" will lead to rejection, they attempt to control, change, ignore, or deny those feelings. Those who attempt to deny their feelings may isolate themselves or create an "acceptable" persona. Initially, this method of coping may prove effective, but eventually some will perceive and become uncomfortable with the schism between who they really are and who other people think they are. This is the case in "Life after High School." Zachary and Sunny, the two central characters, struggle with the incongruence between their public selves and their private selves.

Zachary's conflict revolves around his sexual identity. At about the time he enters puberty, he begins to isolate himself, having as his only friend another brilliant, latently homosexual boy, Tobias. By the time he is in ninth grade, he has thoroughly focused on his intellect and has adopted with girls the prim and proper pose of Clifton Webb, a well-known actor and a closeted homosexual. During Christmas break of his senior year, Zachary apparently takes an enormous risk and acknowledges to himself and to Tobias his homosexuality and his love for Tobias. Tobias' rejection initiates Zachary's quest to make himself heterosexual.

His desperation is understandable not only because he has been rejected but also because of the cultural climate of the 1950s and his own religious convictions. In 1950, government officials, as part of their continuing investigation of citizens purported to have communist affiliations, begin targeting homosexuals ("sex perverts") as threats to national security.[1] Shortly after taking office in 1953, President Eisenhower signs an executive order prohibiting the hiring and permitting the firing of any government employee who is homosexual. The national denunciation and persecution of homosexuals, which continues throughout the decade, is reinforced by the traditional teachings of mainstream religions. A Christian and a practicing member of the Lutheran church, the teenaged Zachary is "afraid of hell" and daily "lacerate[s] his soul," praying "for his sinful soul, for his sinful thoughts, deeds, desires." He understands that his is not "'*a free world.*'" Given the social and political climate as well as his own

---

[1]Homosexuality was brought into the public consciousness in 1948 when Alfred Kinsey released *Sexual Behavior in the Human Male,* revealing that 37 percent of the men studied had some homosexual experience; that 13 percent were more homosexual than heterosexual; and that 4 percent were homosexual. (In 1953, Kinsey released *Sexual Behavior in the Human Female,* revealing that 28 percent of the women studied had homosexual experience and that 3 percent were lesbian.)

Government officials, in the midst of public panic over the spread of communism and the possibility of a nuclear attack, targeted homosexuals as threats to national security:

Feb. 1950	Senator Joseph McCarthy charges that over two hundred communists have infiltrated the U.S. State Department.
Feb. 1950	Undersecretary of State John Peurifoy claims that a "homosexual underground" exists and that homosexuals are "security risks."
Apr. 1950	Guy Gabrielson, National Chairman of the Republican Party, asserts that "sexual perverts" have "infiltrated" the government and may pose a threat as "dangerous" as "the actual Communists."
Dec. 1950	The Senate Subcommittee in Investigations files its report, "Employment of Homosexuals and Other Sex Perverts in Government." The subcommittee concludes "that those who engage in acts of homosexuality and other perverted sex activities are unsuitable for employment in the federal government. This conclusion is based upon the fact that persons who indulge in such degraded activity are committing not only illegal and immoral acts, but they also constitute security risks in positions of public trust."
Apr. 1953	President Eisenhower signs Executive Order 10450, an order which prohibits the hiring of homosexual men and women for federal jobs and permits the firing of employees for "sexual perversion."

For a more detailed discussion, see Kevin Jennings, Becoming Visible: A Reader in Gay and Lesbian History for High School and College Students. Boston: Alyson Publications, 1994.

religious beliefs, it is not surprising that Zachary is terrified by his homosexual feelings and condemns himself as "sick, crazy, 'perverted.'"

Nor is it surprising that Zachary, who has "never to anyone's recollection asked a girl out before," returns to school in January in single-minded pursuit of a heterosexual relationship with Sunny, a popular girl known for her "goodness." Zachary "*seem[s]* to have fallen in love with Sunny" (emphasis added). Around Sunny, he is insecure ("shy"; "stammering"; "nervous"), "humble," and "bold." He "pursue[s]" her with "attentiveness" and "clumsy devotion," "hanging around," "lying in wait," and "waiting for the advantageous moment." Zachary's behavior is more the result of his desperation to be heterosexual than a passion for Sunny. Being with Sunny makes it "possible for [him] to believe" that he can be heterosexual, but that belief is fleeting. Sexual identity is not something that one can change at will, no matter how hard one tries.[2] Had Zachary felt an amorous passion for Sunny, presumably he would have proclaimed his love when he gave her the "coldly glittering" ring. Instead, he speaks "almost formally, as if setting out the basic points of his debating strategy: if Sunny [does] not love him, he [can] love enough for both." He never claims to love her. Being engaged or married to Sunny would be, for Zachary, a symbol of heterosexuality. Unsuccessful in his attempt to conceal or thwart his homosexuality, Zachary returns to Tobias, the one he really loves, and is again rejected.

The complete isolation and alienation that Zachary feels is revealed not only by his suicide but also by its setting. He parks his car, a common symbol for life's journey, in a garage behind "an unoccupied house," assuring not only that he will die, but that he will die as he has lived, alone. The exterior of the car is "plum-colored" or purple, a color long associated with homosexuals. The interior of the car is littered with empty containers: Pepsi bottles, an M&M bag, and a pizza box. These images of emptiness reflect Zachary's own internal void. (Ironically, the 1959 Pepsi slogan was "Be sociable, drink Pepsi.") Just how alone and unloved Zachary feels, having been rejected by Tobias, to whom he professed love, and by Sunny, to whom he proposed marriage, is indicated by his suicide note. He addresses it "To Whom It May (Or May Not) Concern," and he declares that "all others" are "ignorant" of both his death and his life. Zachary abandons his attempt to conceal his true self. He drapes over the steering wheel the parka, a garment that seems symbolic of his attempt to disguise himself as a heterosexual. He has the parka on at the time he proposes to Sunny. When he goes to her house to convince her to go away with him, he again wears the parka, but it is now "soiled." Perhaps the dirt reflects Sunny's spoiling of his plan; perhaps it reflects the foulness of his deceit. By draping the parka (a pocket of which contains the ring he bought for Sunny) over the steering wheel and removing his clothing, Zachary seems to be discarding his attempt to conceal who he really is and his use of deception to direct his life. The powerlessness he feels is evident in his choice to die in the rear seat of the car. It is also evident in his decision to kill himself: literally, he is asphyxiated by carbon monoxide; figuratively, he is suffocated by homophobia.

Zachary's suicide prompts Sunny to dispense with the image that she has created for herself, the image that she began cultivating once she was given the appellation "Sunny" in sixth grade. Like Zachary, Sunny presents a face to the world that is false, a fact she acknowledges: "'God, help him to realize he doesn't love me, doesn't know me.'" All human beings have traits that are less than perfect, and Sunny tries to hide hers, to be worthy of her nickname. She tries to "hide her impatience" with Zachary. She will not tell him to "get lost": "Such words were not part of her vocabulary." Part of her tolerance of Zachary stems from her own "secret vanity." Even Sunny's friends do not believe that she is as good as she appears and "gently" laugh at her. The night of Zachary's visit, she is awakened by him, not only literally but figuratively: She "woke from a thin dissolving sleep." His voice "penetrated her consciousness like a dream voice, felt, not heard." Zachary's death causes a transformation in Sunny. Sunny dies, and Barbara is born. She is still naive, assuming that she was responsible for Zachary's death.

---

[2]For further information on this issue, see "Answers to Your Questions about Sexual Orientation and Homosexuality." *American Psychological Association.* 17 September 2005. <http://www.apa.org/pubinfo/answers.html>.

A wiser person would know that to be false. But, there is a certain amount of bittersweet glory in believing one has that type of power. Ironically, Barbara begins living her new life by "concentrating on academic work" (the type of work that appealed to Zachary) and developing her intellect. The distance she tries to put between her adult self and her adolescent self is revealed by her never having attended a high school reunion and never having told her husband about Zachary.

Sunny and Tobias both find that there *is* life after high school. Sunny found hers. Tobias found his. Nonetheless, they both continue to be affected by their high school experiences. Perhaps it was not possible in "that claustrophobic high school world of the late 1950s" to be who one was, but that did not mean that living one's truth would never be possible. Zachary had been too myopic, too shortsighted to conceive of other alternatives, other possibilities, other people, other relationships. He would forever "remain a high school boy, trapped in his eighteenth year."

Suggestions

Pre-Reading Exercise: Have students watch Douglas Sirk's 1959 remake of *The Imitation of Life*, a film that revolves around two widows, Lora Meredith and Annie Johnson, and their daughters, Susie and Sara Jane, respectively. While each of the characters, in her own way, attempts to deny an essential part of herself, students generally focus their discussion on Sara Jane, a light-skinned young woman who rejects her biracial heritage and her African American mother, choosing to pass for white. After they have read and analyzed "Life after High School," ask students to compare the ideas raised in the film with those raised in the story.

1. Give students questions that will help them examine Zachary's struggle:
    a. Summarize Zachary's religious beliefs.
    b. What apparently happens in Zachary's life during the Christmas recess?
    c. Why does he return from the recess in pursuit of Sunny?
    d. Zachary replies to Sunny's assertion that "it's a free world" by saying, "'Oh, no, it isn't, Sunny. For some of us, it isn't.'" How is it not "a free world" for Zachary?
    e. Zachary tells Sunny, "'When I'm with you, Sunny, it's possible for me to believe.'" What is it possible for him to believe?
    f. Why does he propose marriage to Sunny?
    g. Examine Zachary's suicide note. What does it reveal about his thoughts and feelings?
    h. Consider the items that "litter" Zachary's car. Do any of the items have significance? Explain.
    i. The parka is made of sheepskin. What qualities or characteristics do we usually associate with sheep? Is Zachary sheep-like? Explain.
    j. Examine the three references in the story to the parka (pars. 2, 40, and 98). What is the significance of Zachary's draping the parka over the steering wheel?
    k. What is indicated by the fact that Zachary strips to his underwear and gets in the back seat?
    l. Essentially, Zachary suffocates himself (when inhaled, carbon monoxide prevents oxygen from being absorbed by the blood). Why might it be said that Zachary has literally done to himself what society has figuratively done to him?
    m. What is the significance of Zachary's killing himself on April Fool's day?
    n. Explain why Zachary commits suicide.

2. Once students understand Zachary's turmoil, pose questions that will focus their attention on Sunny/Barbara:
    a. At what age was Barbara given the nickname "Sunny"?

    b. What effect does her nickname have on her?

    c. Compare and contrast "Sunny" and Barbara.

    d. Explain how, "in casting away his young life so recklessly, Zachary Graff freed [Barbara] for hers."

    e. Why has Barbara neither attended a high school reunion nor told her husband about Zachary?

    f. After reading the letter that Zachary had written to Tobias, Barbara feels "as if she'[s] been dealt a blow so hard she [can]not gauge how she'[s] been hurt—or if she'[s] been hurt at all." Explain why she feels this way.

3. Have students answer questions that will focus their attention on the similarities and differences between Zachary and Tobias:

    a. List the ways in which Zachary and Tobias were similar.

    b. List the ways in which they were different.

    c. Consider all of the qualities you identified. Why does Zachary commit suicide while Tobias does not?

    d. Why is the story entitled "Life after High School"?

4. For an extended study of social conformity, "Life after High School" can be teamed with "Barbie Doll" (p. 20), "Mr. Z" (p. 20), "The Unknown Citizen" (p. 35), "Curiosity" (p. 36), "The Lottery" (p. 43), and/or "Harrison Bergeron" (p. 53).

5. To examine the various ways in which people respond to difference, "Life after High School" can be studied in conjunction with "Counting the Mad" (p. 15), "Much Madness Is Divinest Sense" (p. 16), "A Very Old Man with Enormous Wings" (p. 72), "Gimpel the Fool" (p. 95), and/or "What Means Switch" (p. 179).

6. Assign "Mr. Z" (p. 20) and/or "The Fat Girl" (p. 120) along with "Life after High School" to examine the notion of identity,

7. In "Power" (p. 23), Rich makes the point that our power and our pain often stem from the same source. Have students explore this idea by studying "Life After High School" along with "Power" and any of the following: "I Stand Here Ironing" (p. 114), "The Fat Girl" (p. 120), "Islands on the Moon" (p. 144), "Shame" (p. 213), and/or "Daddy Tucked the Blanket" (p. 215).

8. For an examination of the ways in which people respond to loss, "Life after High School" might be studied with "Lot's Wife" (p. 3), "Power" (p. 23), "The Gilded Six-Bits" (p. 63), "Islands on the Moon" (p. 144), and/or "Shame" (p. 213).

9. Focus on the effects of societal expectations and judgments by studying "Life after High School" along with "Barbie Doll" (p. 20) and/or "Mr. Z" (p. 20).

10. To explore the relationship between isolation and suicide, "Life after High School" could be analyzed in conjunction with "Richard Cory" (p. 4) and/or "Barbie Doll" (p. 20).

11. To examine the way in which writers create a surprise ending, "Life after High School" could be assigned with "Richard Cory" (p. 4), "The Lottery" (p. 43), and/or "A Rose for Emily" (p. 193).

Islands on the Moon

Barbara Kingsolver

"Islands on the Moon" revolves around the issue of assumptions, specifically the potential effect of adults' clinging to their childhood assumptions about their parents. As they become mature, most children reevaluate their perceptions of their parents. Age, of course, is no guarantee of maturity. In this short story, Annemarie, a twenty-eight-year-old woman and the mother of a nine-year-old, has neither reconsidered nor analyzed her youthful assumptions about her mother, assumptions that she appears to have developed as a result of her father's death.

As a child, Annemarie responded to her father's death by deciding on some level that she would never be hurt that badly again. She adored her father and felt safe as long as he was alive: He was "devoted and funny" and provided "protection" from poverty. While he was dying, Annemarie, "outside playing hopscotch," was likely too young to understand what "cancer" meant. When he died, she was completely devastated. To avoid the potential pain of future loss, Annemarie emotionally insulated herself, refusing to need anyone, including Magda. She did not "expect anything" from Magda and wanted "nothing in the way of mothering." Tellingly, she continues to refer to her father as "Daddy," but she calls her mother by her first name, not a familiar maternal appellation such as "mom" or "mama." In addition to overtly rejecting her mother as a mother and spurning her attempts to care for her, Annemarie made Magda the target for her grief-based anger. Consequently, she casts her mother in the role of adversary, resenting her actions and assuming many of them to be, at best, inappropriate and, at worst, antagonistic.

Annemarie resents Magda for not providing her with a "normal childhood." Deeming her mother as "vague and useless, no protection from poverty," Annemarie complains about the difficulties caused in her life by Magda's ingenious thrift, environmental concerns, and social activism. As a child, Annemarie's frustration with Magda was understandable. After all, most children would prefer that their mother buy new things instead of "rummag[ing] around in the kitchen drawers until she finds some other thing that will serve just as well." And most adolescents would be more concerned about how they look and fit in with their peers than they are about the welfare of the planet. But Annemarie is an adult. Nonetheless, she does not question her childhood perceptions. If she had, she might have examined Magda's behavior in terms of her experiences. Magda's penchant for saving whatever she could—including "every rubber band and piece of string that entered their door"—may have been a way of coping with poverty. Perhaps it was also a manifestation of her deep sense of loss following her husband's death. The death of her husband may also have increased her awareness of life's fragility and preciousness, leading her to become active in environmental and social causes. Annemarie is too egocentric to attempt to understand her mother's behavior. Instead, she judges it.

She thinks that Magda was and continues to be largely unaffected by her father's death. Annemarie misunderstands Magda's ability to carry on with her life after his death because, in many ways, Annemarie has not gone on with hers. Appropriately, she works for a "service called 'Yesterday!' and really holds the place together." So mired in the past that she cannot move beyond it, she assumes her mother's engagement in the present is an indication that she has "never looked back" and does not "even miss" her father. She notes with some "bitterness" that Magda is uncommitted (she does not "get attached to men"), unconcerned ("'man or no man, it's all the same to her'"), and unencumbered ("'When it comes to men, she doesn't even carry any luggage'"). Annemarie apparently believes that Magda's attitude toward her boyfriends is the same as her attitude toward her father. This assumption deepens her resentment and solidifies her adversarial stance toward Magda.

In fact, when it comes to Magda, Annemarie thinks in terms of assaults and allies. Annemarie assumes that Magda's participation in antiwar demonstrations is designed to "remind" her that she is a "slug" for not "turn[ing] out all gung-ho." She also suspects that Magda became pregnant in order to "one-up" her. These perceptions are, of course, preposterous (Magda has been a social activist for years, and she became pregnant a month before Annemarie did). Nonetheless, they reveal Annemarie's inclination to view Magda's actions as being targeted at her. Assuming that "she was the rock in her mother's road," the obstacle that "got in [her] way," Annemarie may suspect that Magda resents her as much as she resents Magda. Like a child who wants her friends to dislike the same people she dislikes, Annemarie wants those close to her to share her antipathy toward Magda, and she attempts to "make people see" that her childhood was miserable and that her mother is terrible. Despite her efforts, her friends think Magda is "wonderful." Leon, on the other hand, seems to be "influence[d]" by her "stories about growing up with a mother like Magda." Even so, she is fearful that he will "take Magda's side" by thinking Magda's pregnancy is "great" and hers is "awful." To Annemarie, it seems that Magda "always wins" and she always loses.

Annemarie wants to be as distinct from her adversary as possible. Magda, an earth-mother type, has "long," "wavy" hair and wears "loose India-print cotton dresses," moonstone earrings, and sandals. She "paints landscapes on her teakettles," walks "like she's crossing plowed ground," "looks cool" even in abysmal heat, and makes medicinal use of herbs. In the midst of the barren landscape of Island Breezes, Magda's yard, "planted with many things," is fertile. Annemarie, unhappy with having inherited many of Magda's physical attributes (hair, complexion, neck, and fingers), would like to have physical features that "set her apart" from Magda. Unable to alter genetics, she does what she can to alter her appearance, cropping, bleaching, and waxing her hair into spikes. Rejecting Magda's regard for nature, Annemarie revels in the artificial and the manufactured (she wishes the pad in her evaporative cooler were synthetic instead of wood fiber; escapes the heat by taking refuge in her air-conditioned car; etc.).

Ironically, despite her attempts to distinguish herself from Magda, Annemarie's life in ways parallels her perceptions of her mother's life. Both (so Annemarie believes) accidentally became pregnant, Magda at sixteen, Annemarie at eighteen. Just as she did not want her mother to "do one thing" for her, so, too, does Leon not want Annemarie to "do any little thing" for him. Like Annemarie, Leon is an only child who is growing up without his father and who is distanced from his mother. Nonetheless, Annemarie's comment to Kay Kay—"'Oh, Leon's a rock, like me'"—suggests that Annemarie, who believes that she has been a "rock" in her mother's life, may subconsciously think that her son has been an obstacle in her life. Interestingly, none of the families that Annemarie envies for their happiness is comprised of a mother, father, and child: Kay Kay and Connie are "untethered . . . by motherhood"; the traveling jewelers are childless; and the Navarettes are raising their grandson. Whatever Annemarie's true feelings about children are, she, like Magda, is now pregnant and, like Magda, who asserts that the father of her child is "not in the picture," Annemarie has "intended to do [this baby] on her own." Since her husband's death, Magda has not had a committed relationship with a man. Annemarie has never had a successful long-term relationship, but, unlike Magda, who prefers being alone, Annemarie wants to be attached to a man, believing that such a relationship will make her happy.

Yet, she has a predilection for choosing men who cannot provide her with the closeness, compassion, and commitment that she claims to want. This is likely the result of her emotional withdrawal following the death of her father. Like Lone Ranger, her "problem cat," Annemarie "cowers and shrinks from love," rejecting the care offered to her by her mother as well as others who love her. In fact, she "visibly shrugs off Kay Kay's concern." Kay Kay is apparently aware that her friend will reject gestures of love, so she takes care of her "in a carefully offhand way that Annemarie hasn't quite noticed." Despite Annemarie's claim that she wants a man to "take care" of her, she is unwilling to risk having a truly intimate relationship. Consequently, she becomes involved with men who "roll through her life like the drive-in window." Although she has been married to Buddy twice and knows from her experience that he is incapable of providing her with the type of relationship that she wants, Annemarie, pregnant with his child, considers marrying him again.

Since she expects the men in her life to abandon her, Annemarie assumes not only that another marriage to Buddy would end in "divorce number three" but that Leon will leave her to live with his father. The baby that she is carrying, however, will be completely dependent on her, so she can allow herself to love and be loved by it without fear of being abandoned. Ironically, Annemarie's belief that men will abandon her is a self-fulfilling prophecy: Fearing abandonment, she does not trust a man enough to have a truly intimate relationship; consequently, she becomes involved only with men who are not interested in true intimacy, assuring that she will, in fact, be abandoned. She has no more considered the possibility that she is responsible for the types of men and relationships she chooses than she has considered the possibility that she is responsible for the assumptions and feelings she has about Magda.

Magda's asking Annemarie to accompany her to the clinic initiates a series of events that forces Annemarie to discard her childhood assumptions, enabling her to let go of the past and contemplate the future. Appropriately, these events are accompanied by images of light, which is a symbol of illumination, knowledge, and truth. The first reference to light occurs when Magda phones Annemarie, waking her from an unintended nap. Annemarie's having fallen asleep while the "sun is still up" suggests that she has been oblivious to the truth. Indeed, her view of reality, at least in terms of her mother and herself, has been distorted since she was a child, a fact that is illustrated in the description of Annemarie's hundred-foot drive to Magda's trailer: The "sun is reflected so brightly off the road it's like driving on a mirage." A mirage is created by the distortion of light; a misperception is created by the distortion of truth. Thus, the image is a fitting representation of Annemarie's having propelled and guided her life on illusion. Appropriately, light plays a significant role in clarifying Annemarie's illusion that Magda's pregnancy is an act of antagonism. Seeing "reflected" in Magda's eyes the "flickering light" of the sonogram screen, Annemarie realizes that Magda's pregnancy "is not a plan or a plot, it has nothing to do with herself."

Having shed this misperception, Annemarie's eyes are "sensitive" to the "horribly bright" sunlight. She is more willing to communicate with her mother and initiates a conversation even though it feels "awkward" to do so. As a result, she discovers that Magda actively sought to become pregnant with her. Ironically, Annemarie's perception of her mother, a perception that was distorted after her life was "wrecked" by her father's death, is greatly clarified by an automobile wreck. After the accident, beneath a sun that is now described as "unbelievably bright," Annemarie looks at her mother and is struck with the realization that "Magda isn't a very big person." When Annemarie was a child, Magda, an adult, no doubt looked big. Her recognition that Magda is "her own size, if not smaller" is an indication that Annemarie is beginning to see Magda as she really is. The accident also teaches Annemarie a truth that Magda apparently learned when her husband died: Life is a precious, fragile gift, and one should value and do some "great thing . . . with it." With her new appreciation for life, Annemarie suddenly understands Magda's concerns about nuclear war, seeing "how easily [a storm cloud] could grow into something else, tragically roiling up into itself, veined with blinding light: a mushroom cloud." Figuratively, this is exactly what happened to Annemarie: Her grief for her father "roil[ed] up into itself" and grew from a profound anguish into a toxic, blinding anger. In fact, Magda's discussion of her husband's final days and of her decision never to "give anyone that kind of grief again" is a revelation to Annemarie. Like the "unlit streetlamps" in the parking lot outside the window, she has spent most of her life "star[ing] down" as if she had "blind eyes," not seeing what was there for her to see all along, if she had only looked. Appropriately, after Magda's revelation, Annemarie stares out the window, into the darkness. Eventually, the parking lot lights "come on all together with a soft blink." Annemarie understands.

This understanding may well bring Annemarie the happiness for which she has longed. Adult happiness—a state of well being that ranges from periods of contentment to moments of euphoria—cannot be provided by external sources. Rather, it is a by-product of assuming responsibility for oneself and of providing service to others. Unlike Magda, who has long assumed responsibility for herself and served others, Annemarie has believed that life is controlled, to a greater or lesser degree, by extrinsic forces, theorizing that "everyone has some big thing, the rock in their road, that has kept them from greatness." She has looked to men to bring her happiness; she has thought that "get[ting] out" of the trailer court would bring her happiness. Now, her perceptions clarified, she turns her gaze from the past to the future: "Enough time passes, she thinks, and it's tomorrow." Indeed, it is an early Sunday morning in April, the beginning of a new day, a new week, a new season, each a symbol of awakening, renewal, and birth. Annemarie has a new perspective on her life and her mother as well as her baby: "For the first time she lets herself imagine holding a newborn" and thinks about her child growing up with "her mother's second daughter." No longer confused and resentful, she lays her hand on her mother's belly to offer her baby sister affection and reassurance, the gesture of a woman who seems to have matured, understanding that she alone is responsible for her thoughts, feelings, and actions.

Suggestions

Pre-Reading Exercise: Briefly discuss psychologist Albert Ellis's idea that one's feelings are generated by one's thoughts. For the purposes of this assignment, explain Ellis's theory as follows: Person A sees Person B's action, interprets the action, engages in a mental conversation (self-talk), experiences a feeling, engages in more self-talk, experiences more intense feelings, and so forth. The idea can be illustrated with the following diagram (a photo-ready copy, Figure 1, is included in Appendix 2, p. 190).

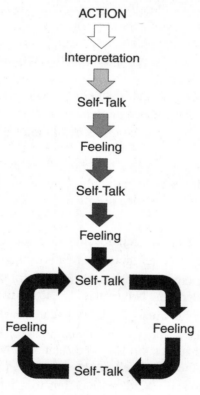

Students can be asked to share their own experience or to create a scenario that illustrates this pattern. As part of their discussion of "Islands on the Moon," students can be asked to use this model to explain Annemarie's feelings toward and response to Magda.

1. One approach to helping students focus on Annemarie's misperceptions is to pose questions that will prompt them to analyze specific relevant details:

   a. What effect did her father's death have on Annemarie? Explain.

   b. What effect does Annemarie believe her father's death had on Magda? Explain why she has this perception.

   c. What did Annemarie want from her mother when she was a child?

   d. Specifically, what did Magda do when Annemarie was a child that she resented then and continues to resent? Why might Magda have developed these traits?

   e. What is indicated by the fact that Annemarie calls her mother by her first name but refers to her father as "Daddy"?

   f. Why does Annemarie believe she was a "rock in her mother's road"?

   g. Explain how Annemarie initially feels about Magda's being pregnant.

   h. What does Annemarie believe to be Magda's motive for participating in anti-nuclear demonstrations?

   i. At the clinic, what does Annemarie realize about Magda's baby?

   j. Was Annemarie an unexpected obstacle in her mother's life? Explain.

   k. How did the death of Annemarie's father actually affect Magda?

   After each group has finished, have the class discuss their answers. During the course of this discussion, encourage students to identify Annemarie's other misperceptions and examine how they are corrected. Finally, have students explain how Annemarie's new understanding of her mother as well as herself is likely to change her.

2. Another approach is to pose more general questions that require students to identify, analyze, and synthesize the details:

   a. Compare and contrast Annemarie and Magda in terms of their looks, experiences, and values.

   b. In what specific ways does Annemarie think her childhood was not "normal"?

   c. Discuss the similarities between Annemarie's childhood and her youthful behavior with Leon's childhood and behavior.

   d. Some form of light is referred to in each of the following paragraphs: 62, 97, 118, 129, 166, 178, 230, and 234. Carefully examine not only the reference to light, but also the context of the reference. Explain what each reference seems to indicate about Annemarie's ability to see or understand her mother.

3. To have students focus on Annemarie's relationships, ask them the following:

   a. What is Annemarie's opinion of her mother's relationships with men?

   b. Explain what Annemarie envies about each of the following relationships: Kay Kay and Connie; the traveling jewelers; the Navarettes.

   c. How does Annemarie respond when people try to care for her? Explain.

   d. Annemarie often feels "she's about to be abandoned" or deserted. Why might she have this fear? How might this fear affect the way she relates to Magda, Leon, and Kay Kay? Is she likely to be abandoned by these people? Explain.

   e. Describe the type of relationship Annemarie claims to want with a man. Is Annemarie likely to have the kind of relationship she claims to want with the type of men she dates? Explain.

4. Introduce students to the idea of internal and external loci of control by asking them to record on a sheet of paper whether they think the following statements are true or false (each of the statements reflects an external locus of control):

    a. The everyday person cannot do much to solve world problems.

    b. Most people succeed because they are in the right place at the right time.

    c. Students often do poorly on tests because their teachers are unclear.

    d. People can't do much to change their personality.

    e. One person's vote doesn't really matter.

    f. Much of a person's behavior is determined by heredity.

    g. People who had a miserable childhood are likely to have a miserable adulthood.

    h. To get rich, people have to take risks.

    i. Some people are just lucky.

    j. People get promoted because their boss likes them.

    Explain to students the difference between an internal and an external locus of control. People who perceive of control as internal believe that the course of their lives is determined primarily by their choices and actions. They tend to be optimistic, active, and autonomous. Those with an external locus of control believe that the course of their lives is often determined by other people (parents, spouses, teachers, etc.), institutions (government, schools, churches, etc.), circumstances (money, health, education, etc.), objects (malfunctioning computers, power outages, flat tires, etc.), and so forth. This outlook can lead to varying degrees of pessimism, passivity, and dependency. Ask students to break up into groups and compare and contrast Annemarie's view of control with Magda's.

5. The correction of youthful misperceptions could be further examined by studying "Islands on the Moon" with "Those Winter Sundays" (p. 8).

6. The idea of a "normal" life or childhood can be further explored by teaming "Islands on the Moon" with "I Stand Here Ironing" (p. 114).

7. To explore further the consequences of living in the past, this story might be studied with "A Rose for Emily" (p. 193).

8. For an examination of the ways in which people respond to loss, this story might be studied with "Lot's Wife" (p. 3), "Power" (p. 23), "The Gilded Six-Bits" (p. 63), "Life after High School" (p. 132), and/or "Shame" (p. 213).

What You Pawn I Will Redeem

Sherman Alexie

The quest for a valued object or person is one of the oldest themes in literature and storytelling. Consider Jason and the Argonauts' journey for the Golden Fleece, Odysseus' expedition for Helen, Gawain's hunt for the Green Knight, and King Arthur's search for the Holy Grail. Quest narratives tend to share certain characteristics:

The quest begins with an initiator who is in need of something or someone important. This object requires a substantial effort to obtain. The initiator calls or imposes upon someone to undertake the quest, or he may plan to go on the quest himself. A long and substantial journey follows, on which the quester may journey alone or with companions. The quester usually faces some difficulty during the course of the journey. The quester may be forced to suspend the quest at any point. Having reached the destination, the quester may seek the possessor and/or the object. The quester may face some sort of test before obtaining the object. Should the quester fail the test, he or she might not obtain the object. The quest is usually complete when the quester returns with or without the object.[1]

While the ostensible goal of a quest is to obtain a person or object, the actual result of most quests is self-knowledge and self-growth. In "What You Pawn I Will Redeem," a story that tackles serious subjects with a great deal of humor, Sherman Alexie adopts many of the conventions of the quest motif while simultaneously challenging several cultural assumptions and norms. Through his quest to redeem his grandmother's pow-wow regalia, Jackson experiences a sort of personal redemption.

At the beginning of the story, Jackson reveals his mistrust of whites as well as his assumption that his reader is white. He states that he is homeless, but he refuses to explain why: "I'm not going to tell you my particular reasons for being homeless, because it's my secret story, and Indians have to work hard to keep secrets from hungry white folks." What Jackson will reveal to his reader is that his attempts to lead an assimilated life were unsuccessful: he flunked out of college; his marriages ended in divorce; and he eventually "went crazy." Now an alcoholic living on the streets, Jackson has abandoned his attempts at assimilation and seems proud of his ability to survive on the fringes of society: "Being homeless is probably the only thing I've ever been good at." Realizing that his reader may not "understand the value of a clean bathroom," Jackson cuts short his discussion and confronts his reader: "Probably none of this interests you. Homeless Indians are everywhere in Seattle. We're common and boring, and you walk right on by us." Annoyed with mainstream society's attitudes toward the dispossessed, Jackson informs his reader that the homeless have "dreams and families" and that he and his friends "matter to each other if [they] don't matter to anybody else." He also announces that he is "not going to let [the reader] know how scared [he] sometimes get[s] of history and its ways" because "silence is the best method of dealing with white folks." Jackson is aware that both he and his heritage have been disappearing "piece by piece" for years. While this scares him, he feels powerless to retrieve what has been lost and to prevent further losses.

All of this changes when Jackson discovers his grandmother's pow-wow regalia hanging in the pawnshop window. Jackson had never seen the regalia, which had been stolen fifty years earlier, but it represents a vital link with his heritage. Told that he can buy the regalia for $999.00 if he can raise that amount in twenty-four hours, Jackson embarks on his "quest." Being impoverished, homeless, jobless, and alcoholic, his chances of succeeding seem non-existent. Nevertheless, he carries on, and tries to raise the money that he needs to achieve his goal.

Jackson's use of the money that he earns, wins, and receives throughout the story suggests that he will not achieve his goal. Rather than save the money he receives from the pawnbroker, he spends it on wine for himself and his "crew." While this is the stereotypical behavior of an alcoholic, it may also reflect the fact that, to Jackson, the money that was given to him is communal, not personal: "Rose of Sharon, Junior, and I carried *our* twenty-dollar bill and *our* five dollars in loose change over to the 7-Eleven" (emphasis added). As the story continues, it becomes evident that his attitude towards money has been culturally shaped. When Jackson wins money with his lottery ticket, he gives part of it to Mary, the young cashier. She tries to refuse, but Jackson explains: "it's tribal. It's an Indian thing. When you win, you're supposed to share with your family." Later, he spends the rest of his lottery winnings on shots for himself and his Indian "cousins" at Big Heart's. Once Jackson's funds are exhausted, his "cousins" buy him drinks because he had "been so generous with [his] money."

Gift-giving is an essential part of most Native American cultures. Tribes of the Pacific Northwest and British Columbia are especially known for holding elaborate gift-giving ceremonies called potlatches. In the past, the host of the potlatch would provide his guests with a great feast and

---

[1]Barrette, Paul E. "The Quest in Classical Literature: Structuralism and Databases." Paper presented at the ACH/ALLC conference in Virginia 1999. http://cheiron.humanities.mcmaster.ca/~barrette/quest_ach_virginia_99.html

then give them most, if not all, of his possessions. In so doing, wealth was redistributed among the community, and the host demonstrated his richness and affirmed or raised his social rank. This attitude is counterintuitive to most Americans because capitalism promotes the idea that power and status are dependent on one's ability to accumulate and retain money and property (think about the popular American board-game of Monopoly). Jackson's use of his money in no way changes the fact that reclaiming his grandmother's regalia is important to him: "I care about it. It's been a long time since I really cared about something." Jackson thinks he must raise money to achieve his goal, but, actually, he must come to terms with part of his "secret story," and become more emotionally vulnerable.

Jackson begins to recount memories of his grandmother, memories that lead him to reevaluate the complicated relationship between his people and white culture. In one vivid recollection, Jackson recounts a story that his grandmother told him when he was 13 about her days as a nurse during World War II. One day, she was tending a wounded Maori soldier, a dark-skinned native of New Zealand. He tells her that it's "funny… How we brown people are killing other brown people so white people will remain free." His grandmother, whose brothers are also fighting on the Allied side "hadn't thought of it that way." She remains optimistic in spite of the Maori's cynicism. The soldier says that even if his legs (which he lost in an artillery attack) will be waiting for him in heaven, they would probably run away from him. Jackson's grandmother replies "you have to get your arms strong… so you can run on your hands." She refuses to think of herself as a victim, and she gives the soldier advice to work with what he has rather than mourning what he's lost. The lesson may have been lost on the 13 year old Jackson, but the 41 year old Jackson may understand it.[2]

Perhaps it is in this mindset that Jackson returns to the pawnshop the next day, in spite of the fact that he does not have the thousand dollars he needs to redeem the regalia. He has only five dollars, the exact amount of money that he had when he entered the pawnshop the day before. The pawnbroker gives him the regalia anyway. Jackson insists that "I wanted to win it," but the pawnbroker replies "You did win it." Although Jackson did not succeed in raising the thousand dollars, he did "work hard" for the money he brought in. The quest had required Jackson to remember painful memories about his family's past and to ask things of people that he normally wouldn't. In order to achieve his quest, he had to recognize "how many good men live in this world… too many to count." By the final scene, Jackson redeems more than his grandmother's regalia. He dances in her regalia in the middle of the street, and "Pedestrians stopped. Cars stopped. The city stopped." Jackson no longer has to disappear or live on the fringes of society, but instead commands the attention and respect of the world to which he previously felt invisible.

Suggestions

Pre-Reading Exercise: Ask students to list and discuss the stereotypes associated with Native Americans, white Americans, and Korean Americans. The stereotypes listed might include some of the following:

kdkdkdkddkdk

Native Americans: alcoholic, crafty, dishonest, irresponsible, lazy, noble, primitive, proud, ruthless, savage, shiftless, spiritual, stoic

White Americans: aggressive, amoral, arrogant, bigoted, clever, cold, dishonest, evil, greedy, hypocritical, power-hungry, racist, untrustworthy

Korean Americans: ambitious, apolitical, clannish, diligent, distant, enterprising, entrepreneurial, exploitative, industrious, isolationist, materialistic, reserved, rude

---

[2] Jackson was 14 in 1972 when his grandmother died of breast cancer (pars. 59 & 216). That means he was born in 1957 or 1958. Assuming he was 18 when he moved to Seattle twenty-three years ago to attend college (par. 2), he is about 41 at the time the story takes place.

This list may be used (and perhaps amended) after students have read the story (see suggestion 6 below).

1.   One way to approach this story is to ask students to compose at least two questions they would like to have answered about it. (Their questions are likely to focus on Jackson's behavior and the pawnshop broker's actions.) Then have them break up into groups and answer their questions. Any they cannot answer should be presented to the class for discussion. During the course of discussion, have students describe and discuss characters other than Jackson and the pawnboker and explain their significance in the story:

   a. Rose of Sharon

   b. Junior

   c. The Aleut cousins

   d. Big Boss

   e. Mary, the cashier at the Korean grocery store

   f. The bartender at Big Heart's

   g. Irene Muse

   h. Honey Boy

   i. Officer Williams

   j. The waitress at the Big Kitchen

2.   Another method is to present students with questions that require analysis and synthesis:

   a. What does Jackson mean when he says that he is "an effective homeless man"?

   b. Describe and discuss the pawnbroker's attitude toward Jackson, his friends, the regalia, and money.

   c. Outline Jackson's actions according to the times indicated in the text. Explain what his actions reveal about his needs and values.

   d. Identify the losses that Jackson experiences within the 24 hours of his quest. How does he react to these losses? What do his reactions reveal about him?

   e. Which characters try to help him in his quest to reclaim his grandmother's regalia? Why do they try to help him?

   f. What does Jackson's grandmother represent to him?

   g. Why is it important to Jackson to "win" his grandmother's regalia?

   h. Jackson tells the pawnbroker that he worked hard for the money he received. Did he? Explain.

   i. Why does the pawnbroker give him the regalia?

   j. Explain Jackson's statement, "I knew that solitary yellow bead was part of me. I knew I was that yellow bead in part."

   k. Is Jackson a likable character? Explain.

3.   Ask students to identify some of the story's themes. Their list may include such themes as alcoholism, alienation, belonging, homelessness, identity, loneliness, loss, mental illness, racism, and redemption. Divide the class into groups, assign each group a different theme, and have the groups determine how the theme they were assigned is developed in the story. Each group should present and discuss its findings with the class.

   Once these discussions are complete, share with students Alexie's comments on humor and ask them to discuss the way he uses humor in the story:

   "'People like to laugh, and when you make them laugh they listen to you. That's how I get people to listen to me now. If I were saying the things I'm saying without a sense of humor, people would turn off right away. I mean I'm saying things people don't like for me to say. I'm saying very aggressive, controversial things, I suppose, about race and gender and sexuality. I'm way left [in my viewpoints], but if you say it funny, people listen. If you don't make `em laugh, they'll walk away. I learned that at a young age.'"

Blewster, Kelley. "Tribal Vision: Sherman Alexie (Interview)." *Biblio* 4.3 (Mar. 1999): 22-3.

4. Provide students with some general characteristics of a quest narrative and ask them to identify and discuss the ones that are evident in the story:

   a. The hero is challenged to obtain an important object
   b. The hero is aware that obtaining the object will be virtually impossible
   c. The hero undertakes a difficult journey in order to obtain the object
   d. The hero goes alone or with companions
   e. The hero receives assistance from his companions or others he meets along the way
   f. The hero is confronted with physical, mental, spiritual, and/or moral test(s)
   g. The hero may or may not pass all of the tests
   h. The hero who fails the test(s) may or may not obtain the object
   i. The hero is changed as a result of his quest, regardless of his success in obtaining the object

5. To have students explore the issue of assumed audience, pose the following questions:

   a. Locate the instances in the first six paragraphs where Jackson directly addresses the reader.
   b. Who does Jackson assume to be his reader?
   c. Describe and explain his attitude toward the reader.
   d. What effect does this attitude have on the reader? Explain.

6. Review with students the list of stereotypes that they compiled before reading the story and add to the list any additional stereotypes they suggest. Once they are satisfied that their lists are complete, have them to name the opposite of each stereotype. Then, ask students to determine which stereotypes or their antitheses are used in the story and to explain how they are used. When students have completed their explanations and discussed their findings, present them with the following excerpt and ask them whether or not Alexie succeeds in doing what he wanted:

   > But what I wanted to do with ["What You Pawn I Will Redeem"] was take these other archetypes and stereotypes--the Korean grocery store owner, the white cop, the white pawn shop owner--and combine them with this portrayal of this homeless Indian man and take these stereotypes, which are so infused with negative ideas about who these people are, and create a story where all of these people in the end are pretty basically decent people.

   > "Sherman Alexie Discusses His New Book *Ten Little Indians*." Host. Steve Inskeep and Renee Montagne. Morning Edition. Washington, D.C. 08/18/2003. http://www.npr.org/templates/story/story.php?storyId=1397737.

7. American culture values the retention of accumulated wealth while many Native American cultures value its redistribution. To explore the differences in these perspectives, students can use InfoTrac to research the potlatch (Subjects Potlatch) or to locate specific articles:

   > Tollefson, Kenneth D. "Potlatching and Political Organization Among the Northwest Coast Indians." *Ethnology* 34 (1995): 53–74

   > Wyels, Joyce Gregory. "Sharing the Box of Treasures." *Americas* (English Edition) 56.1 (Jan.-Feb. 2004): 6-16.

8. To consider the author's thoughts about the story, have students read the *The New Yorker* interview with Sherman Alexie, "Q & A: Redeemers with Sherman Alexie," published online at the same time the magazine ran the story (http://www.newyorker.com/online/content/?030421on_onlineonly01). Other interviews and articles can be located using InfoTrac (Subject: Sherman Alexie).

9. Pair "What You Pawn I Will Redeem" with "Everyday Use" (p. 88) to focus on the issue of heritage.

10. "What You Pawn I Will Redeem" could be studied in conjunction with "Birthday Party" (p. 43) and/or "I Stand Here Ironing" (p. 114) to examine further the notion of narrator reliability.

What Means Switch

Gish Jen

In this delightful story about switching ethnic identity, Jen touches on a broad range of issues. Some have to do with adolescence (acceptance, popularity, friendship, intimacy, love, sexuality, and so forth). Others relate to the family (relationships, expectations, values, etc.). Still others focus on cultural issues such as immigration, assimilation, and ethnic stereotyping.

Suggestions

1. A good, albeit unstructured, entree into the story is simply to ask students whether or not they liked the story and have them explain why. During the course of this discussion, students will undoubtedly pick out themes, analyze characters, and relate personal experiences that parallel those in the story.

2. To focus students' attention on the idea of switching ethnic identity, divide them into groups and have them consider the title of the story:
   a. Look up the word *switch* in a dictionary.
   b. Discuss the ways in which each of the following characters does and/or does not "switch":
      • Mona's mother
      • Mona
      • Sherman
      • Sherman's mother
   c. Explain the significance of the title.

3. Have students examine the relationship between Mona and Sherman:
   a. Mona's opinion of Sherman changes throughout the story. Starting with the moment Mona first sees Sherman, trace and explain these changes.
   b. Locate the points at which Mona's understanding of the relationship differs from Sherman's. Why are their views so different?

4. Mainstream culture tends to place all members of an ethnic minority in one homogeneous lump. In this story, Asians are categorized as one group, even though individual Asian cultures are remarkably different from one another. Ask students to locate the instances in the story where this occurs and to explain the consequences.

5. After students have discussed the story, have them think about the issues Jen raises in terms of their own social or ethnic group: Are there differences or variations among members of the group?

If so, does the general public seem to be aware of the differences? In what ways have they been affected by popular misconceptions?

6. Mona's mother welcomes Sherman into her home, but she becomes infuriated when he hangs his picture of a Japanese flag on the refrigerator. To help students understand the intensity and significance of her reaction, ask them to find out about the Nanking Massacre and the role it continues to play in the relationship between Japan and China. They can conduct their research using InfoTrac (Keyword: Nanking).

7. To examine how people respond to "difference," team "What Means Switch" with "Counting the Mad" (p. 15), "Much Madness Is Divinest Sense" (p. 16), "A Very Old Man with Enormous Wings" (p. 72), and/or "Gimpel the Fool" (p. 95).

8. Explore the issues involved in retaining and/or changing ethnic identity by studying "What Means Switch" along with "Lost Sister" (p. 28), "Persimmons" (p. 30), "Everyday Use" (p. 88), and/or "Mother Tongue" (p. 227).

9. For a discussion of immigration, study "What Means Switch" in conjunction with "Lost Sister" (p. 28), "Persimmons (p. 30)," , and/or "Mother Tongue"(p. 227)

10. "What Means Switch" could be teamed with "Crusader Rabbit" (p. 58) for a study of initiation stories (stories in which the main character comes to understand something about himself, another person, human nature, or society that permanently alters his view of the world).

A Rose for Emily

William Faulkner

"A Rose for Emily" is one of the most famous short stories ever written and certainly one of the most intriguing. It is a marvelous story to use for a study of character motivation. Less experienced readers are prone to dismiss Miss Emily as "crazy," ignoring the reasons for what she does. Granted, a sane person probably would not keep a corpse, much less sleep with it, but being disturbed does not rule out the possibility that a person's actions might be explicable. Miss Emily's actions are not arbitrary: She kills Homer and keeps his body because she is unable to accept change.

This inability to accept change is clearly depicted in Miss Emily's reaction to the death of her father, a man who did not allow his daughter the opportunity to establish a life of her own. Possessive and domineering, he drove away all of Miss Emily's potential suitors, a fact well known by the townspeople: "We thought of them as a tableau, Miss Emily a slender figure in white in the background, her father a straddled silhouette in the foreground, his back to her and clutching a horsewhip, the two of them by the backflung door." By driving away the young men who called on her, Miss Emily's father deprived her of the chance to find love, affection, and companionship with anyone other than himself. When he dies, Miss Emily is left with no sense of security, no sense of identity, and, most important, no love. She is unable to accept this change in her life, and for three days she denies that he is dead.

More profound changes, notably the deterioration of the Old South and the emergence of the New South, take place during Miss Emily's lifetime. The New South is vastly different from the Old South, an era that represents for Miss Emily the last vestiges of the security she had with her father. The differing attitudes of the older and younger generations illustrate clearly the differences between the Old and New South. The older generation, embodying the values of the Old South, feels a paternalistic responsibility for Miss Emily: They know she has no money, so they remit her taxes and send their daughters to her for china-painting lessons. The younger generation is more businesslike. The young man's suggestion that Miss Emily be confronted about the smell coming from her house, a suggestion that appalls the older men, foreshadows the changes the younger generation will make when it comes to power. Indeed, when the younger men, "with [their] more modern ideas," become the city officials, they are not concerned with Miss Emily's financial status. They want her to pay her taxes, and they do not send their daughters to her for china-painting lessons.

Miss Emily will not accept the changes inherent in the New South. When the city officials ask her to pay her taxes, something she has never done, she refuses. She will not allow a mailbox or postal numbers, reflections of the New South's modernization, to be attached to her house. And, even though her once-illustrious neighborhood is now filled with "garages and cotton gins," she does not move. Rather than acknowledge and participate in the growth of the New South, Miss Emily retreats from the world, spending more and more time alone in her house until she eventually becomes a recluse. If she cannot stop the changes, she can at least refuse to witness them. As she grows older, her house, like the dead era to which she clings, rots around her.

In a world of change, Miss Emily clings to the established order, and Homer is part of that order. Homer provides Emily with the love, affection, and security she has not known since her father's death. She apparently thinks they will be married and orders a monogrammed toilet set for him. Homer, a man who is not "the marrying kind," probably changes his mind and tells her he is leaving. Rather than lose another person whom she loves and face the changes that loss would entail, Miss Emily kills him and keeps his body.

Suggestions

1. To get students to focus on the notion of change and Miss Emily's reactions to it, have them work in groups to develop the following lists:

    a. List differences between the older and younger generations.
    b. List examples of the decay in Miss Emily's house.
    c. List the changes that have occurred in Miss Emily's neighborhood.
    d. List examples of Miss Emily's refusal to accept change.

    Once students have reported their lists, discuss with them the implications of these details. You may need to discuss the Old South and the New South. You might devise a "generational chart," placing characters into the appropriate generations:

OLD SOUTH	NEW SOUTH
Emily's father	Homer
Colonel Sartoris	Aldermen
Judge Stevens	Young man who wants to confront Miss Emily about the smell

    Tobe

    After constructing this chart, have students decide whether Miss Emily's values are drawn chiefly from the Old South or the New South. Usually students see quickly that her values are those of the Old South. Thus, Emily can be seen as someone caught in the middle of and in conflict with a great societal change.

2. To have students analyze Miss Emily's character, pose the following questions:

    a. Why does Miss Emily deny her father's death?
    b. What void in her life is filled by Homer?
    c. Why does she order the monogrammed toilet set for Homer?
    d. Why does she kill Homer?

e. Why does she keep Homer's body?

f. Why does she become a recluse?

3. Have students characterize Emily's father and Homer. After they have done this, ask them if Emily's father would have approved of Homer.

4. To explore further the consequences of living in the past, "A Rose for Emily" might be studied with "Islands on the Moon" (p. 144).

5. "A Rose for Emily" can be teamed with "Mother to Son" (p. 7) and/or the poems from "Spoon River Anthology" (p. 16). "A Rose for Emily" also presents a character struggling against forces over which she has little control. In that story, however, great pride causes bizarre responses to the indignities of life. "Mother to Son" presents a character struggling against poverty and other problems of life. The attitude of this character, however, is quite different from the bitter attitude of "Indignation" Jones, and a worthwhile discussion is possible about the different responses that people make toward the indignities of life.

6. To examine the ways in which writers create a surprise ending, "A Rose for Emily" can be assigned with "Richard Cory" (p. 4), "The Lottery" (p. 43), and/or "Life after High School" (p. 132).

The Chrysanthemums

John Steinbeck

"The Chrysanthemums" is a fine, subtle piece of fiction, the complexity of which is not likely to be immediately evident to a first-time reader of the story. It elicits at least two seemingly unrelated interpretations: one, a statement about limitations placed upon women in a society dominated by men; two, a statement about the consequences of "roots," or the lack of them. We say "seemingly" unrelated interpretations because, upon an examination of the rich symbolism of the story, it becomes evident that the two interpretations can be joined. It is the symbolic nature of the chrysanthemums that show the relationship of the two themes.

The very opening description foreshadows the theme of the limitations placed upon women. The valley is "closed off" from the "rest of the world" by a fog that sits "like a lid on the mountains and [makes] the great valley a closed pot." Accordingly, Elisa's role, we come to see, is completely defined for her, regardless of her strengths or abilities. She is responsible for taking care of her house and her husband. She performs her housekeeping duties so well that by two o'clock her house is "hard swept," the windows "hard-polished," the mud-mat "clean," and she is in the garden. Having no children, Elisa is relieved of child-care responsibility, but at the same time denied the outlet children would provide for her nurturing energies. She lavishes these energies on growing chrysanthemums, tending to them, protecting them, and taking pride in them.

We see that Elisa's role is not challenging enough for her when the tinker is introduced in the story. When the tinker presents her with the traditional view that his profession "ain't the right kind of life for a woman," she demands to know how he knows such a thing and tells him he "might be surprised to have a rival sometime." The tinker changes tactics and tries to portray the life he leads as too lonely and too frightening for a woman, but Elisa is not convinced. Indeed, she is excited and, watching the tinker leave, whispers, "That's a bright direction. There's a glowing there."

This encounter makes Elisa realize her strength and worth as a woman. Before the tinker arrives, she is described in terms typically associated with men: Her face is "lean," "strong," "eager," "mature and handsome"; she is "strong" and her work is "over-eager and over-powerful." When the tinker arrives, Elisa is irritated by him, but once he begins talking about her chrysanthemums, the "irritation and resistance" vanish. Elisa takes off her hat and shakes out her "dark pretty hair" and becomes progressively more feminine and more passionate. The changes continue while she gets ready to go out to dinner. She scrubs herself with a pumice stone, "carefully" fixes her hair, puts on makeup, and, dressing slowly, "put[s] on her newest underclothing and her nicest stockings and the dress which was the symbol of her prettiness." Henry seems stunned by the change in her, "blunder[ing]" about how "nice" and "strong and happy" she looks.

Up to this point in the story we have seen a repressed woman who suddenly realizes that she has the strength to do something different with her life; however, when Elisa sees the chrysanthemum sprouts in the middle of the road, her view changes again, and at the end of the story she is crying "weakly—like an old woman." This outcome forces the reader in another direction—Elisa has failed to make a real transformation. The role of the tinker has not been, as we initially thought, that of a catalyst for changing Elisa's life. The tinker's role is to introduce another theme: the consequences of having or not having "roots." He stands in direct opposition to Elisa. He is completely unburdened with the typical duties of life that become, for most, routine and boring. He has no spouse, no house to care for, and no garden. He is so free of obligations to others that he is not even bound by a sense of honesty or decency. In short, he is "rootless." His act of throwing away the chrysanthemum sprouts (or roots) is symbolic of his having thrown aside all the roots of a conventional life, such as the one lived by Elisa. The realization of the symbolic nature of this act enables the reader to connect the two themes: Putting down roots, as Elisa has done, necessarily involves limiting oneself and often creates boredom and a lack of fulfillment. When one has roots, one is not free to follow, at whim, any "bright direction" that may appear. Nor should one, as Elisa learns, think that something is a "bright direction" simply because it differs from one's ordinary life. The tinker's life, after all, has its routine also: He goes "from Seattle to San Diego and back every year."

Suggestions

1. One way to approach a story as subtle as this one is to identify the themes or issues of the story and have students go to the text to find details that support these themes. Have some groups find details that show that a male-dominated society places limitations on women and have other groups find details that show the consequences of roots or the lack of roots. After the groups have reported their findings, discuss with the class as a whole the connection between the two themes.

2. Have students work in groups on questions that will lead them to details that support the themes or issues of the story:

    a. Characterize (describe and discuss) Henry and Elisa's marriage.

    b. Characterize the tinker. What kind of person is he? What are his qualities or characteristics?

    c. What is it about the tinker's life that Elisa envies?

    d. Discuss the changes that seem to occur in Elisa as a result of the tinker's visit.

    e. Why is Elisa crying at the end of the story?

    f. Why is the story called "The Chrysanthemums"?

    After groups have reported their answers to these questions, discuss with the class as a whole the themes that these details reveal.

3.   Because the story is highly symbolic, identify for the students the themes or issues of the story and then ask students to comment on the symbolic implications of the following details:

a.   The description of the valley

b.   Elisa's "planters' hands" or "planting hands"

c.   The tinker's dog

d.   "That's a bright direction. There's a glowing there."

e.   The tinker's throwing away the sprouts

f.   Elisa's wanting to go to the fights

g.   Elisa's crying "weakly—like an old woman"

4.   "The Chrysanthemums" could be assigned in conjunction with "Lot's Wife" (p. 3), "Barbie Doll" (p. 20), "Hills Like White Elephants" (p. 50), and/or "The Fat Girl" (p. 120) for an extended study of the roles of women.

5.   To discuss symbolism, "The Chrysanthemums" can be studied with "The Road Not Taken" (p. 6) and/or "Hills Like White Elephants" (p. 50).

3

Essays

Discussions and Suggestions

Shame

Dick Gregory

and

Daddy Tucked the Blanket

Randall Williams

"Shame" and "Daddy Tucked the Blanket" are both illustrative essays in which the writers reflect on their childhoods, using their own experiences to show the profound effect poverty has on a child. Gregory focuses on the day he learned to feel shame for being poor and illustrates how this new emotion completely altered his attitude and actions. Williams demonstrates how poverty creates frustration and a sense of futility, forces which, in turn, destroy personal relationships.

"Shame" and "Daddy Tucked the Blanket" can be studied together or separately. As students generally have few specific questions about the texts, both essays are excellent to help them identify which details illustrate, explain, or support a point. By examining these essays together, students can compare the types of poverty the authors experienced, the way each learned to feel humiliation, and the effect this lesson had on them.

Suggestions

Pre-Reading Exercise: The notion of shame, as it was felt by Gregory and Williams, is probably foreign to many students. Societal attitudes have changed, and those things that once brought disgrace—unwed motherhood, illegitimacy, divorce, welfare—are no longer as stigmatized as they were in Gregory's childhood. It may be helpful for students to define "shame" and discuss some of the things that might cause it.

Shame

1. In order to help students appreciate how a writer illustrates a point, have them list the details that the writer has chosen in order to show rather than simply tell something. You might want to choose one or more of the following questions:
   a. List those things done by Gregory that show he is in love with Helene.
   b. List those details that show the extent of the poverty in which he lives.
   c. List those actions that show his willingness to work.

2. The exercise above, in which students locate important details to support a conclusion, is an exercise in analysis, as we define it. To have them engage in synthesis, have them answer some of the following questions:
   a. In what way is Helene "a symbol of everything [Richard] want[s]"?
   b. Richard's behavior at school—his inability to concentrate and his constant movement—is interpreted by the teacher as one thing and by Richard as another. How does the teacher view Richard's behavior? How does Richard explain it? Why might their perceptions be so different?
   c. Explain why the school incident made Richard feel such deep shame. Of what is he ashamed? How does this shame alter Richard's attitude and actions?
   d. Why did Helene's memory haunt Richard for so long?

For an examination of the ways in which people respond to loss, "Shame" might be studied with "Lot's Wife" (p. 3), "The Vacuum" (p. 22), "Power" (p. 23), "The Gilded Six-Bits" (p. 63), "Life after High School" (p. 132), "Islands on the Moon" (p. 144), and/or "Shame" (p. 213).

Daddy Tucked the Blanket

1. Williams includes many details that illustrate the severity of his childhood poverty and the way it affected him. One method of having students locate the details is to divide them into groups and ask them to make lists:

   a. List the details that demonstrate the condition of the houses in which Williams and his family lived.

   b. List the actions of Williams and his siblings that show they were ashamed of where they lived.

   c. List the details that show his parents were hard-working and loved their children.

2. Another approach is to pose questions that call for finding specific details:

   a. Why was Williams "ashamed" of where he lived?

   b. Why was it impossible to keep the house clean?

   c. Why was it impossible to fix up the house?

   d. Why was it harder on the girls than the boys to live in a dilapidated house?

   e. Why did Williams' parents frequently argue with each other?

3. In order to have students draw conclusions, you might pose the following questions:

   a. What "freedom" did Williams find when he was sixteen (par. 1)?

   b. Why is it important for us to know that Williams' family was not "shiftless"?

   c. Why is money necessary to "progress up the social ladder"?

   d. What was the significance of Williams' father's tucking the blanket around his mother and weeping?

   e. What did Williams learn in school when he was eight or nine?

   f. Why did Williams cry? Why did the children laugh?

   g. For which moment is Williams "grateful," the moment the children laughed or the moment his mother cried? Why would he be grateful?

Shame and Daddy Tucked the Blanket

1. A comparison of the essays reveals interesting similarities as well as differences. You might pose one or more of the following:

   a. Compare the family situation and the poverty of the children.

   b. Compare the ways the children learned shame and humiliation.

   c. Compare the ways that lesson affected them.

2. To help students develop their critical judgment, have them answer the following question: Which essay do you think is more effective and why? Although this is an opinion question, students should make specific references to the text when justifying their choice.

3. Encourage students to further explore poverty and the issues it raises, especially for children. Students can use InfoTrac to access Denise Rinaldo's "Poor in a Land of Plenty" (*Scholastic Choices* 20.6 (2005): 14–18), an essay that focuses on the experiences and aspirations of three teenagers who grew up in poverty. Or, they can be directed to use InfoTrac (Subject: Poverty) to locate an article of interest to them.

4.   In "Power" (p. 23), Rich makes the point that our power and our pain often stem from the same source. Have students explore this idea by studying "Shame" and "Daddy Tucked the Blanket" along with "Power" and any of the following: "The Fat Girl" (p. 120), "I Stand Here Ironing" (p. 114), "Life after High School" (p. 132), and/or "Islands on the Moon" (p. 144).

5.   To have students examine the idea that a victim is often blamed for being a victim, team "Shame" and "Daddy Tucked the Blanket" with "When Is It Rape" (p. 259). (It is not uncommon for those who are impoverished to be blamed for being poor. They are often dismissed as lazy or shiftless, points that are addressed by both Williams and Gregory.)

A Hanging

George Orwell

and

Death and Justice

Edward Koch

Studying "A Hanging" and "Death and Justice" together allows students to examine not only two different views of capital punishment but also two different types of essays. "A Hanging" is a narrative, and there are no explicit arguments to be examined. Readers can only agree or disagree with Orwell and analyze how effectively his narrative defends his thesis. "Death and Justice," on the other hand, is an expository essay. Consequently, the arguments in it are clearly delineated and supported by a combination of evidence, logic, and belief. Studying these two essays together can also lead to a discussion of capital punishment, a highly controversial topic about which students are likely to have strong opinions.

"A Hanging" is an excellent essay to use in the transition from fiction to nonfiction. It is a narrative, and students can approach it, at least initially, in much the same way they did short stories. Like a short story writer, Orwell involves the reader as a spectator at an execution, only once stepping out of his role as narrator to make an editorial comment. It is in this one paragraph (par. 10) that Orwell's thesis is made explicit: "I saw the mystery, the unspeakable wrongness, of cutting a life short when it is in full tide." Orwell's clear statement of his thesis facilitates the task of explaining what a thesis is and demonstrates how it can be developed through a narrative.

The essay is also excellent for discussing a writer's focus and choice of details. For instance, students invariably ask why the reader is not told what crime the prisoner has committed. Obviously, such information might easily shift the reader's attention away from the "unspeakable wrongness" of capital punishment to a debate about whether or not execution is an appropriate punishment for the prisoner's crime. Recognizing that Orwell omits this information can lead to a discussion regarding the selection of details. Students might also examine the ways in which these details are designed to sway the reader's sympathy. For example, the prisoner is described as a "puny wisp of a man" who is guarded by "six tall Indian warders." These guards prepare the prisoner for the fifty-yard walk to the gallows as if he were a large, aggressive man—"two of them stood by with rifles with fixed bayonets, while the others handcuffed him, passed a chain through his handcuffs and fixed it to their belts, and lashed his arms tight to his sides." Orwell notes that the prisoner is "unresisting, yielding his arms limply to the ropes." Given the physical descriptions of the prisoner and the guards, the extreme precautions taken by the guards are clearly intended to elicit compassion for the condemned man.

In "Death and Justice," Koch also appeals to the reader's emotions, not to gain sympathy for condemned criminals, but to help prove that the death penalty "affirms life" and is necessary. He begins by fostering a sense of outrage in the reader. He cites two cases in which condemned murderers argue that their impending executions should not be carried out because killing is immoral. He also cites the case of a man who admits to murdering a woman, in part because he knew that he would not be executed. Then he systematically notes and refutes the seven major objections of those who oppose the death penalty. During the course of his refutations, Koch continues to appeal to the reader's emotions, noting cases in which the system has failed and convicted murderers have killed again. He also uses analogies and cites studies, statistics, and authorities to support his premise. Students might examine how effectively Koch defends each of his main points.

Suggestions

Pre-Reading Exercise: Before students read "A Hanging," ask them either to summarize an experience that changed an opinion they held or to explain what it would take to convince them that an opinion they hold is wrong. This is designed to make students aware that Orwell's essay is trying to convince them of something and to prepare them for his presentation.

A Hanging

1. Ask students to write down two questions they would like to have answered about the essay. Have them break up into groups of three to four and answer their questions, saving any they could not answer for class discussion.

2. Ask students questions that will help them locate and examine major details:

    a. Examine the descriptions of the prisoner, the guards, and the treatment of the prisoner as he is being readied for the walk to the gallows. What is Orwell trying to accomplish?

    b. What is the effect of the incidents involving the dog?

    c. What is the effect of the prisoner's chanting on the gallows?

    d. Consider the following events: the walk to the gallows, the interruption by the dog, the continued walk, the ascent, the chant, the execution. After having witnessed all of this, why do those involved laugh, tell stories, and have a drink? What is the purpose of including this final incident?

    e. Why are we never told what crime the prisoner committed?

    f. What is Orwell's thesis or main point? Where is it stated?

    > After each student has had ample time to answer the questions, divide the class into groups and assign a different question to each group, perhaps assigning all groups a question regarding Orwell's thesis. Ask the groups to answer their questions in as much detail as possible. When each group reports its findings, ask other groups to comment.

3. If students are interested in finding out more about hanging and other methods of execution (the electric chair, a firing squad, the gas chamber, and a lethal injection), they can be directed to use InfoTrac to access Jonathan Gromer, "Machines of Death," *Popular Mechanics* (Jan. 1998): 52-55.

Death and Justice

1. Divide the class into groups and assign each group two or three of the arguments used by those who oppose capital punishment. Have students answer the following questions about each argument:

    a. What, according to Koch, is wrong with the argument?

    b. What evidence does Koch give to defend his own argument?

    c. Is his defense convincing? Explain.

2. Have each student answer the following questions in writing:

   a. Of the seven objections to the death penalty noted in this essay, which is the most valid and which is the least valid? Explain.

   b. Of Koch's refutations of these arguments, which is the strongest and which is the weakest? Explain.

3. Have students use InfoTrac to explore the validity of one of the anti-capital punishment arguments that Koch refutes as well as the argument(s) Koch offers in response.

A Hanging and Death and Justice

1. Koch argues that people who oppose the death penalty on the grounds that it is barbaric actually "consider death itself . . . barbaric." Ask students to cite details from "A Hanging" to explain how Orwell might respond to this statement.

2. Have students identify the instances in which each writer is trying to appeal to the reader's emotions.

3. Capital punishment is a contentious issue. Encourage students to consider views that contradict their own by having them write down one reason that they oppose or support capital punishment. Next, ask them use InfoTrac to locate one article that refutes their position. After reading it, they should write a short paper in which they summarize it and discuss the strengths of the author's position.

4. Not all condemned prisoners oppose their executions. Some desire it. Students can use InfoTrac to explore this phenomenon and the issues it raises (Keyword: "capital punishment" AND suicide; Keyword: "capital punishement" AND "michael ross").

Mother Tongue

Amy Tan

In "Mother Tongue," Tan explores some of the effects her mother's "broken" or "limited" English has had on both her mother's life and her own. In so doing, she makes two important points about language that students have most likely not considered: Language plays a role in determining one person's perception of another; and the language used in the home has a potential effect on a child's success.

Tan discusses her own experience as the child of immigrant parents to illustrate her points. She supports the notion that language plays a role in our perceptions of others by giving examples of the way in which her mother was judged by her language. She was not taken seriously by service people such as clerks and waiters. Frequently, in order for her to get the results she wanted, she had to rely on her daughter to speak for her. Tan, too, was affected by her language background. Being raised in a home in which "broken English" was spoken and educated in a system in which standard English was demanded, Tan's performance in English was limited, particularly on standardized tests. She generalizes from her experience to suggest that perhaps many other Asian Americans have been handicapped in English studies, and this may partially explain why there are so "few Asian Americans represented in American literature." Up to this point in the essay, she has emphasized the negative effects of "broken" or "fractured" English.

However, the essay ends with Tan showing how she has effectively combined her "mother tongue" and standard English. This dispels the notion that one is necessarily handicapped if the language learned in the home is not standard English. She seems to strike a balance between the position that one must speak standard English in order to succeed and the position that one must speak one's "mother tongue" in order to retain one's identity. Indeed, Tan finds value in all of her Englishes: her mother's English, her own standard English, her English translation of her mother's Chinese, and her mother's "translation of her Chinese if she could speak in perfect English."

Because Tan uses her own experience as the child of immigrant parents to illustrate her points, students may be tempted to limit the relevance of her discussion to recent immigrants and their children. But, the points she makes can be applied to native speakers and their children as well. Native speakers adjust the form of English they use according to the situation and the person with whom they are speaking. In addition, they do not all use grammatically and syntactically correct English. Finally, whether we admit the fact or not, most of us form opinions about others based on the English they use.

Suggestions

1. In order to be sure that students understand the literal meaning of Tan's essay, have them break up into groups and answer the following questions:

    a. Explain what Tan means by "different Englishes."

    b. How does Tan's mother's ability to speak English differ from her ability to understand it?

    c. Why is Tan uncomfortable using the words "broken" or "limited" to describe her mother's English?

    d. How does the English spoken by Tan's mother affect the way she is treated by other people?

    e. Why did Tan have a difficult time on standardized tests?

    f. Why did Tan's teachers steer her toward math and science?

    g. Why does Tan think there are not more Asian American writers represented in American literature?

    h. Why, as a beginning writer, did Tan produce such stilted sentences as "That was my mental quandary in its nascent state"?

    After students have answered these questions, ask them to explain why Tan finally writes stories "using all the Englishes [she] grew up with."

2. Have students apply the concepts discussed or alluded to by Tan:

    a. Have students discuss the differences between formal language (language they might use with a teacher), informal language (language they might use with a parent), and slang (language they might use with a friend).

    b. Have students explain how cultural differences are reflected in language.

    c. Have students explain how one's language skills affect his or her chances for success in the world.

3. To demonstrate how we judge others based on language, excerpt dialogue from one or more short stories and have students discuss the characters based on those excerpts. They might also compare the language used by two characters in the same story.

4. The issues confronting immigrants and/or their children can be explored by studying "Mother Tongue" "along with "Lost Sister" (p. 28), "Persimmons" (p. 30), "What Means Switch" (p. 179), and/or "Myth of the Latin Woman" (p. 232).

5. For a broader examination of retaining and/or changing ethnic identity, "Mother Tongue" could be studied with "Lost Sister" (p. 28), "Persimmons" (p. 30), "Everyday Use" (p. 88), and/or "What Means Switch" (p. 179).

6. Have students consider the role that language plays in ethnic identity. They can use InfoTrac to access the following articles:

    Huiping Ding, Huiping, and Robert M. Boody. "The Other Side of Learning English as a Second Language: Why Isn't My Child Learning Chinese?" *Education* 122.1 (Fall, 2001): 39–45.

    "On Saturday, We Speak Chinese," *Business Week* (Sept 27, 1999): 22-4.

The Myth of the Latin Woman

Judith Ortiz Cofer

In this essay, Judith Ortiz Cofer uses experiences from her own life to demonstrate how a Latina can never fully escape "the myth of the Latin woman," no matter how well educated or eloquent she is. It is because she "so obviously belongs to Rita Moreno's gene pool" that Cofer believes she has been approached on a bus by a tipsy young man (who sang "an Irish tenor's rendition of 'Maria' from *West Side Story*"), accosted in a hotel by a besotted middle-aged man (who sang "Don't Cry for Me, Argentina" as well as an obscene song "about a girl named Maria"), and mistaken for a waitress by an older woman (who tried to order coffee from her). These incidents occurred because Latinas are stereotyped as "sexual firebrands" and "good domestics." According to Cofer, these stereotypes stem from a combination of cultural misunderstanding and media regeneration.

Americans often misinterpret the signal being sent by a Puerto Rican woman's clothing. The fashion of Puerto Rican American women is heavily influenced by the older women in their lives. These women, who either grew up on the island or were influenced by women who did, prefer the bold primary colors of Puerto Rico's natural environment and are accustomed to "showing...skin" in order to "keep cool as well as to look sexy." Women who grew up on the island may also have participated in a complicated and nuanced courtship ritual in which young women dressed in their "best party clothes" and "promenade[ed]" in front of young men they liked. The young men, in turn, expressed their "admiration in the form of *piropos*: erotically charged street poems they composed on the spot." Because women in Puerto Rico were "protected by the traditions, mores, and laws of a Spanish/Catholic system of morality and machismo," they "perhaps felt freer to dress and move more provocatively" than women from countries without this system. In the United States, a "clash is likely to take place" when a Puerto Rican woman "dressed in her idea of what is attractive meets a man from the mainstream culture who has been trained to react to certain types of clothing as a sexual signal." This misunderstanding could be treacherous for adult women: "men on the street would interpret our tight skirts and jingling bracelets as a come-on"; factory bosses would talk to their Latina workers "as if sexual innuendo was all they understood and, worse, often gave them the choice of submitting to advances or being fired."

The media has perpetuated the myth of the Latina as sexual firebrand. For instance, advertisers use "'sizzling' and 'smoldering' as the adjectives of choice for describing the women of Latin America." She blames media stereotyping for the offensive treatment she has sometimes received from insensitive and drunken men, claiming that they would not likely treat a white woman the same way because they would assume that she might be "somebody's wife or mother." To these men, Cofer is "just an Evita or Maria: merely a character in his cartoon-populated universe."

Cofer also discusses a stereotype that is born not out of cultural difference, but out of cultural discrimination. Job opportunities for women who know "little English" and have "few skills" are limited, so most work as domestics, waitresses, and factory laborers. For Latinas, this plight has become fodder for the media: "The big and little screens have presented us with the picture of the funny Hispanic maid, mispronouncing words and cooking up a spicy storm in a shiny California kitchen." Such images reinforce negative stereotypes and make it difficult for Latinas to get the respect that they deserve in all career fields.

Cofer admits that her education has given her the opportunity to defy the stereotypes, but she recognizes that they still present an onerous burden for many of her "Hispanic companeras." By examining and exposing the roots of the "old pervasive stereotypes and myths," she hopes to replace them with "a much more interesting set of realities."

Suggestions

Pre-Reading Exercise: To encourage students to start thinking about the stereotypes of Latin American women, show them a picture of the 2004 billboard that features an obviously ice-cold bottle of Tecate beer with the caption, "Finally, a cold Latina." Next, ask them to write a paragraph explaining the advertisement. Then, have some students read their paragraphs aloud and use their explanations to initiate a discussion of Latina stereotypes. (To locate pictures of the billboard, search for the words *tecate "a cold Latina" .jpg* using Google or a similar internet search engine.)

1. One method of assuring that students understand Cofer's overall point is to divide the class into groups and pose short-answer questions that will call on them to analyze details:

    a. In what way was the neighborhood of Cofer's childhood "a microcosm of [her] parents' *casas* on the island"?

    b. What was the "conflicting message" that Cofer and other girls got from their Puerto Rican mothers?

    c. Why did Cofer often feel "humiliated" when she went to an American friend's party?

    d. Why did she not know how to dress for Career Day?

    e. How did the clothing of Puerto Rican women differ from that of American women?

    f. Why, according to Cofer, might women in Puerto Rico have dressed and moved more provocatively than women in the United States?

    g. Why is a "clash" likely to occur when "a Puerto Rican girl dressed in her idea of what is attractive meets a man from the mainstream culture"?

    h. What appears be the origin of the stereotype that Latinas are "'good domestics'"?

    i. How has the media perpetuated stereotypes about Latinas?

    j. What effect have the stereotypes had on professional Latinas?

    k. How does Cofer think the mainstream society's misconceptions about Latinas can be changed?

2. Another method is to present students with discussion questions that will require them to both analyze and synthesize the text:

    a. Explain how Cofer was isolated from as well as exposed to mainstream American society as a child. Discuss the effect this isolation and exposure had on her as a child.

    b. Describe the types of clothing preferred by the Puerto Rican women who served as Cofer's fashion role models. Explain the cultural origins of their clothing preferences.

    c. Explain how mainstream society might misinterpret certain fashions worn by Puerto Rican women and how that misinterpretation could have contributed to the stereotype that Latinas are "sexual firebrands."

    d. Explain how the stereotype that Latinas are "'good domestics'" likely evolved.

    e. Discuss the "media-engendered image of the Latina in the United States," and explain how it might be "partially responsible for the denial of opportunities for upward mobility among Latinas in the professions"?

    f. Explain how Cofer uses her work to combat the myth of the Latin woman.

3. Have student consider the three incidents that Cofer thinks occurred because the people involved believe the myth of the Latin woman:

    a. Cofer says that that the drunken young man's singing to her on the bus reminded her of "a prime fact of [her] life: you can leave the Island, master the English language, and travel as far as you can, but if you are a Latina, especially one like [her] who so obviously belongs to Rita Moreno's gene pool, the Island travels with you."

     i.   How does Cofer feel about the drunken young man singing "Maria" to her on the bus?

     ii.   Why was she "not quite as amused" as the other passengers?

  b. Cofer notes that "some people, including those who should know better, still put others "'in their place'" and says that "it happened to [her] most recently during a stay at a very classy metropolitan hotel."

     i.   What does it mean to "put one in one's place"?

     ii.   Was the drunken, tuxedoed man "putting [Cofer] in her place" when he stopped her and sang a tune from *Evita* as well as an obscene ditty based on the name "Maria"? Explain.

     iii. Why does Cofer advise the man's daughter "never to ask her father what he had done in the army"?

     iv. Cofer believes that the man "would not have been likely to regale a white woman with a dirty song in public." Do you agree or disagree? Explain.

  c. Cofer says that she has "on occasion been sent to that 'kitchen,' where some think [she] obviously belong[s]" and that "one such incident" occurred when an older woman mistook her for a waitress and tried to order coffee from her.

     i.   What does Cofer mean by being sent to "that 'kitchen'"?

     ii.   Is there any reason other than Cofer's ethnicity that might have caused the woman to mistake her for a waitress? Explain.

     iii. Explain why the incident reminded Cofer "of what [she] had to overcome before anyone would take [her] seriously."

     iv. Cofer notes that she has "almost always taken doubts in [her] abilities as a challenge." Did the woman doubt her abilities? Explain.

     v.   Cofer says that the woman's mistake was "a minor offense," that "it wasn't an intentional act of cruelty," and that the woman was "embarrassed at her little faux pas." Why, then, did the incident so anger her?

     vi. How did she "punish" the woman?

     vii. Cofer does not say whether the woman attended the reading because she had planned to do so or because of her encounter with Cofer. Why might Cofer have omitted this information?

4. To make sure that students understand some of Cofer's more figurative language, have them explain the following statements:

  a. " . . . if you are a Latina, especially one like me who so obviously belongs to Rita Moreno's gene pool, the Island travels with you."

  b. "But with some people, the same things can make you an island—not so much a tropical paradise as an Alcatraz, a place nobody wants to visit. "

  c. "But to him, I was just an Evita or a Maria: merely a character in his cartoon-populated universe."

  d. ". . Latin women pray 'in Spanish to an Anglo God / with a Jewish heritage,' and they are 'fervently hoping / that if not omnipotent, / at least He be bilingual.'"

5. Have students consider compare their own experiences and reactions to Cofer's.

  a. Describe an occasion when you been mistaken or have mistaken someone else for an employee at a store, restaurant, etc.

  b. Why do you think the mistake occurred?

  c. How did you respond to the mistake?

  d. How did the other person respond?

6. Have student explore the way that early films helped establish and perpetuate the myth of the Latin woman. They might be asked to research such 1930s and 1940s actresses as Dolores Del Rio, Lupe Velez, and Maria Montez (all of whom played the role of the hot-blooded Latina seductress) as well as Carmen Miranda (who starred in musical-comedies speaking heavily accented English and wearing outrageous costumes and headdresses). Students can search for information using the Internet Movie Database (www.imdb.com) as well as Google.

7. Students can be asked to use InfoTrac to investigate the stereotyping of other ethnic groups by the mass media in general (Keyword: Stereotype AND "mass media") or the film industry in particular (Keyword: Stereotype AND "Motion Pictures"). Alternatively, students can be directed to specific articles that are accessible through InfoTrac:

> Jonathan J. Cavallero, "Gangsters, Fessos, Tricksters, and Sopranos: The Historical Roots of Italian American Stereotype Anxiety," *Journal of Popular Film and Television* 32.2 (2004): 50-64.
>
> Richard H. Curtiss and Delinda C. Hanley, "Dr. Jack Shaheen Discusses Reel Bad Arabs: How Hollywood Vilifies a People, *Washington Report on Middle East Affairs* 20.5 (2001): 103
>
> Jonathan Kay, "Jews, Blacks, and Aliens: In *Independence Day*, Racial Stereotypes Save the Day," *Saturday Night* 111.9 (1996): 133.

8. The issues confronting immigrants and/or their children can be explored by studying this essay along with "Lost Sister" (p. 28), "Persimmons" (p. 30), "What Means Switch" (p. 179), and/or "Mother Tongue" (p. 227).

9. To examine how "signals" can be wrongly perceived as sexual, team "The Myth of the Latin Woman" with "When Is It Rape?" (p. 259)

Making the Grade

Kurt Wiesenfeld

Grades are a subject that is generally of keen interest to students. They have received them, in one form or another, since they started school. This essay provides them the opportunity to think about the significance of grades in what is likely a new light.

  In "Making the Grade," Kurt Wiesenfeld, a physics professor at Georgia Institute of Technology, addresses the "disgruntled-consumer approach" that some students have developed toward grades, arguing that the "attitude is not only self-destructive, but socially destructive." Students who ask for a better grade than the one they deserve are indifferent "toward grades as an indication of personal effort and performance." They hold the professor, not themselves, responsible for their losing a scholarship, being suspended, becoming depressed. These students are not concerned with the connection between actions and consequences. They value grades, not learning ("the one thing college actually offers"). When the grades that students receive do not accurately reflect their performance, then they graduate without the expertise they need, get jobs they are not truly qualified to perform, and make errors that affect others. Students must receive the grades they have earned: "it's necessary to help preserve a minimum standard of quality that our society needs to maintain safety and integrity."

Suggestions

Pre-Reading Exercise: Have students write a brief paper explaining what grades are supposed to indicate and why they are used in colleges and universities.

1. Students are likely to have a fairly good grasp of Wiesenfeld's points. Pose some questions that direct attention to a few points they may have skimmed over:

    a. Fully explain what Wiesenfeld means by a "disgruntled-consumer approach" (par. 3). What does he think has caused some students to develop this attitude?

    b. What does Wiesenfeld mean when he says grades are "intrinsically worthless" (par. 6)? In what way(s) are grades valuable? Explain.

    c. In paragraph 8, Wiesenfeld asserts that "their attitude is not only self-destructive, but socially destructive." Whose attitude is he referring to? In what way(s) is it self-destructive? Socially destructive? Explain.

    d. How is giving appropriate grades a form of "quality control" (par. 8)?

    e. What is a degree supposed to indicate?

2. Invite students to further explore some of the issues Wiesenfeld raises:

    a. Do you think that a professor is responsible for a student's "losing a scholarship, flunking out or deciding whether life has meaning" (par. 6)? Explain.

    b. Wiesenfeld provides some examples of "real-world consequences of errors and lack of expertise." What are some other examples?

    c. Is it fair for teachers to judge students "according to their performance, not their desires or 'potential'"? Explain.

    d. Do you agree that accurate grades are "necessary to help preserve a minimum standard of quality that our society needs to maintain safety and integrity" (par. 11)? Explain.

3. Present students with the following scenarios and ask them what they would do:

    a. Up until this semester, you have made an A in every class in your major. This term's class, you made A's on all the tests and quizzes, but you blanked on the final exam and got a C for the semester. What do you do?

    b. You made a D on every chemistry test you took throughout the term. You know you made a D on the final exam because you went to your professor's office and reviewed the test. When you get your end of term grade report, you are surprised to see that you received an A for the class. What do you do?

    c. You struggled all term in your math class. You never missed a class, attended all of the supplemental instruction sessions, went to the math lab almost every day, and studied math at least two hours every night. Your final average is 6/10's of a point from a C. What do you do?

    d. You are a straight A psychology student with a love of drawing. You want to take a drawing class, but you are concerned that you might earn a low grade and pull down your GPA. Do you take the drawing class? Explain.

4. According to most academics, grade inflation is a serious problem in secondary schools as well as colleges and universities. Have students explore and discuss the issue. Information can be located using InfoTrac (Keyword: grade inflation).

5. Initiate a class discussion with the following question: What is the value of learning? To fully explore the question, students will need to define *value* as well as *learning*.

6. "Making the Grade" can be teamed with the short story "Harrison Bergeron" (p. 53) for a discussion of the difference between effort and achievement, potential and fulfillment.

What Is Child Pornography?

George Will

Disgusting Doesn't Make It "Speech"

Ann Coulter

and

Should a Man Be Put in Jail for What He's Thinking?

Leonard Pitts, Jr.

This series of articles focuses on the case of Brian Dalton and raises issues about which students are likely to have strong and possibly emotional opinions. Dalton was on probation for child pornography when it was discovered that his journal contained several sexual fantasies he had written about molesting children. Though Dalton had neither distributed his writing nor shown any inclination to do so, the state of Ohio charged him with pandering child pornography. Dalton pled guilty. Typically, those who plead guilty (instead of being found guilty by a jury or a judge) cannot appeal their conviction. At the time these articles were written, Dalton's course of legal action was unclear, and no one knew whether or not Dalton would be permitted to appeal. Nevertheless, each of these writers has strong opinions about the Dalton case and the issues it raises.

For George Will, the Dalton case is "puzzling." Questioning the propriety, not to mention the legality, of convicting a man for the contents of his personal diaries, Will traces the evolution of federal law with respect to child pornography. In 1969 the Supreme Court ruled that "the mere private possession of obscene material cannot constitutionally be made a crime." In 1982 the Court upheld a New York law that "criminalized depicting sexual performances by children when the promotion involved materials depicting such performances." Then in 1990, the Court held that the mere possession of child pornography can be proscribed because the state has "compelling interests in protecting the physical and psychological well-being of minors and in destroying the market for the exploitative use of children." Will notes that Dalton pleaded guilty to the charges, "thereby discarding a chance to contest his conviction." Were Dalton able to appeal his conviction, Will believes he would prevail.

Ann Coulter disagrees. After alluding to Will's essay in her first sentence, Coulter claims to be "The Only Person in America who says Ohio wins." While Will's reasoning is based on the legal significance of relevant Supreme Court decisions, Coulter's reasoning is based on her own sensibilities and her disdain for the Supreme Court. According to Coulter, "states can do anything that isn't prohibited by the Constitution." She makes this statement as if it were well-established, incontrovertible fact. Such is not the case. While her claim seems to be supported by the Tenth Amendment ("The powers not delegated to the United States by the Constitution, nor prohibited by it to the states, are reserved to the states respectively, or to the people"), it is clearly contradicted by the Ninth Amendment ("The enumeration in the Constitution, of certain rights, shall not be construed to deny or disparage others retained by the people"). She defines "speech" as the communication of an idea (as opposed to the expression of an idea), arguing that writings that are not intended to be shared are not "speech" and concluding that Dalton's writings are not speech. Aware, perhaps, of the weakness of that argument, Coulter shifts her focus, pointing out that not all speech is Constitutionally protected. Indeed, she says, obscenity is not protected. Referring to the same Supreme Court cases referenced by George Will, Coulter declares that the Supreme Court's obscenity rulings have been "incomprehensible, contradictory." She concludes her impassioned but rather erratic essay by suggesting that the government's reading of a citizen's private journal is not "authoritarian" if that citizen is a "convicted and paroled child pornographer."

Unlike Coulter, who seems to lose sight of her original point, Leonard Pitts, Jr. boils all of the issues down to one simple question, the question he uses as the title of his essay: "Should a man be put in jail for what he's thinking?" Brian Dalton's incarceration has shown that a man *can* be put in jail for what he's thinking, and that, Pitts argues, "represents a clear and present danger" to the rights of all Americans. Pitts spends no time reviewing Supreme Court decisions, no time defining speech or pornography. Instead, he acknowledges that some ideas and the people who espouse them are abhorrent, but he cautions us not to allow our revulsion to obscure the fact that disallowing some free speech endangers all free speech: "If government is allowed to do it to 'them,' what stops government from doing it to you?" Pitts recognizes that there is "nothing preordained about the rights we take for granted" and warns that "they can be nibbled away until they are gone."

Suggestions

Pre-Reading Exercise: Have students watch *Minority Report* (2002), a film in which a team of detectives is charged with stopping murders *before* they occur. Before students watch the film, have them answer the questions provided below:

   a. Is thinking about murdering someone the moral equivalent of actually doing it?
   b. Should the state take action against individuals who think about murdering someone?
   c. Should the state take action against individuals who write a piece of fiction about murdering someone?
   d. Should the state take action against individuals who talk with a friend about murdering someone?
   e. At what point, short of actual murder, should the state intervene?

   > After they have watched the film, discuss their answers and any changes of opinion they may have had.

What Is Child Pornography?

1. Students are likely to find this emotionally-charged subject matter difficult to analyze precisely because it is emotionally-charged. Pose questions that will help them keep their focus on the issues.
   a. What is Will's opinion of Brian Dalton?
   b. What crime did the state of Ohio accuse Brian Dalton of committing?
   c. Why will Brian Dalton most likely be unable to appeal his conviction?
   d. Will thinks that Dalton's conviction would be overturned (if he were able to appeal it). Examine the evidence that Will provides to support his opinion:

      > Summarize each of the Supreme Court decisions that Will mentions.

      > Locate the instances in which Will points the reader's attention to specific words in the Supreme Court rulings. Why does Will emphasize these specific words?

   e. Does Will adequately support his argument? Explain.
   f. Based on the rulings on this subject, do you agree or disagree with Will that Dalton's conviction would have been overturned? Explain.
2. If students have read Ann Coulter's "Disgusting Doesn't Make It 'Speech'," ask them to compare and contrast Will's attitude toward the Supreme Court and its rulings with Coulter's attitude.

Disgusting Doesn't Make It "Speech"

1. Pose questions that will prompt students to look at the substance of Coulter's argument:

    a. Coulter claims that "the states can do anything that isn't prohibited by the Constitution." Why does she offer no evidence to support her assertion? Do you think her assertion is correct? Explain.

    b. According to Coulter, "the only question is whether Dalton's private journal is protected by the First Amendment." Is this "the only question"? Explain.

    c. Coulter argues that journal writings are not a form of speech. Summarize her argument and analyze her logic. Is her argument valid? Explain.

    d. What does Coulter find "ridiculous" the Supreme Court's definition of obscenity?

    e. In paragraph 7, Coulter says, "Dalton was either pandering child pornography or he was talking to himself—which isn't obviously protected by the Constitution." She then shifts her attention to the Supreme Court, devoting eight paragraphs to its rulings. She does not mention the Dalton case again until the final paragraph of her essay (par. 16). Does her discussion of the Supreme Court and its rulings support her assertion that Dalton's conviction would not be overturned? Explain.

2. If students have read George Will's "What Is Child Pornography?," ask them to compare and contrast Will's attitude toward the Supreme Court and its rulings with Coulter's attitude. If they have not read Will's essay, ask them to discuss Coulter's opinion of the Supreme Court and its rulings in the cases that she mentions.

Should a Man Be Put in Jail for What He's Thinking?

1. Pose questions that will help students examine why Pitts is fearful of what happened to Dalton:

    a. What does Pitts think about Dalton?

    b. How, according to Pitts, does what happened to Dalton represent "a clear and present danger to the rights you and I enjoy as United States citizens"?

    c. Fully explain Pitts's observation: ". . . some would willingly allow the same intrusion upon others . . . because we find them and their beliefs abhorrent. In allowing that intrusion, such people seldom see that they are betrayed by their own revulsion, induced to make a narrow argument and miss its broad implication: If government is allowed to do it to 'them,' what stops government from doing it to you?"

2. Have students consider the significance of the title:

    Twice in the essay, Pitts presents the question, "Can a man be put in jail for what he is thinking?" Yet, he titles the essay "Should a Man be Put in Jail for What He's Thinking?" What is the difference in meaning in the questions? Explain the significance of the title.

3. To further examine the issue of free speech and abhorrent ideas, have students watch *Skokie* (1981), a true story about the 1978 neo-Nazi plan to march in Skokie, Illinois, a city with a large population of World War II concentration camp survivors. Discussion of the film could be followed up with a short research project about the 1980 rally in Skokie of the KKK and other white supremacist groups.

What Is Child Pornography?, *Disgusting Doesn't Make It "Speech"*, *and Should a Man Be Put in Jail for What He's Thinking?*

1. Have students discuss each writer's tone as well as the effect it had on them as they were reading the essay.

2. Ask students to compare and contrast the effectiveness of these three essays:

    a. Which of these three essays best achieves its purpose? Explain.

    b. Which essay did you personally like the most? Explain.

3. Divide the class into groups, and ask each to write an essay using one of the following as the introduction:

    > George Will is a leading conservative thinker and a consistent contributor to the national press. He expresses himself clearly and forthrightly and is never reluctant to voice controversial or unpopular opinions, tending to argue logically and rarely emotionally, even when his opinions displease not only his reader but also, one suspects, himself. In "What Is Child Pornography?," Will keeps his emotions almost consistently in check. His sedate tone invites the reader to analyze the strength of his arguments on logical, not emotional, grounds.

    > A conservative political analyst and writer, Ann Coulter is well-known for her blistering assaults on people and agendas that she considers liberal. Coulter seems to have written "Disgusting Doesn't Make It 'Speech'" more to affirm the opinions of those who agree with her than to change the opinions of those who do not.

    > Leonard Pitts is a social commentator and syndicated columnist who can be neatly labeled as neither a conservative nor a liberal. An independent thinker, Pitts frequently addresses comments and questions directly to his reader. In "Should a Man Be Put in Jail for What He's Thinking?," Pitts uses a conversational tone to warn his readers against taking their rights for granted.

4. Have students use InfoTrac (Keyword: "Brian Dalton") to find out what has happened to Brian Dalton since these articles were published. Ask them to write a short paper explaining their view of what has transpired in the case. They can read their papers and discuss their opinions in class.

5. Have students watch the film *Nineteen Eighty-Four* (1984), an adaptation of George Orwell's novel about a state that monitors and punishes any unacceptable ideas held by its citizens. Students can examine the parallels between the issues raised in the essays and those raised in the film.

Starved Out

Cynthia Fox

Five percent of American females and one percent of American males suffer from anorexia nervosa, bulimia nervosa, or a binge eating disorder.[1] According to the National Mental Illness Screening Project, roughly "one in ten college women have a clinical or nearly clinical eating disorder, including 5.1 percent who suffer from bulimia nervosa." Without proper treatment, many of the more than five million Americans afflicted with an eating disorder will die. In fact, approximately one thousand women in the United States die each year of anorexia nervosa (National Eating Disorders Screen Project). Nonetheless, insurance companies generally refuse to pay for treatment until a person with anorexia is in immediate

---

[1]Over ninety percent of those who have an eating disorder are female:
- 0.5 to 1.0 percent suffer from anorexia nervosa,
- 1 to 3 percent have bulimia nervosa, and
- 0.7 to 4 percent experience binge-eating disorder.

Source: *National Institute of Mental Health,* "Women Hold Up Half the Sky" (July 1999), 17 Sept. 2005 <http://www.nimh.nih.gov/publicat/womensoms.cfm>.

danger of dying. Even then, the treatment they will cover is far short of the treatment needed. In "Starved Out," Fox examines the insurance industry's stance and the impact it is having on people seeking treatment for anorexia.

According to Fox, the industry's position is based on finances, not medicine. Fox supports her assertion by contrasting the coverage that insurance companies provided before and after they adopted the managed-care system. Insurers used to permit severely anorexic patients to remain in the hospital until they reached their ideal body weight, a process that can take from two to seven months. Now, they will cover treatment only when the patient is about to die and, even then, will permit only two to fourteen days of hospitalization. Consequently, by the time anorexics are actually admitted to the hospital, they are so severely malnourished that their cognitive functions are impaired. Until they are renourished, talk therapy, a crucial part of treatment, will be ineffective. Nevertheless, most patients, unable to pay for hospitalization out-of-pocket, are forced to leave the hospital well before they are physically and mentally prepared to do so. The new policies are economically efficient but medically unsound.

While the insurance industry is obviously influenced by financial considerations, they may also be affected by the cultural myths and biases regarding eating disorders. Prejudices are, after all, often insidious and far-reaching. The question posed by the unnamed congressman reflects societal misunderstanding of anorexia: "'How am I supposed to convince a small-business man he has to pay for this girlie disease?'" It is doubtful that the congressman would have had the same dismissive attitude had the illness in question had an overtly biological basis. Fox does not explicitly analyze the causes of anorexia, some of which are biological. She frames her discussion of the insurance industry's stance toward anorexia with the story of Jayme Porter, a twenty-year-old severely anorexic college student who is not receiving proper treatment.

In telling Jayme's story, Fox includes details that provide some insight into the causes of Jayme's anorexia. Biological factors seem to have contributed to her disorder. Studies have found that anorexics often have abnormally low levels of the neurotransmitters serotonin and norepinephrine and that the levels do not increase after recovery. Reduced levels of one or both of these neurotransmitters are also typically found in people who are clinically depressed as well as those who are obsessive–compulsive[2] Jayme is taking Prozac, an antidepressant that regulates serotonin. The medication has helped her become less obsessive–compulsive: She now allows people to sit on the sofa without being so concerned about the cushions being "squashed." Although she has overcome her "obsessive neatness," she continues to talk to her mother four times a day. Psychopharmacology has helped Jayme, but she is in need of additional treatment to address the other causes of her disorder.

Like most anorexics, Jayme and Julie appear to have grown up in a dysfunctional home. Their parents placed a good deal of emphasis on success and perfection, and the girls learned their lessons well. Julie won "speech contests while Jayme won sheep-showing contests." Trophies, concrete evidence of their accomplishments, filled their childhood bedrooms. Each was one of two in their graduating class to go to college. The primacy of success is evident in the sisters' descriptions of their rapid weight loss: "'I had to be thinnest.'" Galen and Kay Porter, aware that the need to succeed played a role in their daughters' development of anorexia, believe that each girl's illness was triggered by her realization that she was not achieving a goal or excelling in anything.

The desire to win may have created a competitive relationship between Jayme and Julie, each striving to be the best and receive from their parents the concomitant accolades and affection. Now adults, the sisters, who "have had to compete for attention and money," "almost never speak to each other," a division that insures noncompetitive interaction with their parents. In a healthy family, of course, competition between adult siblings is not necessary.

---

[2]For an analysis of the role of neurotransmitters in depression, see Charles B. Nemeroff, "The Neurobiology of Depression," *Scientific American* 278.6 (1998): 42-50. 17 Sept. 2005 <www.lib.calpoly.edu/infocomp/ modules/05_evaluate/WIC2b.html >.

There is also the oblique suggestion that the dysfunction in the Porter household may also have included alcohol abuse. Galen Porter has "prided himself on 'always having fun,'" a not uncommon euphemism for the temporary escape provided by excessive drinking. Galen's daughters seem to have acquired a taste for alcohol. Jayme "used to go drinking *every night* with boyfriends" [emphasis added]. And, Julie has attended Alcoholics Anonymous. Galen and Kay also appear to be adept at not acknowledging painful realities: They "can pretend their problems don't exist." Children of substance abusers learn to hide their "weaknesses" and suppress their feelings. Some find that focusing their attention on their bodies helps them avoid dealing with painful emotions.

Self-restriction provides anorexics with a sense of power over their lives. Weight gain is equated with the loss of that control. Jayme, like most anorexics, has developed her own methods of measuring any changes in her body size and of assuring that she does not gain weight. She checks everyday "to make sure her forearm fits in a circle formed by her thumb and finger." This form of checking is Jayme's gauge of success. She attempts to burn as many calories as possible, working out at the gym and walking "wearing a twenty pound knapsack." When Jayme looks in the mirror and sees her "'skeleton," she gets a "rush." The "rush" is the headiness of success, power, and control. When anorexics feel helpless, they often attempt to reestablish their sense of control by restricting their food intake. Having learned that Dr. Pryor's clinic will likely close, Jayme feels powerless. She responds by restricting her food intake, eating "an apple for breakfast instead of the juice, yogurt, meat, cereal, milk, and two fruits prescribed."

The toll that Jayme's self-starvation has taken on her body is clear. When she is admitted to the hospital, she is near death, lacking even the strength to lift the sheets over herself. She has no subcutaneous layer of fat, making her skin translucent and enabling the nurses to "see the outlines of her organs through her skin." Devoid of any insulating fat, her body cannot retain heat, so she is hypothermic. Her lack of nutrition has caused a severe electrolyte imbalance and heart disease ("If she sat up, her heart rate would go to 180, then would slow to thirty-two beats a minute, and when she tried to get out of bed, it went off the charts").

Despite having almost died, Jayme does not see the damage she has done and is doing to her body. She perceives herself as "strong" and, ignoring the fact that she has stopped menstruating and that her boyfriends have been frightened away by her weight loss, she believes that she will get married and have children. Her misperceptions are likely the result of denial as well as impaired cognition. Jayme's self-starvation has deprived her body of the nourishment it needs, and the functioning of her brain, like the functioning of her heart, has been affected. Jayme's inability to process and comprehend is evident in her response to being told that Dr. Pryor's clinic will likely close: she "doesn't understand," asking "'I'll still be able to see Dr. Pryor, right?'"

Jayme obviously needs the same type of intensive treatment that her sister received. Julie attended "group therapy, psychotherapy, nutrition and body image class, [and] AA." During treatment, she was also constantly monitored. As a result of treatment, she has relinquished her rituals, her need to please, and her obsessive–compulsive behavior ("Her house is as cheerfully unkempt as Jayme's is Spartan"). Galen and Kay Porter tried to find help for Jayme, eventually remortgaging their house to pay for her hospitalization. Fox says only that Jayme was discharged from the program for being "noncompliant." She does not explain the form of Jayme's noncompliance, nor does she examine the possibility that Jayme's behavior was motivated by a desire to be dismissed and thus spare her parents further indebtedness.

The insurance industry's refusal to cover adequate treatment for anorexics places those in need of assistance at great risk. They cannot be hospitalized until they are in danger of dying, and then they must be released before they can be treated for their anorexia. Many, if not most, cannot afford to pay for treatment, and those who can may be unable to find the specialized programs they need. The lack of insurance reimbursement has caused many treatment facilities to close, a trend that will likely continue.

As a result of the insurance companies' policies, the number of anorexics who are able to receive treatment will decrease. The number who will die will increase.

Works Consulted

Eating Disorders. National Mental Illness Screening Project. 28 Aug. 1999.
       <http://www.nmisp.org/eat/eat-faq.htm>.

Eating Disorders: Anorexia and Bulimia Nervosa. New York Online Access to Health (NOAH). May
       1998. 30 Sept. 1999 <http://www.noah.cuny.edu/wellconn/eatdisorders.html>.

Etiology. Academy for Eating Disorders. 30 Aug. 1999 <http://www.acadeatdis.org/>.

Nemeroff, Charles B. "The Neurobiology of Depression," *Scientific American* 278.6 (1998): 42-50. 24
       Nov. 1999 <http://www.scientificamerican.com/ 1998/0698issue/0698nemeroff.html>.

Reiff, Dan and Kim Reiff. *Eating Disorders: Nutrition Therapy in the Recovery Process.* Aspen, CO:
       Aspen Pub., 1990. Rpt. *What Causes Eating Disorders.* Eating Disorder Recovery Online. 3 Oct.
       1999 <http://www.edrecovery.com/ whatcauses.html>.

"Serotonin and Eating Disorders." *Medical Sciences Bulletin,* Oct. 1998. 9 Sept. 1999
       <http://pharminfo.com/pubs/msb/seroton.html>.

Understanding Eating Disorders. National Depressive and Manic-Depressive Association 15 March
       1998. 18 Aug. 1999 <http://www.ndmda.org/eating.htm>.

United States. Dept. of Health and Human Services. National Institute of Mental Health. *Women Hold Up
       Half the Sky,* July 1999. 30 Sept. 1999 <http://www.nimh.nih.gov/publicat/womensoms.cfm>.

West, Caroline, LPC, Eating Disorders Specialist. Personal Interview. 2 Sept. 1999.

What Causes Eating Disorders. Anorexia Nervosa and Related Eating Disorders (ANRED). 30 Sept.
       1999 <http://www.anred.com/causes.html>.

Suggestions

Pre-Reading Exercises: One somber but highly effective exercise makes graphically clear the potential effects of severe anorexia. Without preface, show students an image of "The Bristol Schoolgirl," a sixteen-year-old girl who died in 1888 of anorexia.[1] Ask students to record their feelings and/or thoughts on paper. There is no "wrong" response. Students are free to write whatever they would like. When students have completed their response, ask for volunteers to share their writing with the class.

Another approach is to ask students what options people have if they are very ill and their insurance company refuses to pay for adequate treatment. Students are usually unaware of the options and may have never considered the question. Posing this question encourages them to think critically and to consider the role of insurance coverage in health care. They can return to their responses after they have analyzed the essay and examined Jayme Porter's situation.

During this discussion, share with students the advice of Larry Levitt, director of the Changing Healthcare Marketplace Project, and ask them to explain the likely rational for his recommendations.[2] Levitt recommends that people first contact their insurance plan's customer service department and try to resolve the dispute directly. They need to keep written documentation of phones calls, conversations, and so forth. If these attempts prove unsuccessful, they should contact their state insurance department. Their

[1]Reproductions are available in various books and Web sites devoted to eating disorders. One such site is Kathryn Sylva and Robin Lasser's "The Bristol Schoolgirl," *Eating Disorders / Disordered Culture,* 17 Sept. 2005 <http://www.eating.ucdavis.edu/history/bristol.html>.
[2]Consumers Unaware of HMO Independent Review. Health Central News Archives 16 Nov. 1998. 17 Sept. 2005 < http://www.personalmd.com/news/a1998111613.shtml>.

state may have a state-run independent review-board that mediates such health insurance disputes. If not, the department will take their complaint and may be willing to act as mediator.

1. Have students closely examine the text for details that illustrate the effects of Jayme's anorexia.
    a. One approach is to pose questions:
        - Locate details that reveal Jayme's lack of physical health.
        - Locate details that reveal Jayme's lack of mental health.
        - Locate details that reveal Jayme's inability to process and comprehend information.
    b. Another approach is to provide students with a list of the signs and consequences of anorexia. Then, have them examine the text and locate details that show which ones apply to Jayme:

    Danger signs
    - Loss of a significant amount of weight
    - Continuing to diet although thin
    - Feeling fat, even after losing weight
    - Intense fear of weight gain
    - Loss of monthly menstrual periods
    - Preoccupation with food, calories, fat contents, and nutrition
    - Preferring to diet in isolation
    - Cooking for others
    - Hair loss
    - Cold hands and feet
    - Fainting spells
    - Exercising compulsively
    - Lying about food
    - Depression, anxiety
    - Weakness, exhaustion
    - Periods of hyperactivity
    - Constipation
    - Growth of fine body hair on arms, legs, and other body parts
    - Heart tremors
    - Dry, brittle skin
    - Shortness of breath

    Medical Consequences
    - Shrunken organs
    - Bone mineral loss, which can lead to osteoporosis
    - Low body temperature
    - Low blood pressure
    - Slowed metabolism and reflexes
    - Irregular heartbeat, which can lead to cardiac arrest

SOURCE: Common Eating Disorders: Anorexia Nervosa. Rutgers University Health Services, Feb. 23, 2003. 2005 Sept. 17 <http://health.rutgers.edu/brochures/eatingdisorders.htm >.

2. Pose questions that will lead students to examine the details that relate to the Porter family and reach conclusions about Jayme's upbringing.

    a. Describe the town in which Jayme grew up.

    b. How do the Porters' define success?

    c. How does their definition differ from the definition of their community?

    d. What is the Porters' attitude toward success?

    e. Did Julie and Jayme meet their parents' expectations of success? Explain.

    f. How might Jayme and Julie's need to succeed been a cause of their anorexia?

    g. List actions taken by Kay and Galen Porter. What seems to be the primary concerns of each parent?

    h. Describe the relationship between Jayme and Julie.

    i. Describe the relationship that each daughter has with her parents.

3. Once students have a firm understanding of anorexia and the effect it is having on Jayme, have them address questions about the insurance industry:

    a. Fully explain why insurance companies generally refuse to pay for adequate treatment of anorexia.

    b. How has Jayme been affected by her insurance company's policy?

    c. How have Jayme's parents been affected?

    d. Does Fox provide any evidence that anorexia can be treated effectively? Explain.

    e. According to Dr. Pat Santucci, there is "such bias" about eating disorders. What are these biases?

4. This exercise provides students with an opportunity to work with information contained in a table. Distribute the following table and ask students to analyze the information it contains. What conclusions can they draw from their analysis? Ask them to discuss their conclusions in light of "Starved Out."

1 to 4 percent	Percentage of high school and college girls who have either anorexia or bulimia
0.5 to 1 percent	Percentage of girls who had bulimia or anorexia in 1976
33-23-33	Average measurements of a contemporary fashion model
36-18-33	Projected measurements of a Barbie doll, in inches, if she were a full-size human being
5'4"/142 lbs.	The average height and weight of an American woman
5'9"/110 lbs.	The average height and weight of a model
33 percent	Percentage of American women who wear a size 16 or larger
80 percent	Percentage of women who diet
25 percent	Percentage of men who diet
50 percent	Percentage of American women on a diet at any one time
50 percent	Percentage of nine-year-old girls who have ever dieted
$10 billion	Revenues of the diet industry in 1970
$33 billion	Revenues of the diet industry today
10 percent	Percentage of teenagers with eating disorders who are boys

Source: Karen S. Schneider, Shelley Levitt, Danelle Morton, and Paula Yoo, "Mission Impossible: Deluged by Images from TV, Movies, and Magazines, Teenage Girls Do Battle with an Increasingly Unrealistic Standard of Beauty—and Pay a Price," *People,* 3 June 1996: 64.

5. To explore the idea of success and the various ways in which people define it, "Starved Out" can be studied with "Richard Cory" (p. 4) and/or "Warren Pryor" (p. 5).

6. As a research project, students might be asked to write short papers on any of the following topics:

   a. Advertising and body image (InfoTrac Keyword: Advertising and body image)

   b. The Bristol schoolgirl (Google Search: Bristol schoolgirl anorexia 1888)

   c. Bulimia (InfoTrac Subject: Bulimia)

   d. Catherine of Siena (InfoTrac Subject: Catherine of Siena)

   e. Mental health coverage (InfoTrac Keyword: Mental health coverage)

   f. Twiggy (Google Search: Twiggy model)

   g. Weight Loss Industry (InfoTrac Subject: Weight Loss Industry)

A Brief History of Anorexia Nervosa in Western Culture

In "The Prehistory of Anorexia Nervosa," Jules R. Bemporad provides a historical overview of self-starvation and finds that anorexia is used to "express deeper psychological issues" primarily when specific social factors exist: a perception that the soul and body are separate; a degree of affluence that assures survival; and an esteem for women that is based on their "aesthetic, cultural, or spiritual attributes."

According to Bemporad, nothing is known about self-starvation in western culture prior to the Hellenistic age. Gnosticism, a religious movement that flourished during the second and third centuries, taught that the soul was divine and imprisoned by the human body. By the end of the third century, gnostics had all but disappeared, but their belief in the dichotomy between the spirit and the body had taken firm root in orthodox Christianity and led those in search of spiritual transcendence to deprive their bodies of nourishment and care. In A.D. 383, an aristocratic Roman woman, a follower of St. Jerome, died as a result of her continued fasting. She is the first person who is known to have died from self-starvation (Ranke-Heinemann, 1900). After the fall of Rome, Western Europe plunged into the so-called Dark Ages, a period when a lack of food and an abundance of aggression made survival itself difficult. Women were again valued for their biological ability to procreate, and anorexic practices seem to have vanished.

During the Middle Ages and the Renaissance, as society once again became relatively affluent and women were again valued for their nonbiological attributes, spiritually motivated self-starvation resurfaced. In *Holy Anorexia,* Rudolph Bell examines 261 cases of women starving themselves between 1206–1934, but well over two-thirds of these cases occurred between the thirteenth and seventeenth centuries. Among the "holy anorexics" of this time are Margaret of Cortona (c. 1247–1297), Catherine of Siena (c. 1333–1380), and Columba of Rieti (c. 1467–1501). The number of women fasting themselves to actual or near death diminished after 1600.

As Bemporad points out, this was likely the result of both the Catholic Church and the Reformation. The Church determined that people could only communicate with Christ through intermediaries such as priests, so it was no longer acceptable for young Catholic women to claim a direct relationship with Christ. The rise in Puritanism lead to a general depreciation of aesthetics and an emphasis on utility. Women were not valued for their beauty but for their function. Despite these cultural shifts, the practice of self-starvation among women never disappeared entirely.

In the seventeenth century, Richard Morton, an English physician, wrote what is generally considered the first detailed description of anorexia, a disorder he termed "nervous atrophy." Unable to isolate any pathological reasons for the illness, he concluded that the reasons must be psychological.

By the nineteenth century, the industrial revolution had a profound effect on American society. One of the most notable effects was the emergence of an affluent middle class with a desire for leisure as well as beauty and art. The valuing of women for their aesthetic qualities escalated, as did the instances of their self-starvation. Physicians began to notice and publish articles about the phenomenon. In 1873, two well-known physicians, Ernest Charles Lasegue ("On Hysterical Anorexia") and Sir William Whitney Gull (Communication to the London Clinical Society, October 24, 1873) each published an article about anorexia. Morton, Lasegue, and Gull all attributed the condition to psychological forces. During the World Wars and the Depression, times when life was difficult, instances of self-starvation decreased.

By the 1950s, the number of women with anorexia began to increase, a trend that has not only continued but accelerated. Hilde Burch, a pioneer in the field of eating disorders, maintains that the increase is a fundamental result of "the changing status of (and expectations for) women":

> Girls whose early upbringing has prepared them to become "clinging-vine" wives suddenly are expected at adolescence to prove themselves as women of achievement. This seems to create severe personal self-doubt and basic uncertainty. In their submissive way, they "choose" the fashionable dictum to be slim as a way of proving themselves as deserving respect (9).

Women who attempt to attain society's "ideal" body image put themselves at great risk. Models are typically 15 percent underweight (23 percent thinner than the average American woman). Sometimes, anorexics use obsessing over food and weight as a means of avoiding feelings such as fear, sadness, and anger. Often, anorexics are perfectionists who, despite their many accomplishments, feel inadequate. For some, their feelings of inadequacy lead them to believe that they deserve no pleasures, including eating. For others, exercising rigid control over their weight and food intake makes them feel successful. At the core of anorexia seems to be the issue of power. Anorexics often feel they have no power over their lives or their surroundings. Many come from dysfunctional homes where they were allowed no autonomy or where expectations were high and anything less than perfection was not tolerated. Control over one's body—one's weight and size—becomes an expression of power and a seizure of control . . . frequently in the only permissible or possible realm.

Works Cited

Bell, Rudolph. *Holy Anorexia.* Chicago: The University of Chicago Press, 1985.

Bemporad, Jules R. "Self-Starvation through the Ages: Reflections on the Pre-History of Anorexia Nervosa." *The International Journal of Eating Disorders,* 19 (1996): 217-37.

Burch, Hilde. "Four Decades of Eating Disorders." *Handbook of Psychotherapy for Anorexia Nervosa and Bulmia.* Eds. David M. Garner and Paul E. Garfinkel. NY: The Guildford Press, 1985.

Zimmerman, Jill S. "An Image to Heal." *The Humanist,* 57 (1997): 20-6.

Heavy Judgment: A Sister Talks about the Pain of Living Large

Deborah Gregory

Beauty may be in the eye of the beholder,[1] but, more often than not, the beholder's perceptions are shaped by the culture in which he or she lives. The same is true of body size, especially women's body size. Primitive cultures valued obesity in women. Food was often scarce, and women needed excess body fat to see them through periods of famine and ensure their fertility. As civilizations developed and food became more plentiful, the ideals of feminine beauty changed. The ancient Egyptians, Greeks, and Romans valued thinness in women, and aristocratic women in those societies attempted to attain the ideal by depriving themselves of food. After the collapse of the Roman Empire, there was no centralized government in Europe and survival was difficult. The full-bodied woman again gained favor, a trend that continued through the Middles Ages and the Renaissance, despite the relative affluence of the times.

During the eighteenth century, this began to change, at least for the upper class. While artists continued to depict peasant women as robust, they began to portray their wealthier counterparts as thin. By the late nineteenth century, women's magazines were sending strong messages about body size, standardized sizes had been introduced, and clothing was being mass-produced. Nonetheless, such full-bodied women as Lillie Langtry and Lillian Russell were quite popular and praised for their beauty. In the 1890s, American illustrator Charles Dana Gibson began depicting the ideal young American woman as tall, thin, and athletic. By the 1920s, the Gibson Girl had given way to the It Girl, Clara Bow. Bow personified the image of the flapper, a thin, boyish look that women dieted and bound their breasts to attain. With the depression and World War II, the ideals for women became more mature and the body size slightly heavier. This change is reflected in the sex symbols of the 1940s and 1950s (such as Rita Hayworth, Betty Grable, and Marilyn Monroe).

By the mid-1950s, thinness was again being emphasized. The Barbie Doll, whose real-life proportions would be 36-18-33, was introduced in 1959. Four years later, Weight Watchers was founded. In 1967, Twiggy, a 5' 7" English model who weighed 97 pounds, came to the United States and became an instant celebrity. Young women strove to look like her. Since then, the "ideal" female body has grown progressively thinner. According to Deborah Gregory's "Heavy Judgment," society's preference for thinness has become so profound that women who are not thin are routinely treated with disdain. To support her assertions, Gregory offers not only her personal experience but also statistics, studies, guidelines, documentaries, publications, and interviews.

Indeed, Gregory felt the sting of discrimination when she was suddenly proclaimed too fat to be a model. Lest any think, though, that the discrimination is isolated to the entertainment industry, Gregory provides examples of large women outside the industry who have experienced discrimination, both professionally and socially. Referring to studies comparing the social and financial status of overweight men and women, Gregory demonstrates that overweight people suffer financially and socially and that overweight women suffer demonstrably more than overweight men. Since a higher percentage of African American and Latino women are overweight than white women, it stands to reason that these populations are disproportionately harmed by society's demand that women be thin.

According to Gregory, the discrimination suffered by overweight women stems from society's mistaken assumption that people who are overweight are character deficient. In fact, people do not have complete control over their size and shape. Gregory explains that weight is determined by a number of factors, both biological and psychological. Ironically, one factor that contributes to weight-gain is

---

[1]Cf. Plato's *Symposium:* "Remember how in that communion only, beholding beauty with the eye of the mind, he will be enabled to bring forth, not imagees of beauty, but realities (for he has hold not of an image but of a reality), and bringing forth and nourishing true virtue to become the friend of God and be immortal, if mortal man may."

low-calorie dieting: Once the dieter begins to eat normally, they will not only gain back the weight they lost, but "an additional 20 percent above that." Genetically, African American women are predisposed to being overweight. In addition, "Black women may use food and body size to fight personal trauma." Because of the emphasis society places on body size, many women have a self-esteem that fluctuates with their weight. Society's rejection of overweight women can lead women who are overweight to feel ashamed and reject themselves.

Suggestions

Pre-Reading Exercise: One approach is to have students focus on language and the way in which it is used to describe as well as to judge.

Ask students to list words that are used to describe people who are overweight (e.g., blubbery, chubby, corpulent, fat, fleshy, heavy, large, obese, portly, potbellied, plump, pudgy, roly-poly, rotund, stocky, stout, tubby, thick, weighty, etc.). Then, ask them to list words that are used to describe people who are underweight (e.g., anorexic, emaciated, gaunt, lean, scrawny, skeletal, skinny, slender, slim, svelte, thin, willowy, etc.).

When students have completed their lists, instruct them to rank the words on their lists according to the sizes they denote. Then, ask them to go through their list and identify which words are "objective" and which are "judgmental." After they have read the articles, have them pick from their lists the words that Gregory and Fox use to describe body sizes and discuss what each author's word choice reveals about her perceptions.

Another approach is to have each student list two to three celebrities whom they believe to be remarkably beautiful or good looking. Once students have completed their lists, ask them to choose one of the people they identified and to list the qualities that make that person so good looking. Collect the lists and create an alphabetized master list of the qualities they identified. (Alphabetizing the list discourages students from thinking that the order of qualities reflects the instructor's preferences, beliefs, etc.) This master list can be used as the basis for discussion after students have examined Gregory's essay or it can be used as suggested in exercise three.

1. To have students examine the development of Gregory's argument, assign each group a section of the essay to outline and critique for the class. Students might be directed to consider questions such as the following:

   a. What is the main idea of the section?

   b. List the points that she uses to develop the main idea. Are her points logical? Explain.

   c. How does she support each of her points? (Analysis? Authorities? Definitions? Examples? Facts? Information? Statistics? Studies? etc.) Is her support valid? Explain.

   d. Are there any opposing points or counter-arguments that Gregory overlooks or minimizes? Explain.

   e. Evaluate her organization. (Does each sentence lead logically to the next? Does each paragraph lead logically to the next? etc.)

   f. After each group presents its analysis to the class, discussion should focus on how well Gregory's overall thesis is supported.

2. Students might be asked to analyze Gregory's use of her source material. Have them look up the word *obesity* in a general dictionary and a medical dictionary. Also, have them read "Maintain Healthy Weight" from the *1990 Dietary Guidelines for Americans*. This section is included in Appendix 2 and can be reproduced and distributed to students.

   Gregory claims that the medical community is "struggling to define obesity"; however, medical dictionaries provide a consistent definition: *obesity* is the condition of exceeding by 20 percent or more one's recommended weight. (Nonmedical dictionaries are far less precise, defining the word as the condition of being grossly overweight.)

Actually, the medical community appears to be trying to determine exactly what constitutes a healthy weight. Gregory notes that the *1990 Dietary Guidelines for Americans* include "three criteria for determining the appropriateness of a person's weight: disease risk factors, weight tables (which group men and women together) and body-fat distribution." In an apparent attempt to minimize the significance of the weight–height tables, Gregory quotes a member of the *Dietary Guidelines* committee as saying, "'The most important factor [in assessing a person's weight-related health risks] is whether the person has a medical condition that would improve with weight loss. . . .'" Interestingly, the *Dietary Guidelines for Americans* makes no such distinction: "Whether your weight is 'healthy' depends on how much of your weight is fat, where in your body the fat is located, and whether you have weight-related medical problems, such as high blood pressure, or a family history of such problems." The *Dietary Guidelines* further states,

> If your weight is within the range in the table, if your waist-to-hip ratio does not place you at risk, and if you have no medical problem for which your doctor advises you to gain or lose weight, there appears to be no health advantage to changing your weight. If you do not meet all of these conditions, or if you are not sure, you may want to talk to your doctor about how your weight might affect your health and what you should do about it.

The impression given by Gregory is that one's risk of weight-related disease is the fundamental factor in determining one's healthy weight. This may or may not be true, but it is not the conclusion published in the *1990 Dietary Guidelines for Americans*.

3. To encourage students to consider the relationship between culture and beauty, have them examine various artistic representations of women. Students might be asked to consider works such as the following:

    Botticelli's *Venus* (fifteenth century)

    Titian's Venus and the Lute Player (sixteenth century)

    Peter Paul Rubens' Bacchus (seventeenth century)

    François Boucher's Naiads and Triton (eighteenth century)

    Gustave Courbet's Woman with a Parrot (nineteenth century)

    Pierre-Auguste Renoir's Apres le Bain (early-twentieth century)

    Fernando Botero's Bagno (late-twentieth century)

(The pieces listed above are frequently reproduced and easily accessible. Obviously, the works of art that might be used for this assignment are by no means limited to these seven paintings.)

Explain to students that the lists they created as part of the pre-reading exercise were merged to create a master list. Distribute the master list, divide the class into groups, and give each group a reproduction to examine. Have students evaluate the beauty of each woman according to the criteria delineated on the master list. When all of the groups have completed the task, have each one share its evaluation and discuss why the woman would or would not be considered beautiful by today's standards. These presentations should lead to a discussion of the influence of culture on perceptions of beauty.

4. A good exercise in synthesis is to have students research the lengths to which people will go to be "beautiful" and then relate their findings to Gregory's essay. Gregory asserts that health ought to be one's primary concern. However, people have often sacrificed their health and comfort in order to attain their society's preferred look. (e.g., despite the fact that prolonged exposure to the ultraviolet rays seriously damages the skin and can lead to skin cancer, many white Americans not

only spend hours lying in the sun in order to darken their skin, some also regularly go to tanning salons.)

Students might be asked to locate information on body modification in non-Western societies. This can be done by assigning each student a specific modification or a specific culture to research and directing them to prepare a report to present to the class. Common forms of body alteration are body piercing, breast modification, foot binding, head flattening, neck elongation, scarification, and tattooing. Some of the many societies that practice or have practiced body mutilation are the Aborigines of Australia (nasal piercing for bone-ornament), the Ainu of northern Japan (ear piercing for ninkari), the Chinese (foot binding), the Kayapo of the Amazon (scarification), the Kwakiutl of the Northwest Coast (head flattening), the Mangbettu of Central Africa (head shaping), the Masai of East Africa (ear piercing for adornment and elongation), the Maori of New Zealand (tattooing), the Padaung of Myanmar (neck elongation), and the Sara of Southern Sudan (lip piercing for labret).

To have students focus on body modification in the West, have them research the history of body-shaping apparel (e.g., corsets, girdles, and brassieres) and body mutilation and modification (branding, piercing, and tattooing as well as abdominoplasty, cervicofacial rhytidectomy, liposuction, otoplasty, and rhinoplasty).

5. To engage in a research project that relates specifically to weight, students can use InfoTrac (Keyword: "set point" weight) to explore the idea of a "set point" (the theory that each individual's body has a point which it "sets" as its correct weight and attempts to maintain).

6. The influence of social pressure can be explored by teaming "Heavy Judgement" with "Barbie Doll" (p. 20) and "Mr. Z" (p. 20), and/or "Life after High School" (p. 132).

Starved Out and Heavy Judgment

1. Both Gregory and Jayme suffer socially because of their body size (discrimination, rejection, criticism, etc.). Have students compare and contrast the types of discrimination they experience.

2. Health figures prominently in the discussions of both essays. Have students compare and contrast Gregory and Jayme's physical and mental health.

3. "Barbie Doll" (p. 20) and "The Fat Girl" (p. 120) be assigned along with "Starved Out" and "Heavy Judgment" in order to explore further the value American society places on physical beauty.

4. To encourage students to consider the relevance of body size and "acceptability" in terms of celebrity, assign them a short research project. They should choose two or three of the celebrities they identified during the pre-reading exercise and locate a fan Web page that includes "vital statistics" such as height and weight. With that information, they should use the formula reprinted in their book to determine the person's Body-Mass Index (BMI). (The formula for the BMI is included in the note on *height-body-mass index*, p. 258). Their findings can be discussed in class.

5. While *obese* and *anorexic* have very specific medical definition, terms such as *fat, overweight, thin, skinny,* and *scrawny* are quite subjective. According to Ellen Creager, some female celebrities are so underweight that they meet the American Psychological Association's weight criteria for anorexia nervosa (a BMI of 17.5 or below): Cameron Diaz, Calista Flockhart, Elle Macpherson, Kate Moss, Julia Roberts, Diana Ross, and Niki Taylor. (Source: Creager, Ellen. "It Takes Effort—and Maybe Anorexia—to Be Model-Thin." *Detroit Free Press*, 21 July 1998. 17 Sept. 2005 <http://www.freep.com/news/health/qstar21.htm>).

Locate pictures of six to ten famous women of varying sizes and shapes. Block out the faces so that students do not know who the women are. Show the pictures to students, asking them to note on a sheet of paper their opinion of each woman's body size (does the woman need to gain weight, lose weight, or stay the way she is?). Once all of the pictures have been shown, tally up the students' opinions and use them as a springboard for class discussion.

Include female celebrities whose BMI may indicate that they are either over- or under-weight: Roseanne Barr, Kathy Bates, Delta Burke, Nell Carter, Kim Coles, Cameron Diaz, Conchata Farrel, Calista Flockhart, Aretha Franklin, Star Jones, Wynona Judd, Ricki Lake, Elle Macpherson, Kate Moss, Kathy Najimy, Jessye Norman, Rosie O'Donnell, Julia Roberts, Linda Ronstadt, Diana Ross, Niki Taylor, Liz Torres, and Oprah Winfrey.

6. Eating disorders are most commonly associated with adolescent and adult females, but they are becoming more and more prevelent among boys and men. Students can use InfoTrac to explore this phenomenon and the issues it raises (Keyword: eating disorders boys; Keyword: eating disorders men).

When Is It Rape?

Nancy Gibbs

The topic of date rape moved to the forefront of public discussion in April, 1991 when William Kennedy Smith was charged with sexual battery. In July (the month after Gibbs published this article), the Indianapolis police revealed that Mike Tyson had been accused of rape. Kobe Bryant was charged with sexual assaul in 2003. And, a year later, In 2004, another woman accused William Kennedy Smith of rape.[1] Since then, the topic has continued to receive attention due in part to the increase in the number of sexual assaults involving the use of so-called "date rape drugs": Gamma-hydroxybutyrate (GHB, Goop), flunitrazepam (Rohypnol, Roofies), and ketamine (Special K). A person who drinks a beverage that has been laced with a tiny dose of these colorless and odorless drugs will usually be incapacitated within a half hour. When the drug wears off, the person often has only a vague memory of what happened. Thus, the date rape drugs impede a woman's ability to resist a sexual assault as well as her ability to recall the details of the assault. Without these details, authorities have an extraordinarily difficult time prosecuting alleged rapists (Woodworth). Most people would likely agree that a man is committing rape if he clandestinely slips some "Goop" into a woman's drink, waits until she is intoxicated, and then forces her to have sex. Sometimes the situation is not so clear.

In "When Is It Rape?" Gibbs discusses the contentiousness surrounding the phrase "date rape" as well as the crime it supposedly denotes. Initially, Gibbs' approach seems relatively straightforward, but, by the end of the article, students are sometimes confused as to her overall point. Constructing an informal outline helps them look closely at the text and identify the topics she covers. Once they have done this, students should be able to see how Gibbs' ideas connect. They should also be prepared to explore the issues she raises, the support she offers, and the analysis she provides.

In discussing the prevalence of rape, Gibbs sites statistics but fails to provide her source(s), making it difficult for the reader to verify the accuracy of Gibbs' information and to ascertain the validity of the studies from which they were gleaned. According to Gibbs, "experts" estimate that 25 percent of women will be raped at some point in their lifetime, 20 percent of these crimes are committed by strangers, 10 percent of rapes will be reported to police, and less than 5 percent of rapists will be

---

[1] On Dec. 11, 1991, Smith was acquitted of sexual assault and battery. On Feb. 10, 1992, Tyson was found guilty of one count of rape, and two counts of deviate sexual conduct; on March 6, he was sentenced to six years in prison and fined $30,000. On Sept. 1, 2004, the charges against Bryant were dismissed. On Jan. 4, 2005, the charges against Smith were dismissed.

incarcerated. The assertion that one in four women will be raped is often made and is typically drawn from the work of Mary Koss, a psychology professor who directed *Ms.* magazine's study of rape on college campuses.

Based on interviews with over 3,500 randomly selected college women, Koss concluded that 15.4 percent had been raped and 12.1 percent had experienced an attempted rape.[2] Koss' methodology has been criticized by some scholars, leading them to assert that her estimates are too high.[3] Since Koss' findings were published in 1985, other studies have been conducted to determine the prevalence of sexual violence against women. To avoid any ambiguity with regard to the meaning of rape, researchers usually specify their definitions.

The results of these studies indicate that Koss' findings (and Gibbs' statistics) are inaccurate, but not nearly as inaccurate as one might wish:

- 22 percent of women surveyed have been "forced to do something sexual" in their lifetime. (Michael 223)

- 18 percent of women surveyed have experienced a completed or attempted rape at some time in their life. (Tjaden and Thoennes 6)

- 35 percent of women who were raped and/or sexually assaulted during the survey years (1992–1994) were between 18–24 years old, the traditional ages of college students (8 percent were 12–14 years old; 12 percent were 15–17; 21 percent were 18–21; 14 percent were 22–24 ; 9 percent were 25–29 ; 13 percent were 30–34; 9 percent were 35–39; 13 percent were 40 or older). (Perkins 3)

- At least 86 percent of women who have been raped and/or physically assaulted since age 18 were assaulted by someone they knew. (Tjaden and Thoennes 8) Note: The following total exceeds 100 percent because some victims had multiple perpetrators:

  - 75 percent by an intimate (current or former husband, cohabiting partner, boyfriend, date)
  - 17 percent by an acquaintance (friend, neighbor, coworker, etc.)
  - 9 percent by a relative other than a husband
  - 14 percent by a stranger

- 9 percent of sexual assaults were committed by perpetrators who had a weapon. (Rennison 7)

- 68 percent of rape/sexual assaults were not reported. (Rennison 9)

Indeed, Gibbs is correct in her assertion that women are often victims of sexual assault and that the majority of their assailants are not strangers.

While there is general agreement that *rape* denotes forced sexual intercourse, there are four primary positions regarding the application of the word to instances of "date rape." Gibbs presents each of these positions without explicitly evaluating them. Thus, students are able to analyze each position and identify its weakness(es) with little guidance from the writer. Gibbs first relays the opinion of those who believe that the word *rape* should be used to denote only acts of sexual intercourse that are forced on a victim by a predatory stranger.

According to those who hold this opinion, *date* is a situation in which sex might occur, and no judge can truly know "whether there was genuine mutual consent." Implicit in this position is the assumption that women are likely to make false allegations and that an act of violence must be perpetrated by a person unknown to the victim in order for the act to be considered a true crime. In fact,

---

[2] Koss' findings are summarized in Robin Warshaw, *I Never Called It Rape* (New York: HarperPerennial, 1988).

[3] For example, see Nara Schoenberg and Sam Roe, "The Making of an Epidemic," Part 1 *Toledo Blade*, 10 Oct. 1993: 3+; Part 2 *Toledo Blade*, 11 Oct. 1993: 4+. See also, Katie Roiphe, *The Morning After: Sex, Fear, and Feminism* (Boston: Little, Brown, 1993).

few false complaints are filed. According to the 1996 FBI Uniform Crime Report, only 8 percent of rape complaints were determined to be "unfounded" (Sec. 2, 24).

The notion that one's assailant must be a stranger in order to be considered a rapist appears to be illogical. The majority of women who are forced to have nonconsensual sexual intercourse know their assailants. The same is true of the majority of people who are murdered (FBI Sec. 2, 17). There also seems to be a lack of logic in arguing that a crime should be defined according to a court's ability to *know* whether or not an allegation is true. Judges and juries rely daily on evidence, not omniscience, to determine the innocence or guilt of defendants. As Koch points out in "Death and Justice," "If government functioned only when the possibility of error didn't exist, government wouldn't function at all."

A less extreme view is taken by those who acknowledge that date rape exists but argue that it is not as horrible a crime as street rape. Those who hold this opinion believe that date rape is an instance of "a man go[ing] too far on a date without a woman's consent." This phrase minimizes the crime in the same way that saying someone "had a little too much to drink" minimizes that person's drunkenness. The phrase also reveals a belief that men are unable to control their sexual urges and are, therefore, not really responsible for their actions. This is, of course, one of the prevalent myths regarding rape and has been a successful defense in a number of rape cases. In fact, it is this type of thinking that led the man charged in Florida with raping a woman at knife point to be acquitted: "his victim had been wearing lace shorts and no underwear" (par. 13).

The contention that date rape is less "ghastly" than "street rape" is refuted by those who argue that "rape is rape, and any form of forced sex . . . is a crime." This may be true in terms of general denotation, but the American judicial system does delineate levels of crimes (e.g., first degree murder, second degree murder, voluntary manslaughter, involuntary manslaughter, etc.). Rape (like assault) is a category and that can be subdivided by type. These subdivisions are based not on the relationship between the victim and the assailant, but on the circumstances surrounding the crime (e.g., Was the rape premeditated? Was the victim threatened with a weapon? Did the rapist inflict additional physical injury?). A variety of elements are considered in determining the classification of any crime, and rape is no exception.

The argument that the word *rape* is appropriately applied to everything from forced sex to "inappropriate innuendo" is befuddling. Those who hold this belief appear to have conflated the four fundamental definitions of the noun (and the verb) *rape*. The first three denotations are literal and denote specific physical actions: forced sex, abduction, and theft and destruction. The fourth definition of *rape* is figurative and denotes nonphysical violations that are outrageous and cause damage or harm. (The literal and figurative denotations are used in the expression, "A rape victim is raped twice: first by a man and then by the justice system.") Translating the argument that inappropriate innuendo is rape into a syllogism makes readily apparent the argument's fallacy:

Major Premise:	Rape = harmful action
Minor Premise:	Inappropriate innuendo = harmful action
Conclusion:	Therefore, rape = inappropriate innuendo

The major premise is sound, but the minor premise is not. Innuendo may be inappropriate. It may be offensive. It may even be outrageous. But, an innuendo is not likely to do psychological harm or damage. By analyzing this argument as well as the other three positions that Gibbs presents, students come to see that the use of the word *rape* to describe "date rape" reflects politics and acculturation.

Students are aware that they have been socialized to view men as sexually aggressive and women as sexually passive and can usually identify songs, movies, television shows, advertisements, and so forth that contain those messages. The effect of these messages is clearly seen in the study of Rhode Island sixth- to ninth-graders mentioned by Gibbs. She does not cite her source, but a 1996 study of eighth grade students in North Carolina revealed similar patterns (Boxley, Lawrance, and Gruchow). According to this study, approximately one-third of male adolescents believe in a number of rape myths. In fact, according to this study, male adolescents are at least twice as likely as females to believe the following:

- "A woman who goes to the home or apartment of a man on their first date implies that she is willing to have sex."
- "A woman who is stuck-up and thinks she is too good to talk to guys on the street deserves to be taught a lesson."
- "If a girl is making out and she lets things get out of hand, it is her own fault if her partner forces sex on her."
- "In the majority of rapes, the victim is loose or has a bad reputation."

That one third of young men believe the rape myths suggest that the problem with date rape stems from far more than intoxication and poor communication. It seems to stem from belief in the stereotypes about men and women. This may also explain why a woman and a man can have differing views of the same sexual encounter, with the woman defining it as rape and the man defining it as sex.

Works Consulted

Boxley, Jeanne, Lynette Lawrance, and Harvey Gruchow. "A Preliminary Study of Eighth Grade Students' Attitudes toward Rape Myths and Women's Roles." *Journal of School Health,* 65 (1995): 96–101.

Koss, Mary and Cheryl Oros. "Sexual Experiences Survey: A Research Instrument Investigating Sexual Aggression and Victimization." *Journal of Consulting and Clinical Psychology,* 50 (1982): 455-7.

Michael, R., J. Gagnon, E. Lauman, and G. Kolata. *Sex in America: A Definitive Survey.* New York: Warner Books, 1994.

Perkins, Craig A. *Age Patterns of Victims of Serious Crimes.* United States. Dept. of Justice. Bureau of Justice Statistics. NCJ-162031. Washington, DC: GPO, 1997.

Rennison, Callie M. *Criminal Victimization in 1998, Changes 1997–1998 with Trends 1993–1998.* United States. Dept. of Justice. Bureau of Justice Statistics. NCJ-176353. Washington, DC: GPO, 1999.

Roiphe, Katie. *The Morning After: Sex, Fear, and Feminism.* Boston: Little, Brown, 1993.

Schoenberg, Nana and Sam Roe. "The Making of an Epidemic." Part 1 *Toldeo Blade,* 10 Oct. 1993: 3+; Part 2 *Toldeo Blade* 11 Oct. 1993: 4+.

Tjaden, Patricia and Nancy Thoennes. *Prevalence, Incidence, and Consequences of Violence against Women: Findings from the National Violence against Women Survey.* United States. Dept. of Justice. Office of Justice. National Institute of Justice. NCJ-172837. Washington, DC: GPO, 1998.

United States. Dept. of Justice. Federal Bureau of Investigation. *Uniform Crime Report for the United States,* 1996. Washington, DC: GPO, nd. 12 Oct. 1999 <http://www.fbi.gov/ucr.htm>.

Warshaw, Robin. *I Never Called It Rape.* New York: HarperPerennial, 1988.

Woodworth, Terrance. *DEA Congressional Testimony before the House Commerce Committee Subcommittee on Oversight and Investigations.* 11 March 1999. United States. Department of Justice. Drug Enforcement Administration. Office of Diversion Control. 3 Oct. 99 <http://www.usdoj.gov/dea/pubs/cngrtest/ct990311.htm>.

Suggestions

Pre-Reading Exercise: Students can be helped to assess their own knowledge of rape by giving them a brief quiz:

A.   What is the percentage of women who have experienced an attempted or completed rape?

    1. <5 percent   2. 5–10 percent   3. 11–20 percent   4. 21–30 percent

B.   How many rapists have a weapon ((knife, gun, etc.) when committing rape?

    1. 1 out of 11   2. 4 out of 11   3. 8 out of 11   4. 10 out of 11

C.   What percentage of rapes are not reported to police?

    1. <25 percent   2. 25–50 percent   3. 51–75 percent   4. >75 percent

D.   By whom are women most frequently raped?

    1. a relative   2. an intimate   3. an acquaintance   4. a stranger

This quiz might be followed by asking students to define the word *rape*. During discussion of the article, both their answers to the quiz and their definitions can be examined.

1.   Students need to look closely at the text to understand Gibbs' thesis and the relevancy of her main points. Have them construct an informal outline of the article:

    Synopsis (par. 1)

    Terminology (par. 2)

    Myths about rape (par. 3)

    Gender-based perceptions regarding "date rape" (par. 4)

    Disagreement about denotation of *rape* (par. 5)

    Four positions on the appropriate definition of *rape* (pars. 6–8)

    Illustration: date rape (pars. 9–11)

    Typical reaction of a victim; typical action of an assailant (par. 12)

    Treatment of a rape victim (pars. 13–14)

    Changes in perception of rape (par. 15)

    Use of the word *rape* as a political weapon (par. 16)

    Illustration: false accusation (pars. 17–18)

    Communication of consent (par. 19)

    Impediments to communication; acculturation (par. 20)

    Conclusions (pars. 21–22)

    Once they have completed this process, students generally have a good grasp of Gibbs' thesis, main points, development, and organization.

2.   Have students examine each of the four positions regarding the appropriate use of the word *rape:*

a.   Summarize how each of the four groups believes that rape should be defined, explain the reasons given for this belief, and analyze the validity of the reasons.

    Students' responses can be used as the basis for a class discussion. As the discussion progresses, students will most likely provide their own opinions, but, if they do not do so, the following questions can be posed:

b.   Should "rape" be a category with varying classifications or should it be a word that is used exclusively to denote a sexual assault by a stranger? Explain and defend your answer.

c.   If there are to be classifications, how should they be delineated? Explain.

d. If rape is to be used solely to denote a sexual assault by a stranger, how should a sexual assault by an acquaintance be denoted? Explain.

3. Once students have a clear understanding of the four positions, divide the class into four groups and assign each group one of the four positions. Provide them with a scenario and ask them to explain how someone with their assigned point of view would likely respond.

A good scenario to use is from the ninety-second film that was shown prior to many London screenings of Kubrick's film, *Eyes Wide Shut* (1999). The film, produced for Women against Rape, presents scenes from a date but contains no dialogue. Instead, each scene is accompanied by short statements:

"You call."

"You meet."

"You drink."

"You dance."

"You flirt."

"You leave."

"Nightcap, coffee?"

"You touch."

"You kiss."

"She stops."

"You don't."

When first presenting this to students, stop reading here. After students have written and shared their responses, reread the statements, including the ones that follow.

The film then shows a picture of the man holding the woman down.

"What are you doing?" it asks.

The audience is then informed that two out of three rape victims know their attacker. (*Source*: UK Film Highlights Date Rape Campaign." *BBC Online Network*, 10 Sept. 1999. 11 Nov. 1999 <http://news.bbc.co.uk/hi/english/uk/newsidpercent5F443000/443144.stm>.)

4. Have students examine the stories of the thirty-two-year-old woman in Tampa and the male freshman at a liberal arts college.

a. One approach would be to pose specific questions for students to answer:

• Why did the woman in Tampa not raise an alarm when she awoke with the man on top of her?

• She knew she felt violated. Why was she confused about whether or not it was rape?

• If the man heard her say "no," why did he not stop?

• Why did the male freshman have sex with his former friend when he knew it was not a good idea?

• He knows he feels violated. Why is he afraid?

• If his friend believed she had been raped, why did she not press charges?

• In what ways are the experiences of the woman in Tampa and the male freshman similar? Explain.

• In what ways are their experiences dissimilar? Explain.

b. Another approach would be to have students stage a trial of the man who allegedly raped the woman in the Tampa hotel and of the woman who allegedly defamed the male freshman. To do this, divide the class into four groups, assigning one group the woman in Tampa, one group her alleged rapist, one group the male freshman, and one group his alleged defamer. Instruct each group to examine the allegations presented in the text, develop their person's view of the events, and form a defense for her or him. The basic events cannot be changed: Groups can only develop their character's view or interpretation of the events.

Give the groups fifteen to twenty minutes to complete their tasks. When time is up, the two opposing groups should present their cases to the jury (the other two groups). The teacher should act as cross-examiner, questioning any discrepancies, inconsistencies, and so forth. After each side has presented its case and been cross-examined, the jury should discuss what has been said and arrive at a conclusion. The plaintiff and defendant groups should not be privy to the jury's deliberations or verdict until the remaining trial has been conducted and concluded. Then, each jury can present its findings, and the class can discuss the process and the experience.

5. Either have students identify all of the beliefs they have heard articulated about rape or provide them with the following list:

- Rape is a crime of passion—the assailant just couldn't control his sexual urges.
- Rapists look like criminals.
- Rapists are sexual perverts.
- Women provoke rape by the way they dress and/or act—they "ask for it."
- Women who engage in heavy petting but don't want to go all the way deserve what they get.
- Women really want to be raped.
- Women who have been sexually active can't be raped (or, only virgins can be raped).
- Women say "no" when they mean "yes."
- Women can't be raped against their will.
- Women often falsely accuse men of rape.
- Women who allow a man to pay for everything on a date owe him something.
- Women aren't raped by men they know.
- Women who are young and attractive are the only ones who are raped.
- A man who is intoxicated when he assaults a woman can't be charged with rape.
- A woman who is intoxicated when she is assaulted can't claim she has been raped.

Have students get into groups and determine which of the myths are stated or assumed by anyone in the essay. During the discussion of the groups' findings, students might be asked to also discuss each of the myths.

6. Students might be asked to examine the "character question" as it relates to rape trials. To do this, they might use InfoTrac to locate information about the trials of William Kennedy Smith and Mike Tyson. Patricia Bowman, Kennedy's accuser, was depicted as having a "wild streak." Desiree Washington, on the other hand, was a Miss America contestant, an honor student, and a Sunday school teacher. Have students examine the two cases and determine what influence—if any—the characters of the women involved might have had on the jury's decision.

7. After reading and discussing the essay, students might be asked to watch and discuss a film that relates to the issue of rape. Three such films are *In Your Dreams* (1997), *A Reason to Believe* (1995), and *Girls Town* (1996).

In Your Dreams. Jamie and Clare, university students, have an enjoyable first date. Jamie walks Clare to her apartment and leaves. He is soaked in a downpour and returns to her apartment, asking to stay the night. The next day, Jamie is arrested for rape. At the trial, Jamie's point of view and Clare's point of view are presented. Was it rape?

A Reason to Believe. Charlotte attends a party at her boyfriend's fraternity house while he is out of town. Realizing she is drunk, she goes to his room to sleep, but she is soon joined by Jim, a fraternity brother with whom she had danced, and is forced into a sexual encounter. Charlotte feels guilty and ashamed and has a great deal of difficulty revealing what happened. When she does, she is not believed. Jim genuinely believes that what occurred between them was sex, not rape.

Girls Town. Three high school friends, trying to understand why Nikki (one of their group) committed suicide, steal her journal and discover that she had been raped. The film focuses on the evolution of the relationship between the three surviving friends as they struggle with their own lives and reveal their own secrets.

8. The controversy surrounding the definition of rape is not new, but the laws have changed. Have students compare and contrast their state's definition of rape with the definition from *Bouviers Law Dictionary,* 1856 Edition. A photo-ready copy of Bouviers' definition appears in Appendix 2 (p. 194). Students can locate their state's laws through Cornell Law School's Legal Information Institute at <http://www.law.cornell.edu/statutes.html> or Washburn School of Law's WashLaw Web, Search State Law at <http://www.washlaw.edu/uslaw/statelaw.html>.

9. To help students consider the influence of culture on perceptions of rape, present them with the following scenarios, each of which is based on stories from the Old Testament. Would they consider these instances of rape? Why or why not?

   - A powerful king sees a beautiful woman, sends his soldiers to bring her to him, and has sex with her. (David and Bathsheba, 2 Samuel 11:2–4)

   - A woman gives her husband one of her slaves and tells him to have sex with her. (Abram and Hagar, Genesis 16:1–5)

   - A woman plies a man with vast quantities of alcohol and, when he is sufficiently intoxicated, crawls into bed with him and has sex. (Lot's daughters and Lot, Genesis 19:30–36)

   - A man coaxes his nurse to his bed, overpowers her, and has sex with her. (Amnon and Tamar, 2 Samuel 13:13–15)

   - To keep from being sexually assaulted himself, a man gives his wife to those assailing him. As a result of the repeated assaults, his wife dies. (Levite and his wife, Judges 19:22–28)

   - A man offers his daughters to those who are attempting to sexually assault his guests. (Lot offers his daughters, Genesis 19:5–8; cf. Levite's host offers his daughter, Judges 19:22–28)

   (Punishments for adultery and rape are specified in Deuteronomy 22.)

10. To examine how "signals" can be wrongly perceived as sexual, team "When Is It Rape?" with "The Myth of the Latin Woman" (p. 232)

11. To have students examine the idea that a victim is often blamed for being a victim, team this essay with "Shame" (p. 213) and "Daddy Tucked the Blanket" (p. 215). (It is not uncommon for those who are impoverished to be blamed for being poor. They are often dismissed as *lazy* or *shiftless,* points that are addressed by both Williams and Gregory.)

Time for a Change on Drugs: Americans Are Ahead of Politicians on This One

Molly Ivins

and

Legalization of Narcotics: Myths and Reality

Joseph A. Califano

These essays by Ivins and Califano focus on the legalization of drugs, an issue that has been the subject of public debate for at least thirty years. In 1972, the National Commission on Marihuana and Drug Abuse released its report and made a variety of recommendations, one of which was the decriminalization of marijuana:

> Marihuana's relative potential for harm to the vast majority of individual users and its actual impact on society does not justify a social policy designed to seek out and firmly punish those who use it. This judgment is based on prevalent use patterns, on behavior exhibited by the vast majority of users, and on our interpretations of existing medical and scientific data. This position also is consistent with the estimate by law enforcement personnel that the elimination of use is unattainable (par. 7).

In the past few years, conservatives such as William F. Buckley have spoken out in favor of drug legalization. This unanticipated advocacy has intensified the debate and elicited reactions ranging from outrage to approval. Ivins and Califano have decidedly different points of view regarding drug legalization. Their essays provide students with the opportunity to examine opposing views and to analyze each writer's focus, main points, supporting details, and tone. Students may initially equate critique with disagreement. Whether or not one agrees with a writer's position is, of course, irrelevant. What matters is how well the writer develops and supports his or her ideas.

In "Time for a Change on Drugs," Molly Ivins, a political commentator and humorist, suggests that mainstream politicians may be edging toward acknowledging a truth the public has long known: The war on drugs is not working. The people are ready for a reasonable policy, says Ivins, pointing to the legalization of marijuana for medical use in five states as well as the election of Jesse Ventura (a candidate "elected in large part by young people who like his libertarian straight talk on drugs"). She disparages both liberals and conservatives for having lacked the courage to address the drug issue in an open, honest, reasonable manner. Liberals have been deathly afraid of being labeled "'soft on drugs'" while conservatives have been using the "cheap scare" of drugs so long that "they're hooked on it." Now that "respected and respectable" leaders have begun to question the usefulness of the war on drugs, mainstream politicians might become more willing to engage in thoughtful dialogue. Ivins encourages politicians to "consider decriminalizing marijuana," reconsider "mandatory minimum sentences," and immediately address the disparity in sentencing for crimes involving crack cocaine and those involving powder cocaine. Ivins concludes that the government's attempt to prohibit drugs have been as futile as its attempt to prohibit alcohol. Despite the seriousness of her subject and the earnestness of her observations, Ivins' article is humorous. The humor, of course, stems from her tone as well as her sense of irony and use of language.

Joseph A. Califano, the president and chairperson of the National Center on Addiction and Substance Abuse at Columbia University and the former Secretary of Health, Education, and Welfare in the Carter administration, argues that the legalization of drugs would cause "long-lasting, permanent damage." To prove his thesis, Califano attempts to disprove "myths" about drug use and legalization. Many of the problems with Califano's article are obvious (sweeping generalizations, unsupported assertions, unnamed sources, etc.). Some are less obvious (inaccurate statistics, misrepresented findings, etc.) and would likely be unrealized by readers who did not attempt to verify Califano's supporting evidence. A commentary on each of Califano's counterarguments follows the Suggestions. This commentary provides detailed information that supports, refutes, and amends Califano's points.

Works Consulted

Buckley, William F., Jr., Robert B. Duke, Ethan A. Nadelmann, Kurt L. Schmoke, Robert W. Sweet, and Thomas Szasz. "The War on Drugs Is Lost: A Panel Discussion." *National Review,* 12 Feb. 1996: 34+.

U.S. National Commission on Marihuana and Drug Abuse. "A Social Control Policy for Marihuana." *The Report of the National Commission on Marihuana and Drug Abuse.* 1972. 9 Sept. 1999 <http://www.-druglibrary.org/schaffer/library/studies/nc/ncrec2.htm>.

Suggestions

Pre-Reading Exercise: President Reagan initiated the "war on drugs" in 1982. Many students have grown up hearing the phrase, but many may have given little thought to its significance. Ask students to write a paragraph that addresses questions such as the following: What is the "war on drugs"? How long has it been waged? What is its purpose? How well is it succeeding? Why are some drugs illegal while other drugs are legal? In what ways are illicit drugs a problem for society?

Time for a Change on Drugs

1.   As a political commentator and humorist, Ivins makes no pretense about offering an "objective" view of politicians or political issues. She simply offers her opinions. Sometimes she supports her view; other times, she does not. Have students examine Ivins's approach:

   a.   Identify the words and phrases that Ivins uses to create a sense of camaraderie or friendship with her reader.

   b.   Who is Ivins's intended audience? Explain.

   c.   Summarize Ivins's opinion of politicians. Which of her opinions does she support? Which does she not support?

   d.   Summarize Ivins's opinion of America's current drug policy. Which of her opinions does she support? Which does she not support?

   e.   In Ivins' opinion, what changes need to be made in America's drug policy? Which of her opinions does she support? Which does she not support?

   f.   What effect does her (lack of) support have on your response to her essay? Explain.

2.   Two excerpts that address the issue of "medical marijuana" are reproduced in Appendix 2 (page 195). The first excerpt is from a 1998 article written by Dr. Linda Bayer, a senior writer and strategic analyst for the White House Office of National Drug Control Policy; the second is from a 1999 press release from the White House Office of National Drug Control Policy. Reproduce the excerpts for students and ask them to compare and contrast them. The pieces are quite different in terms of purpose, tone, and content. In addition, they *seem* to contradict each other. Students might be asked to do a bit of research to find out why the Department of Health and Human Services is funding research into "potential medical uses of marijuana's constituent cannabinoids" if, as Dr. Bayer states, medical marijuana has been available for fifteen years.

3.   According to Ivins, Mike Gray (author of *Drug Crazy: How We Got into This Mess and How We Can Get out of It)* "makes a strong case that the war on drugs is just as disastrous a failure as was Prohibition, with exactly the same consequences in the growth of enormous criminal empires." As a research project, students might be asked to discover and write a brief report on the impact that

Prohibition had on the crime. They could look into bootlegging or moonshining, or they could investigate some of the more prominent gangsters of the period: Charles Dion O'Bannion, Al Capone, Vito Genovese, Meyer Lansky, Lucky Luciano, Salvatore Maranzano, Joe (Giuseppe) Masseria, George "Bugs" Moran, Bugsy Siegel, Johnnie Torrie, Roger Touhy, and Frankie Yale. Student findings could be presented to the class. During the ensuing discussion, students could be asked to compare and contrast the Prohibition-era role of gangsters in the alcohol trade with the current role of organized crime and gangs in the drug trade.

4. For a study of tone, "Time for a Change on Drugs" is an excellent work with which to team "What Would Freud Say" (p. 37).

Legalization of Narcotics

1. This is an outstanding article to use in teaching students the need to maintain a healthy skepticism, especially when reading a heavily opinionated piece. One approach is to have students get into groups and critique each of Califano's refutations. Have them consider such questions as the following:

   a. What, if anything, does Califano's phrasing of the myth reveal about his own opinions (regarding drugs and/or the people who believe the myth)?

   b. Identify each of Califano's main assertions and examine his defense of it. Does he support his assertions? Explain. Is his support credible? Explain.

   When students have completed their tasks, have the class share their critiques of the article. ("Commentary on 'Legalization of Narcotics: Myths and Reality'" follows the Suggestions and addresses many of the questions students are likely to raise.)

2. Another approach is to reproduce the related figures and tables that are included in Appendix 2 (pp. 196–214), distribute them to students, and have students examine Califano's points in light of the information they provide:

Figure 2	Estimated numbers of past year users of illicit drugs: 1979–1994, by drug and year. (Line chart)
Figure 3	Percentages reporting past year use of illicit drugs: 1979–1994, by drug and year. (Column chart)
Figure 4	Percentages reporting past month use of any illicit drug with past month use of any illicit drug other than marijuana: 1979–1994. (Line chart)
Figure 5	Average age of past month users of illicit drugs: 1979–1994. (Column chart)
Figure 6	Percentages of 12–17 year-olds reporting past month drug use: 1979–1994, by year and drug. (Column chart)
Figure 7	Mean age of first use: 1968–1997, by drug. (Line chart)
Table 2	Percentage of convicted prison and jail inmates who reported using drugs at the time of their offense, by substance.
Figure 8	Type of crimes committed by offenders reporting being under the influence of drugs or drugs and alcohol at the time of their offense. (Column chart)
Table 3	Type of crimes committed by offenders reporting being under the influence of drugs or drugs and alcohol at the time of their offense.
Figure 9	Apparent gallons of alcohol consumed per person in the United States: 1850–1945. (Line chart)
Figure 10	Apparent gallons of alcohol consumed per person in the United States: 1850–1996. (Line chart)

Time for a Change on Drugs and Legalization of Narcotics

1. Have students compare and contrast the tone of these two essays. (Remind them to point to specific words or phrases that reveal to them the author's attitude.) During class discussion of their findings, students can be asked to explain whether or not the writers' tone is appropriate, given their purposes in writing their essays.

2. Have students examine, explain, and evaluate how each writer uses Prohibition to support his/her point. (Student may need to do some research on Prohibition before they can address this issue.)

3. Ivins refers to a letter sent to U.N. Secretary General Kofi Annan by participants in the 1998 UN General Assembly Special Session (UNGASS). This letter, dated June 1, 1998, asks Annan to "initiate a truly open and honest dialogue regarding the future of global drug control policies—one in which fear, prejudice and punitive prohibitions yield to common sense, science, public health and human rights." Reproduce the letter for students (see Appendix 2, p. 215) and ask them to write a response to this letter from Califano's point of view.

4. "Crusader Rabbit" (p. 58), a story that deals with heroin addiction, can be assigned along with "Time for a Change on Drugs" and "Legalization of Narcotics."

5. Ask students to outline the effects that methamphetamine has on a user's health, to discuss the steps various states have taken to curb its production, and to explain what Califano and Ivins might say about those steps. Students can locate a great deal of information using InfoTrac (Keyword: methamphetamine AND health; Keyword: methamphetamine AND laws).

Commentary on Legalization of Narcotics: Myths and Reality

Myth: There has been no progress in the war on drugs.

Reality: The U.S. Department of Health and Human Services' National Household Drug Survey . . . reports that, from 1979 to 1994, marijuana users dropped from 23,000,000 to 10,000,000, while cocaine users fell from 4,400,000 to 1,400,000. The drug-using segment of the population also is aging. In 1979, 10 percent were over age 34; today, almost 30 percent are. The number of hardcore addicts has held steady at around 6,000,000. . . .

Comments

Califano does not demonstrate that the "war on drugs" has caused a decline in drug use. Instead, citing statistics from the 1994 National Household Survey on Drug Abuse *(NHSDA)*, he notes that the number of marijuana users and cocaine users has fallen and that the "drug-using segment of the population also is aging." This information is essentially correct (see Figures 2–4, Appendix 2, pp. 196–198).

The *NHSDA* reports that the age of illicit drug users continues to rise (see Figures 5–6, Appendix 2, pp. 199–200). The report also notes that the "heavy drug-using cohorts of the 1970s, including those with severe problems, continue to get older. . . . Nevertheless, in 1994 the rate of current illicit drug use was highest among persons 18–21 and 16–17 years old. Heavy drinking was most prevalent among persons age 18–21 and 22–25" (*NHSDA 1994* 3).

While Califano's statements regarding marijuana use are fundamentally correct, he seems to ignore *NHSDA* findings that do not support his position. Most notably, marijuana use by adolescents began to increase in 1992 and "nearly doubled" between 1992 and 1994 (*NHSDA* 4). This suggests that the use of marijuana among young people is increasing, not decreasing.

According to Califano, the *NHSDA* "reports that, from 1979 to 1994 . . . cocaine users fell from 4,400,000 to 1,400,000." In fact, the *NHSDA* only began to estimate the number of weekly cocaine users in 1985:

- No change in the number of weekly cocaine users has been detected since the survey first estimated this in 1985, indicating a continuing demand for drug abuse treatment services. However, the number of occasional cocaine users has declined dramatically. (2)

- Frequent cocaine use, defined as use on a weekly basis during the past year, has not changed significantly since it was first estimated in 1985, suggesting a continuing demand for drug abuse treatment services. In 1994, 0.3 percent of the population was a frequent cocaine user, the same rate as in 1985. Since 1985, estimates of the number of weekly cocaine users have ranged from 476,000 (in 1993) to 862,000 (in 1988). (3)

- The estimated number of occasional cocaine users (people who used in the past year but less often than monthly) has sharply declined from 8.1 million (4.2 percent of the population) in 1985 to 2.4 million (1.2 percent) in 1994. (13)

Califano also states that the number of "hardcore addicts has held steady at around 6 million." He does not site his source. The 1994 *NHSDA* report notes that its data "have limitations with respect to estimating heavy drug use":

Other researchers have estimated that there are over 2 million frequent cocaine users and over a half million heroin addicts in the United States (Rhodes 1993). These estimates were developed by using various data sources and making a number of assumptions (many of which are of uncertain validity). (31)

Clearly, the difference between Califano's number—6 million—and that of other researchers—2.5 million—is significant.

Myth: Whether to use drugs and become hooked is an adult decision.

Reality: It is children who choose. . . .

Comments

Califano's phrasing of this "myth"—"Whether to use drugs and become hooked is an adult decision"—appears to equate "us[ing] drugs" with "becom[ing] hooked" on drugs. There is, of course, a difference between use and addiction, a distinction that is consistently made by agencies such as the U.S. Department of Health and Human Services. In fact, the U.S. Dept. of Health and Human Services not only acknowledges its inability to make reliable estimates regarding "'hard-core' drug use," it also distinguishes between "occasional use," "monthly use," and "weekly use":

> For 1994-A and prior years, occasional drug use is defined as use in the past year but less often than monthly; for 1994-B, occasional use is defined as use in the past year but on fewer than twelve days. For 1994-A and prior years, monthly or weekly use refer to a tendency within the past year and do not necessarily imply use in the past month or in the past week; for 1994-B, monthly use is defined as use on twelve or more days in the past year and weekly use is defined as use on fifty-one or more days in the past year. (*NHSDA* 74, n. 2)

Califano provides no source or statistics to support his assertion that "an individual who does not smoke, use drugs, or abuse alcohol by twenty-one is virtually certain never to do so." The 1998 *NHSDA* does, however, include information regarding the mean age of first use (see Figure 7, Appendix 2, p. 201).

Myth: Legalized drugs would be only for adults and not available to children.

Reality: Nothing in the American experience gives any credence to the ability to keep legal drugs out of the hands of children. . . .

Comments

Califano again fails to site his sources.

To support his assertion that drug legalization would make drugs more available to children, Califano points out that children use alcohol and nicotine, despite the fact that both drugs are legal only for adults. Califano does not address a central question: Do we determine which substances adults are and are not permitted to consume based on our concern that children might also consume them? If so, would it not then be necessary to outlaw other substances that are potentially or actually harmful? While Califano's point is well taken in terms of accessibility, it ignores the reality that our laws do distinguish between the rights of children and the rights of adults.

Myth: Legalization would reduce crime and social problems.

Reality: Any short-term reduction in arrests from repealing drug laws would evaporate quickly. . . . The U.S. Department of Justice reports that criminals commit six times as many homicides, four times as many assaults, and almost one and a half times as many robberies under the influence of drugs as they do in order to get money to buy drugs.

Comments

Califano seems to misrepresent the Department of Justice's statistics. He merges two catagories: offenders under the influence of drugs at the time of the offense and offenders who committed a crime in order to get money to buy drugs.

According to the U.S. Department of Justice's Bureau of Justice Statistics (BJS):

Overall, 10 percent of Federal prison inmates in 1991, 17 percent of State prison inmates in 1991, and 13 percent of convicted jail inmates in 1989 said they committed their offense to obtain money for drugs. . . . Inmates incarcerated for robbery, burglary, larceny, and drug trafficking most often committed their crime to obtain money for drugs. Inmates who committed homicide, sexual assault, assault, and public-order offenses were least likely to commit offense to obtain money for drugs. (*Drugs and Crime Facts* 1994, 8).

The Bureau of Justice Statistics (BJS) reports that 27 percent of jail inmates and 31 percent of prison inmates reported using drugs at the time of their offense (see Table 2, Appendix 2, p. 202).

Most of the offenders who were under the influence of drugs at the time of the offense committed drug-related crimes (see Figure 8 and Table 3, Appendix 2, p. 203).

The BJS National Crime Victimization Survey asks victims of rape, robbery, and assault about their perceptions of their assailant's drug and alcohol use. Thirty percent believed their assailant was under the influence at the time of the offense: drugs only, 4.3 percent; both drugs and alcohol, 6.1 percent; alcohol only, 18.0 percent; not sure which, 1.6 (*Drugs and Crime Facts 1994*, 4).

Of the homicides committed in the seventy-five most populous counties in the United States in 1988, "circumstances involving illegal drugs, such as a drug scam or dispute over drugs, accounted for 18 percent of the defendants and 16 percent of the victims" (*Drugs and Crime Facts 1994*, 9).

The Department of Justice urges caution in interpreting drug/crime statistics, noting that "the drug/crime relationship is difficult to specify" because:

- Most crimes result from a variety of factors (personal, situational, cultural, economic), so even when drugs are a cause, they are likely to be only one factor among many.

- What is meant by "drug-related" varies from study to study; some studies interpret the mere presence of drugs as having causal relevance while other studies interpret the relationship more narrowly: Reports by offenders about their drug use may exaggerate or minimize the relevance of drugs; drug use measures, such as urinalysis that identifies only very recent drug use, are limited. (*Drug-Related Crime,* 3)

Myth: The American experience with prohibition of alcohol supports drug legalization.

Reality: This ignores two important distinctions: Possession of alcohol for personal consumption was not illegal, and . . . the public and political consensus favoring Prohibition was short-lived. . . .

Comments

Califano does not cite his sources, but according to data from the National Institute of Alcohol and Alcoholism (NIAA), the "apparent per capita consumption of alcohol" was lower the year that Prohibition ended than it was the year it began. By focusing only on the years 1919 and 1934, Califano seems to misrepresent the changing patterns of alcohol consumption in the United States. Per capita consumption of alcohol had reached 2.5 gallons in 1860, had fallen to 1.72 in 1880, had risen to 2.6 in 1910, and had dropped to 1.96 in 1919 (see Figures 9–10, Appendix 2, p. 204). This data is, of course, based on alcohol sales data and, consequently, does not include the consumption of nontaxed alcohol (i.e., black market alcohol or moonshine). Prior to Prohibition, legal sales of alcohol may well have been affected by a variety of factors, including the Civil War and the Temperance Movement. During Prohibition, people who chose to drink made their own wine, beer, and whiskey or bought their liquor from unregulated sources. When Prohibition ended, the Depression was in full swing, and people who did not want to pay the tax on alcohol may well have made their own alcohol or bought it from those who did. The government would have had little ways of estimating this type of commerce (but it did employ revenuers to search out and destroy moonshine stills).

Califano is correct that the number of deaths due to cirrhosis declined from 1910 to 1929. However, according to the NIAA, his numbers are incorrect: The number of men per 100,000 who died from cirrhosis fell from 22.2 in 1911 to 10.9 in 1934, not from 29.5 to 10.7 (*Age-Adjusted Death Rates of Liver Cirrhosis*). Califano gives no reason for choosing 1911 as the date to begin his comparison, but the number of deaths from cirrhosis were higher that year than others (see Figures 11–12, Appendix 2, p. 205). Had he chosen to begin his comparison in 1920, the first full year after Prohibition took effect, he would have noted that the death rate for men dropped from 11.2 percent to 10.9 percent in 1934. A .03 percent decline is admittedly less dramatic than a 19.2 percent decrease.

Califano ignores the fact that cirrhosis is caused not only by alcohol abuse, but also by malnutrition and infections (such as hepatitis). In 1970, the government began to keep records distinguishing between alcohol-related liver cirrhosis, specified liver cirrhosis without mention of alcohol, and unspecified liver cirrhosis without mention of alcohol. Prior to that time, no distinction was made.

Califano claims that "alcohol, unlike illegal drugs such as heroin and cocaine, has a long history of broad social acceptance." Certainly alcohol has a long tradition. For instance, Proverbs 31:6–7 advises, "Give strong drink to one who is perishing, and wine to those in bitter distress; let them drink and forget their poverty, and remember their misery no more."

Opium, too, has a long tradition and is mentioned by the Greek physician Pedanius Dioscorides (A.D. 40–90) in *De Materia Medica*. By the 1700s, opium was widely used as a painkiller and was socially acceptable. (In the late 1700s, Samuel Taylor Coleridge wrote *Kubla Khan* while using opium. In 1822, Thomas De Quincey published "Confessions of an English Opium Eater." The first Opium War began in 1839 when the Chinese tried to stop British traders from importing opium.) Morphine was isolated from opium in the early 1800s. Heroin was derived from morphine in the late 1890s.

Cocaine's history is relatively short. It was not extracted from coca leaves until the mid-1800s. Coca-Cola, first marketed in the 1880s, contained cocaine. Cocaine remained part of the formula for Coca-Cola until 1905, when it was removed and replaced with caffeine. In fact, many perfectly legal and easily accessible tonics contained opiates and cocaine. However, this fact was not always noted on their labels. In 1906, the Pure Food and Drug Act took effect, requiring that a product's label identify its contents. The Harrison Act of 1914 established governmental control of opium, cocaine, and their derivatives. Alcohol was prohibited five years later.

Califano asserts that no "crime wave" was generated by Prohibition. In fact, the bootlegging industry flourished during Prohibition, generating huge profits for gangsters such as Al Capone and leading to the organization of crime. (Today, organized crime deals primarily in drug trafficking and gambling.) Many Americans supported the repeal of Prohibition precisely because the government was unable to enforce the law in large urban areas such as New York and Chicago. The Association against the Prohibition Amendment argued not only that the sale of alcohol would generate tax revenue, but also that repeal of the Amendment would create jobs. The country was, of course, in the midst of the Depression, and jobs were badly needed.

Myth: Greater availability and legal acceptability of drugs would not increase use.

Reality: This defies not only experience, but human nature. In the 1970s, the U.S. de facto decriminalized marijuana. . . . The result was a soaring increase in marijuana use, particularly among youngsters. Today, just 11 percent of Americans report seeing drugs available in the area where they live; after legalization, there could be a place to purchase drugs in every neighborhood.

Comments

Califano fails to demonstrate a cause-and-effect relationship between the *"de facto"* decriminalization of marijuana and the rise in its usage.

Interestingly, in 1992, teenagers began to perceive less risk in using marijuana occasionally, to find it more readily available, and to use it more frequently (see Figure 13, Appendix 2, p. 206). While they also began to perceive less risk in using cocaine occasionally, they have found that it is becoming only slightly easier to obtain, and they have not increased their usage (see Figure 14, Appendix 2, p. 207). What is unclear is the relationship between perceived risk, availability, and use. (Does a perception of less risk lead to increased usage that leads to increased availability? Does increased usage lead to a perception of less risk and greater availability? Does greater availability lead to increased usage that leads to a perception of less risk? etc.)

Califano asserts that legalization of drugs would cause the rate of use to increase. Alcohol is a legal drug, and, according to the *NHSDA,* neither its use nor its abuse appears to be increasing:

- Alcohol usage (in the past month) declined from 1979 to 1992, from 61 percent of the population in 1979 to 48 percent of the population in 1992. Since then, the rate has increased to 53 percent in 1994. Heavy alcohol use has changed little since 1990, remaining at about 5 percent each year. (14)
- Following a decrease from 37.3 percent in 1979 to 15.7 percent in 1992, the rate of current alcohol use among youth 12–17 years old has stabilized (18.0 percent in 1993 and 16.3 percent in 1994). (14)

In fact, per capita consumption of alcohol has been steadily declining since the mid-1980s (see Figure 10, Appendix 2, p. 204).

Myth: Legalization will save money by allowing the government to spend less on law enforcement and permit taxation of drug sales.

Reality: While legalization temporarily might take some of the burden off the criminal justice system, such a policy would impose heavy additional costs on the health care and social service systems, schools, and the workplace.

Comments

Califano claims that any law enforcement money saved and any tax money generated by legalizing drugs would be offset by the additional costs such an action would have on "the health care and social service systems, schools, and the workplace." He provides neither discussion nor evidence to support his claim that legalizing drugs would cost more money than continuing the war on them.

Drug related arrests have increased substantially since 1980 (see Table 4 and Figure 15, Appendix 2, pp. 208–209). In 1993, there were 1,364,881 adult jail and prison inmates. That same year, total government expenditures for corrections, judicial, legal, and police costs were 9.7 billion ($9,754,200,000) (*Sourcebook* 4). The cost per inmate was $71,465.00 (*Sourcebook* 464). The federal government's drug control budget for 1994 was 12.1 billion dollars *(Drug and Crime Facts).*

Myth: Drug use is an issue of civil liberties.

Reality: This is a convenient misreading of John Stuart Mill's On Liberty. . . . Mill's conception of freedom does not extend to the right of individuals to enslave themselves or to decide that they will give up their liberty. . . . [Individual drug abuse and addiction] does affect others directly. . . .

Comments

In discussing Mills, Califano does not distinguish between use and addiction, asserting that Mills would not support the right of an individual to "enslave" himself or herself to drugs. Use of drugs does not invariably lead to addiction.

Califano draws an analogy between the state's interest in banning "lead paint, asbestos insulation, unsafe toys, and flammable fabrics," and its interest in banning "cocaine, heroin, marijuana, methamphetamines, and hallucinogens." The analogy seems imperfect. The government did not ban paint, insulation, toys, or fabric. Perhaps a closer analogy would be between the state's interest in banning manufactured items that are potentially unsafe and in banning manufactured drugs that are potentially unsafe. If one assumes that all manufactured drugs are potentially unsafe and should, consequently, be banned, one would necessarily be forced to concede the banning of such legal drugs as alcohol. Additionally, one would have to reconsider drugs that are not "manufactured" (marijuana, hashish, peyote, etc.).

Myth: Legalization works well in European countries.

Reality: The ventures of Switzerland, England, the Netherlands, and Italy into drug legalization have had disastrous consequences. . . .

Comments

The Swiss permitted users to possess, sell, buy, and use drugs in "Needle Park," or Platzspitz. The mistake, says columnist Arnold S. Trebach of the *Washington Post,* was that the Swiss government went too far by allowing public use of drugs and by not restricting the park to residents of Zurich (17). Platzspitz was closed down in 1992. In January, 1994, the Swiss implemented a heroin prescription experiment which, after three years, seems to have substantially improved the health of program participants as well as dramatically decreased their involvement in criminal activities (Uchtenhagen).

In the Netherlands, the 1976 Opium Act distinguished between "soft drugs" (marijuana and hashish) and "hard drugs" (heroin, cocaine, and amphetamines) and permitted the use of "soft drugs" in regulated coffee houses. According to the Dutch Ministry of Health, Welfare, and Sport, the results have been positive:

> There were 2.4 drug-related deaths per million inhabitants in the Netherlands in 1995. In France this figure was 9.5, in Germany 20, in Sweden 23.5 and in Spain 27.1. According to the 1995 report of the European Monitoring Centre for Drugs and Drug Addiction in Lisbon, the Dutch figures are the lowest in Europe. The Dutch AIDS prevention programme was equally successful. Europe-wide, an average of 39.2 percent of AIDS victims are intravenous drug users. In the Netherlands, this percentage is as low as 10.5 percent. The number of addicts in the Netherlands has been stable—at 25,000—for many years. Expressed as a percentage of the population, this number is approximately the same as in Germany, Sweden and Belgium (5).

In its *1998 Annual Report on the State of the Drugs Problem in the European Union,* the European Monitoring Centre for Drugs and Drug Addiction (EMCDDA) provides the following figures for problem drug usage in selected European Union countries before 1996 (20):

COUNTRY	YEAR	PREVALENCE
Italy	1992	190,000–313,000
France	1993	160,000
Denmark	1996	12,500
Sweden	1992	14,000–20,000
Netherlands	1993	25,000–28,000
Germany	1995	100,000–150,000
Austria	1993	10,000–15,000
Finland	1995	5,300–10,500

(*Note:* The definitions of "problem usage" and methodologies vary.)

This information is reproduced in Appendix 2 (see Table 5, p. 210). Based on the estimates provided by the EMCDDA, the countries with the largest number of problem drug users are Italy, Germany, and France (see Figure 16, Appendix 2, p. 211). However, the country with the highest percentage of problem drug users is Luxembourg (see Figures 17–18, Appendix 2, p. 212).

The EMCDDA also provides statistics on the percentage of AIDS cases in Europe from 1985–1997 that are related to injecting drug use (28):

Spain	65.4	France	23.8	Denmark	7.9
Italy	62.4	Luxembourg	15.7	Belgium	6.5
Portugal	43.5	Germany	14.2	U. Kingdom	6.5
Ireland	43	Sweden	11.5	Greece	4
Austria	25.5	Netherlands	10.9	Finland	3.7

This table is reproduced in Appendix 2 (Table 6, p. 213) and is followed by a chart containing the same information (Figure 19, p. 214).

Works Consulted

European Monitoring Centre for Drugs and Drug Addiction. *1998 Annual Report on the State of the Drugs Problem in the European Union.* Luxembourg: Office for Official Publications of the European Communities, 1998.

Kerr, Austin, ed. *Temperance and Prohibition.* Ohio State. Dept. of History Web Projects. 25 Sept. 1999 <http://www.cohums.ohio-state.edu/history/projects/prohibition/Contents.htm>.

Manning, Michael, Sarah Smith, and Eric Chernoff. "History." *North Carolina Moonshine.* 25 Sept. 1999 <http://metalab.unc.edu/moonshine/drink/historical.html>.

Nadelmann, Ethan A. "Switzerland's Heroin Experiment." *National Review* 10 July 1995: 46–47. Rpt. The Lindesmith Center. Online Library. 15 Aug. 1999
<http://www.lindesmith.org/library/tlcnr.html>.

Steiny, Don. *A History of Drug Use and Prohibition.* 'Lectric Law Library. 25 Sept. 1999
<http://lectlaw.com/files/drg09.htm>.

Sterling, Eric. "Is the Bill of Rights a Casualty in the War on Drugs?" The Colorado Bar Association, 92nd Annual Convention. Aspen, Colorado. 14 Sept. 1990. Rvsd. 5 Nov. 1990. 13 Aug. 1999
<http://user.intersatx.net/jc/sterling.html>.

The Netherlands. Dutch Ministry of Health, Welfare and Sport. "Drug Policy." Documentation April 1997. 23 Aug. 1999 <http://www.minvws.nl/pdf/!d1eng.pdf>.

Trebach, Arnold S. "Lessons from Needle Park." *Washington Post,* 17 March 92: A17+.

Uchtenhagen, A. "Summary of the Synthesis Report." *Programme for a Medical Prescription of Narcotics: Final Report of the Research Representatives.* Eds. A. Uchtenhagen, A. Gutzwiller, and A. Dobler-Mikola. Zurich: Institute for Social and Preventive Medicine at the University of Zurich, 1997. 10 Oct. 1999 <http://www.zorgstad.nl/drugs/schweiz/summary.htm>.

United States. Dept. of Health and Human Svcs. National Institutes of Health. National Institute of Alcohol and Alcoholism. *Age-Adjusted Death Rates of Liver Cirrhosis by Sex: Death Registration States, 1910–1932, and United States, 1933–1995* April 1999. 23 Aug. 1999
<http://silk.nih.gov/silk/niaaa1/database/cirmrt1.txt>.

———. *Apparent per Capita Ethanol Consumption for the United States, 1850–1996* May 1999. 23 Aug. 1999 <http://silk.nih.gov/silk/niaaa1/database/consum01.txt>.

United States. Dept. of Health and Human Svcs. Substance Abuse and Mental Health Svcs. Admin. Office of Applied Studies. *1994 National Household Survey on Drug Abuse.* Washington, DC: GPO, 1995. 21 Aug. 1999 <http://www.samhsa.gov/oas/p0000016.htm>.

————.*1998 National Household Survey on Drug Abuse.* Washington, DC: GPO, 1999. 28 Aug. 1999 <http://www.samhsa.gov/oas/NHSDA/98SummHtml/TOC.htm>.

————.*Statistics Sourcebook, 1998.* Ed. Beatrice Rouse. Washington, DC: GPO, 1999. 22 Aug. 1999 <http://www.samhsa.gov/oas/oasftp.htm>.

United States. Dept. of Health and Human Svcs. Substance Abuse and Mental Health Svcs. Admin. The National Clearinghouse for Drug and Alcohol Information. *Prevention Online.* 2 Oct. 1999 <http://www.health.org/>.

United States. Dept. of Justice. Bureau of Justice Statistics. *Drug-Related Crime.* NCJ–149286. Washington, DC: GPO, 1994. 28 Aug. 1999 <http://www.ojp.usdoj.gov/bjs/abstract/drc.htm>.

————.*Drugs and Crime Facts* 17 May 1999. By Tina Dorsey. NCJ-165148. 28 Aug. 1999\ <http://www.ojp.usdoj.gov/bjs/dcf/contents.htm>.

————.*Drugs and Crime Facts, 1994.* NCJ-154043. Washington, DC: GPO, 1995. 28 Aug. 1999 <http://www.ojp.usdoj.gov/bjs/abstract/dcfacts. htm>.

————.*Sourcebook of Criminal Justice Statistics, 1996.* NCJ 165361. Washington, DC: GPO, 1997. 28 Aug. 1999 <http://www.ojp.usdoj.gov/bjs/abstract/socjs96.htm>.

United States. Dept. of Justice. Federal Bureau of Investigation. *Uniform Crime Report for the United States, 1996.* Washington, DC: GPO, nd. 12 Oct. 1999 <http://www.fbi.gov/ucr.htm>.

Wilkinson, Alec. Moonshine: A Life in Pursuit of White Liquor. New York: Knopf, 1985.

The Prisoner's Dilemma

Stephen Chapman

In "The Prisoner's Dilemma," Chapman compares the method of punishment used in the West (imprisonment) with those methods used in Islam (flogging, amputation, and stoning), arguing that "At least in regard to cruelty, it's not at all clear that the system of punishment that has evolved in the West is less barbaric than the grotesque practices of Islam" (par. 8). Students often have a difficult time determining Chapman's thesis, not only because it is placed in the middle of the essay, but also because it contains qualifiers and negatives. They also tend to look for a statement in which Chapman advocates adopting the Islamic practices. Obviously, he is suggesting no such thing. After all, he considers the methods "grotesque" and notes that "no one, of course, would think of copying the medieval practices of Islamic nations. . . ." The writer is simply trying to make the reader understand the cruelties of prison life and to consider the possibility that it is as barbaric as the Islamic methods. Once the students understand what Chapman is trying to do, they can discuss the validity of his argument and ask themselves the questions he poses in paragraph 8.

Suggestions

Pre-Reading Exercise: Choose one of the following three questions and have students respond to it:

a. What do you consider to be the objectives of imprisonment? How well do you think our prison system achieves these objectives?

b. Describe what you know about the conditions of our prisons.

c. The Eighth Amendment to the United States Constitution prohibits eleven cruel and unusual punishments. What punishments do you consider "cruel and unusual"?

1. One approach is to begin by having students put in writing Chapman's thesis. Circulate around the room and read their responses. The majority of students will probably have difficulty finding or explaining his thesis. Ask them to underline the topic sentence of each paragraph and explain in one or two sentences the substance of paragraphs 1–2, 3–13, 14–17, and 18–19. (Paragraphs 1–2 explain the Islamic system of punishment; paragraphs 3–13 discuss the Western system of punishment, its ideals and its shortcomings; paragraphs 14–17 examine Islamic practices in light of Western goals; paragraphs 18–19 conclude that Western punishments are as cruel as those of Islam and perhaps more dangerous because our cruelties have been hidden from public view.) This approach allows the students to gain an overview of the essay's structure and to see some of the major points that support Chapman's thesis.

2. Another way to help students pinpoint Chapman's thesis is to break them up into groups and pose questions that require textual analysis:

    a. What is the only type of criminal punishment used in the United States?

    b. How is the intended criminal punishment in the United States different from the actual punishment?

    c. According to Chapman, people of all political persuasions agree that prisons in the United States are a disgrace. How does he support his assertion?

    d. What are some of the horrors of prison life in the United States?

    e. Why might someone prefer to lose a hand rather than spend ten years in a typical United States prison?

    f. What are some of the barbaric methods of punishment that were, until recently, used in the West?

    g. Why were the barbaric methods of the West replaced by incarceration?

    h. What five functions does imprisonment supposedly perform? Which of these functions are actually performed?

    i. How well do Islamic practices perform the five intended functions of Western imprisonment?

    After the questions have been answered, ask each group to locate Chapman's thesis and to explain whether or not he is suggesting that the West adopt Islamic methods of punishment.

3. Another approach is to identify the thesis for the students. Have them break up into groups and ask them the following question: Is Chapman suggesting that the West adopt Islamic methods of punishment? They must support their answers with textual evidence.

4. Jonathan Alter and Pat Wingert's "The Return of Shame" (*Newsweek*, Feb. 6, 1995: 20-6) explores the use of public shame as a method of deterance and rehabilitation. Have students read the article and explain how Chapman might reply to it. Students can use InfoTrac to find the article (Keyword: "The Return of Shame").

Violent Crime: Myths, Facts, and Solutions

D. Stanley Eitzen

In "Violent Crime: Myths, Facts, and Solutions," Eitzen debunks various illusions about violent crime, outlines the social variables that contribute to it, analyzes the responses of conservatives and progressives to fighting crime, and presents long-term and short-term solutions to the problem. Initially, he delineates and examines five popularly held beliefs about crime, attempting to prove that each is false: America ranks relatively low among industrialized nations in the amount of violent crime; this country is experiencing "a crime wave"; perpetrators of violent crime are "found throughout the age structure"; the streets are the most dangerous place in the United States; and violent criminals are genetically predisposed toward violence. Poverty, unemployment, racial segregation, family instability, and economic disparity are identified as factors that increase the rate of violent crime.

Eitzen maintains that the crime problem cannot be solved by "after the fact" measures such as incarceration. It can only be solved by preventing at-risk young people from becoming criminals. In the short term, Eitzen supports removing "predatory sociopaths" from society, implementing strict gun control laws, restoring order to the inner cities, making the criminal justice system equitable, rehabilitating criminals, and legalizing drugs. In the long term, he argues that society must eradicate poverty, support the family, commit to "full and decent employment," and invest heavily in the education of at-risk children. Unless we implement preventative programs, Eitzen concludes, we will not deter crime, but increase it.

"Violent Crime: Myths, Facts, and Solutions" is an address that Eitzen presented at the 1995 symposium "The Shadow of Violence: Unconsidered Perspectives," Hastings College. Thus, it provides students with the opportunity to examine not only the issue of violent crime, but also the way that a speech (intended to be heard) differs from an essay (intended to be read). Eitzen's title clearly delineates the outline of his talk making it easier for his listeners without prepared texts before them to follow his thoughts. He explicitly enumerates his ideas, beginning his discussions of each myth, each social variable, each fact about prisons, each short-term solution, and each long-term solution with a number. His transitions are also explicitly stated and adhere to the outline he presents in his title. In addition, he avoids using extensive references to studies and statistics that might prove interesting to readers but would be lost on listeners.

Suggestions

Pre-Reading Exercise: Have students consider their own opinions about violent crime before they read this text. Read each of the beliefs that Eitzen classifies as myths, and ask students to record whether the statement is true or false.

1. Pose questions that will require students to analyze and synthesize the details of the text:
    a. What five popular beliefs about crime does Eitzen assert are myths? What evidence does he offer to prove each one false? Is the evidence convincing? Explain.
    b. Why is there a "relatively high probability of criminal behavior—violent criminal behavior—among young, black, impoverished males in the inner cities"?
    c. Why does Eitzen object to "indiscriminately" imprisoning criminals?
    d. Why are "after the fact" solutions to the crime problem not effective?
    e. What steps does Eitzen believe should be taken to decrease violent crime?

2. Once students have answered these questions, encourage them to explore their own opinions. Working individually, they should answer the following questions in regard to each of the measures (immediate and long term) that Eitzen believes will protect society from violent crime:
    a. Do you think that this measure would help reduce the rate of violent crime? Explain.
    b. Do you support or oppose this proposal? Explain.

    When everyone has finished, discuss each of the proposals and list students' reasons on the board or on a transparency for supporting or opposing it. After all of the proposals have been discussed, have students cast votes for or against each of the measures. Rank the measures according to the number of favorable votes they received. Ask students to discuss the obstacles that stand in the way of implementing the three proposals they most support.

3. For further analysis of our prison system, have students read "The Prisoner's Dilemma" (p. 271). Does Chapman's essay support or refute Eitzen's assertion that "The prison experience tends to increase the likelihood of further criminal behavior"?

4. Have students break up into groups and identify some alternatives to incarceration. When the groups are finished, reunite the class and write their alternatives on the board. Assign each group one alternative. The groups are responsible for researching their alternative, finding out about its use and effectiveness, and presenting their findings to the class. Students can use InfoTrac to locate the information they need. They can start with a general Keyword Search ("Alternatives to Imprisonment") and progress to more specific Keyword Searches as need be.

A Nasty Business

Bruce Hoffman

and

Torture's Allure and Effect

Darius Rejali

In "A Nasty Business" by Bruce Hoffman and "The Allure and Effect of Torture" by Darius Rejali, both authors discuss the relationship between torture and the gathering of military information (oftentimes making use of the same historical examples), but they come to substantially different conclusions about the nature of that relationship. Rejali argues that torture is an ineffective and unreliable method for gathering good intelligence and that it demeans the individuals who inflict it as well as the governments who endorse it. While Hoffman agrees that the use of torture is morally questionable, he believes that it may be the only way to gather the intelligence necessary to wage an effective war against a highly unconventional enemy. Both authors establish their credibility, but Hoffman develops a more effective argument than Rejali.

The importance of having the reader accept an author as credible is lost on neither Rejali nor Hoffman. Both attempt to show that they are trustworthy and knowledgeable. Early in his essay, Rejali explains that he learned about torture "while growing up in Iran under Mohammad Reza Shah Pahlavi" (par. 3) and that he has spent 20 years researching "modern torture and the bureaucracies that sponsored and practiced it in Germany, Japan, France and Britain" (par. 4). In the subsequent paragraphs, he emphasizes his education and expertise by using phrases such as "[m]y research shows" (par. 6) and "my research has shown" (par. 7). Like Rejali, Hoffman tries to establish his credibility early on, but his efforts are less overt. Indeed, he so seamlessly weaves his credentials into his discussion of *The Battle of Algiers* that the focus of the paragraph never shifts away from the film. He succeeds in establishing himself as an academic expert on terrorism (for five years, he taught a graduate course "which considered the difficulties democracies face in countering terrorism"), and he suggests that he has some association with governmental agencies that are involved in fighting terrorism (he has "long" worked with "soldiers, spies, and students"). Referring to past experience and acquired knowledge is an effective and legitimate way of establishing credentials, but an author's expertise is not the only element to be considered in assessing the validity of an argument. An effective argument is clearly focused, logically organized, fully developed, and well supported.

Rejali's thesis is clear but broad: "the history of modern torture tells us that governments can't license [torture]—even in the cause of spreading democracy—without reducing the quality of their intelligence, compromising their allies and damaging their military and bureaucratic capabilities" (par. 1). Given this thesis, the reader justifiably expects Rejali to use research pertaining to the "history of modern torture" to prove that the institutional use of torture has a negative impact on a government's "intelligence," its "allies," and its "military and bureaucratic capabilities." To fulfill these expectations, Rejali should have main points that relate directly to his thesis and arrange his ideas so that one leads logically to the next. Instead, his essay is at times almost stream-of-consciousness, with one point leading tangentially to another point. This lack of cohesion is frustrating to readers who are trying to analyze and understand his argument. Equally as frustrating is the vagueness of Rejali's evidence. While he frequently refers to "research," "studies," and experts, he identifies only half of his sources by name. The remainder of his sources are referred to in generic terms such as "one prisoner in Chile" (par. 28), "a doctor attached to a French torture unit" (par. 52), and "clinical psychiatrists and some torturers in colonized nations" (par. 10). References of this sort are suspicious because they do not really document a source, leaving readers with no way to conduct their own investigation of the evidence. Even when Rejali does provide specific information about his sources, he oftentimes does not explain how the research of these experts supports his claims. For example, in paragraph 14, Rejali asserts that ""torture induces a dynamic that breaks down professionalism" and then claims that his assertion is supported by the findings of "Yale psychologist Stanley Milgram" as well as a book entitled *Violence Workers: Police Torturers and Murderers Reconstruct Brazilian Atrocities*. He fails to explain how his point is supported by Milgram's findings and/or the book's evidence. Students will be challenged (and perhaps frustrated) by Rejali's essay not because his ideas are particularly complex but because his presentation lacks focus, organization, and development.

Hoffman is more circumspect than Rejali in his discussion of torture, suggesting that, despite the 9/11 attacks, "Americans still do not appreciate the enormously difficult—and morally complex— problem that the imperative to gather 'good intelligence' entails" (par. 1). Progressing logically from one point to the next, he explores the problem by focusing on two specific conflicts: the battle between the Algerian *Front de Libération Nationale* (FLN) and the French authorities; and the struggle between the Tamil Tigers and the Sri Lankan government. Throughout the essay, Hoffman explicitly identifies his sources of information and establishes their credibility. He also makes clear the connection between the information and his thesis. For example, Hoffman states, "Rarely have the importance of intelligence and the unpleasant ways in which it must often be obtained been better or more dearly elucidated than in the 1966 movie *The Battle of Algiers*" (par. 2). A non-documentary film might seem like a less than reputable source, but Hoffman explains that he recommends and refers to the film because of its "verisimilitude" (par. 4) and general accuracy ("The events depicted on celluloid closely parallel those of history" (par. 5)). Still, the reader needs to remember that the lines he quotes are bits of dialogue from the film, and, while instructive, are not necessarily the words spoken by the historical figures. He moves from discussing the cinematic portrayal of historical events to discussing the actual historical events and their aftermath: the use of torture helped the French army win the Battle of Algiers, but it lead to their "eventual political defeat" (par. 6). Nevertheless, the army's actions demonstrate, according to Hoffman, that "only information can effectively counter terrorism" (par. 7).

To explain the lengths to which civil and military authorities must "often resort" to "get that information," Hoffman discusses his conversation with Thomas, "a much decorated, battle-hardened Sri Lankan army officer charged with fighting the LTTE" (pars. 7, 8). Before discussing his conversation, Hoffman illustrates the "professionalism, capability, and determination" of the Tigers: they staged a chemical-weapons attack five years before the attack on the 1995 nerve-gas attack on a Tokyo subway; they carried out several seaborne suicide missions against Sri Lankan navy vessels ten years before the 2000 seaborne attack on the USS Cole; and "they are believed to have developed their own embryonic air capability—designed to carry out attacks similar to those of September 11" (par. 7). By comparing the Tigers' assaults to more recent and perhaps more familiar assaults, Hoffman contextualizes the Tigers' activities, making their ruthless nature concrete and comprehensible. The clearly organized comparisons also demonstrate that Sri Lanka is fighting conflicts and enemies similar to those being fought by the

United States and suggests that the Sri Lankan experience might provide valuable insight for Americans. To Thomas, an intelligence officer who "merciless[ly] . . . discharged his duties," the issue is simple: "terrorism can be "fought only by thoroughly 'terrorizing' the terrorists—that is, inflicting on them the same pain that they inflict on the innocent" (par.8). Thomas extracts information from "recalcitrant terrorists" by giving them a choice: talk or die (par. 8). (In paragraph 56 of his essay, Rejali mentions that this was the approach advocated by Yves Godard during the Battle of Algiers.) Whether or not such an ultimatum constitutes torture is highly debatable. What is not debatable is Thomas's presumption that those who are brought before him are guilty of terrorism and have information of value, a fact that Hoffman never addresses. He does, however, make clear his own lack of comfort with Thomas' methods. Drawing together the "enormously difficult" and "morally complex" issues that he refers to in his thesis and explores throughout the essay, Hoffman concludes with a pointed question: "In the quest for timely, 'actionable' intelligence will the United States, too, have to do bad things—by resorting to measures that we would never have contemplated in a less exigent situation?"

Hoffman's argument is far more effective and thought-provoking than Rejali's. Both writers articulate a clear thesis, but only Hoffman keeps his essay focused on his thesis, organizes his points logically, and develops his ideas fully. While he incorporates fewer sources than Rejali, he explores them in greater depth and shows how they relate directly to the point he is making. Each example provides information that is built upon by the next example. Rejali, on the other hand, so frequently veers away from his thesis that the reader has a difficult time following his argument. This is not to say that Rejali makes no good points. He does. He simply fails to explicate them fully and to make clear how they support this thesis. By comparing these essays, students will gain valuable insight into the roles that focus, organization, support, and development play in creating an effective argument.

Suggestions

Pre-Reading Exercises

1. Have students watch and discuss the 1966 film, *The Battle of Algiers*. Doing this before students have read the essays will enable them to view the film without being influenced by the opinions of Rejali or Hoffman. Rejali believes that it misrepresents the facts: "Unlike in the famous movie, which portrays the Algerian population as united behind the FLN and assumes that torture is why the French won the battle, the real Battle of Algiers was a story of collaboration and betrayal by the local population." Hoffman, on the other hand, believes the film clearly elucidates "the importance of intelligence and the unpleasant ways in which it must often be obtained."

2. Prompt students to start thinking about the subject of these essays by asking them to define in writing the noun *torture*. Have them read aloud what they wrote, discuss the various ideas, and come to a consensus on the meaning(s) of the word. After students have read the essays, have them explain how each of the authors might respond to their definition(s).

A Nasty Business

1. One approach is to direct students' attention to the final sentence of the first paragraph: "But the experiences of other countries, fighting similar conflicts against similar enemies, suggest that Americans still do not appreciate the enormously difficult—and morally complex—problem that the imperative to gather "good intelligence" entails." Then, ask students to divide up into groups and outline the evidence and arguments that Hoffman uses to prove his point. When all the groups have completed their work, each should present and discuss its findings with the class.

2. Another approach is to pose questions that call on students to analyze and synthesize details from the text and then to identify Hoffman's thesis and determine whether or not he succeeds in proving it: What does Godard mean, "'Intelligence is capital'" (par. 1)?

a. How does Hoffman establish that Godard is a credible source of information?

b. Explain the "differences between police officers and soldiers in training and approach" (par. 2).

c. Why does Hoffman think *The Battle of Algiers* should be seen by those who "want to understand how to fight terrorism" (par. 3)?

d. How does Hoffman account for the film's "verisimilitude" (par. 4)?

e. Hoffman states that Massu's approach, "at least strategically, was counterproductive" (par. 6). What "approach" did Massu use? Why was it "counterproductive"?

f. How does Hoffman support his assertion that the "Tigers are unique in the annals of terrorism and arguably eclipse even bin Laden's al Qaeda in professionalism, capability, and determination" (par. 7)?

g. How does Thomas extract information from the suspects who are brought before him?

h. What is it that Thomas thinks Hoffman "couldn't possibly understand" (par. 9)? Why does he think Hoffman could not understand?

i. What impact did the terrorist attacks of September 11, 2001 have on Hoffman's thoughts about terrorists and the need to gather good intelligence?

j. What might Thomas have said about the prisoner abuse at Abu Ghraib?

k. Does Hoffman support the abuse and/or torture of terror suspects? Explain.

l. What is Hoffman's thesis in this essay? Does he succeed in proving it? Explain.

3. Have students examine and draw conclusions about Hoffman's portrayal of himself and of Thomas:

a. Characterize (describe) Thomas.

b. Describe and explain Thomas's attitude toward Hoffman.

c. How does Hoffman depict himself? (Look closely at the words Hoffman uses to describe his reactions, thoughts, and feelings.)

d. What might Hoffman be trying to accomplish by portraying himself and Thomas as he does?

4. Encourage students to discuss their own opinions:

a. Is it torture or abuse or neither to give someone a "talk or die" choice? Explain.

b. Is it torture or abuse or neither to flick "a few drops of gasoline . . . into a plastic bag," place it over the suspect's head, and cinch it "tight around his neck with a web belt" (par. 8)? Explain.

c. Do you agree with Hoffman's assertion that "the struggle against Osama bin Laden and his minions . . . depend on good intelligence" (par. 1)? Explain.

d. Do you think that "the intelligence requirements of counterterrorism" should "take precedence over democratic ideals" (par. 6)? Explain.

5. Have students work individually to identify some of the claims that Hoffman makes but does not support and then discuss with them whether or not those claims need to be supported.

Students will likely wonder how he knows that "members of the IRA; the Tamil Tigers, in Sri Lanka; and 1960s African-American revolutionaries" have "assiduously studied" *The Battle of Algiers* (par. 3)? They will probably point out that he does provide a source for his assertion that *The Battle of Algiers* is supposedly "one of Prabhakaran's favorite films" (par. 7)? And, in all likelihood, they will question his statement that "the U.S. Army has enlisted Hollywood screenwriters to help plot scenarios of future terrorist attacks" (par. 3). His statements about *The Battle of Algiers* being a favorite of terrorists need to be supported, if only because he finds their view of the film to be exceedingly significant. His comment about the military's requesting the assistance of screenwriters did not need to be supported at the time his essay was published

(January, 2002): that assistance, having been widely publicized in October, 2001, was common knowledge.

Students who are interested in learning more about screenwriter's developing scenarios for the military can be directed to two articles that are accessible through InfoTrac:

> Peter Bart, "Mixing the Real and the Surreal," Variety, Oct 15, 2001: 6.

> Karen Brandon, "To Help Military, Hollywood Writers Imagine Novel Terror Strikes," Chicago Tribune (via Knight-Ridder/Tribune News Service), Oct 14, 2001.

6. According to Hoffman, "Massu remained forever unrepentant: he insisted that the ends justified the means used to destroy the FLN's urban insurrection. The battle was won, lives were saved, and the indiscriminate bombing campaign that had terrorized the city was ended. To Massu, that was all that mattered. To his mind, respect for the rule of law and the niceties of legal procedure were irrelevant given the crisis situation enveloping Algeria in 1957" (par. 6).

On November 23, 2000 (a little over a year before Hoffman's essay was published), *Le Monde* published an interview with the then 92-year-old Massu in which he states that "Morally, torture is something pretty dismal" and that a formal apology from France to Algeria "would be positive."

Students can be directed to use InfoTrac to find out for themselves whether or not Hoffman's claim that Massu was "forever unrepentant" is true. Have them do a Keyword search "in entire article content": Jacques Massu. This search will lead them to articles that deal with Massu as well as the French reaction to General Paul Aussaresses's memoirs, *Services Spéciaux, Algérie* 1955-1957 [*Special Services, Algeria 1955-1957*]. (The English edition of the book, entitled *The Battle of the Casbah: Terrorism and Counter-Terrorism in Algeria 1955-1957*, is in print.)

7. The Liberation Tigers of Tamil Eelam (LTTE) still operate in Sri Lanka. To have students compare different views of the Tigers, direct them to some websites of their supporters and their opponents:

- EelamWeb: http://www.eelamweb.com/
- Sinhaya: http://www.sinhaya.com/
- South Asian Terrorism Portal: http://www.satp.org/satporgtp/countries/shrilanka/terroristoutfits/Ltte.htm
- TamilTigers: http://www.tamiltigers.net/

Students can conduct further research on the LTTE by using InfoTrac (Keyword: Liberation Tigers of Tamil Eelam).

The Allure and Effect of Torture

1. Encourage students to analyze the content of the essay by having them answer in writing questions such as these:

   a. What does Rejali mean by "stealthy" torture techniques (par. 4)? Why do democratic governments prefer these techniques?

   b. What, according to Rejali, is wrong with the view that "more physical pain stimulates more compliance" (par. 9)?

   c. Rejali argues that torture cannot be done "professionally" (par. 14). Summarize the points he offers in evidence.

   d. What evidence does Rejali offer to support his claim that torture is "inferior" to other methods of intelligence gathering (par. 19)?

e. How does Rejali support his claim that torture is not an effective tool "in intelligence" because "one must gather information about things that one does not know" (par. 25)?

f. Why is torture not an effective "shortcut" to gathering intelligence (par. 29)?

g. Rejali maintains that the "leaders of dictatorships" and the "leaders of democracies" sign on to the Geneva Conventions for different reasons (par. 36). What are those reasons?

h. Why, according to Gen. Massu, was the use of torture effective in Algiers but not in Vietnam?

i. How did the FLN unintentionally help the French military identify "all its sympathizers" (par. 44).

j. How did the French unknowingly help the FLN "liquidate the infrastructure" of their rival, the more moderate MNA (par. 46)?

k. What negative effects does Rejali believe the use of torture had on the judicial system? On the doctors "whose task it was to monitor torture" (par. 52)? On the military?

When the groups have answered all of the questions, reassemble the class and have students discuss their answers. Then, ask them to decide how well Rejali supports his thesis: "the history of modern torture tells us that governments can't license this corruption—even in the cause of spreading democracy—without reducing the quality of their intelligence, compromising their allies and damaging their military and bureaucratic capabilities" (par. 1).

2. Divide the class into groups, assign each group three of four of the statements listed below, and ask all of the groups to determine how well Rejali supports the claims they have been assigned. The groups should present their conclusions to the class for further discussion.

a. ". . . stealthy techniques appeared more often in the wars of democracies than in those of dictatorships" (par. 4).

b. ". . . torture during interrogations rarely yields better information than traditional human intelligence" (par. 6).

c. ". . . anyone who tortures is necessarily corrupted by the experience and is often turned into a sadist" (par. 6).

d. ". . . a democracy that legalizes the use of torture in its desperation to gain information loses something more important—the trust of its people, the foundation of a democracy" (par. 7).

e. ". . . institutionalizing torture . . . only ends up destroying all the individuals involved—and the military and political goals of the government in whose name torture is carried out" (par. 7).

f. "The history of torture demonstrates that [torture] does not" produce "better results than [other methods] at an army's disposal" (par. 8).

g. ". . . torture induces a dynamic that breaks down professionalism" (par. 14).

h. "No matter how professional torturers may think they are, they have no choice but behaving like sadists" (par. 15).

i. ". . . coercive interrogation undermines other professional policing skills" (par. 17).

j. ". . . competition between intelligence agencies that conduct torture tears bureaucracies apart" (par. 18).

k. ". . . good intelligence requires humans willing to trust government enough to work with it" (par. 21).

l. "Torture is a sign that a government either does not enjoy the trust of the people it governs or cannot recruit informers for a surveillance system" (par. 23).

m. ". . . torture to obtain information is a sign of institutional decay and desperation" (par. 23).

n. ". . . prisoners who tell the truth under torture normally provide less detailed information than that obtainable through noncoercive interrogation" (par. 26).

o. "Real torture—not the stuff of television—takes days, if not weeks" (par. 29).

p. "The priority in America's war on terror should be on developing human intelligence" (par. 35).

q. "Leaders of dictatorships sign on to the Geneva Conventions only out of prudential fear of what other states might do to their POWs. Leaders of democracies sign on to them because they understand the evil that lurks in the heart of all human beings" (par. 36).

r. "Unrestrained power leaves behind a legacy of destruction that takes generations to undo" (par. 37).

s. ". . . the French won [Battle of Algiers] by applying overwhelming force in an extremely constrained space, not by superior intelligence gathered through torture" (par. 40).

t. "The real significance of the Battle of Algiers, however, is the startling justification of torture by a democratic state" (par. 41).

u. "What made the difference for the French in Algiers was not torture, but the accurate intelligence obtained through public cooperation and informants" (par. 44).

v. "Torture forced a politics of extremes, destroying the middle that had cooperated with the French" (par. 49).

w. "The judicial system also collapsed under the weight of torture. Judges and prefects found themselves unable to deny warrants to armed men who tortured and killed for a living" (par. 50).

x. "As oversight failed, the French military government arrested more people for flimsier reasons" (par. 52).

y. "Torture drifted headlong into sadism, continuing long after valuable information could be retrieved" (par. 54).

z. "The French military also fragmented under the competition associated with torture" (par. 55).

aa. "Soldiers trained in stealthy techniques of torture take these techniques back into civilian life as policemen and private security guards" (par. 62).

bb. ". . . once soldiers get away with torture, they repeat it" (par. 66).

cc. "democracies that have tortured . . . lost their wars because the brutality they licensed reduced their intelligence, compromised their allies and corrupted their military and government, and they could not come to terms with that" (par. 68.)

3. Have students answer questions that will require students to engage in synthesis:

   a. What point is Rejali attempting to make in his second paragraph?

   b. How does Rejali attempt to demonstrate that he is qualified to authoritatively discuss torture?

   c. Why does Rejali refer to the Greeks and Romans and the Italian city-states (par. 37)?

   d. Does Rejali consider it torture to give people who are being interrogated the "simple draconian choice: Talk or die" (par. 56)? Explain.

   e. Rejali never provides an explicit definition of torture. Based on his essay, how does he appear to define it?

   f. Rejali contends that it was not torture that enabled the French to win the Battle of Algiers. Does he succeed in proving that torture was of no value in Algiers? Explain.

   g. Does Rejali succeed in proving that "The French won the Battle of Algiers primarily through force, not by superior intelligence gathered through torture" (par. 60)?

4. Divide the class into groups and present students with the following list of the countries that are mentioned in the essay (the numbers delineate all of the paragraph(s) in which the country, its government, and/or its people are mentioned):

Brazil (pars. 14 &18)	Iran (pars. 3 & 67)
Britain (pars. 4 & 57)	Iraq (pars. 2, 5, 7, 22, 23, 60, & 61)
Chile (pars. 26 & 28)	Japan (pars. 4 & 19)
China (par. 21)	Soviet Union (par. 21)
France (pars. 4, 30, & 38-60)	United States (pars. 2, 3, 5, 7, 25,
Germany (pars. 4, 18, 33, 34, & 57)	32, 35, 58, 62 & 63)

Have students work in groups and answer the following questions for each of the countries listed:

a. Does Rejali state or suggest that this country has permitted the use of torture? If he does, answer the remaining questions. (If he does not, skip the following questions and move on to the next country.)

b. What evidence does Rejali provide to show that this country has allowed torture? Is his evidence valid? Explain.

c. What form of government was in effect at the time torture was permitted? (If that information is not supplied in the essay, simply write "unknown.")

    When all of the groups are finished, reassemble to class and have students discuss their findings. Students can be asked to use InfoTrac to further investigate the use of torture by the countries listed above (Keyword: torture AND [*the name of the country being researched*]).

5. Direct students to investigate some of Rejali's identified sources and determine whether or not they are accurately represented in the essay:

• The March 2003 report prepared by the Pentagon (par. 2.)

   • A copy of the memo published by the *Wall Street Journal* is available online at http://www.antiwar.com/lobe/?articleid=2769.

   • The report is discussed by Jess Bravin, "Pentagon Report Set Framework For Use of Torture" (*Wall Street Journal - Eastern Edition*, 6/7/2004: A1). Bravin's article can be accessed through ProQuest (http://proquest.umi.com/pqdweb?did=647393661&sid=1&Fmt=3&clientId=12526&RQT= 309&VName=PQD) or the *Wall Street Journal Online* (http://online.wsj.com/article/0,,SB108655737612529969-,00.html)

• The Justice Department's August 2002 memo (par. 2)

   • The memo is posted online by the *Washington Post*: http://www.washingtonpost.com/wp-srv/nation/documents/dojinterrogationmemo20020801.pdf

• Anne Applebaum's article (par. 2)

   • Anne Applebaum, "So Torture Is Legal?" (*Washington Post*, June 16, 2004, Page A27) is posted on the Washington Post website: http://www.washingtonpost.com/wp-dyn/articles/A44874-2004Jun15.html.

   • The line that Rejali attributes to Applebaum is actually from William Pfaff, "When Laws Get In The Way of Torture" (*International Herald Tribune*, June 12, 2004). Available on Algora Publishing's website: http://www.algora.com/Clippings/The%20United%20States/IHT_06_12_04.htm.

• Yale psychologist Stanley Milgram (par. 14)

- Milgram presents some of his findings about obedience to authority in his 1963 film, *Obedience* (available from Pennsylvania State University Audio Visual Services < http://www.medianet.libraries.psu.edu/htbin/wwform/175?TEXT=R42864942-42869253-/CA/WWI770.HTM>). Students can conduct their own research using InfoTrac (Keyword: milgram AND obedience; Subject: Milgram, Stanley)
- Seymour Hersh's article (par. 22)
  - Seymour Hersh, "The Gray Zone," (*New Yorker*, May 24, 2004). Available on the *New Yorker* website: http://www.newyorker.com/fact/content/?040524fa_fact

6. Rejali notes that Defense Secretary Donald Rumsfeld "ordered a 'high-value' detainee in Iraq held in secret, in part to keep him from being seen by the International Red Cross" (par. 2). Have students investigate this issue using InfoTrac (Keyword: rumsfeld AND iraq AND "red cross"). Or send them directly to one or both of these articles:

   Johanna McGeary, "The Scandal's Growing Stain: Abuses by U.S. Soldiers in Iraq Shock the World and Roil the Bush Administration," *Time*, May 17, 2004: 26.

   Thom Shanker and Andrea Elliott, "Rumsfeld Admits He Told Jailers to Keep Detainee in Iraq Out of Red Cross View", *The New York Times,* June 18, 2004: A10

7. Have students use InfoTrac to research the significance of the Geneva Conventions as they relate to the prisoners being held at Guantanamo and in Iraq (Keyword: "geneva convention" AND guantanamo; Keyword: "geneva convention" AND iraq). Or send them directly to this article: John Barry, Michael Hirsh, and Michael Isikoff, "The Roots of Torture," *Newsweek*, May 24, 2004: 26-34.

The Allure and Effect of Torture and A Nasty Business

1. In their essays, Hoffman and Rejali address some of the same issues and use some of the same examples. Have students compare and contrast the essays by posing questions such as the following:
   a. Compare and contrast the ways that Rejali and Hoffman seek to establish their credentials.
   b. List Rejali's reasons for objecting to the use of torture. Are his objections based on "'humane considerations'" (Hoffman, par. 4)? Explain.
   c. Rejali and Hoffman both discuss the use of torture in the Battle of Algiers. Do they come to the same conclusions about the effects of its use? Explain.
   d. Do Rejali and Hoffman share the same opinion of the film, *The Battle of Algiers?* Explain.
   e. Compare and contrast the differences that Rejali and Hoffman see between the work of police and the work of the military.
   f. Would Rejali and Hoffman agree that the most "actionable" information comes from human intelligence gathered from the indigenous population? Explain.
   g. How might Rejali respond to Hoffman's assertion that "the intelligence requirements of counterterrorism can suddenly take precedence over democratic ideals"?
   h. How does Rejali characterize torturers? Does Thomas fit his description? Explain.
2. If they have not already done so, have students watch and discuss the film *The Battle of Algiers*. To explore the veracity of the film, direct them to InfoTrac to read reviews and articles about the film (Keyword: Battle of Algiers). Or send them directly to this article: Gary Crowdus, "Terrorism and Torture in The Battle of Algiers: An Interview with Saadi Yacef," *Cineaste* 29.3 (2004): 30-8.

3.   Have students examine and report on the use of torture in countries other than those mentioned in the essays. They can be directed to conduct their research using InfoTrac (Keyword: torture AND [*the name of the country being researched*]). Assign each student one of the countries listed below:

Argentina	Egypt	Kenya	Spain
Armenia	El Salvador	Mexico	Turkey
Bosnia	Georgia	Myanmar	Uganda
Chad	Guatemala	Pakistan	Uzbekistan
Congo	India	Russia	Vietnam
Croatia	Indonesia	Saudi Arabia	Zambia
Czech Republic	Israel	South Africa	Zimbabwe
East Timor	Jordan		

4.   For further discussion of the methods that the United States has employed in the war on terrorism, have students use InfoTrac to research the treatment of prisoners at Guantánamo Bay and/or Abu Ghraib (Keyword: guantanamo AND abuse; Keyword: abu ghraib AND abuse).

5.   The United States has been accused having terror suspects interrogated by countries known to use torture. Have students use InfoTrac to investigate these allegations (Keyword: outsourcing AND torture; Keyword: torture AND proxy).

6.   To facilitate additional consideration of the ethical questions raised by the use of torture, direct students to InfoTrac (Keyword: torture AND terror).

4
Textbook Chapters
Discussions and Suggestions

Suggestions for Teaching Students How to Read Textbook Chapters

Teaching students to read textbook chapters may seem like a daunting task at first, primarily because students, who have been reading textbooks for years, are likely to insist that they already know how to read them. When asked to explain how they go about reading an assigned chapter, students rarely outline a process: They usually respond that they "just read it." There are several methods of reading textbooks, and the processes can be applied to most, if not all textbooks, no matter the level or subject.

Before students begin to read any textbook chapters, they should first examine the textbook itself. To do this, they should read the preface in order to determine the author's intent in writing the book, glance over the table of contents to see what material will be covered and how it is arranged, and thumb through the book itself to find out how the text is laid out and what types of apparatus or study aids are included.

Because *An Introduction to Critical Reading* is the only textbook all of the students in the class are likely to have, they should examine it in order to learn the process. They may be asked either to read the preface to the student, the preface to the instructor, or both. The preface to the student explains why the pieces in the anthology were selected and makes clear the authors' belief that thinking and questioning are essential parts, not only of reading, but also of living. The preface to the instructor introduces the rationale for the anthology and the pedagogical approach presented in the instructor's manual. If students have worked with some of the pieces in the anthology before textbook chapters are discussed, they will already know how the anthology is arranged, how the text is laid out, and what study aids are included.

If they have not yet worked with the anthology, they should complete the process of examining the textbook. A quick scan of the table of contents reveals that the anthology is divided by genre: poetry, fiction, essays, and textbook chapters. Looking through the book, students should notice that the text is spaciously laid out (allowing plenty of room for marginal comments), that notes containing definitions and explanations accompany many selections, and that a glossary, an index, and a list of acknowledgments are provided. After students have completed their examination of *An Introduction to Critical Reading,* they should discuss the process and what they gained from it. Such a discussion could be initiated by asking them to explain how understanding the authors' intentions might have affected (or might affect) their approach to the pieces in the anthology.

After a textbook has been examined, the assigned chapter should be previewed. First, students should note and consider the title of the chapter. To provide themselves with a purpose for reading the chapter (beyond merely completing their assignment), they might generate a series of questions based on the title. For example, the history chapter that is reproduced in the anthology is entitled "Presidency in Crisis." Students could turn this into a number of questions: In what way was the presidency in crisis? What caused the crisis? How was the crisis resolved? What effect did it have on the presidency?

Once they have composed their questions, students should scan the chapter, noting the headings and subheadings, both of which are usually printed in boldface type in textbooks. The headings and subheadings provide the student with an idea of how the chapter is organized and how the questions they posed will be addressed. If a list of learning objectives, an overview, and/or a summary are provided, students should read them after reviewing the chapter's headings and subheadings. Study aids such as these supply a synopsis of the issues that are dealt with in the chapter. Reading these introductory materials first helps students avoid getting so caught up in details that they lose track of the large issues.

Review questions, if provided, should also be read before the chapter itself. These questions alert students to the concepts that the author thinks are most important.

After previewing the assigned chapter, students are ready to read it, but they need to read it actively, not passively. One way for students to remain engaged in the text is to turn section headings into questions. Once students have composed questions, they can read the section in order to answer them. After they have read the section, they should paraphrase what they have read and try to answer their questions. If they cannot, then they should reread the section. The process and value of summarizing can be easily demonstrated in class.

Before discussing the need to summarize each section of a textbook chapter, have students read a section of one of the textbook chapters in class that they have not yet been assigned. Then, ask them to write a summary of what they have just read. More often than not, students will be unable to provide more than a cursory summary of the section. After the need for summary has been discussed, choose another section, have students turn the section heading into a question, and ask them to read the section, keeping in mind that they will be asked to summarize it and to answer the question they have formulated. The process of summarizing, section by section, helps students identify what they need to reread, ensures that they have really understood what they have read, and prepares them for examinations. The more they summarize, the more actively engaged in the text they will be and the more they will be able to remember what they have read.

In addition to summarizing, students should be encouraged to outline, highlight, and annotate their textbook chapters. A skeleton outline can be constructed using the author's chapter title, section headings, and subheadings. After students have read and summarized a section, they should outline the main ideas and important details it contains. Because this concept is more easily grasped when it is illustrated as it is explained, photo-ready outlines are included in Appendix 2. These can be reproduced on transparencies and discussed in conjunction with the assigned chapter. Outlining helps students keep their attention focused on the chapter, distinguish main points from supporting details, and connect the main points. The finished product also helps them study for exams.

Highlighting can also be useful, but only if done carefully and sparingly. Too often students highlight their texts indiscriminately. Ask students to define the noun *highlight* and to explain, in light of that definition, the purpose of highlighting. Their discussion should lead them to conclude that only points and details of great significance ought to be highlighted. Since main points and important details are often evident only after an entire section has been read, students should be encouraged to highlight a section not when they first read it, but when they reread it. Students will find that marking essential words or phrases is more helpful than marking entire sentences. If they highlight entire sentences or series of sentences, they will be forced to reread a great deal of text when they review their chapters. Their reviews will be less time-consuming and more effective if they can scan through their chapters, locating and explaining to themselves the importance of highlighted words or phrases. If they are unable to explain the significance, they need to reread the relevant portion of the text.

Annotating a text also helps students identify important information and review for exams. Annotations take a variety of forms, and no one way is the right way. Some students prefer to make marginal notes that identify the main idea covered in the adjacent text. This approach enables them to locate information quickly. Other students find writing questions in the margins of their textbook to be an effective study aid. This method is especially helpful if there is little or no apparatus in the chapter. When reviewing for an exam, students can cover the text with a sheet of paper, read and answer the questions they have posed, and then check the accuracy and completeness of their responses.

Students may express some reluctance about the laboriousness of examining a textbook, previewing chapters, composing questions, summarizing sections, outlining, highlighting, and annotating. Granted, they may not need to employ all of these techniques for every textbook they read. They do, however, need to be aware of the techniques, and they need to realize that the methods they use will depend on their interests, their aptitude, the subject matter, and the textbook itself. They also need to realize that reading a textbook chapter carefully and employing any methods necessary to understand and retain the information it presents is a wise investment of their time and energy.

"Presidency in Crisis"

from *The American Past: A Survey of American History*

Joseph R. Conlin

This is an excellent chapter to use after students have worked with the other chapter in the anthology. Students should have learned not only how to develop their own study aids but also how to use the apparatus provided by the authors. This chapter, like many they will be asked to read, contains minimal apparatus: section headers are printed in all capitals and are boldfaced, subsection headers are italicized and are boldfaced, and interesting facts are enclosed in boxes. The chapter contains no learning objectives, no marginal notations, no list of key concepts, no chapter summary, and no review questions. To learn the material it presents and prepare for an examination, students must rely on themselves and the study aids they develop. For this reason, no specific content questions are included in the suggestions. Rather, the suggestions focus primarily on reinforcing the skills of annotating, highlighting, and outlining. Because students have to generate virtually all of the study aids for this chapter, devoting two or more class meetings to it may be helpful.

Suggestions

Pre-Reading Exercise: Have students preview the chapter and identify the study aids it includes. Ask them what types of study aids they might develop to help themselves learn the material presented in the chapter and to review for exams. Have them construct a series of questions based on the section and subsection headings. Later, as they read, they should try to answer their questions.

1. Reproduce the subsection entitled "Political Savvy" on a transparency. Read the subsection aloud, stopping after each paragraph to ask students what highlights and annotations they believe should be made. Record their responses on the transparency. When the subsection has been completed, ask students to explain how their highlights and annotations would help them learn the material and review for exams.

2. Divide the students into groups, assigning each group a different subsection of the chapter and providing each with a transparency of the section that it has been assigned. Have each group highlight and annotate its section. When the groups have finished, project their transparencies onto the screen and ask them to discuss their work.

3. Show students a skeleton outline of the chapter (a photo ready outline is printed in Appendix 2, p. 216). Have them work as a class to outline the first section, "The Nixon Presidency." Then, divide the class into five groups, assign each group a different subsection of "Nixon's Vietnam," and have the groups outline their section on a transparency. When the students are finished, each group should present and explain its outline. Encourage students to discuss the strengths and weaknesses of each outline.

    If time permits, each of the five groups can be assigned a different subsection of "Nixon Kissinger Foreign Policy" to outline on a transparency and the process can be repeated. Otherwise, students can be asked to outline the section as homework.

4.   To help students assess and improve their ability both to outline and to develop review questions, divide them into groups A, B, C, and D and refer them to the section entitled "Watergate and Gerald Ford."

Groups A and B should outline the first five subsections and develop review questions for the last four subsections; groups C and D should develop review questions for the first five subsections and outline the last four subsections. (If this takes the whole class period, collect the outlines and questions, and redistribute them at the beginning of the next class.)

Have groups A and C exchange questions and groups B and D exchange questions. Tell students to close their books and, using only the outlines they developed, to answer the questions they have received. When all groups are finished, have students discuss the effectiveness of their outlines and the comprehensiveness of the questions they received.

5.   Have students divide into groups and summarize the main point made in each of the subsections of "Quiet Crisis." When they are finished, have them compare and discuss their summaries. Then, ask them to explain the overall point that is being made in the section.

6.   Once students have examined the entire chapter, have them work in groups to explore the theme of the chapter, "Presidency in Crisis." Ask them to explain what lead to the crises in leadership in each of the three administrations.

7.   Based on the descriptions given, have students write brief character sketches on Nixon, Ford, and Carter. What are their qualities and characteristics? This assignment should call for students' drawing conclusions about the actions of these men as well as identifying the characterizing words and phrases that are provided by the author.

8.   The questions Conlin provides in the Test Bank accompanying *The American Past* are reproduced in Appendix 3, p. 222. Some of these questions might be used to test students' understanding of the material presented in the chapter.

"Business Ethics and Social Responsbility"

from *Contemporary Business*

Louis E. Boone and David L. Kurtz

This chapter provides a great deal of apparatus designed to help students understand and learn the material it presents. The chapter's title page presents a list of learning goals. Students who take note of these goals before reading the chapter will have a clear understanding of their objectives at the outset. The chapter opens with a scenario that raises some of the issues that will be dealt with in the chapter. Following the scenario is a chapter overview. This overview defines the terms used in the chapter title and explains the importance of a company's being ethical and socially responsible. The chapter itself is divided into sections and subsections: section headers are printed in boldface capital letters; in a slightly smaller font than the section headings, the subheadings are printed in boldface upper- and lower-case letters. Within the text, key terms are boldfaced when they are introduced. In addition, "Concept Check" boxes appear periodically throughout the chapter, allowing students to test their comprehension and retention of information. Figures and tables are used throughout the chapter to illustrate or clarify concepts being discussed. The chapter concludes with a "Summary of Learning Goals," two lists of business terms, review questions, projects and applications, and experiential as well as web-based exercises.

Suggestions

1. If students have discussed the way in which a textbook chapter should be approached, have them identify the apparatus used in this chapter and explain the function of each one. Class discussion might revolve around how the apparatus could be most effectively used.

2. After outlining has been discussed, illustrate the way in which this chapter might be formally outlined. In Appendix 2 (pp. 217–219) are templates for a formal outline of the entire chapter as well as a formal outline of the section "The New Ethical Environment." Reproduce the template and the formal outline on transparencies. Use the template to show students how formal outlines are often based on a chapter's headings and subheadings. Then, use the outline of "The New Ethical Environment" to show students how additional information is added to create a formal outline. Have students work in groups to create a formal outline of one of the other section in the chapter. After they have completed the task, the groups can compare and contrast their outlines, discussing the strengths and weakness of each.

3. Discuss with students highlighting and annotating (see the essay, "Suggestions for Teaching Students How to Read Textbook Chapters," p. 165). Reproduce on transparencies a few pages from the chapter and have the students, working as a class, highlight and annotate the pages, discussing why they chose to highlight what they did and the purpose of the annotations they made. Then, give each group a transparency of a different page and a marker and ask them to highlight and annotate the page. Bring the class back together and project each group's transparency onto the screen. Have group members discuss why they highlighted and annotated what they did.

4. In order to have students come to terms with the content of the chapter, divide them into groups and have them answer the review questions at the end of the chapter.

5. Once students have a handle on the material presented in the chapter, pose one of the discussion questions presented at the end of the chapter. Ask each student to answer the question in writing and then discuss their responses.

6. The questions that Boone and Kurtz provide in the Test Bank accompanying *Contemporary Business* are reproduced in Appendix 3, p. 231. Some of these questions might be used to test students' understanding of the material presented in the chapter.

Appendix 1
Articles for the Instructor

Attention Deficit Hyperactivity Disorder

National Institute of Mental Health

(Edited)

Imagine living in a fast-moving kaleidoscope, where sounds, images, and thoughts are constantly shifting. Feeling easily bored, yet helpless to keep your mind on tasks you need to complete. Distracted by unimportant sights and sounds, your mind drives you from one thought or activity to the next. Perhaps you are so wrapped up in a collage of thoughts and images that you don't notice when someone speaks to you.

For many people, this is what it's like to have Attention Deficit Hyperactivity Disorder, or ADHD. They may be unable to sit still, plan ahead, finish tasks, or be fully aware of what's going on around them. To their family, classmates or coworkers, they seem to exist in a whirlwind of disorganized or frenzied activity. Unexpectedly—on some days and in some situations—they seem fine, often leading others to think the person with ADHD can actually control these behaviors. As a result, the disorder can mar the person's relationships with others in addition to disrupting their daily life, consuming energy, and diminishing self-esteem.

ADHD, once called hyperkinesis or minimal brain dysfunction, is one of the most common mental disorders among children. It affects 3 to 5 percent of all children, perhaps as many as two million American children. Two to three times more boys than girls are affected. On the average, at least one child in every classroom in the United States needs help for the disorder. ADHD often continues into adolescence and adulthood, and can cause a lifetime of frustrated dreams and emotional pain.

But there is help . . . and hope. In the last decade, scientists have learned much about the course of the disorder and are now able to identify and treat children, adolescents, and adults who have it. A variety of medications, behavior-changing therapies, and educational options are already available to help people with ADHD focus their attention, build self-esteem, and function in new ways.

What Are the Symptoms of ADHD?

ADHD is not like a broken arm, or strep throat. Unlike these two disorders, ADHD does not have clear physical signs that can be seen in an x-ray or a lab test. ADHD can only be identified by looking for certain characteristic behaviors, and these behaviors vary from person to person. Scientists have not yet identified a single cause behind all the different patterns of behavior—and they may never find just one. Rather, someday scientists may find that ADHD is actually an umbrella term for several slightly different disorders.

At present, ADHD is a diagnosis applied to children and adults who consistently display certain characteristic behaviors over a period of time. The most common behaviors fall into three categories: inattention, hyperactivity, and impulsivity.

Inattention. People who are inattentive have a hard time keeping their mind on any one thing and may get bored with a task after only a few minutes. They may give effortless, automatic attention to activities and things they enjoy. But focusing deliberate, conscious attention to organizing and completing a task or learning something new is difficult.

Hyperactivity. People who are hyperactive always seem to be in motion. They can't sit still. Sitting still through a lesson can be an impossible task. Hyperactive teens and adults may feel intensely restless.

They may be fidgety or they may try to do several things at once, bouncing around from one activity to the next.

Impulsivity. People who are overly impulsive seem unable to curb their immediate reactions or think before they act. Their impulsivity may make it hard for them to wait for things they want or to take their turn.

Not everyone who is overly hyperactive, inattentive, or impulsive has an attention disorder. Since most people sometimes blurt out things they didn't mean to say, bounce from one task to another, or become disorganized and forgetful, how can specialists tell if the problem is ADHD?

To assess whether a person has ADHD, specialists consider several critical questions: Are these behaviors excessive, long-term, and pervasive? That is, do they occur more often than in other people the same age? Are they a continuous problem, not just a response to a temporary situation? Do the behaviors occur in several settings or only in one specific place like the playground or the office? The person's pattern of behavior is compared against a set of criteria and characteristics of the disorder. These criteria appear in a diagnostic reference book called the *DSM* (short for the *Diagnostic and Statistical Manual of Mental Disorders*).

According to the diagnostic manual, there are three patterns of behavior that indicate ADHD. People with ADHD may show several signs of being consistently inattentive. They may have a pattern of being hyperactive and impulsive. Or they may show all three types of behavior.

According to the *DSM*, signs of inattention include:

Becoming easily distracted by irrelevant sights and sounds
Failing to pay attention to details and making careless mistakes
Rarely following instructions carefully and completely
Losing or forgetting things like toys, or pencils, books, and tools needed for a task

Some signs of hyperactivity and impulsivity are:

Feeling restless, often fidgeting with hands or feet, or squirming
Running, climbing, or leaving a seat in situations where sitting or quiet behavior is expected
Blurting out answers before hearing the whole question
Having difficulty waiting in line or for a turn

Because everyone shows some of these behaviors at times, the *DSM* contains very specific guidelines for determining when they indicate ADHD. The behaviors must appear early in life, before age seven, and continue for at least six months. In children, they must be more frequent or severe than in others the same age. Above all, the behaviors must create a real handicap in at least two areas of a person's life, such as school, home, work, or social settings. So someone whose work or friendships are not impaired by these behaviors would not be diagnosed with ADHD. Nor would a child who seems overly active at school but functions well elsewhere.

What Can Look Like ADHD?

Underachievement at school due to a learning disability
Attention lapses caused by *petit mal* seizures
A middle ear infection that causes an intermittent hearing problem
Disruptive or unresponsive behavior due to anxiety or depression

What Causes ADHD?

Scientists are finding more and more evidence that ADHD does not stem from home environment, but from biological causes.

One disappointing theory was that all attention disorders and learning disabilities were caused by minor head injuries or undetectable damage to the brain, perhaps from early infection or complications at birth. Based on this theory, for many years both disorders were called "minimal brain damage" or "minimal brain dysfunction." Although certain types of head injury can explain some cases of attention disorder, the theory was rejected because it could explain only a very small number of cases. Not everyone with ADHD or LD (learning disabilities) has a history of head trauma or birth complications.

Another theory was that refined sugar and food additives make children hyperactive and inattentive. As a result, parents were encouraged to stop serving children foods containing artificial flavorings, preservatives, and sugars. However, this theory, too, came under question. In 1982, the National Institutes of Health (NIH), the federal agency responsible for biomedical research, held a major scientific conference to discuss the issue. After studying the data, the scientists concluded that the restricted diet only seemed to help about 5 percent of children with ADHD, mostly either young children or children with food allergies.

ADHD is not usually caused by:

Too much TV

Food allergies

Excess sugar

Poor home life

Poor schools

In recent years, as new tools and techniques for studying the brain have been developed, scientists have been able to test more theories about what causes ADHD.

Using one such technique, NIMH scientists demonstrated a link between a person's ability to pay continued attention and the level of activity in the brain. Adult subjects were asked to learn a list of words. As they did, scientists used a PET (positron emission tomography) scanner to observe the brain at work. The researchers measured the level of glucose used by the areas of the brain that inhibit impulses and control attention. Glucose is the brain's main source of energy, so measuring how much is used is a good indicator of the brain's activity level. The investigators found important differences between people who have ADHD and those who don't. In people with ADHD, the brain areas that control attention used less glucose, indicating that they were less active. It appears from this research that a lower level of activity in some parts of the brain may cause inattention.

Brain scan images produced by positron emission tomography (PET) show differences between an adult with Attention Deficit Hyperactivity Disorder and an adult free of the disease.

The next step will be to research why there is less activity in these areas of the brain. Scientists at NIMH hope to compare the use of glucose and the activity level in mild and severe cases of ADHD. They will also try to discover why some medications used to treat ADHD work better than others, and if the more effective medications increase activity in certain parts of the brain.

Researchers are also searching for other differences between those who have and do not have ADHD. Research on how the brain normally develops in the fetus offers some clues about what may disrupt the process. Throughout pregnancy and continuing into the first year of life, the brain is constantly developing. It begins its growth from a few all-purpose cells and evolves into a complex organ made of billions of specialized, interconnected nerve cells. By studying brain development in animals and humans, scientists are gaining a better understanding of how the brain works when the nerve cells are connected correctly and incorrectly. Scientists at NIMH and other research institutions are tracking clues to determine what might prevent nerve cells from forming the proper connections. Some of the factors they are studying include drug use during pregnancy, toxins, and genetics.

Research shows that a mother's use of cigarettes, alcohol, or other drugs during pregnancy may have damaging effects on the unborn child. These substances may be dangerous to the fetus' developing brain. It appears that alcohol and the nicotine in cigarettes may distort developing nerve cells. For example, heavy alcohol use during pregnancy has been linked to fetal alcohol syndrome (FAS), a condition that can lead to low birth weight, intellectual impairment, and certain physical defects. Many children born with FAS show much the same hyperactivity, inattention, and impulsivity as children with ADHD.

Drugs such as cocaine—including the smokable form known as crack—seem to affect the normal development of brain receptors. These brain cell parts help to transmit incoming signals from our skin, eyes, and ears, and help control our responses to the environment. Current research suggests that drug abuse may harm these receptors. Some scientists believe that such damage may lead to ADHD.

Toxins in the environment may also disrupt brain development or brain processes, which may lead to ADHD. Lead is one such possible toxin. It is found in dust, soil, and flaking paint in areas where leaded gasoline and paint were once used. It is also present in some water pipes. Some animal studies suggest that children exposed to lead may develop symptoms associated with ADHD, but only a few cases have actually been found.

Other research shows that attention disorders tend to run in families, so there are likely to be genetic influences. Children who have ADHD usually have at least one close relative who also has ADHD. And at least one-third of all fathers who had ADHD in their youth bear children who have ADHD. Even more convincing: the majority of identical twins share the trait. At the National Institutes of Health, researchers are also on the trail of a gene that may be involved in transmitting ADHD in a small number of families with a genetic thyroid disorder.

Types of Professionals Who Make the Diagnosis

Adults who think they may have ADHD can also seek a psychologist, psychiatrist, or neurologist. But at present, not all specialists are skilled in identifying or treating ADHD in adults.

Within each specialty, individual doctors and mental health professionals differ in their experience with ADHD. So in selecting a specialist, it's important to find someone with specific training and experience in diagnosing and treating the disorder.

Steps in Making a Diagnosis

Adults are diagnosed for ADHD based on their performance at home and at work. When possible, their parents are asked to rate the person's behavior as a child. A spouse or roommate can help rate and evaluate current behaviors. But for the most part, adults are asked to describe their own experiences. One symptom is a sense of frustration. Since people with ADHD are often bright and creative, they often report feeling frustrated that they're not living up to their potential. Many also feel restless and are easily bored. Some say they need to seek novelty and excitement to help channel the whirlwind in their minds. Although it may be impossible to document when these behaviors first started, most adults with ADHD can give examples of being inattentive, impulsive, overly active, impatient, and disorganized most of their lives.

Until recent years, adults were not thought to have ADHD, so many adults with ongoing symptoms have never been diagnosed. People go for decades knowing that something is wrong, but not knowing what it is. Psychotherapy and medication for anxiety, depression, or manic depression fail to help much, simply because the ADHD itself is not being addressed. Yet half the children with ADHD continue to have symptoms through adulthood. The recent awareness of adult ADHD means that many people can finally be correctly diagnosed and treated.

A correct diagnosis lets people move forward in their lives. Once the disorder is known, they can begin to receive whatever combination of educational, medical, and emotional help they need.

An effective treatment plan helps people with ADHD and their families at many levels. For adults with ADHD, the treatment plan may include medication, along with practical and emotional support.

What Are the Educational Options?

Students with ADHD often need to learn techniques for monitoring and controlling their own attention and behavior. For example, a student who loses track of what he is supposed to be doing can look for instructions on the blackboard, raise his hand, wait to see if he remembers, or quietly ask another student. The teacher can frequently stop to ask students to notice whether they are paying attention to the lesson or if they are thinking about something else. The students record their answer on a chart. As students become more consciously aware of their attention, they begin to see progress and feel good about staying better focused. The process helps make students aware of when they are drifting off, and they can return their attention to the lesson faster.

Because schools demand that students sit still, wait for a turn, pay attention, and stick with a task, it's no surprise that many students with ADHD have problems in class. Their minds are fully capable of learning, but their hyperactivity and inattention make learning difficult. As a result, many students with ADHD repeat a grade or drop out of school early. Fortunately, with the right combination of appropriate educational practices, medication, and counseling, these outcomes can be avoided.

What Treatments Are Available?

For decades, medications have been used to treat the symptoms of ADHD. Three medications in the class of drugs known as stimulants seem to be the most effective in both children and adults. These are methylphenidate (Ritalin), dextroamphetamine (Dexedrine or Dextrostat), and pemoline (Cylert). For many people, these medicines dramatically reduce their hyperactivity and improve their ability to focus, work, and learn. The medications may also improve physical coordination, such as handwriting and ability in sports.

Unfortunately, when people see such immediate improvement, they often think medication is all that's needed. But these medicines don't cure the disorder, they only temporarily control the symptoms. Although the drugs help people pay better attention and complete their work, they can't increase knowledge or improve academic skills. The drugs alone can't help people feel better about themselves or cope with problems. These require other kinds of treatment and support.

For lasting improvement, numerous clinicians recommend that medications should be used along with treatments that aid in these other areas. There are no quick cures. Many experts believe that the most significant, long-lasting gains appear when medication is combined with behavioral therapy, emotional counseling, and practical support. Some studies suggest that the combination of medicine and therapy may be more effective than drugs alone. NIMH is conducting a large study to check this.

Use of Stimulant Drugs

Stimulant drugs, such as Ritalin, Cylert, and Dexedrine, when used with medical supervision, are usually considered quite safe. Although they can be addictive to teenagers and adults if misused, these medications are not addictive in children. They seldom make children "high" or jittery. Nor do they sedate the child. Rather, the stimulants help children control their hyperactivity, inattention, and other behaviors.

Different doctors use the medications in slightly different ways. Cylert is available in one form, which naturally lasts five to ten hours. Ritalin and Dexedrine come in short-term tablets that last about three hours, as well as longer-term preparations that last through the school day.

Nine out of ten improve on one of the three stimulant drugs. So if one doesn't help, the others should be tried. Usually a medication should be tried for a week to see if it helps. If necessary, however, the doctor will also try adjusting the dosage before switching to a different drug.

Other types of medication may be used if stimulants don't work or if the ADHD occurs with another disorder. Antidepressants and other medications may be used to help control accompanying depression or anxiety. In some cases, antihistamines may be tried. Clonidine, a drug normally used to treat hypertension, may be helpful in people with both ADHD and Tourette's syndrome. Although stimulants tend to be more effective, Clonidine may be tried when stimulants don't work or can't be used. Clonidine can be administered either by pill or by skin patch and has different side effects than stimulants. The doctor works closely with each patient to find the most appropriate medication.

The Medication Debate

As useful as these drugs are, Ritalin and the other stimulants have sparked a great deal of controversy. Most doctors feel the potential side effects should be carefully weighed against the benefits before prescribing the drugs. While on these medications, some children may lose weight, have less appetite, and temporarily grow more slowly. Others may have problems falling asleep.

Another debate is whether Ritalin and other stimulant drugs are prescribed unnecessarily for too many children. Remember that many things, including anxiety, depression, allergies, seizures, or problems with the home or school environment can make children seem overactive, impulsive, or inattentive. Critics argue that many children who do not have a true attention disorder are medicated as a way to control their disruptive behaviors.

Myths about Stimulant Medication

Stimulants can lead to drug addiction later in life.

Stimulants help many children focus and be more successful at school, home, and play. Avoiding negative experiences now may actually help prevent addictions and other emotional problems later.

Responding well to a stimulant drug proves a person has ADHD.

Stimulants allow many people to focus and pay better attention, whether or not they have ADHD. The improvement is just more noticeable in people with ADHD.

Medication should be stopped when the child reaches adolescence.

Not so! About 80 percent of those who needed medication as children still need it as teenagers. Fifty percent need medication as adults.

Treatments to Help People with ADHD Learn to Cope

Medication can help to control some of the behavior problems that may have led to family turmoil. But more often, there are other aspects of the problem that medication can't touch. Even though ADHD primarily affects a person's behavior, having the disorder has broad emotional repercussions. For some children, being scolded is the only attention they ever get. They have few experiences that build their sense of worth and competence. If they're hyperactive, they're often told they're bad and punished for being disruptive. If they are too disorganized and unfocused to complete tasks, others may call them lazy. And if they have a related conduct disorder, they may get in trouble at school or with the law. Facing the daily frustrations that can come with having ADHD can make children fear that they are strange, abnormal, or stupid.

Psychotherapy works to help people with ADHD to like and accept themselves despite their disorder. In psychotherapy, patients talk with the therapist about upsetting thoughts and feelings, explore self-defeating patterns of behavior, and learn alternative ways to handle their emotions. As they talk, the therapist tries to help them understand how they can change. However, people dealing with ADHD usually want to gain control of their symptomatic behaviors more directly. If so, more direct kinds of intervention are needed.

Cognitive-behavioral therapy helps people work on immediate issues. Rather than helping people understand their feelings and actions, it supports them directly in changing their behavior.

Social skills training can also help students learn new behaviors. In social skills training, the therapist discusses and models appropriate behaviors like waiting for a turn or asking for help, then gives students a chance to practice. For example, a student might learn to "read" other people's facial expression and tone of voice, in order to respond more appropriately.

Support groups connect people who have common concerns. Many adults with ADHD find it useful to join a local or national support group. Members of support groups share frustrations and successes, referrals to qualified specialists, and information about what works. There is strength in numbers—and sharing experiences with others who have similar problems helps people know that they aren't alone.

Can ADHD Be Outgrown or Cured?

Even though most people don't outgrow ADHD, people do learn to adapt and live fulfilling lives. With effective combinations of medicine, new skills, and emotional support, people with ADHD can develop ways to control their attention and minimize their disruptive behaviors. And although we know that half of all children with ADHD will still show signs of the problem into adulthood, we also know that the medications and therapy that help children also work for adults.

All people with ADHD have natural talents and abilities that they can draw on to create fine lives and careers for themselves. In fact, many people with ADHD even feel that their patterns of behavior give them unique, often unrecognized, advantages. People with ADHD tend to be outgoing and ready for action. Because of their drive for excitement and stimulation, many become successful in business, sports, construction, and public speaking. Because of their ability to think about many things at once, many have won acclaim as artists and inventors. Many choose work that gives them freedom to move around and release excess energy. But some find ways to be effective in quieter, more sedentary careers. Others who own their own business find it useful to hire support staff to provide day-to-day management.

Further Reading Regarding Adult Attention Disorders

Adelman, P., and Wren, C. *Learning Disabilities, Graduate School, and Careers: The Student's Perspective.* Lake Forest, IL: Learning Opportunities Program, Barat College, 1990.

Hallowell, E., and Ratey, J. *Driven to Distraction.* New York: Pantheon Books, 1994.

Hartmann, T. *Attention Deficit Disorder: A New Perception.* Lancaster, PA: Underwood-Miller, 1993.

Kelly, K., and Ramundo, P. *You Mean I'm not Lazy, Stupid, or Crazy?!* Cincinnati, OH: Tyrell and Jeremy Press, 1993.

Weiss, G., and Hechtman, L. (eds). *Hyperactive Children Grown Up.* 2d ed. New York: Guilford Press, 1992.

Weiss, L. *Attention Deficit Disorder in Adults.* Dallas, TX: Taylor Pub. Co., 1992.

Wender, P. *The Hyperactive Child, Adolescence, and Adult: Attention Deficit Disorder through the Lifespan.* New York: Oxford University Press, 1987.

Dyslexia

Sally E. Shaywitz

One hundred years ago, in November 1896, a doctor in Sussex, England, published the first description of the learning disorder that would come to be known as developmental dyslexia. "Percy F., . . . aged 14, . . . has always been a bright and intelligent boy," wrote W. Pringle Morgan in the "British Medical Journal," "quick at games, and in no way inferior to others of his age. His great difficulty has been—and is now— his inability to learn to read."

In that brief introduction, Morgan captured the paradox that has intrigued and frustrated scientists for a century since: the profound and persistent difficulties some very bright people face in learning to read. In 1996 as in 1896, reading ability is taken as a proxy for intelligence; most people assume that if someone is smart, motivated and schooled, he or she will learn to read. But the experience of millions of dyslexics like Percy F. has shown that assumption to be false. In dyslexia, the seemingly invariant relation between intelligence and reading ability breaks down.

Early explanations of dyslexia, put forth in the 1920s, held that defects in the visual system were to blame for the reversals of letters and words thought to typify dyslexic reading. Eye training was often prescribed to overcome these alleged visual defects. Subsequent research has shown, however, that children with dyslexia are not unusually prone to reversing letters or words and that the cognitive deficit responsible for the disorder is related to the language system. In particular, dyslexia reflects a deficiency in the processing of the distinctive linguistic units, called phonemes, that make up all spoken and written words. Current linguistic models of reading and dyslexia now provide an explanation of why some very intelligent people have trouble learning to read and performing other language-related tasks.

In the course of our work, my colleagues and I at the Yale Center for the Study of Learning and Attention have evaluated hundreds of children and scores of men and women for reading disabilities. Many are students and faculty at our university's undergraduate, graduate and professional schools. One of these, a medical student named Gregory, came to see us after undergoing a series of problems in his first-year courses. He was quite discouraged.

Although he had been diagnosed as dyslexic in grade school, Gregory had also been placed in a program for gifted students. His native intelligence, together with extensive support and tutoring, had allowed him to graduate from high school with honors and gain admission to an Ivy League college. In college, Gregory had worked extremely hard and eventually received offers from several top medical schools. Now, however, he was beginning to doubt his own competence. He had no trouble comprehending the intricate relations among physiological systems or the complex mechanisms of disease; indeed, he excelled in those areas requiring reasoning skills. More problematic for him was the

Source: United States. Department of Health and Human Services. National Institute of Health. *Attention Deficit Hyperactivity Disorder.* NIH 96-3572 Washington, DC: GPO, 1996.

simple act of pronouncing long words or novel terms (such as labels used in anatomic descriptions); perhaps his least well-developed skill was rote memorization.

Both Gregory and his professors were perplexed by the inconsistencies in his performance. How could someone who understood difficult concepts so well have trouble with the smaller and simpler details? Could Gregory's dyslexia—he was still a slow reader—account for his inability to name body parts and tissue types in the face of his excellent reasoning skills?

It could, I explained. Gregory's history fit the clinical picture of dyslexia as it has been traditionally defined: an unexpected difficulty learning to read despite intelligence, motivation and education. Furthermore, I was able to reassure Gregory that scientists now understand the basic nature of dyslexia.

Over the past two decades, a coherent model of dyslexia has emerged that is based on phonological processing. The phonological model is consistent both with the clinical symptoms of dyslexia and with what neuroscientists know about brain organization and function. Investigators from many laboratories, including my colleagues and I at the Yale Center, have had the opportunity to test and refine this model through ten years of cognitive and, more recently, neurobiological studies.

The Phonological Model

To understand how the phonological model works, one has first to consider the way in which language is processed in the brain. Researchers conceptualize the language system as a hierarchical series of modules or components, each devoted to a particular aspect of language. At the upper levels of the hierarchy are components involved with semantics (vocabulary or word meaning), syntax (grammatical structure) and discourse (connected sentences). At the lowest level of the hierarchy is the phonological module, which is dedicated to processing the distinctive sound elements that constitute language.

The phoneme, defined as the smallest meaningful segment of language, is the fundamental element of the linguistic system. Different combinations of just forty-four phonemes produce every word in the English language. The word "cat," for example, consists of three phonemes: "kuh," "aah," and "tuh." (Linguists indicate these sounds as |k|, |ae| and |t|.) Before words can be identified, understood, stored in memory or retrieved from it, they must first be broken down, or parsed, into their phonetic units by the phonological module of the brain.

In spoken language, this process occurs automatically, at a preconscious level. As Noam Chomsky and, more recently, Steven Pinker of the Massachusetts Institute of Technology have convincingly argued, language is instinctive—all that is necessary is for humans to be exposed to it. A genetically determined phonological module automatically assembles the phonemes into words for the speaker and parses the spoken word back into its underlying phonological components for the listener.

In producing a word, the human speech apparatus—the larynx, palate, tongue and lips— automatically compresses and merges the phonemes. As a result, information from several phonemes is folded into a single unit of sound. Because there is no overt clue to the underlying segmental nature of speech, spoken language appears to be seamless. Hence, an oscilloscope would register the word "cat" as a single burst of sound; only the human language system is capable of distinguishing the three phonemes embedded in the word.

Reading reflects spoken language, as my colleague Alvin M. Liberman of Haskins Laboratories in New Haven, Conn., points out, but it is a much harder skill to master. Why? Although both speaking and reading rely on phonological processing, there is a significant difference: speaking is natural, and reading is not. Reading is an invention and must be learned at a conscious level. The task of the reader is to transform the visual percepts of alphabetic script into linguistic ones—that is, to recode graphemes (letters) into their corresponding phonemes. To accomplish this, the beginning reader must first come to a conscious awareness of the internal phonological structure of spoken words. Then he or she must realize that the orthography—the sequence of letters on the page—represents this phonology. That is precisely what happens when a child learns to read.

In contrast, when a child is dyslexic, a deficit within the language system at the level of the phonological module impairs his or her ability to segment the written word into its underlying phonological components. This explanation of dyslexia is referred to as the phonological model, or sometimes as the phonological deficit hypothesis.

According to this hypothesis, a circumscribed deficit in phonological processing impairs decoding, preventing word identification. This basic deficit in what is essentially a lower-order linguistic function blocks access to higher-order linguistic processes and to gaining meaning from text. Thus, although the language processes involved in comprehension and meaning are intact, they cannot be called into play, because they can be accessed only after a word has been identified. The impact of the phonological deficit is most obvious in reading, but it can also affect speech in predictable ways. Gregory's dilemma with long or novel words, for example, is entirely consistent with the body of evidence that supports a phonological model of dyslexia.

That evidence began accumulating more than two decades ago. One of the earliest experiments, carried out by the late Isabelle Y. Liberman of Haskins Laboratories, showed that young children become aware between four and six years of age of the phonological structure of spoken words. In the experiment, children were asked how many sounds they heard in a series of words. None of the four year olds could correctly identify the number of phonemes, but 17 percent of the five year olds did, and by age six, 70 percent of the children demonstrated phonological awareness.

By age six, most children have also had at least one full year of schooling, including instruction in reading. The development of phonological awareness, then, parallels the acquisition of reading skills. This correspondence suggested that the two processes are related. These findings also converge with data from the Connecticut Longitudinal Study, a project my colleagues and I began in 1983 with 445 randomly selected kindergartners; the study continues in 1996 when these children are age nineteen and out of high school. Testing the youngsters yearly, we found that dyslexia affects a full 20 percent of schoolchildren—a figure that agrees roughly with the proportion of Liberman's six year olds who could not identify the phonological structure of words. These data further support a connection between phonological awareness and reading.

During the 1980s, researchers began to address that connection explicitly. The groundbreaking work of Lynette Bradley and Peter E. Bryant of the University of Oxford indicated that a preschooler's phonological aptitude predicts future skill at reading. Bradley and Bryant also found that training in phonological awareness significantly improves a child's ability to read. In these studies, one group of children received training in phonological processing, while another received language training that did not emphasize the sound structure of words. For example, the first group might work on categorizing words by their sound, and the second group would focus on categorizing words according to their meaning. These studies, together with more recent work by Benita A. Blachman of Syracuse University, Joseph E. Torgesen of Florida State University and Barbara Foorman of the University of Houston, clearly demonstrate that phonological training in particular—rather than general language instruction—is responsible for the improvements in reading.

Such findings set the stage for our own study, in the early 1990s, of the cognitive skills of dyslexic and nondyslexic children. Along with Jack M. Fletcher of the University of Texas-Houston and Donald P. Shankweiler and Leonard Katz of Haskins Laboratories, I examined 378 children from seven to nine years old on a battery of tests that assessed both linguistic and nonlinguistic abilities. Our results as well as those of Keith E. Stanovich and Linda S. Siegel of the Ontario Institute for Studies in Education made it clear that phonological deficits are the most significant and consistent cognitive marker of dyslexic children.

One test in particular seemed quite sensitive to dyslexia: the Auditory Analysis Test, which asks a child to segment words into their underlying phonological units and then to delete specific phonemes from the words. For example, the child must say the word "block" without the "buh" sound or say the word "sour" without the "s" sound. This measure was most related to a child's ability to decode single words in standardized tests and was independent of his or her intelligence, vocabulary and reasoning skills. When we gave this and other tests of phonemic awareness to a group of fifteen year olds in our Connecticut Longitudinal Study, the results were the same: even in high school students, phonological awareness was the best predictor of reading ability.

If dyslexia is the result of an insufficiently developed phonological specialization, other consequences of impaired phonological functioning should also be apparent—and they are. Ten years ago the work of Robert B. Katz of Haskins Laboratories documented the problems poor readers have in naming objects shown in pictures. Katz showed that when dyslexics misname objects, the incorrect responses tend to share phonological characteristics with the correct response. Furthermore, the misnaming is not the result of a lack of knowledge. For example, a girl shown a picture of a volcano calls it a tornado. When given the opportunity to elaborate, she demonstrates that she knows what the pictured object is—she can describe the attributes and activities of a volcano in great detail and point to other pictures related to volcanoes. She simply cannot summon the word "volcano."

This finding converges with other evidence in suggesting that whereas the phonological component of the language system is impaired in dyslexia, the higher-level components remain intact. Linguistic processes involved in word meaning, grammar and discourse— what, collectively, underlies comprehension—seem to be fully operational, but their activity is blocked by the deficit in the lower-order function of phonological processing. In one of our studies, Jennifer, a very bright young woman with a reading disability, told us all about the word "apocalypse." She knew its meaning, its connotations and its correct usage; she could not, however, recognize the word on a printed page. Because she could not decode and identify the written word, she could not access her fund of knowledge about its meaning when she came across it in reading.

Of course, many dyslexics, like Gregory, do learn to read and even to excel in academics despite their disability. These so-called compensated dyslexics perform as well as nondyslexics on tests of word accuracy—they have learned how to decode or identify words, thereby gaining entry to the higher levels of the language system. But they do so at a cost. Timed tests reveal that decoding remains very laborious for compensated dyslexics; they are neither automatic nor fluent in their ability to identify words. Many dyslexics have told us how tiring reading is for them, reflecting the enormous resources and energy they must expend on the task. In fact, extreme slowness in making phonologically based decisions is typical of the group of compensated dyslexics we have assembled as part of a new approach to understanding dyslexia: our neuroimaging program.

The Neurobiology of Reading

The phonological model incorporates a modular scheme of cognitive processing in which each of the component processes used in word identification is carried out by a specific network of brain cells. Until recently, however, researchers have had no firm indication of how that scheme maps onto the actual functional organization of the human brain. Unlike many other functions, reading cannot be studied in animals; indeed, for many years the cerebral localization of all higher cognitive processes could be inferred only from the effects of brain injuries on the people who survived them. Such an approach offered little to illuminate the phenomena my colleagues and I were interested in. What we needed was a way to identify the regions of the brain that are engaged when healthy subjects are reading or trying to read.

Our group became quite excited, then, with the advent in the late 1980s of functional magnetic resonance imaging (fMRI). Using the same scanning machine that has revolutionized clinical imaging, fMRI can measure changes in the metabolic activity of the brain while an individual performs a cognitive task. Hence, it is ideally suited to mapping the brain's response to stimuli such as reading. Because it is noninvasive and uses no radioisotopes, fMRI is also excellent for work involving children.

Since 1994, I have worked with several Yale colleagues to use fMRI in studying the neurobiology of reading. Bennett A. Shaywitz, Kenneth R. Pugh, R. Todd Constable, Robert K. Fulbright, John C. Gore and I have used the technique with more than two hundred dyslexic and nondyslexic children and adults. As a result of this program, we can now suggest a tentative neural architecture for reading a printed word. In particular, the identification of letters activates sites in the extrastriate cortex within the occipital lobe; phonological processing takes place within the inferior frontal gyrus; and access to meaning calls on areas within the middle and superior temporal gyri of the brain.

Our investigation has already revealed a surprising difference between men and women in the locus of phonological representation for reading. It turns out that in men phonological processing engages the left inferior frontal gyrus, whereas in women it activates not only the left but the right inferior frontal gyrus as well. These differences in lateralization had been suggested by behavioral studies, but they had never before been demonstrated unequivocally. Indeed, our findings constitute the first concrete proof of gender differences in brain organization for any cognitive function. The fact that women's brains tend to have bilateral representation for phonological processing explains several formerly puzzling observations: why, for example, after a stroke involving the left side of the brain, women are less likely than men to have significant decrements in their language skills, and why women tend more often than men to compensate for dyslexia.

As investigators who have spent our entire professional lives trying to understand dyslexia, we find the identification of brain sites dedicated to phonological processing in reading very exciting—it means that we now have a possible neurobiological "signature" for reading. The isolation of such a signature brings with it the future promise of more precise diagnosis of dyslexia. It is possible, for example, that the neural signature for phonological processing may provide the most sensitive measure of the disorder. Furthermore, the discovery of a biological signature for reading offers an unprecedented opportunity to assess the effects of interventions on the neuroanatomic systems serving the reading process itself.

Putting It in Context

The phonological model crystallizes exactly what we mean by dyslexia: an encapsulated deficit often surrounded by significant strengths in reasoning, problem solving, concept formation, critical thinking and vocabulary. Indeed, compensated dyslexics such as Gregory may use the "big picture" of theories, models and ideas to help them remember specific details. It is true that when details are not unified by associated ideas or theoretical frameworks—when, for example, Gregory must commit to memory long lists of unfamiliar names—dyslexics can be at a real disadvantage. Even if Gregory succeeds in memorizing such lists, he has trouble producing the names on demand, as he must when he is questioned on rounds by an attending physician. The phonological model predicts, and experimentation has shown, that rote memorization and rapid word retrieval are particularly difficult for dyslexics.

Even when the individual knows the information, needing to retrieve it rapidly and present it orally often results in calling up a related phoneme or incorrectly ordering the retrieved phonemes. Under such circumstances, dyslexics will pepper their speech with many um's, ah's and other hesitations. On the other hand, when not pressured to provide instant responses, the dyslexic can deliver an excellent oral presentation. Similarly, in reading, whereas nonimpaired readers can decode words automatically, individuals such as Gregory frequently need to resort to the use of context to help them identify specific words. This strategy slows them further and is another reason that the provision of extra time is necessary if dyslexics are to show what they actually know. Multiple-choice examinations, too, by their lack of sufficient context, as well as by their wording and response format, excessively penalize dyslexics.

But our experience at the Yale Center suggests that many compensated dyslexics have a distinct advantage over nondyslexics in their ability to reason and conceptualize and that the phonological deficit masks what are often excellent comprehension skills. Many schools and universities now appreciate the circumscribed nature of dyslexia and offer to evaluate the achievement of their dyslexic students with essays and prepared oral presentations rather than tests of rote memorization or multiple choices. Just as researchers have begun to understand the neural substrate of dyslexia, educators are beginning to recognize the practical implications of the disorder. A century after W. Pringle Morgan first described dyslexia in Percy F., society may at last understand the paradox of the disorder.

The Myths of Dyslexia

Mirror writing is a symptom of dyslexia.

In fact, backwards writing and reversals of letters and words are common in the early stages of writing development among dyslexic and nondyslexic children alike. Dyslexic children have problems in naming letters but not in copying letters.

Eye training is a treatment for dyslexia.

More than two decades of research have shown that dyslexia reflects a linguistic deficit. There is no evidence that eye training alleviates the disorder.

More boys than girls are dyslexic.

Boys' reading disabilities are indeed identified more often than girls', but studies indicate that such identification is biased. The actual prevalence of the disorder is nearly identical in the two sexes.

Dyslexia can be outgrown.

Yearly monitoring of phonological skills from first through twelfth grade shows that the disability persists into adulthood. Even though many dyslexics learn to read accurately, they continue to read slowly and not automatically.

Smart people cannot be dyslexic.

Intelligence is in no way related to phonological processing, as scores of brilliant and accomplished dyslexics—among them William Butler Yeats, Albert Einstein, George Patton, John Irving, Charles Schwab and Nicholas Negroponte—attest.

Further Reading

"The Alphabetic Principle and Learning to Read." Donald P. Shankweiler and Alvin M. Liberman in *Phonology and Reading Disability.* Edited by D. P. Shankweiler and I. Y. Liberman. University of Michigan Press, 1989.

Learning to Read. Edited by Laurence Rieben and Charles A. Perfetti. Lawrence Erlbaum Associates, Hillsdale, NJ, 1991.

"Evidence that Dyslexia May Represent the Lower Tail of a Normal Distribution of Reading Ability." Sally E. Shaywitz, Michael D. Escobar, Bennett A. Shaywitz, Jack M. Fletcher and Robert Makuch in *New England Journal of Medicine*, Vol. 326, No. 3, pages 145–150; January 16, 1992.

"Sex Differences in the Functional Organization of the Brain for Languages." Bennett A. Shaywitz, Sally E. Shaywitz, Kenneth R. Pugh, R. Todd Constable, Pawel Skudlarski, Robert K. Fulbright, Richard A. Bronen, Jack M. Fletcher, Donald P. Shankweiler, Leonard Katz and John C. Gore in *Nature*, Vol. 373, pages 607–609; February 16, 1995.

"Toward a Definition of Dyslexia." G. Reid Lyon in *Annals of Dyslexia*, Vol. 45, pages 3–27; 1995.

Source: Shaywitz, Sally. "Dyslexia." *Scientific American* Nov. 1996.

Appendix 2
Photo-Ready Material

TABLE 1.   Categories of feelings.[*]

GLAD	BAD	MAD	SAD	FEAR
Appreciated	Ashamed	Angry	Apathetic	Anxious
Calm	Degraded	Annoyed	Bewildered	Apprehensive
Cheerful	Dependent	Bitter	Bored	Critical
Close	Embarrassed	Disgusted	Defeated	Distant
Comfortable	Foolish	Enraged	Depressed	Distrustful
Confident	Guilty	Envious	Dismayed	Edgy
Consoled	Helpless	Frustrated	Excluded	Frightened
Content	Humiliated	Furious	Gloomy	Nervous
Daring	Inadequate	Hateful	Hopeless	Panicky
Delighted	Inferior	Hostile	Hurt	Submissive
Energetic	Insignificant	Impatient	Lethargic	Suspicious
Excited	Mortified	Irritated	Listless	Tense
Gratified	Powerless	Jealous	Lonely	Threatened
Hopeful	Rejected	Resentful	Melancholy	Unsure
Intimate	Self-conscious	Revengeful	Miserable	Wary
Joyful	Shy	Spiteful	Misfortunate	Weak
Loving	Stupid	Sullen	Sorrowful	Worried
Nurturing	Timid	Vulnerable		
Patient	Unimportant			
Playful	Unlovable			
Pleased	Unloved			
Proud	Unvalued			
Relaxed	Unwanted			
Relieved	Unworthy			
Satisfied	Weak			
Sentimental				
Serene				
Tender				
Thankful				
Trusting				
Valuable				
Wanted				

*Secondary feelings can be generated by more than one primary emotion. (For example, hostility can be generated by shame ("bad"), anger ("mad"), as well as fear.) This table is not meant to rigidly classify secondary feelings. Rather, it is meant to help students as they think about and examine emotions.

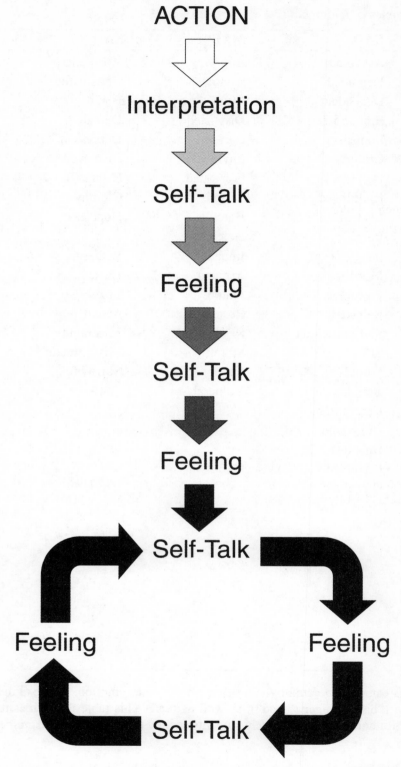

FIGURE 1.   An illustration of self-talk, based loosely on the theory of psychologist Albert Ellis.

Excerpt from

"Maintain Healthy Weight"

Dietary Guidelines for Americans, 1990

If you are too fat or too thin, your chances of developing health problems are increased. Being too fat is common in the United States. It is linked with high blood pressure, heart disease, stroke, the most common type of diabetes, certain cancers, and other types of illness. Being too thin is a less common problem. It occurs with anorexia nervosa and is linked with osteoporosis in women and greater risk of early death in both women and men.

Whether your weight is "healthy" depends on how much of your weight is fat, where in your body the fat is located, and whether you have weight-related medical problems, such as high blood pressure, or a family history of such problems.

What is a healthy weight for you? There is no exact answer right now. Researchers are trying to develop more precise ways to describe healthy weight. In the meantime, you can use the guidelines suggested below to help judge if your weight is healthy.

See if your weight is within the range suggested in the table for persons of your age and height. The table shows higher weights for people 35 years and above than for younger adults. This is because recent research suggests that people can be a little heavier as they grow older without added risk to health. Just how much heavier is not yet clear. The weight ranges given in the table are likely to change based on research under way.

Ranges of weights are given in the table because people of the same height may have equal amounts of body fat but differ in muscle and bone. The higher weights in the ranges are suggested for people with more muscle and bone.

Weights above the range are believed to be unhealthy for most people. Weights slightly below the range may be healthy for some small-boned people but are sometimes linked to health problems, especially if sudden weight loss has occurred.

Research also suggests that, for adults, body shape as well as weight is important to health. Excess fat in the abdomen is believed to be of greater health risk than that in the hips and thighs. There are several ways to check body shape. Some require the help of a doctor; others you can do yourself.

Suggested Weights for Adults

Height (without shoes)	Weight in Pounds (without clothes)	
	19 to 34 years	35 years years
5'0"	97–128	108–138
5'1"	101–132	111–143
5'2"	104–137	115–148
5'3"	107–141	119–152
5'4"	111–146	122–157
5'5"	114–150	126–162
5'6"	118–155	130–167
5'7"	121–160	134–172
5'8"	125–164	138–178
5'9"	129–169	142–183
5'10"	132–174	146–188
5'11"	136–179	151–194
6'0"	140–184	155–199
6'1"	144–189	159–205
6'2"	148–195	164–210
6'3"	152–200	168–216
6'4"	156–205	173–222
6'5"	160–211	177–228
6'6"	164–216	182–234

Note: The higher weights in the ranges generally apply to men, who tend to have more muscle and bone; the lower weights more often apply to women, who have less muscle and bone.

Source: Derived from National Research Council, 1989.

A look at your profile in the mirror may be enough to make it clear that you have too much fat in the abdomen. Or you can check your body shape this way:

- Measure around your waist near your navel while you stand relaxed, not pulling in your stomach
- Measure around your hips, over the buttocks, where they are largest
- Divide the waist measure by the hips measure to get your waist-to-hip ratio

Research in adults suggests that ratios close to or above one are linked with greater risk for several diseases. However, ratios have not been defined for all populations or age groups.

If your weight is within the range in the table, if your waist-to-hip ratio does not place you at risk, and if you have no medical problem for which your doctor advises you to gain or lose weight, there appears to be no health advantage to changing your weight. If you do not meet all of these conditions, or if you are not sure, you may want to talk to your doctor about how your weight might affect your health and what you should do about it.

Heredity plays a role in body size and shape as do exercise and what you eat. Some people seem to be able to eat more than others and still maintain a good body size and shape.

Source: United States, Department of Agriculture and Department of Health and Human Services. "Maintain Healthy Weight." *Dietary Guidelines for Americans.* 3rd ed. Home and Garden Bulletin No. 232. Washington, DC: GPO, 1990. 17 Sept. 2005 <http://www.nal.usda.gov/fnic/dga/weight.htm>.

The Definition of *Rape*

from

Bouviers Law Dictionary, 1856 Edition

(references to case law have been omitted)

RAPE, crim. law. The carnal knowledge of a woman by a man forcibly and unlawfully against her will. In order to ascertain precisely the nature of this offence, this definition will be analyzed.

2.   Much difficulty has arisen in defining the meaning of carnal knowledge, and different opinions have been entertained some judges having supposed that penetration alone is sufficient, while other's deemed emission as an essential ingredient in the crime. But in modern times the better opinion seems to be that both penetration and emission are necessary. It is, however, to be remarked, that very slight evidence may be sufficient to induce a jury to believe there was emission. In Scotland, emission is not requisite.

3.   By the term man in this definition is meant a male of the human species, of the age of fourteen years and upwards; for an infant, under fourteen years, is supposed by law incapable of committing this offence. But not only can an infant under fourteen years, if of sufficient mischievous discretion, but even a woman may be guilty as principals in the second degree. And the husband of a woman may be a principal in the second degree of a rape committed upon his wife, as where he held her while his servant committed the rape.

4.   The knowledge of the woman's person must be forcibly and against her will; and if her consent has not been voluntarily and freely given, (when she has the power to consent), the offence will be complete, nor will any subsequent acquiescence on her part do away the guilt of the ravisher. A consent obtained from a woman by actual violence, by duress or threats of murder, or by the administration of stupefying drugs, is not such a consent as will shield the offender, nor turn his crime into adultery or fornication.

5.   The matrimonial consent of the wife cannot be retracted, and, therefore, her husband cannot be guilty of a rape on her as his act is not unlawful. But, as already observed, he may be guilty as principal in the second degree.

6.   As a child under ten years of age is incapable in law to give her consent, it follows, that the offence may be committed on such a child whether she consent or not.

Source: Bouvier, John. "Rape." *A Law Dictionary.* 6th ed. 1856. The Constitution Society. 17 September 2005 <http://www.constitution.org/bouv/bouvier.htm>.

Medical Marijuana

Excerpts from Two Articles

The following excerpts address the issue of "medical marijuana." The first paragraph is from a 1998 article written by Dr. Linda Bayer, a senior writer and strategic analyst for the White House Office of National Drug Control Policy; the second is from a 1999 press release from the White House Office of National Drug Control Policy.

The medical marijuana referendum are something of a hoax because Marinol—the real "medical marijuana"—has been available for fifteen years. The active form of cannabis, THC, can be prescribed legally by physicians and taken in measured doses as well as guaranteed purity. It isn't prescribed often because new and better medications—like ondansetron and grenisetron—(with fewer adverse side effects) have been invented, but that's beside the point. No one argues that patients should have the right to bypass pure forms of penicillin so they can grow it on moldy bread at home. We don't need to endanger our entire pure food and drug system, which has made American medicine among the safest in the world, for a drug that is already available.

Source: Linda Bayer, "U.S. Drug Policy Is Sound, Despite What Molly Ivins Might Think," *Oregonian,* 25 Nov. 1998: B11.

The federal government is committed to ensuring that the analysis of the medical efficacy and safety of cannabinoids takes place within the context of medicine and science. To that end, the Department of Health and Human Services announced on May 21, 1999, new procedures to facilitate further research into the potential medical uses of marijuana's constituent cannabinoids. Such research will allow science to better explore what benefits might actually exist for the use of cannabinoid-based drugs, and what health risks such use entails. It will also facilitate the development of an inhaler or alternate rapid-onset delivery system for THC or other cannabinoid drugs.

Source: United States, Office of the President, Office of National Drug Control Policy, *Statement on California Medical Marijuana Bill (SB 848)* (21 July 1999).
28 Aug. 1999 <http://www.whitehousedrugpolicy.gov/news/press/1999/072199.html>.

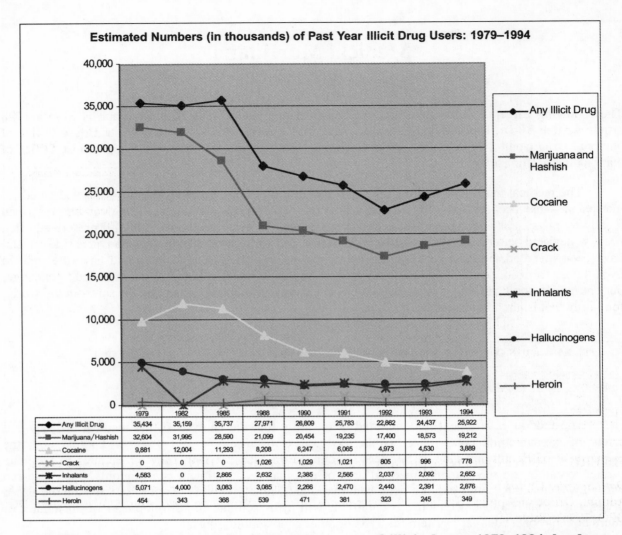

Estimated Numbers (in thousands) of Past Year Illicit Drug Users: 1979–1994

	1979	1982	1985	1988	1990	1991	1992	1993	1994
Any Illicit Drug	35,434	35,159	35,737	27,971	26,809	25,783	22,862	24,437	25,922
Marijuana/Hashish	32,604	31,995	28,590	21,099	20,454	19,235	17,400	18,573	19,212
Cocaine	9,881	12,004	11,293	8,208	6,247	6,065	4,973	4,530	3,889
Crack	0	0	0	1,026	1,029	1,021	805	996	778
Inhalants	4,583	0	2,865	2,632	2,385	2,565	2,037	2,092	2,652
Hallucinogens	5,071	4,000	3,083	3,085	2,266	2,470	2,440	2,391	2,876
Heroin	454	343	368	539	471	381	323	245	349

FIGURE 2.   Estimated numbers of past year users of illicit drugs: 1979–1994, by drug and year.

Data Source: United States, Dept. of Health and Human Svcs., Substance Abuse and Mental Health Svcs. Admin., Office of Applied Studies. *1994 National Household Survey on Drug Abuse* (Washington, DC: GPO, 1995): Table 4A.

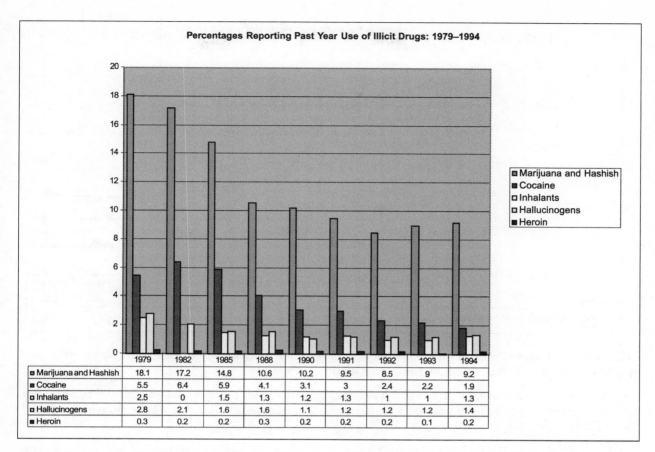

FIGURE 3.   Percentages reporting past year use of illicit drugs: 1979–1994, by drug and year.

Data Source: United States, Dept. of Health and Human Svcs., Substance Abuse and Mental Health Svcs. Admin., Office of Applied Studies. *1994 National Household Survey on Drug Abuse* (Washington, DC: GPO, 1995): Table 4B.

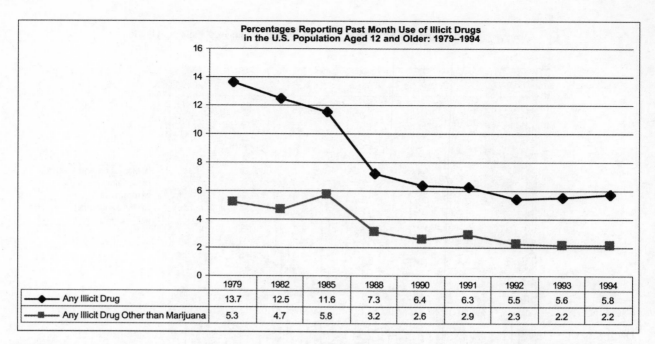

FIGURE 4.   Comparison of percentages reporting past month use of any illicit drug with past month use of any illicit drug other than marijuana: 1979–1994.

Data Source: United States, Dept. of Health and Human Svcs., Substance Abuse and Mental Health Svcs. Admin., Office of Applied Studies. *1994 National Household Survey on Drug Abuse* (Washington, DC: GPO, 1995): Table 5B.

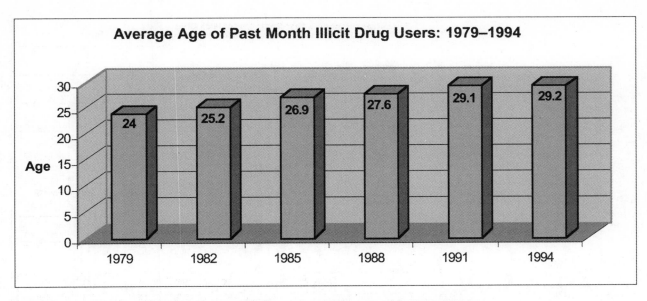

FIGURE 5.   Average age of past month users of illicit drugs: 1979–1994.

Data Source: United States, Dept. of Health and Human Svcs., Substance Abuse and Mental Health Svcs. Admin., Office of Applied Studies. *1994 National Household Survey on Drug Abuse* (Washington, DC: GPO, 1995): Figure 2.

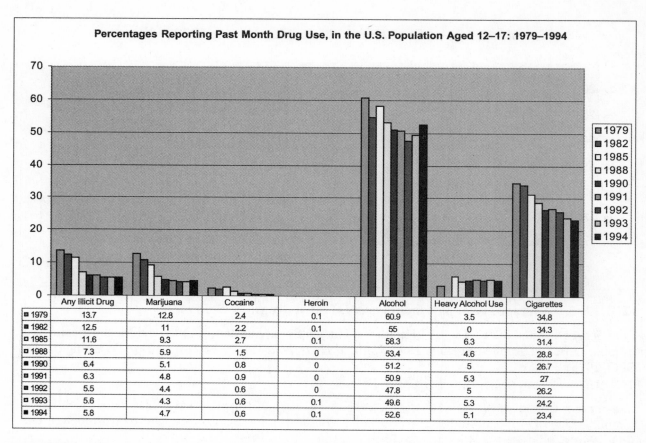

FIGURE 6.   Percentages of 12–17 year-olds reporting past month drug use: 1979–1994, by year and drug.

Data Source: United States, Dept. of Health and Human Svcs., Substance Abuse and Mental Health Svcs. Admin., Office of Applied Studies. *1994 National Household Survey on Drug Abuse* (Washington, DC: GPO, 1995): Tables 6–11.

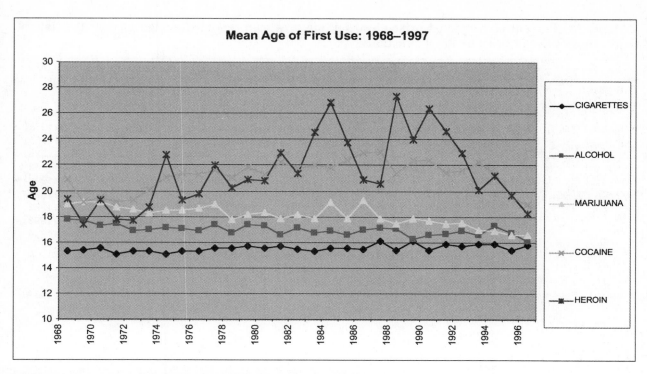

FIGURE 7.   Mean age of first use: 1968–1997, by drug.

Data Source: United States, Dept. of Health and Human Svcs., Substance Abuse and Mental Health Svcs. Admin., Office of Applied Studies. 1998 National Household Survey on Drug Abuse (Washington, DC: GPO, 1999): Tables 41–42, 45–47.

TABLE 2.   Percent of convicted prison and jail inmates who reported using drugs at the time of their offense: Breakdown by illicit substance.

	Jail Inmates, 1989	Prison Inmates, 1991
Any drug	27%	31%
Marijuana	9	11
Cocaine /crack	14	14
Heroin/opiates	5	6

Data Source: United States, Dept. of Justice, Bureau of Justice Statistics, *Drug-Related Crime*, NCJ–149286 (Washington, DC: GPO, 1994): 5.

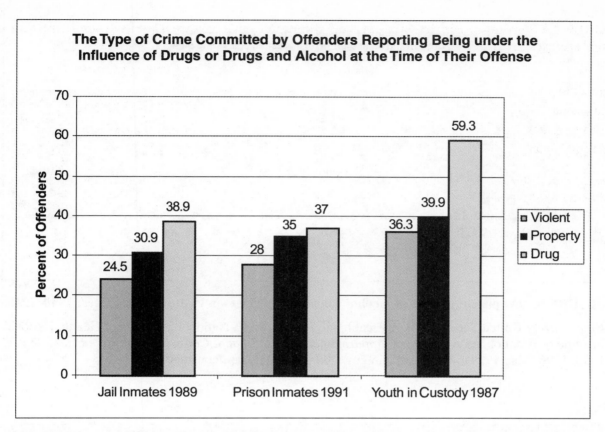

FIGURE 8. Type of crimes committed by offenders reporting being under the influence of drugs or drugs and alcohol at the time of their offense.

Data Source: United States, Dept. of Justice, Bureau of Justice Statistics, *Drug-Related Crime,* *NCJ–149286* (Washington, DC: GPO, 1994): 2.

TABLE 3. Type of crimes committed by offenders reporting being under the influence of drugs or drugs and alcohol at the time of their offense.

	Violent Crimes	Property Crimes	Drug Crimes
Jail Inmates 1989	24.5	28	36.3
Prison Inmates 1991	28	35	37
Juveniles 1987	36.3	39.9	59.3

Data Source: United States, Dept. of Justice, Bureau of Justice Statistics, *Drug-Related Crime*, NCJ–149286 (Washington, DC: GPO, 1994): 2.

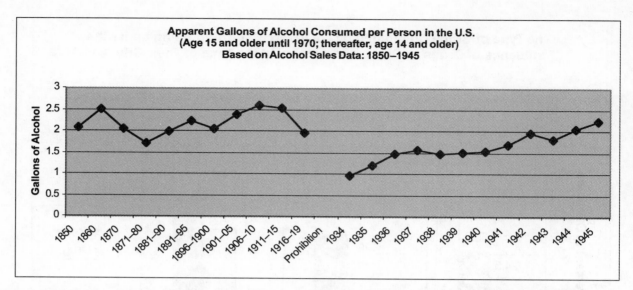

FIGURE 9.   Apparent gallons of alcohol consumed per person in the United States: 1850–1945.

Data Source: United States, Dept. of Health and Human Svcs., National Institutes of Health, National Institute of Alcohol and Alcoholism, *Apparent per Capita Ethanol Consumption for the United States, 1850–1996* (May 1999). <http://silk.nih.gov/silk/niaaa1/database/consum01.txt>.

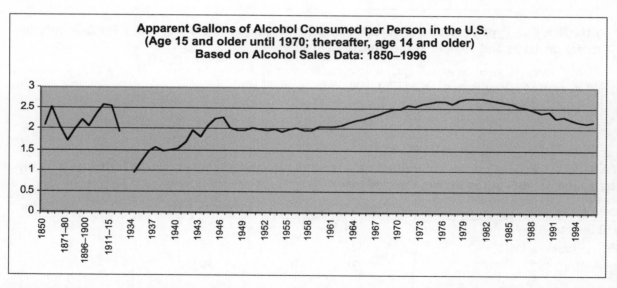

FIGURE 10.   Apparent gallons of alcohol consumed per person in the United States: 1850–1996.

Data Source: United States, Dept. of Health and Human Svcs., National Institutes of Health, National Institute of Alcohol and Alcoholism, *Apparent per Capita Ethanol Consumption for the United States, 1850–1996* (May 1999). <http://silk.nih.gov/silk/niaaa1/database/consum01.txt>.

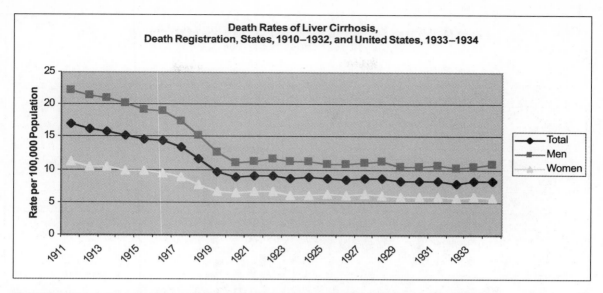

FIGURE 11.   Death rates of liver cirrhosis in the United States: 1910–1934.

Data Source: United States, Dept. of Health and Human Svcs., National Institutes of Health, National Institute of Alcohol and Alcoholism, *Age-Adjusted Death Rates of Liver Cirrhosis by Sex: Death Registration States, 1910–1932, and United States, 1933–1995* (April 1999). <http://silk.nih.gov/silk/niaaa1/database/cirmrt1.txt>.

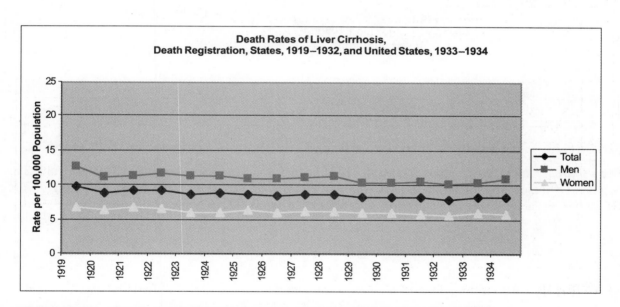

FIGURE 12.   Death rates of liver cirrhosis in the United States: 1919–1934.

Data Source: United States, Dept. of Health and Human Svcs., National Institutes of Health, National Institute of Alcohol and Alcoholism, *Age-Adjusted Death Rates of Liver Cirrhosis by Sex: Death Registration States, 1910–1932, and United States, 1933–1995* (April 1999). <http://silk.nih.gov/silk/niaaa1/database/cirmrt1.txt>.

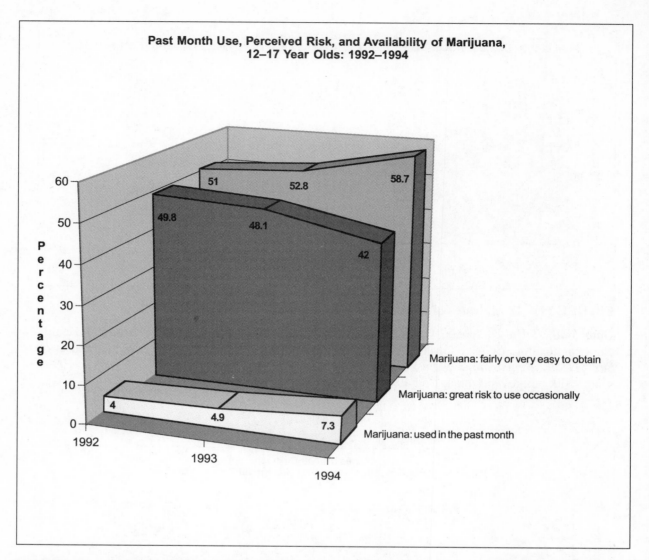

FIGURE 13.   Past month use, perceived risk, and availability of marijuana to 12–17 year-olds.

Data Source: United States, Dept. of Health and Human Svcs., Substance Abuse and Mental Health Svcs. Admin., Office of Applied Studies, *1994 National Household Survey on Drug Abuse* (Washington, DC: GPO, 1995): Tables 7, 13, 14. <http://www.samhsa.gov/oas/p0000016.htm>.

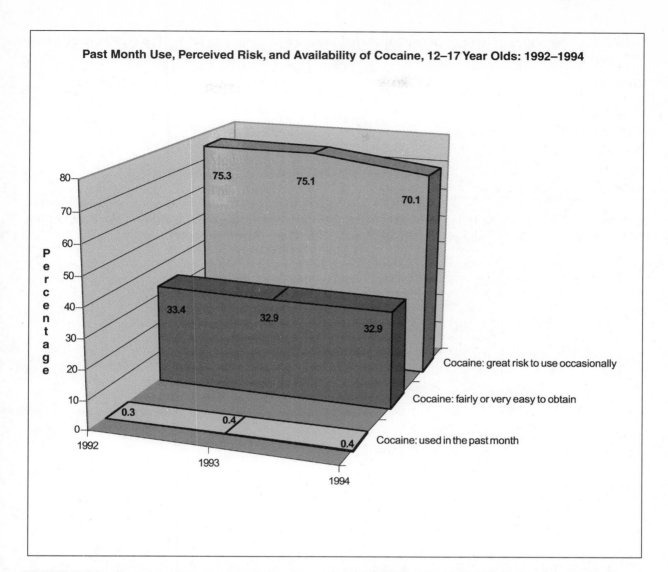

FIGURE 14.   Past month use, perceived risk, and availability of cocaine to 12–17 year-olds.

Data Source: United States, Dept. of Health and Human Svcs., Substance Abuse and Mental Health Svcs. Admin., Office of Applied Studies, *1994 National Household Survey on Drug Abuse* (Washington, DC: GPO, 1995): Tables 8, 13, 16. <http://www.samhsa.gov/oas/p0000016.htm>.

TABLE 4.   Percentage changes in the estimated number of drug arrests by type, 1995 over 1980, 1985, and 1990.

Drug Type	1995/1980	1995/1985	1995/1990
Total	**154.1**	**81.9**	**35.5**
Heroin/Cocaine	741.5	163.1	5.7
Marijuana	48.8	30.6	79.8
Synthetic	50.6	69.3	39.3
Other	153.6	120.8	57.4

Data Source: United States, Dept. of Justice, Federal Bureau of Investigation, *Uniform Crime Report for the United States*, 1996 (Washington, DC: GPO, nd.): 276. <http://www.fbi.gov/ucr.htm>.

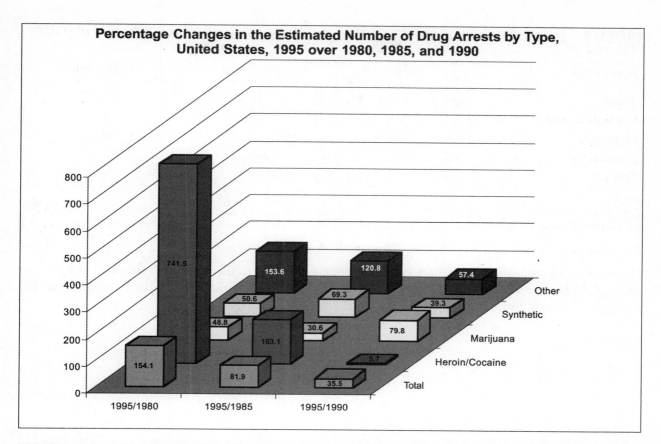

FIGURE 15.   Percentage changes in the estimated number of drug arrests by type, 1995 over 1980, 1985, and 1990.

Data Source: United States, Dept. of Justice, Federal Bureau of Investigation, *Uniform Crime Report for the United States, 1996* (Washington, DC: GPO, nd.): 276. <http://www.fbi.gov/ucr.htm>.

TABLE 5.   Problem drug usage in selected European Union countries before 1996.

	Year	Prevalence
Italy	1992	190,000–313,000
France	1993	160,000
Denmark	1996	12,500
Sweden	1992	14,000–20,000
Netherlands	1993	25,000–28,000
Germany	1995	100,000–150,000
Austria	1993	10,000–15,000
Finland	1995	5,300–10,500

(*Note:* The definitions of "problem usage" and methodologies vary.)

Data Source: European Monitoring Centre for Drugs and Drug Addiction, *1998 Annual Report on the State of the Drugs Problem in the European Union* (Luxembourg: Office for Official Publications of the European Communities, 1998): 20.

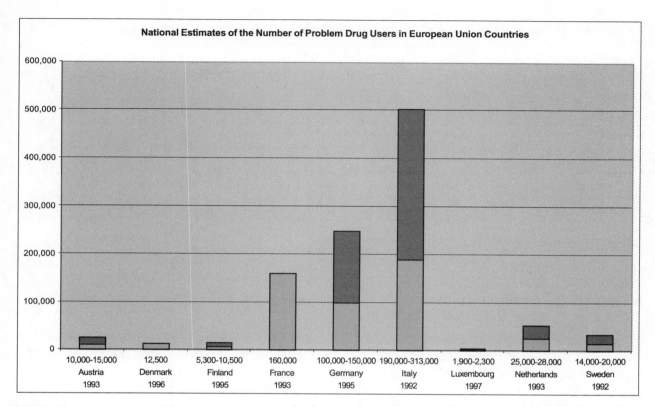

FIGURE 16. **National estimates of the number of problem drug users in European Union countries.**

Data Source: European Monitoring Centre for Drugs and Drug Addiction, *Highlights and Summaries of the Annual Report on the State of the Drugs Problem in the European Union, 1998.* (18 Dec. 1998) <http://www.emcdda.org/html/annual_report.html>.

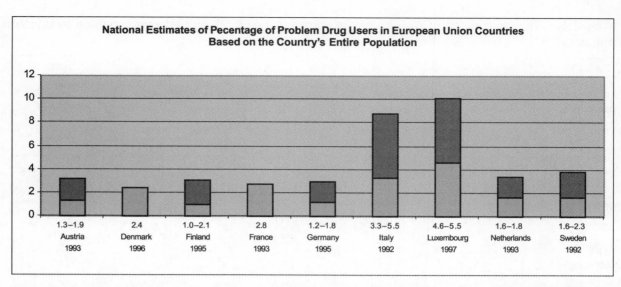

FIGURE 17.   National estimates of the percentages of problem drug users in European Union countries, based on the country's entire population.

Data Source: European Monitoring Centre for Drugs and Drug Addiction, *1998 Annual Report on the State of the Drugs Problem in the European Union* (Luxembourg: Office for Official Publications of the European Communities, 1998): 20.

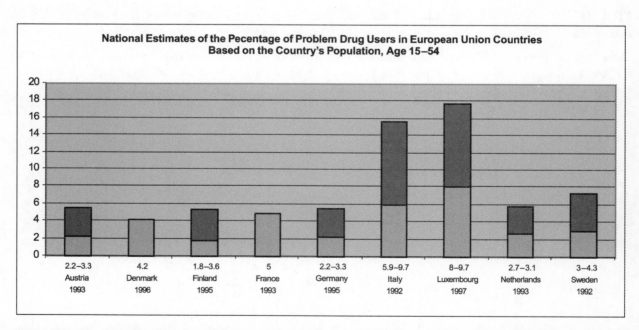

FIGURE 18.   National estimates of the percentages of problem drug users in European Union countries, based on the country's population, age 15–54.

Data Source: European Monitoring Centre for Drugs and Drug Addiction, *1998 Annual Report on the State of the Drugs Problem in the European Union* (Luxembourg: Office for Official Publications of the European Communities, 1998): 20.

TABLE 6. **The percentage of AIDS cases in Europe from 1985–1997 that are related to injecting drug use.**

Country	Percentage
Spain	65.4
Italy	62.4
Portugal	43.5
Ireland	43
Austria	25.5
France	23.8
Luxembourg	15.7
Germany	14.2
Sweden	11.5
Netherlands	10.9
Denmark	7.9
Belgium	6.5
U. Kingdom	6.5
Greece	4
Finland	3.7

Data Source: European Monitoring Centre for Drugs and Drug Addiction, *1998 Annual Report on the State of the Drugs Problem in the European Union* (Luxembourg: Office for Official Publications of the European Communities, 1998): 28.

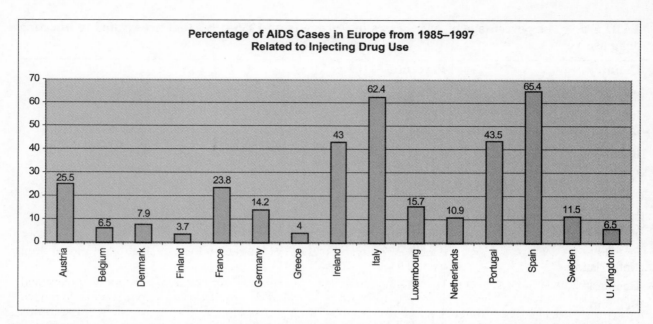

FIGURE 19. **Percentage of AIDS cases in Europe from 1985–1997 that are related to injecting drug use.**

Data Source: European Monitoring Centre for Drugs and Drug Addiction, *1998 Annual Report on the State of the Drugs Problem in the European Union* (Luxembourg: Office for Official Publications of the European Communities, 1998): 28.

Public Letter to Kofi Annan

June 1, 1998

Mr. Kofi Annan
Secretary General
United Nations
New York, New York
United States

Dear Secretary General,

On the occasion of the United Nations General Assembly Special Session on Drugs in New York on June 8–10, 1998, we seek your leadership in stimulating a frank and honest evaluation of global drug control efforts.

We are all deeply concerned about the threat that drugs pose to our children, our fellow citizens and our societies. There is no choice but to work together, both within our countries and across borders, to reduce the harms associated with drugs. The United Nations has a legitimate and important role to play in this regard—but only if it is willing to ask and address tough questions about the success or failure of its efforts.

We believe that the global war on drugs is now causing more harm than drug abuse itself.

Every decade the United Nations adopts new international conventions, focused largely on criminalization and punishment, that restrict the ability of individual nations to devise effective solutions to local drug problems. Every year governments enact more punitive and costly drug control measures. Every day politicians endorse harsher new drug war strategies.

What is the result? U.N. agencies estimate the annual revenue generated by the illegal drug industry at $400 billion, or the equivalent of roughly eight per cent of total international trade. This industry has empowered organized criminals, corrupted governments at all levels, eroded internal security, stimulated violence, and distorted both economic markets and moral values. These are the consequences not of drug use per se, but of decades of failed and futile drug war policies.

In many parts of the world, drug war politics impede public health efforts to stem the spread of HIV, hepatitis and other infectious diseases. Human rights are violated, environmental assaults perpetrated and prisons inundated with hundreds of thousands of drug law violators. Scarce resources better expended on health, education and economic development are squandered on ever more expensive interdiction efforts. Realistic proposals to reduce drug-related crime, disease and death are abandoned in favor of rhetorical proposals to create drug-free societies.

Persisting in our current policies will only result in more drug abuse, more empowerment of drug markets and criminals, and more disease and suffering. Too often those who call for open debate, rigorous analysis of current policies, and serious consideration of alternatives are accused of "surrendering." But the true surrender is when fear and inertia combine to shut off debate, suppress critical analysis, and dismiss all alternatives to current policies. Mr. Secretary General, we appeal to you to initiate a truly open and honest dialogue regarding the future of global drug control policies—one in which fear, prejudice and punitive prohibitions yield to common sense, science, public health and human rights.

Sincerely,

Participants in the 1998 United Nations General Assembly Special Session

Source: United Nations General Assembly Special Session. "UNGASS: Public Letter to Kofi Annan." *Drug Policy Around the World.* June 1, 1998. Drug Policy Alliance. 17 Sept. 2005 <http://www.drugpolicy.org/global/ungass/letter/index.cfm>.

Skeleton Outline
of "Presidency in Crisis"

from

The American Past:
A Survey of American History

I.   Presidency in Crisis
  A. The Nixon Presidency
      1.   Odd Duck
      2.   Political Savvy
      3.   The Warren Court
  B. Nixon's Vietnam
      1.   Vietnamization
      2.   Expansion of the War
      3.   Falling Dominos
      4.   Bottom Line
  C. Nixon–Kissinger Foreign Policy
      1.   The Long Crusade
      2.   Premises of Détente
      3.   Rapprochement with China
      4.   Soviet Policy
      5.   Shuttle Diplomacy
  D. Watergate and Gerald Ford
      1.   A New Definition of Liberalism
      2.   The Election of 1972
      3.   The Watergate Cover-Up
      4.   The Imperial Presidency
      5.   Resignation
      6.   A Ford, Not a Lincoln
      7.   A Tank Half Empty
      8.   OPEC and the Energy Crisis
      9.   Whip Inflation Now!
  E. Quiet Crisis
      1.   Peacemaking
      2.   The End of Détente
      3.   The Economy Under Carter: More of the Same
      4.   Malaise

Formal Outline Template of "Business Ethics and Social Responsbility"

from

Contemporary Business

II. Business Ethics and Social Responsibility
  A. Concern for Ethical and Societal Issues
  B. The New Ethical Environment
    1. Individuals Make a Difference
    2. Development of Individual Ethics
    3. On-the-Job Ethical Dilemmas
      a. Conflict of Interest
      b. Honest and Integrity
      c. Loyalty vs. Truth
      d. Whistle-Blowing
  C. How Organizations Shape Ethical Conduct
    1. Ethical Awareness
    2. Ethical Reasoning
    3. Ethical Action
    4. Ethical Leadership
  D. Acting Responsibily to Satisfy Society
    1. Responsibilities to the General Public
      a. Public Health Issues
      b. Protecting the Environment
      c. Developing the Quality of the Workforce
      d. Corporate Philanthropy
    2. Responsibilities to Customers
      a. The Right to Be Safe
      b. The Right to Be Informed
      c. The Right to Choose
      d. The Right to Be Heard
    3. Responsibilities to Employees
      a. Workplace Safety
      b. Quality of Life Issues
      c. Ensuring Equal Opportunity on the Job
      d. Age Discriimination
      e. Sexual Harassment and Sexism
    4. Responsibilities to Investors and the Financial Community

Formal Outline of The New Ethical Environment, a section of "Business Ethics and Social Responsbility"

from

Contemporary Business

II. Business Ethics and Social Responsibility
  B. The New Ethical Environment
    1. Individuals Make a Difference
    2. Development of Individual Ethics
      a. Stages of moral and ethical development
        i.   Preconventional
        ii. Conventional
        iii. Post Conventional
      b. Factors influencing stage of moral and ethical development
        i.   Personal experience
        ii. Background (family, educational, cultural, religious)
    3. On-the-Job Ethical Dilemmas
      a. Conflict of Interest
        i.   Definitions
          a) A situation in which a person has influence or control over an action that would benefit one associate while potentially harming another associate
          b) A situation in which when a person has influence or control over an action that would be personally beneficial but is not necessarily beneficial to his/her company or customers
        ii. Ethical handling of conflicts of interest
          a) Avoid them
          b) Disclose them
      b. Honest and Integrity
        i.   Definitions
          a) Honesty: Telling the truth
          b) Integrity: Adhering to ethical principles
        ii. Advantages of behaving with honesty and integrity
          a) Inspires trust
          b) Helps build long-term relationships with associates
        iii. Examples of behavior that is dishonest and lacks integrity
          a) Misrepresenting credentials on a resume or application
          b) Taking home supplies from the office
          c) Doing personal business while on company time
          d) Lying to avoid punishment
          e) Deceiving others into believing one's performance is better than it is

    c. Loyalty vs. Truth

      i. Conflicts between loyalty and truth arise when the truth about a company is negative

      ii. Resolving conflicts between loyalty and truth

        a) Choosing to be loyal instead of truthful

        b) Choosing not to volunteer negative information but providing it if directly asked

        c) Choosing to actively disclose negative information

    d. Whistle-Blowing

      i. Definition: An employee's informing the media or government officials of an organization's illegal, immoral, or unethical practice(s).

      ii. Reasons for Whistle-Blowing

        a) Organizational

          i. The organization fails to solve the problem

          ii. The employee thinks the organization will not address the problem

        b) Employee thinks the problem could result in significant harm to the public

      iii. Protection of Whistle-Blowers

        a) State and federal laws

        b) The Sarbanes-Oxley Act of 2002

        c) U.S. Department of Labor

C. How Organizations Shape Ethical Conduct

Appendix 3
Textbook Chapter Test Bank Questions and Answers

CHAPTER 49

PRESIDENCY IN CRISIS

The Nixon, Ford, and Carter Administrations, 1968–1980

MAJOR THEME: The Nixon, Ford, and Carter presidencies were beset by scandal, financial problems, and international tensions. Presidential leadership fell to new lows.

STUDENT "HOOKS"

1. Nixon failed to make the Supreme Court more conservative.
2. Nixon escalated the Vietnam conflict while reducing ground forces despite his promise to end it.
3. The Nixon-Kissinger foreign policy opened relations with China and improved relations with the U.S.S.R.
4. Watergate was Nixon's downfall.
5. The emerging power of the Middle East and the oil crisis baffled Americans.
6. The Carter presidency was an unhappy time for America.

CHAPTER OUTLINE

The Nixon Presidency (p. 722)
    Odd Duck (p. 722)
    Political Savvy (p. 723)
    The Warren Court (p. 724)
Nixon and Vietnam (p. 725)
    Vietnamization (p. 725)
    Expansion of the War (p. 725)
    Falling Dominoes (p. 726)
    The Bottom Line (p. 72)
Nixon–Kissinger Foreign Policy (p. 726)
    The Long Crusade (p. 727)
    Premises of Détente (p. 727)
    Rapprochement with China (p. 728)
    Soviet Policy (p. 728)
    Shuttle Diplomacy (p. 728)
Watergate and Gerald Ford (p. 729)
    A New Definition of Liberalism (p. 729)
    The Election of 1972 (p. 730)
    The Watergate Cover-Up (p. 731)
    The Imperial Presidency (p. 731)
    Resignation (p. 732)
    A Ford, Not a Lincoln (p. 732)
    A Tank Half-Empty (p. 733)
    OPEC and the Energy Crisis (p. 733)
    Whip Inflation Now! (p. 734)
Quiet Crisis (p. 735)
    Peacemaking (p. 735)
    The End of Détente (p. 736)
    The Economy Under Carter: More of the Same (p. 736)
    Malaise (p. 736)

SIDEBARS

Affirmative Action (p. 723)

Lyndon Johnson saw affirmative action as vigorous recruitment of minorities by universities and employers. Under President Nixon, the concept was expanded to one that favored minority-owned businesses for federal contracts.

Griswold and Roe (p. 724)
The "right" to privacy was first introduced in *Griswold v. Connecticut* (1965), but it became much more controversial in the *Roe v. Wade* (1973) case that legalized abortion based on the right of privacy.

Cleanup (p. 725)
This box gives a comparison of the type of garbage removed from the streets of Chicago in 1912 and in 1968.

Principled Foreign Policy (p. 726)
The American defeat in Vietnam caused Americans to be so bitter that as late as 1990, the United States insisted that Pol Pot was the legal ruler of Cambodia.

Kissinger on the Cold War (p. 727)
This box gives an excerpt from the memoirs of Henry Kissinger on his description of how the two superpowers acted toward one another.

Constitutional Contradiction? (p. 732)
There is a contradiction between the Twenty-fifth Amendment and Article II, Section 1 of the Constitution. Actually, Gerald Ford and Nelson Rockefeller may have held office illegally because of this technical issue. The matter was never tested, and it remains unclear today.

Persistence (p. 732)
Richard Nixon in 1972 was the seventh person to run for president three times as a candidate of a major party. The other people and their dates are listed.

Jimmy Carter and the Segregationists (p. 736)
Jimmy Carter, as a businessman, was asked to join the White Citizens' Council in the 1950s. He told them he would flush the $5 membership fee down the toilet before he would give it to the organization.

HOW THEY LIVED: Sex: From No No to Obsession (pp. 730-731)
The traditional American code of sexual morality was Christian sexual morality plus the prohibition in polite society, of talking about sex in any way but impenetrable euphemisms. The traditional code was enforced after 1873 by the Comstock Law, named for Anthony Comstock, head of the New York Society for the Suppression of Vice. Challenges came soon after the law, especially by people like Margaret Sanger who promoted birth control, but not much progress was made in changing the law or society's view. The "sexual revolution" began in the 1960s with the introduction of the "pill," a safe and almost 100 percent effective pill that prevented pregnancy. Gradually, the old laws were repealed and restrictions were eased. Sex, and anything related to it, became the rage. A decline in casual sex occurred in the 1980 with the emergence of Acquired Immune Deficiency Syndrome (AIDS), first thought to be a disease only of homosexuals, but which soon appeared among all groups in society.

KEY DATES

1873	Congress passes the "Comstock" law designed to control the dissemination of information about sexual activity.
1952	Dwight Eisenhower almost drops Richard Nixon as his vice presidential candidate because of questions about Nixon's financial dealings.
1956	President Eisenhower considers dropping Nixon from the ticket for a second term.
1960	Eisenhower humiliates Nixon while he is running for president by saying he could not remember any contributions Nixon made to Eisenhower's administration.
	The birth control pill is introduced.
1967	The Twenty-Fifth Amendment to provide for the selection of a vice president is added to the constitution.
1968	In *Miranda v. Arizona* the Supreme Court provides new protections for persons accused of crimes. Earl Warren resigns as Chief Justice so Johnson can name a replacement, but it fails.
1969	In the spring, Nixon begins to bomb neutral Cambodia to strike at sanctuaries where the Viet Cong and North Vietnamese are hiding.
	The Supreme Court allows the publication of *Fanny Hill*, an 18th century novel considered

	obscene by many people.
1970	Nixon reduces American forces in Vietnam to 335,000.
	Nixon sends ground forces intoCambodia, unleashing violent pro-test in America, especially on college campuses.
1971	President Nixon places controls on wages and prices because inflation is threatening his chances for reelection.
	Nixon expands the war into Laos.
	The American table tennis team is invited to visit the People's Republic of China.
1972	Nixon reduces American forces in Vietnam to 24,000.
	A cease-fire in Vietnam is negotiated by Henry Kissinger and Le Duc Tho of North Vietnam.
	Nixon goes to China on a goodwill visit, the first thawing of the Cold War between China and the United States.
	Just months after the China trip, Nixon goes to the Soviet Union, where he signs a preliminary strategic arms limitation treaty (SALT).
	In the election for president Nixon defeats Democrat George McGovern by a landslide.
	In June, burglars are arrested while involved in a break-in of the Democratic party headquarters in the Watergate building in Washington, DC.
1973	Nixon names Kissinger secretary of state.
	In January the Paris Accords go into effect, which requires the United States to withdraw all troops from Vietnam in 60 days while the North Vietnamese release all prisoners of war.
	The Yom Kippur War occurs when Egypt and Syria attack Israel.
	Vice President Spiro Agnew is forced to resign from the presidency in October, and Gerald Ford is selected to replace him.
	An oil crisis occurs when the oil-producing nations of the Middle East withhold oil in protest of the Yom Kippur War.
1974	Information becomes available that Kissinger was aware and may have instigated and aided an overthrow of the president of Chile, Salvador Allende.
	On August 9, President Nixon resigns from office after impeachment proceedings have begun in the House of Representatives.
1975	The Communist organization in Laos, the Pathet Lao, takes control of the country.
	The South Vietnamese government collapses and the North Vietnamese take control of South Vietnam.
	With about 6 percent of the world's population, the United States consumes a third of the world's annual production of oil.
1976	Pol Pot takes control in Cambodia and creates a criminal regime as bad as the Nazis in Germany.
1977	President Anwar Sadat of Egypt takes an unprecedented step by traveling to Israel and addressing the Israeli Knesset, or parliament.
	President Carter sets back the strategic arms limitation talks with completely new proposals.
1978	The Senate narrowly ratifies an agreement with Panama that will transfer sovereignty of the Panama Canal back to Panama.
	Sadat of Egypt and Begin of Israel meet with President Carter at Camp David to negotiate their differences.
1979	In March, Israel and Egypt sign a treaty, the first between the two nations.
	President Carter withdraws from the Senate a treaty on arms limitation (SALT-II) when the Soviet Union invades Afghanistan.
	Oil consumption is higher than ever and a higher proportion of oil is being imported.
	China and the United States establish full diplomatic relations.
	The divorce rate is 5.3 per 1,000 marriages, compared to 2.5 in 1965.
1980	Inflation in America reaches almost 20 percent.
1982	A Vietnam War memorial is erected in Washington, DC.
1999	On December 31, control of the Panama Canal returns to Panama.

ESSAY QUESTIONS

1. "Whatever else may be said of Richard Nixon, he earned everything he ever got." Comment.
   ANSWER: PAGES: 722-725, 729-733

2. How did President Nixon's pursuit of the Vietnamese War differ from that of Lyndon B. Johnson? Was Nixon's Vietnam policy a success?
   ANSWER: PAGES: 725-729

IDENTIFICATIONS

Richard Milhous Nixon (p. 722)
John F. Kennedy (p. 722)
"Tricky Dicky" (p. 722)
Barry Goldwater (p. 722)
Six Crises (p. 723)
H. R. Haldeman (p. 723)
John Ehrlichman (p. 723)
Spiro T. Agnew (p. 723)
George Wallace (p. 723)
"nattering nabobs of negativism" (p. 723)
New Federalism (p. 723)
Family Assistance Plan (p. 723)
"Silent Majority" (p. 723)
Earl Warren (p. 724)
Brown v. Board of Education of Topeka (1954) (p. 724)
Miranda v. Arizona (1968) (p. 725)
Abe Fortas (p. 725)
Warren Burger (p. 725)
Vietnamization (p. 725)
George Aiken (p. 974)
Henry A. Kissinger (p. 725)
Kent State University incident (p. 726)
Jackson State College (p. 726)
Tonkin Gulf Resolution (p. 726)
Pathet Lao (p. 726)
Khmer Rouge (p. 726)
Pol Pot (p. 726)
Prince Sihanouk (p. 726)
Paris Accords of 1973 (p. 726)
Nguyen Van Thieu (p. 726)
Ho Chih Minh City (p. 726)
Agent Orange (p. 726)
Vietnam War Memorial (p. 726)
détente (p. 727)
Realpolitik (p. 728)
Mao Zedong (p. 728)
Zhou Enlai (p. 728)
Hua Guofeng (p. 728)
Deng Xiaoping (p. 728)
Strategic Arms Limitation Talks (SALT) (p. 728)
Leonid Brezhnev (p. 728)
Yom Kippur War of 1973 (p. 728)
Anwar Sadat (p. 729)
Fidel Castro (p. 729)
Salvador Allende (p. 729)
Agostin Pinochet (p. 729)
election of 1972 (p. 730)
George McGovern (p. 730)

Watergate burglary (p. 731)
Committee to Reelect the President (CREEP)(p. 731)
John Mitchell (p. 731)
James E. McCord (p. 731)
Howard Hunt (p. 731)
John Sirica (p. 731)
Robert Woodward (p. 731)
Carl Bernstein (p. 731)
"Deep Throat" (p. 731)
Sam Ervin (p. 731)
"dirty tricks" (p. 731)
"enemies list" (p. 731)
"affirmative action" (p. 723 box)
"politically correct" (p. 723 box)
Eugene v. Debs (p. 732 box)
Norman Thomas (p. 732 box)
"double standard" (p. 730 box)
Anthony "Comstock (p. 730 box)
Margaret Sanger (p. 730 box)
"the pill" (p. 730 box)
"sexual revolution" (p. 730 box)
Acquired Immune Deficiency Syndrome (AIDS) (p. 731 box)
Griswold v. Connecticut (1965) (p. 724 box)
Donald Segretti (p. 731)
G. Gordon Liddy (p. 731)
J. Edgar Hoover (p. 732)
Daniel Ellsberg (p. 732)
"imperial presidency" (p. 732)
Spiro Agnew (p. 732)
Twenty-fifth Amendment (p. 732)
Gerald Ford (p. 732)
Ronald Reagan (p. 733)
Nelson A. Rockefeller (p. 732 box)
Organization of Petroleum Exporting Countries (OPEC) (p. 733)
WIN! ("Whip Inflation Now!") (p. 734)
James "Jimmy" Earl Carter (p. 734)
Rosalyn Carter (p. 735)
White Citizens' Councils (p. 736 box)
Menachem Begin (p. 736)
Camp David Accords (p. 736)
Zbigniew Brzezinski (p. 736)
Strategic Arms Limitation Talks II (SALT II) (p. 736)
Three Mile Island incident (p. 736)
The China Syndrome (p. 736)
Bert Lance (p. 736)
Andrew Young (p. 736)

FILL-INS

1. Richard Nixon wrote of overcoming obstacles in the autobiographical book, _____, which he hoped would further his political career.
   ANSWER: *SIX CRISES*. PAGE: 723

2. Before he left office, Lyndon Johnson tried to replace Chief Justice Earl Warren with a long-time crony from Texas, _____.
   ANSWER: ABE FORTAS. PAGE: 725

3. In foreign affairs, President Nixon in his early presidential years relied less on his secretary of state than on special advisor _____.
   ANSWER: HENRY A. KISSINGER. PAGE: 725

4. The Vietnam War cost the United States more than any other war in American history except _____.
   ANSWER: WORLD WAR II. PAGE: 726

5. Henry A. Kissinger was roundly criticized for covertly assisting Agostín Pinochet, a repressive dictator, to come to power in the South American nation of _____.
   ANSWER: CHILE. PAGE: 729

6. The Democratic presidential candidate in 1972, _____, as Republican Kevin Phillips had predicted, represented the party's left wing.
   ANSWER: GEORGE MCGOVERN. PAGE: 730

7. _____, the name of a fashionable apartment-office complex in Washington, gave its name to the scandal that toppled Richard Nixon from the presidency.
   ANSWER: WATERGATE. PAGE: 731

8. Robert Woodward and Carl Bernstein, reporters for the newspaper, _____, uncovered key acts in the campaign to force Nixon's removal from the presidency.
   ANSWER: THE *WASHINGTON POST*. PAGE: 731

9. President _____ succeeded Nixon but could not win re-election in 1976.
   ANSWER: GERALD FORD. PAGE: 732

MULTIPLE CHOICE

1. Richard Nixon's chief interests lay in
   a. foreign affairs.
   b. domestic affairs.
   c. administration.
   d. platform politicking.
   e. campaigning throughout the country.
   ANSWER: A. PAGE: 723

2. Nixon's first vice president was Spiro Agnew, previously
   a. mayor of Los Angeles.
   b. secretary of state.
   c. governor of Maryland.
   d. congressman from Michigan.
   e. senator from Maryland.
   ANSWER: C. PAGE: 723

3. Nixon's second vice president was Gerald Ford, previously
   a. mayor of Los Angeles.
   b. secretary of state.
   c. governor of Maryland.
   d. congressman from Michigan.
   e. senator from Michigan.
   ANSWER: D. PAGE: 732

4. The bombing of Cambodia in 1971 led to riots at many universities and deaths at two,
   a. Kent State, Ohio, and Fullerton State, California.
   b. Fullerton State and Jackson State, Mississippi.
   c. Kent State and Jackson State.
   d. Kent State and Sump State, Florida.
   e. Kent State and Michigan State.
   ANSWER: C. PAGE: 726

5. Pol Pot's reign of terror in Cambodia was brought to an end by
   a. massive American military intervention.
   b. United Nations economic sanctions.
   c. an invasion by the North Vietnamese.
   d. a goodwill mission by the National Council of Churches.
   e. none of the above.
   ANSWER: C. PAGE: 726

6. Communist China hinted its interest in friendly relations with the United States by
   a. inviting an American Ping-Pong team to play in China.
   b. sending President Nixon condolences on the death of his mother.
   c. complimenting Henry Kissinger on his peacemaking in the Middle East.
   d. lifting restrictions on tobacco imports.
   e. increasing cultural exchanges.
   ANSWER: A. PAGE: 728

7. A Nixon administration employee involved in the "dirty tricks" campaign was
   a. Henry A. Kissinger.
   b. G. Gordon Liddy.
   c. Patrick Buchanan.
   d. Gerald Ford.
   e. Nelson Rockefeller.
   ANSWER: B. PAGE: 731

8. President Ford was challenged in the 1976 Republican primary elections by
   a. Spiro T. Agnew.
   b. Ronald Reagan.
   c. George Bush.
   d. Donald Segretti.
   e. Barry Goldwater.
   ANSWER: B. PAGE: 734

9. James Earl Carter was the first
   a. state governor to become president since Franklin D. Roosevelt.
   b. convicted felon to run for president and win.
   c. president to come directly from Congress since John F. Kennedy.
   d. unmarried president since James Buchanan.
   e. Southern Democrat to win since the Civil War.
   ANSWER: A. PAGES: 734-735

10. For advice on foreign policy matters, President Carter relied on
    a. Henry A. Kissinger.
    b. Zbigniew Brzezinski.
    c. Lillian Carter.
    d. William Rogers.
    e. Hamilton Jordan.
    ANSWER: B. PAGE: 736

11. Richard Nixon's qualifications for the presidency included
    a. the affability of Franklin D. Roosevelt.
    b. the charm of Dwight D. Eisenhower.
    c. the pluck of Harry Truman.
    d. the sophistication of John F. Kennedy.
    e. none of the above.
    ANSWER: C. PAGES: 722-723

12. *Silent Majority* was Richard Nixon's term for
    a. Republicans.
    b. white Americans.
    c. grass-roots conservatives disgusted win noisy pressure groups.
    d. the soldiers killed in Vietnam.
    e. religious Americans.
    ANSWER: C. PAGE: 723

13. Under Chief Justice Warren Burger,
    a. the work of the Warren Court was upended.
    b. the decisions of the Warren Court were moderated.
    c. the Supreme Court remained committed to judicial activism.
    d. three justices were impeached and convicted.
    e. no changes were made in judicial philosophy.
    ANSWER: B. PAGE: 725

14. Nixon's Vietnam policy included
    a. a slow but steady withdrawal of American troops.
    b. improvement of the army of South Vietnam.
    c. expansion of the war into Cambodia.
    d. increase in the number of troops and the number of conflicts with the enemy.
    e. a, b, and c.
    ANSWER: E. PAGES: 725-726

15. One result of sending American ground troops into Cambodia in 1970 was
    a. an increase in the power of the Khmer Rouge, the Cambodian Communists.
    b. a brief escalation of protest in the United States.
    c. an increase in American commitment to the war.
    d. the repeal of the Tonkin Gulf Resolution.
    e. a, b, and d.
    ANSWER: E. PAGES: 725-726

16. When faced with the Southeast Asian refugee problem, the United States
    a. closed the doors to would-be immigrants.
    b. blamed it on Pol Pot.
    c. admitted some 600,000 displaced people to the United States.
    d. threatened Vietnam with renewed intervention.
    e. all of the above.
    ANSWER: C. PAGE: 726

17. Nixon's openness toward China
    a. was a surprise because he had been a staunch anticommunist.
    b. should have been expected, given his previous statements.
    c. reflected his belief that the great powers all had to get along.
    d. was urged on him by Henry A. Kissinger.
    e. a, c, and d.
    ANSWER: D. PAGE: 728

18. The dramatic improvement in American relations with China under Nixon
    a. proved to be a gold mine for American exporters.
    b. encouraged the Soviet Union to cooperate with the United States.
    c. was short-lived.
    d. a, b, and c.
    e. none of the above.
    ANSWER: B. PAGE: 728

TRUE-FALSE

1. Although the phrase "Affirmative Action" originated during the Johnson administration, it was interpreted to mean preferential treatment for members of certain groups only under Nixon.
   ANSWER: T. PAGE: 723
2. President Nixon radically reduced the number of American soldiers in Vietnam.
   ANSWER: T. PAGE: 725
3. Pol Pot, the head of the Pathet Lao, terrorized the population of Laos with tacit American support.
   ANSWER: F. PAGE: 726
4. Richard Nixon imagined a world of economic superpowers balancing one another peacefully.
   ANSWER: F. PAGE: 727
5. Virtually no labor unions, once the workhorses of the Democratic party, supported George McGovern in 1972.
   ANSWER: T. PAGE: 730
6. During his brief presidency, Gerald Ford was the target in two assassination attempts, both by women.
   ANSWER: T. PAGE: 733
7. President Jimmy Carter ran for the presidency as an outsider, with no ties to the Washington establishment.
   ANSWER: T. PAGES: 734-735
8. Carter's greatest achievement as president was to save the peace between Egypt and Israel.
   ANSWER: T. PAGES: 735-736
9. Détente with the Soviet Union was shored up during the Carter administration.
   ANSWER: F. PAGE: 736
10. Jimmy Carter was oblivious to what critics called a malaise of the spirit in America during his presidency.
    ANSWER: F. PAGE: 737

MATCHING: ALL THE PRESIDENT'S MEN

Match each individual with the appropriate description. Answers may be used more than once or not at all.
a. Nixon's choice as chief justice of the Supreme Court
b. Nixon's second vice president
c. Nixon political functionary who hatched fantastic schemes in election campaign of 1972
d. Nixon's first vice president
e. Nixon's tough-talking White House aide
f. Nixon's trusted foreign policy advisor and collaborator
g. Nixon's attorney general
h. Arrested Watergate burglar who intimated early on that Nixon administration was involved in the scheme
i. Nixon Supreme Court appointee who became known as a liberal justice
j. Not one of the president's men

1. Spiro T. Agnew
   ANSWER: D. PAGE: 723
2. H. R. Haldeman
   ANSWER: E. PAGE: 723
3. James McCord
   ANSWER: H. PAGE: 731
4. Gerald Ford
   ANSWER: B. PAGE: 732

5. George McGovern
   ANSWER: J. PAGE: 730
6. G. Gordon Liddy
   ANSWER: C. PAGE: 731
7. John Mitchell
   ANSWER: G. PAGE: 731
8. Henry A. Kissinger
   ANSWER: F. PAGE: 725
9. Warren Burger
   ANSWER: A. PAGE: 725

SUGGESTED WEB LINKS

http://www.old.smh.com.au/news/0202/21/world/world11.html
For information on Nixon's trip to China.

http://www.gwu.edu/~nsarchiv/coldwar/interviews/episode-16/laird1.html
This is an interview with former defense secretary Melvin Laird on the matter of détente with the Soviet Union.

http://affiliate.timeincmags.com/time/special/moy/1973.html
This is the story on John Sirica from *Time Magazine* when it named him "Man of the Year."

http://www.civnet.org/resources/teach/basic/part8/55.htm
This site provides much information on President Carter's policy of human rights in foreign policy.

Chapter 2: Business Ethics and Social Responsibility

Completion

Completion 2

Directions: Complete the following using the terms listed.

A. corporate philanthropy
B. Occupational Safety and Health Administration
C. consumerism
D. integrity
E. social audits
F. social responsibility
G. business ethics
H. sexual harassment
I. code of conduct
J. conflict of interest
K. product liability
L. family leave
M. boycott
N. whistleblowing
O. green marketing

1. A formal statement that defines how the organization expects and requires employees to resolve ethical questions: _____.

     ANS: I   DIF: 2   REF: p. 48   OBJ: TYPE: KN

2. The act of an organization giving something back to the communities in which it earns profits: _____.

     ANS: A   DIF: 2   REF: p. 56   OBJ: TYPE: KN

3. The main federal regulatory force in setting workplace safety and health standards: _____.

     ANS: B   DIF: 2   REF: p. 60   OBJ: TYPE: KN

4. The standards of conduct and moral values governing actions and decisions in the work environment: _____.

     ANS: G   DIF: 2   REF: p. 40   OBJ: TYPE: KN

5. A situation where a business decision may be influenced by the potential for personal gain: _____.

     ANS: J   DIF: 2   REF: p. 45   OBJ: TYPE: KN

6. Management's acceptance of the obligation to consider profit, consumer satisfaction, and societal well-being of equal value in evaluating the firm's performance: _____.

     ANS: F   DIF: 2   REF: p. 51   OBJ: TYPE: KN

7. Some firms measure social performance by conducting _____.

ANS: E   DIF: 2   REF: p. 51   OBJ: TYPE: KN

8. Inappropriate actions of a sexual nature in the workplace: _____.

ANS: I   DIF: 2   REF: p. 62   OBJ: TYPE: KN

9. Having _____ means adhering to deeply felt ethical principles in all business situations.

ANS: D   DIF: 2   REF: p. 45   OBJ: TYPE: KN

10. In a _____, consumers refuse to buy a company's products.

ANS: M   DIF: 2   REF: p. 51   OBJ: TYPE: KN

11. The public demand that a business consider the needs and wants of its customers in making decisions is called _____.

ANS: C   DIF: 2   REF: p. 57   OBJ: TYPE: KN

12. _____ refers to the responsibility of manufacturers for injuries and damages caused by their goods.

ANS: K   DIF: 2   REF: p. 57   OBJ: TYPE: KN

13. Many organizations now offer _____ to help employees deal with family matters.

ANS: L   DIF: 2   REF: p. 61   OBJ: TYPE: KN

14. _____ is an employee's disclosure to government authorities of illegal, immoral, or unethical practices of his or her employer.

ANS: N   DIF: 2   REF: p. 46   OBJ: TYPE: KN

15. A strategy that emphasizes a firm's commitment to environmentally safe products and production is called _____.

ANS: O   DIF: 2   REF: p. 54   OBJ: TYPE: KN

Essay Questions

1. What are business ethics and why are they important?

ANS: Business ethics are standards of conduct and moral values that govern actions and decisions in the work environment. They are important because a company cannot prosper in the long-run without considering ethics.

DIF: 1   REF: p. 40   OBJ: TYPE: KN

2. Why is it often difficult in business to decide what is right or wrong in a given situation?

ANS: Businesses have many responsibilities-to customers, to employees, to investors, and to society as a whole. Sometimes conflicts arise in trying to serve the divergent needs of separate constituencies. A business may be faced with a conflict between the firm's desire for profits and its responsibility to customers and the law. Conflict may also arise between ideal decisions and those that are practical in given situations.

DIF: 3   REF: p. 40-41   OBJ: TYPE: AP

3. Explain how technology has impacted business ethics.

    ANS: Technology seems to have expanded the range and impact of unethical behavior. For instance, technology has made it easier for people to access data from a variety of locations. That, in turn, has increased the potential for someone to steal or manipulate data, or even shut down the system.

    DIF: 2   REF: p. 41   OBJ: TYPE: KN

4. List and briefly describe the three stages of moral and ethical development.

    ANS: The three stages of moral and ethical development are pre-conventional, conventional and post-conventional. In the pre-conventional stage, individuals primarily consider their own needs and desires in making decisions. They obey rules only because there are afraid of the consequences. The next stage is the conventional stage. Individuals are aware of and act in response to their duties to others (family or an organization, for example). Self-interest still plays a role. The final stage is the post-conventional stage. In this stage the individual is able to move beyond self-interest and take the larger needs of society into account as well.

    DIF: 3   REF: p. 42-43   OBJ: TYPE: KN

5. When does a conflict of interest pose an ethical challenge? How should a conflict of interest be handled?

    ANS: A conflict of interest exists when a person is faced with a situation in which an action benefiting one person or group has the potential to harm another. A conflict of interest can pose an ethical challenge when it involves the person's own interests and someone to whom he or she has a duty. The best way to handle a potential conflict of interest is to avoid it and/or to disclose it.

    DIF: 2   REF: p. 45   OBJ: TYPE: KN

6. How could loyalty versus truth create an ethical dilemma for a businessperson?

    ANS: Businesses expect their employees to be loyal and to act in the best interests of the company. An ethical conflict can arise when an individual must decide loyalty to the company and truthfulness in business relationships.

    DIF: 2   REF: p. 46-47   OBJ: TYPE: AP

7. What is a code of conduct and what is it designed to do?

    ANS: A code of conduct is designed to improve ethical awareness among employees, to help them to identify ethical problems when they occur and some guidance about how they should respond. A code of conduct can be quite basic-listing the rules, regulations, and laws employees are expected to follow-or may be more elaborate-listing corporate values and frameworks for resolving ethical dilemmas.

    DIF: 2   REF: p. 48   OBJ: TYPE: AP

8. Why is ethical leadership so important?

    ANS: Without supervisors and managers demonstrating ethical behavior, employees are not as likely to follow a set of ethical standards. Companies where managers set good examples have fewer incidences of unethical behavior, and employees report higher levels of satisfaction.

    DIF: 2   REF: p. 49-50   OBJ: TYPE: AP

9. The development of a corporate culture to support business ethics happens on four levels. Explain each of the four levels.

ANS: Ethical awareness is the foundation of an ethical climate. Employees need help in identifying ethical problems, and guidance in how to respond. Ethical reasoning involves ethics training programs to provide employees with the tools they need to evaluate ethical dilemmas and arrive at suitable decisions. Ethical action involves the structures and procedures that firms establish to enable their employees to follow ethical behavior. Companies encourage ethical action by providing support for employees faced with dilemmas. Ethical leadership charges each employee at every level with the responsibility for being an ethical leader. This principle requires that employees be personally committed to the company's core values and be willing to base their actions on them.

DIF: 3   REF: p. 47-52   OBJ: TYPE: AP

10. What is a social audit? Who conducts one?

ANS: A social audit is a formal procedure to identify and evaluate all company activities that relate to social issues such as conservation, employment practices, environmental protection, and philanthropy. The audit informs management about how well the company is performing in these areas. Social audits are often conducted internally by firms. Outside groups-such as environmental organizations and labor unions-also conduct social audits.

DIF: 2   REF: p. 51   OBJ: TYPE: AP

11. List the four classifications of social responsibilities of a business.

ANS: The four classifications of social responsibilities of business are those to the general public, those to customers, those to employees, and those to investors and the financial community.

DIF: 2   REF: p. 52   OBJ: TYPE: KN

12. What are the objectives of the consumerism movement?

ANS: Consumerism refers to the movement calling for businesses to consider the needs of consumers when making decisions. President Kennedy summarized many of the consumers of the consumerism movement in a speech in which he listed four basic consumer rights: the right to safety, the right to be informed, the right to choose, and the right to be heard.

DIF: 3   REF: p. 57-59   OBJ: TYPE: AP

13. What is green marketing?

ANS: It is a marketing strategy that promotes enviornmental friendly products and production methods.

DIF: 1   REF: p. 54   OBJ: TYPE: KN

14. List the major responsibilities business has to its workers.

ANS: The major responsibilities to workers are a safe work environment, recognizing quality of life issues, ensuring equal employment opportunity, and prohibiting age discrimination, sexual harassment, and sexism.

DIF: 2   REF: p. 60-63   OBJ: TYPE: KN

15. Why do investors expect a firm to act ethically and exhibit social responsibility?

    ANS: Even though the primary purpose of a firm is to make a profit, investors also expect the firm to act ethically as well as legally and exhibit social responsibility. Investors know that the failure of a firm to act ethically, legally, or without a sense of social responsibility can result in substantial monetary losses to investors. For instance, ethical or legal problems can cause a sudden and substantial drop in a company's stock price.

    DIF: 2   REF: p. 64-65   OBJ: TYPE: KN

16. List the constituencies to which businesses are responsible.

    ANS: Businesses are responsible to customers, employees, investors, and society.

    DIF: 1   REF: p. 41   OBJ: TYPE: KN

Multiple Choice

1. When management considers social and economic issues in decision making, the company is practicing _____.
   a. business ethics
   b. social responsibility
   c. consumerism
   d. social welfare

   ANS: B   DIF: 1   REF: p. 40   OBJ: TYPE: KN

2. For a company to prosper over the long term, it _____.
   a. must consider business ethics
   b. should maximize profits
   c. should minimize social responsibility
   d. should maximize revenues

   ANS: A   DIF: 1   REF: p. 40   OBJ: TYPE: KN

3. Why should a company act in an ethical manner?
   a. Because the government will take action if a firm fails to act ethically
   b. Because acting ethically always maximizes profits in the short-run
   c. Because acting ethically will help a company to prosper in the long-run
   d. Because the right thing to do is always the cheaper alternative

   ANS: C   DIF: 3   REF: p. 40   OBJ: TYPE: AP

4. Businesses should _____.
   a. do what is right regardless of profits
   b. find the balance between doing what is right and what is profitable
   c. do whatever is profitable
   d. do whatever is in the company's best interests

   ANS: B   DIF: 1   REF: p. 41   OBJ: TYPE: KN

5. Which of the following statements is correct?
    a. Setting ethical standards is easy.
    b. Setting ethical standards is always clear-cut.
    c. Doing what is right can sometimes be difficult.
    d. Social and ethical problems affect only a few companies.

    ANS: C   DIF: 1   REF: p. 41   OBJ: TYPE: KN

6. A company removes a profitable product from the market because it may be dangerous. This company is demonstrating _____.
    a. ethical behavior
    b. short-run thinking
    c. how not to run a business
    d. social welfare

    ANS: A   DIF: 2   REF: p. 41   OBJ: TYPE: AP

7. Are seeking profits and upholding high principles of right and wrong mutually exclusive goals? Today, a growing number of businesses of all sizes are saying _____.
    a. it depends on the social and economic implications of each decision
    b. the priority is for profits which are the primary purpose of most businesses
    c. yes
    d. no

    ANS: D   DIF: 2   REF: p. 41   OBJ: TYPE: KN

8. In today's business environment, who can make the difference in ethical expectations and behavior?
    a. Everyone
    b. No one
    c. Only managers
    d. Only the CEO

    ANS: A   DIF: 1   REF: p. 41   OBJ: TYPE: KN

9. In order for a company to operate to a high set of ethical standards, _____ must be involved.
    a. the CEO
    b. managers
    c. only customers
    d. everyone

    ANS: D   DIF: 2   REF: p. 47   OBJ: TYPE: KN

10. Technology has _____ ethical issues.
    a. expanded the range of
    b. reduced the range of
    c. made little difference on the range of
    d. eliminated most

    ANS: A   DIF: 1   REF: p. 43   OBJ: TYPE: KN

11. Which type of company typically experiences the highest-cost abuses of ethics?
    a. Large firms
    b. Small firms
    c. Internet firms
    d. Manufacturing firms

    ANS: D   DIF: 2   REF: p. 43   OBJ: TYPE: KN

12. Which of the following has expanded the range and impact of unethical behavior?
    a. Workplace diversity
    b. An aging population
    c. Technology
    d. Government regulation

    ANS: C   DIF: 2   REF: p. 43   OBJ: TYPE: KN

13. Theft of intellectual property-such as copyrighted or patented material-is a growing problem today. Approximately what percentage of intellectual property thefts is believed to be committed by insiders?
    a. Less than 10 percent
    b. About 25 percent
    c. About 50 percent
    d. About 67 percent

    ANS: D   DIF: 2   REF: p. 43   OBJ: TYPE: KN

14. What is the most common excuse given by individuals for not acting ethically?
    a. Everyone does it.
    b. It violates company policy.
    c. It didn't violate my personal values and morals.
    d. It is easy to get away with.

    ANS: A   DIF: 2   REF: p. 44   OBJ: TYPE: AP

15. Many people rationalize unethical acts because they _____.
    a. know they can get away with it
    b. are fundamentally unethical
    c. have no personal or moral values
    d. feel pressured on their jobs to meet performance goals

    ANS: D   DIF: 2   REF: p. 44   OBJ: TYPE: AP

16. Katsuko decides not to take office supplies home because she fears she'll be fired if she's caught since it's against company rules. Which stage of ethical development is Katsuko in?
    a. Pre-conventional
    b. Conventional
    c. Post-conventional
    d. Concentrations stage

    ANS: A   DIF: 2   REF: p. 44   OBJ: TYPE: AP

17. Tanisha wouldn't make personal long-distance phone calls at work because it will end up costing her employer money. Which stage of ethical development is Tanisha in?
    a. Pre-conventional
    b. Conventional
    c. Post-conventional
    d. Concentrations stage

    ANS: B   DIF: 2   REF: p. 44   OBJ: TYPE: AP

18. Al makes a point of turning off his computer when he's not using it because it saves his employer money and saves energy. Which stage of ethical development is Al in?
    a. Pre-conventional
    b. Conventional
    c. Post-conventional
    d. Concentrations stage

    ANS: C   DIF: 2   REF: p. 44   OBJ: TYPE: AP

19. When an individual considers the interests and expectations of others in making decisions and follows rules because it is part of belonging to the group, which stage of ethical development is this individual in?
    a. Pre-conventional
    b. Conventional
    c. Post-conventional
    d. Concentrations stage

    ANS: B   DIF: 2   REF: p. 44   OBJ: TYPE: KN

20. When a businessperson is faced with a situation where his or her decision may be influenced by the potential for personal gain, it is called _____.
    a. whistle blowing
    b. honesty and integrity
    c. cultural consequences
    d. a conflict of interest

    ANS: D   DIF: 1   REF: p. 45   OBJ: TYPE: KN

21. Your supervisor asks you to conceal information from the outside auditors examining the company's financial records. What is your ethical challenge?

    a. Loyalty versus truth.
    b. Conflict of interest.
    c. Honesty and integrity.
    d. You have none.

    ANS: A   DIF: 2   REF: p. 46   OBJ: TYPE: AP

22. Outside auditors are examining your company's financial records. You know that there may be an error and will tell them about it, if they ask. They don't ask. Your _____ could be questioned.

    a. loyalty
    b. truthfulness
    c. integrity
    d. Nothing you've done could be called into question.

    ANS: C   DIF: 1   REF: p. 45   OBJ: TYPE: AP

23. An investment advisor wants to recommend a stock that he or she also owns. How should the advisor best deal with this potential conflict of interest?

    a. He or she should not make the recommendation.
    b. He or she should make a negative recommendation.
    c. He or she should disclose the fact that he or she owns the stock while making the recommendation.
    d. He or she should make a positive recommendation and then sell the stock.

    ANS: C   DIF: 2   REF: p. 45   OBJ: TYPE: AP

24. How should a businessperson deal with a conflict of interest?

    a. Disclose it
    b. Avoid it
    c. Disclose it or avoid it
    d. Not worry about it

    ANS: C   DIF: 1   REF: p. 45   OBJ: TYPE: KN

25. During a meeting with government regulators, Nicole voluntarily points out a potential problem with a new drug her company is testing. Nicole has shown _____.

    a. honesty
    b. loyalty
    c. truthfulness
    d. integrity

    ANS: D   DIF: 2   REF: p. 45   OBJ: TYPE: AP

26. When a businessperson refuses to accept responsibility for mistakes, he or she is showing a lack of
    _____.
    a. integrity
    b. honesty
    c. truthfulness
    d. loyalty

    ANS: A   DIF: 1   REF: p. 45   OBJ: TYPE: KN

27. Bob takes responsibility for something his assistant failed to do. Bob has shown _____.
    a. integrity
    b. honesty
    c. truthfulness
    d. loyalty

    ANS: A   DIF: 1   REF: p. 45   OBJ: TYPE: KN

28. Two traits that are highly valued by employers and that are the most important qualities sought in job
    applicants are _____.
    a. honesty and loyalty
    b. honesty and integrity
    c. integrity and loyalty
    d. competence and commitment

    ANS: B   DIF: 2   REF: p. 45   OBJ: TYPE: KN

29. _____ goes beyond truthfulness.
    a. Honesty
    b. Loyalty
    c. Integrity
    d. Competence

    ANS: C   DIF: 1   REF: p. 45   OBJ: TYPE: KN

30. Whistleblowers _____.
    a. are demonstrating unethical behavior
    b. are acting in their own self-interest
    c. are placing ethical standards above personal self-interest
    d. are being disloyal

    ANS: C   DIF: 1   REF: p. 46   OBJ: TYPE: KN

31. Serena's boss tells her, in confidence, that Jade will be laid off when the company announces a round of job cuts next week. Afterwards, Jade asks Serena if there is any truth to the rumor of impending job cuts and if she knows anything about her status. What is Serena's ethical challenge?
    a. Conflict of interest
    b. Loyalty versus truth
    c. Honesty versus integrity
    d. Serena faces no ethical challenge.

    ANS: B   DIF: 2   REF: p. 46   OBJ: TYPE: AP

32. How many steps (or levels) are there in the development of a corporate culture that supports ethical decision making?
    a. One
    b. Two
    c. Three
    d. Four

    ANS: D   DIF: 1   REF: p. 47   OBJ: TYPE: KN

33. Development of a corporate culture to support business ethics occurs on each of the following levels EXCEPT _____.
    a. ethical leadership
    b. ethical awareness
    c. ethical success
    d. ethical reasoning

    ANS: C   DIF: 2   REF: p. 47   OBJ: TYPE: KN

34. Which of the following is the first step in the development of a corporate culture designed to support ethical behavior?
    a. Ethical leadership
    b. Ethical awareness
    c. Ethical reasoning
    d. Ethical action

    ANS: B   DIF: 2   REF: p. 47   OBJ: TYPE: KN

35. A formal statement that defines how the organization expects and requires employees to resolve ethical questions is _____.
    a. a code of conduct
    b. an organizational culture
    c. the Ethics Challenge
    d. an ethical environmental statement

    ANS: A   DIF: 2   REF: p. 48   OBJ: TYPE: KN

36. Which of the following can help to improve ethical reasoning?
    a. A code of conduct
    b. Practical training sessions
    c. Ethical environment statement
    d. Organization culture

    ANS: B   DIF: 1   REF: p. 48   OBJ: TYPE: KN

37. Ethical reasoning _____.
    a. is incorporated into the company's code of conduct
    b. helps resolve black and white ethical dilemmas
    c. helps resolve gray areas
    d. can be successfully taught in the classroom

    ANS: C   DIF: 2   REF: p. 48   OBJ: TYPE: KN

38. Games such as the Ethics Challenge can help to improve _____.
    a. ethical awareness
    b. ethical reasoning
    c. ethical leadership
    d. ethical action

    ANS: B   DIF: 2   REF: p. 49   OBJ: TYPE: AP

39. Macrohard, Inc. provides support for employees faced with ethical dilemmas. An ethics officer is available in the Human Resources Office or through an employee hotline. This is an example of _____.
    a. ethical leadership
    b. ethical awareness
    c. ethical action
    d. ethical reasoning

    ANS: C   DIF: 3   REF: p. 49   OBJ: TYPE: AP

40. A company hands out cards to employees designed to help them make ethical decisions. This is an example of _____.
    a. ethical leadership
    b. ethical awareness
    c. ethical action
    d. ethical reasoning

    ANS: C   DIF: 3   REF: p. 49   OBJ: TYPE: AP

41. When a firm strives to have each individual personally committed to the company's core values and be willing to base their actions on them, this is _____.
    a. ethical leadership
    b. ethical awareness
    c. ethical action
    d. ethical reasoning

    ANS: A   DIF: 2   REF: p. 49   OBJ: TYPE: KN

42. The sales manager decides to double each salesperson's monthly quota. What impact is this action likely to have on the company's ethical climate?
    a. It will improve.
    b. It will remain the same.
    c. It will deteriorate.
    d. It will initially deteriorate and then improve.

    ANS: C   DIF: 2   REF: p. 49   OBJ::   TYPE: AP

43. Development of a corporate culture to support business ethics happens on four levels. The foundation of an ethical climate is _____.
    a. ethical leadership
    b. ethical awareness
    c. ethical action
    d. ethical reasoning

    ANS: B   DIF: 2   REF: p. 47   OBJ: TYPE: KN

44. If employees believe that their company's ethics program is designed primarily to protect upper management from being blamed for any misconduct, how are they likely to respond?
    a. Their ethical standards will remain the same.
    b. Their ethical standards will improve.
    c. Their ethical standards will deteriorate.
    d. It is impossible to tell what will happen.

    ANS: C   DIF: 3   REF: p. 50   OBJ: TYPE: AP

45. Hi-Way Construction has five plant sites with each site employing about 300 employees. The general manager and several supervisors at the Gamma site were fired recently and face charges for bribery and for not using acceptable materials for several government contracts. Rather than close down the Gamma site, top management decides to take steps intended to create the correct ethical climate. They must begin with Hi-Way's code of conduct and use it to establish the basic level of _____.
    a. ethical leadership
    b. ethical awareness
    c. ethical action
    d. ethical compliance

    ANS: B   DIF: 3   REF: p. 47   OBJ: TYPE: AP

46. Hi-Way Construction has five plant sites with each site employing about 300 employees. The general manager and several supervisors at the Gamma site were fired recently and face charges for bribery and for not using acceptable materials for several government contracts. Rather than close down the Gamma site, top management decides to take steps intended to create the correct ethical climate.

Mike was an employee at Gamma site for ten years. Though Mike worried about his family's security should he lose his job, Mike went to the government authorities and informed them of the faulty construction. Mike's action is called _____.

  a. ethical compliance
  b. good intentions
  c. whistleblowing
  d. ethical allegations

ANS: C   DIF: 3   REF: p. 46   OBJ: TYPE: AP

47. Historically, which of the following were considered a measure for evaluating a firm's social performance?

  a. Employment opportunities
  b. Product safety standards
  c. Industrial safety standards
  d. Pollution control standards

ANS: A   DIF: 1   REF: p. 51   OBJ: TYPE: KN

48. Which of the following would be least likely to be a factor in evaluating a firm's social performance?

  a. Providing a safe, healthy workplace
  b. Respecting the cultural diversity of employees
  c. Holding company-sponsored social events
  d. Producing safe, high-quality products

ANS: C   DIF: 1   REF: p. 51   OBJ: TYPE: AP

49. A formal procedure that identifies and evaluates all company activities relating to social issues is known as a(n) _____.

  a. ethical profile
  b. social audit
  c. social inventory
  d. mission analysis

ANS: B   DIF: 1   REF: p. 51   OBJ: TYPE: KN

50. Which of the following organizations would be least likely to conduct a social audit of a business?

  a. The firm itself
  b. Religious organizations
  c. Environmental organizations
  d. The government

ANS: D   DIF: 2   REF: p. 51   OBJ: TYPE: AP

51. The Wright Tire Co. uses a company-wide team of employees to identify all company activities related to social issues, to report on how the firm is responding to those issues, and to evaluate how effectively the firm has met those issues. The Wright Tire team is conducting a(n) _____.
    a. environmental impact audit
    b. government-mandated audit
    c. internal accounting audit
    d. social audit

    ANS: D   DIF: 2   REF: p. 51   OBJ: TYPE: AP

52. All of the following issues deal with the social responsibility of business to the general public EXCEPT _____.
    a. acid rain
    b. building profitable products
    c. building safe products
    d. saving energy

    ANS: B   DIF: 1   REF: p. 52   OBJ: TYPE: KN

53. Three health-related issues that relate to business responsibilities are _____.
    a. smoking, acid rain, and AIDS
    b. alcohol abuse, AIDS, and pollution
    c. AIDS, smoking, and alcohol abuse
    d. pollution, the greenhouse effect, and acid rain

    ANS: C   DIF: 2   REF: p. 52-53   OBJ: TYPE: KN

54. Pollution _____.
    a. is of concern only to business
    b. can only occur in forests or oceans
    c. primarily occurs as the result of natural forces
    d. is the destroying or tainting of a natural environment

    ANS: D   DIF: 1   REF: p. 53   OBJ: TYPE: KN

55. Which of the following statements about acid rain is UNTRUE?
    a. Wind can carry the sulfur created from burning fossil fuels all over the world.
    b. Acid rain can pollute ground water.
    c. Acid rain kills fish and trees.
    d. Countries around the world have come to an agreement about what should be done about acid rain.

    ANS: D   DIF: 2   REF: p. 53   OBJ: TYPE: KN

56. Reprocessing used materials so they can be reused is known as _____.
    a. rotation
    b. recycling
    c. ecology
    d. conversion

    ANS: B   DIF: 1   REF: p. 54   OBJ: TYPE: KN

57. AIDS represents a challenge to business because _____.
    a. sick people make poor employees
    b. you can get the disease from someone else's coffee
    c. many people have the disease without knowing it
    d. it makes good positive public relations a difficult assignment

    ANS: C   DIF: 2   REF: p. 53   OBJ: TYPE: KN

58. The doctrine of "the right to be heard" as put forth by former President John F. Kennedy in his speech on consumer rights would be best reflected by _____.
    a. product safety
    b. disclosure of true annual interest rates on revolving charge accounts
    c. disclosure of sodium content on labels of processed foods
    d. a firm establishing a consumer appeals board

    ANS: D   DIF: 3   REF: p. 59   OBJ: TYPE: AP

59. The public demand that businesses give proper consideration to consumer wants and needs in making its decisions is known as _____.
    a. consumerism
    b. political activism
    c. conservation
    d. ethics

    ANS: A   DIF: 1   REF: p. 57   OBJ: TYPE: KN

60. Consumerism _____.
    a. has become a major social and economic movement
    b. is concerned with equal employment opportunity
    c. as a movement has had little effect on society
    d. is a movement basically concerned with industrial safety

    ANS: A   DIF: 2   REF: p. 57   OBJ: TYPE: KN

61. All of the following are current social issues related to business's responsibilities to employees EXCEPT _____.
    a. sexual harassment
    b. discrimination against older workers
    c. discrimination against workers who earn minimum wage
    d. quality of life issues

    ANS: C   DIF: 2   REF: p. 59   OBJ: TYPE: KN

62. Star Corporation allowed Tamika to take 60 days off from work to care for her seriously ill child. Tamika's time off work falls within the realm of _____.
    a. sick leave
    b. maternity leave
    c. professional leave
    d. family leave

    ANS: D   DIF: 2   REF: p. 61   OBJ: TYPE: AP

63. All of the following groups are specifically identified by federal equal employment opportunity laws EXCEPT _____.
    a. Vietnam-era veterans
    b. obese persons
    c. handicapped persons
    d. persons over age 40

    ANS: B   DIF: 2   REF: p. 62   OBJ: TYPE: KN

64. The Age Discrimination in Employment Act and its amendments protect workers _____.
    a. between the ages of 45 and 65
    b. aged 40 and over
    c. between the ages of 40 and 70
    d. aged 65 and older

    ANS: B   DIF: 2   REF: p. 62   OBJ: TYPE: KN

65. According to many experts, the next round of equal employment opportunity protection will extend to _____.
    a. genetics
    b. obesity
    c. tobacco use
    d. alcohol use

    ANS: A   DIF: 1   REF: p. 62   OBJ: TYPE: KN

66. Approximately what percentage of managerial and professional positions is currently held by women?
    a. About 50 percent
    b. About 33 percent
    c. About 25 percent
    d. Less than 25 percent

ANS: A   DIF: 2   REF: p. 64   OBJ: TYPE: KN

67. Which of the following would not be included in an effective sexual harassment prevention program?
    a. Developing a complaint procedure employees can follow
    b. Creating an atmosphere in which harassed employees can come forward
    c. Exempting employees in certain job classifications
    d. Punishing those reporting sexual harassment

ANS: D   DIF: 3   REF: p. 63-64   OBJ: TYPE: KN

68. Which federal agency is designed to protect investors from the financial misdeeds of companies?
    a. The Federal Trade Commission (FTC)
    b. The Justice Department
    c. The Securities and Exchange Commission (SEC)
    d. The Equal Employment Opportunity Commission (EEOC)

ANS: C   DIF: 1   REF: p. 64   OBJ: TYPE: KN

69. Zardoz, Inc. uses questionable accounting practices to artificially inflate its profits. Which federal agency might become involved?
    a. The Federal Trade Commission (FTC)
    b. The Justice Department
    c. The Securities and Exchange Commission (SEC)
    d. The Equal Employment Opportunity Commission (EEOC)

ANS: C   DIF: 1   REF: p. 64   OBJ: TYPE: KN

70. Companies that adhere to high ethical standards _____.
    a. often make poorer investments in the long run
    b. often make better investments in the long run
    c. always make higher profits
    d. always make lower profits

ANS: B   DIF: 2   REF: p. 64   OBJ: TYPE: AP

71. Which of the following is an ethical issue dealing with a company and its direct relations with investors and the financial community?
    a. Questionable accounting practices
    b. Being insensitive to cultural differences among employees
    c. Forcing older workers to retire
    d. Paying women less than men

    ANS: A   DIF: 1   REF: p. 64   OBJ: TYPE: KN

72. Businesses have responsibilities
    a. only to investors.
    c. to investors, customers, and employees.
    b. to investors and customers.
    d. to investors, customers, employees, and society.

    ANS: D   DIF: 1   REF: p. 41   OBJ: TYPE: KN

73. Business ethics begins
    a. with the individual employee.
    b. with the government.
    c. with a code of conduct.
    d. with a firm's customers.

    ANS: A   DIF: 2   REF: p. 41   OBJ: TYPE: AP

74. According to recent surveys, what percentage of Americans admire business executives?
    a. Less than 25%.
    b. Between 25% and 50%.
    c. Between 50% and 75%.
    d. More than 75%.

    ANS: A   DIF: 1   REF: p. 41   OBJ: TYPE: KN

75. Approximately _____ percent of companies have set up ethics standards and codes of conducts.
    a. 25
    b. 50
    c. 75
    d. virtually 100

    ANS: C   DIF: 1   REF: p. 42   OBJ: TYPE: KN

76. The minimum requirements for an ethics compliance program includes all of the following except
    a. high-level personnel responsible for compliance.
    b. substantial discretionary authority given to compliance officials.
    c. establishment of systems to monitor, audit, and report misconduct.
    d. consistent enforcement of ethical codes.

    ANS: B   DIF: 3   REF: 42   OBJ: TYPE: KN

77. Each year, U.S. organizations lose _____ to fraud.
    a. less than $100 million
    b. between $100 million and $300 million
    c. between $300 million and $500 million
    d. more than $500 million

    ANS: C   DIF: 1   REF: p. 43   OBJ: TYPE: KN

78. What percentage of American workers knew of, or suspected unethical behavior at their companies?
    a. Around one-quarter.
    b. Around one-third.
    c. Around one-half.
    d. Around three-quarters.

    ANS: B   DIF: 2   REF: p. 43   OBJ: TYPE: KN

79. Under the Sarbanes-Oxley Act _____ must personally certify the validity of a company's financial statements.
    a. the CEO
    b. the chief financial officer
    c. neither the CEO nor chief financial officer.
    d. both the CEO and chief financial officer

    ANS: D   DIF: 1   REF: p. 42   OBJ: TYPE: KN

80. If an individual looks out only for his or her own interests when making decisions, he or she is at the _____stage of ethical development
    a. pre-conventional
    b. conventional
    c. post-conventional
    d. concentrations

    ANS: A   DIF: 1   REF: p. 44   OBJ: TYPE: KN

81. Even though his company doesn't specifically have a policy forbidding it, Sean doesn't use his office computer for personal business. Sean is at the _____ stage of ethical development.
    a. pre-conventional
    b. conventional
    c. post-conventional
    d. concentrations

    ANS: B   DIF: 2   REF: p. 44   OBJ: TYPE: AP

82. If an individual follows personal principles for resolving ethical delimmas and considers personal, group and societal interests, he or she is at the _____ stage of ethical development.
    a. pre-conventional
    b. conventional
    c. post-conventional
    d. concentrations

    ANS: C   DIF: 1   REF: p. 44   OBJ: TYPE: KN

83. A pharmaceutical company has been asked by a developing nation to cut the price of a drug in half to make it more affordable. This price cut, however, means that the pharmaceutical company will be selling the drug at a loss. What ethical dilemma does the company face?
    a. A conflict of interest.
    b. A question of integrity.
    c. A question of loyalty.
    d. It faces no dilemma.

    ANS: A   DIF: 2   REF: p. 44   OBJ: TYPE: AP

84. Harold knows of a defect in a product his company sells. He will disclose the defect but only if the customer specifically asks about it. Harold's _____ could be called into question.
    a. loyalty
    b. truthfulness
    c. integrity
    d. whistleblowing

    ANS: C   DIF: 2   REF: p. 45   OBJ: TYPE: AP

85. Mica learns that her company is secretly discharging untreated waste into the city sewer systems. She informs the local EPA office. All of the following describe Mica's ethical situation except
    a. she is acting as a whistleblower.
    b. she has a conflict of interest.
    c. she is showing integrity.
    d. she is showing loyalty.

    ANS: D   DIF: 2   REF: p. 45-46   OBJ: TYPE: AP

86. One of the best measures of _____ is how well a company focuses on the welfare of its investors, customers, and employees and how well it performs in the long-run.
    a. ethical awareness
    b. ethical reasoning
    c. ethical action
    d. ethical leadership

    ANS: D   DIF: 1   REF: p. 50   OBJ: TYPE: KN

87. Providing the necessary tools for employees to evaluate options and arrive at suitable decisions is called
    a. ethical awareness.
    b. ethical reasoning.
    c. ethical action.
    d. ethical leadership.

ANS: B   DIF: 1   REF: p. 48   OBJ: TYPE: KN

88. Providing structures and approaches will help to foster _____ among employees.
    a. ethical awareness
    b. ethical reasoning
    c. ethical action
    d. ethical leadership

ANS: C   DIF: 1   REF: p. 49   OBJ: TYPE: KN

89. After meeting with employees, a manager realizes that she has set performance goals unrealistically high for her department's employees. If she makes employee performance goals more realistic, what will likely happen to the department's ethical climate?
    a. It will improve.
    b. It will stay about the same
    c. It will deteriorate.
    d. It will deteriorate initially and then improve.

ANS: A   DIF: 2   REF: p. 49   OBJ: TYPE: AP

90. A group urges its members not to buy the products of a particular firm because of the firm's employment practices. The group is conducting a
    a. green marketing campaign.
    b. boycott.
    c. social audit.
    d. mission analysis.

ANS: B   DIF: 1   REF: p. 51   OBJ: TYPE: AP

91. A strategy that promotes environmentally friendly products and production methods is called
    a. consumerism.
    b. recycling.
    c. ethical awareness.
    d. green marketing.

ANS: D   DIF: 1   REF: p. 54   OBJ: TYPE: KN

92. Alcohol ads appearing in magazines
    a.   are illegal.
    b.   shouldn't appear as though the company is encouraging underage drinking.
    c.   are unethical.
    d.   cannot contain color.

    ANS: B   DIF: 2   REF: p. 53   OBJ: TYPE: KN

93. What percentage of corn and soybeans currently grown in the U.S. have been genetically engineered?
    a.   Less than 25 percent.
    b.   Between one-third and one-half.
    c.   Between one-half and three-quarters.
    d.   More than three-quarters.

    ANS: B   DIF: 1   REF: p. 55   OBJ: TYPE: KN

94. The U.S. is currently in a trade dispute with _____ over genetically engineered agricultural products.
    a.   the European Union
    b.   the United Nations
    c.   Canada
    d.   Japan

    ANS: A   DIF: 1   REF: p. 55   OBJ: TYPE: KN

95. In the U.S. most new jobs require _____ and the gap between the highest-paid and lowest-paid workers has been _____.
    a.   high-school degrees only; increasing.
    b.   high-school degrees only; decreasing.
    c.   college-educated workers; increasing.
    d.   college-education workers; decreasing.

    ANS: C   DIF: 2   REF: p. 56   OBJ: TYPE: KN

96. College graduates, on average, earn _____ more than high school graduates.
    a.   between one-quarter and one-half
    b.   between one-half and three-quarters
    c.   between three-quarters and 100 percent
    d.   over 100 percent

    ANS: B   DIF: 2   REF: p. 56   OBJ: TYPE: KN

97. All of the following are examples of corporate philanthropy EXCEPT
   a. supporting the local public radio station.
   b. sponsoring a Red Cross blood drive.
   c. paying local property taxes.
   d. giving employees release time to participate in volunteer activities.

   ANS: C   DIF: 2   REF: p. 56   OBJ: TYPE: AP

98. All of the following are business responsibilities to customers EXCEPT
   a. the right to be heard.
   b. the right to be safe.
   c. the right to be informed.
   d. the right to low prices.

   ANS: D   DIF: 1   REF: p. 57   OBJ: TYPE: KN

99. Which federal agency is responsible for ensuring the safety of prescription drugs?
   a. The FDA.
   b. The FTC.
   c. The SEC.
   d. The FCC.

   ANS: A   DIF: 1   REF: p. 58   OBJ: TYPE: KN

100. Which federal agency is responsible for setting workplace health and safety standards?
   a. The FTC.
   b. The FDA.
   c. OSHA.
   d. The FCC.

   ANS: C   DIF: 1   REF: p. 60   OBJ: TYPE: KN

101. _____ producing industries have the highest number of worker injuries and illnesses (per 100 workers) and in recent years this rate has been _____.
   a. Goods; rising.
   b. Goods; falling
   c. Service; rising.
   d. Service; falling

   ANS: B   DIF: 2   REF: p. 61   OBJ: TYPE: AP

True/False

1. Social and ethical issues affect every company.

   ANS: T   DIF: 1   REF: p. 40   OBJ: TYPE: KN

2. Organizations wishing to prosper cannot do so without considering business ethics.

   ANS: T   DIF: 1   REF: p. 40   OBJ: TYPE: KN

3. Halting the production and sale of a potentially dangerous product, even if it hurts profits, is an example of ethical behavior.

    ANS: T   DIF: 2   REF: p. 41   OBJ: TYPE: AP

4. Putting profits ahead of safety is an example of reasonable business behavior.

    ANS: F   DIF: 2   REF: p. 41   OBJ: TYPE: AP

5. Businesses must find a balance between doing what is right and doing what is profitable.

    ANS: T   DIF: 1   REF: p. 41   OBJ: TYPE: KN

6. Setting appropriate ethical standards is a fairly straightforward task for most managers.

    ANS: F   DIF: 1   REF: p. 41   OBJ: TYPE: KN

7. All companies consistently set and meet high ethical standards.

    ANS: F   DIF: 1   REF: p. 41   OBJ: TYPE: KN

8. With training, both managers and operative employees learn that deciding what is right or wrong in a given situation is a clear-cut choice.

    ANS: F   DIF: 1   REF: p. 41   OBJ: TYPE: KN

9. Individual employees have little influence over ethical expectations and behavior.

    ANS: F   DIF: 1   REF: p. 41   OBJ: TYPE: KN

10. A single employee acting ethically will have little influence on his or her co-workers.

    ANS: F   DIF: 2   REF: p. 41   OBJ: TYPE: AP

11. Small companies appear to experience the highest-cost abuses of ethics.

    ANS: T   DIF: 1   REF: p. 43   OBJ: TYPE: KN

12. Technology has expanded the range and impact of unethical behavior.

    ANS: T   DIF: 1   REF: p. 43   OBJ: TYPE: KN

13. Insiders are responsible for less than half of all thefts of intellectual property.

    ANS: F   DIF: 2   REF: p. 43   OBJ: TYPE: KN

14. Some employees rationalize questionable or unethical behavior by saying, "everyone does it."

    ANS: T   DIF: 1   REF: p. 44   OBJ: TYPE: KN

15. Employees can avoid many ethical conflicts on the job by being truthful as well as being loyal to their companies.

    ANS: F   DIF: 1   REF: p. 46   OBJ: TYPE: KN

16. Some people engage in activities that are contrary to their personal and moral values because they feel pressured on their jobs.

    ANS: T   DIF: 1   REF: p. 44   OBJ: TYPE: KN

17. Pre-conventional behavior is the term used to describe an employee's disclosure to the media or government authorities of illegal, immoral, or unethical practices of the organization.

    ANS: F   DIF: 1   REF: p. 44   OBJ: TYPE: KN

18. An employee refrains from "padding" his or her expense account because if the employee is caught, he or she will be fired. This person is at the conventional stage of moral and ethical development.

    ANS: F   DIF: 2   REF: p. 44   OBJ: TYPE: AP

19. An employee refrains from "padding" his or her expense account because it hurts the company. This person is at the conventional stage of moral and ethical development.

    ANS: T   DIF: 2   REF: p. 44   OBJ: TYPE: AP

20. A person takes actions that will help his or her company, as well as protect the environment. This person is at the post-conventional stage of moral and ethical development.

    ANS: T   DIF: 2   REF: p. 44   OBJ: TYPE: AP

21. Pre-conventional behavior is the term for an employee's disclosure to the media or government authorities of illegal, immoral, or unethical practices of the organization.

    ANS: F   DIF: 1   REF: p. 44   OBJ: TYPE: KN

22. It is not easy to distinguish between right and wrong in many business situations.

    ANS: T   DIF: 1   REF: p. 44   OBJ: TYPE: KN

23. On-the-job ethical dilemmas are very rare, but can be quite significant.

    ANS: F   DIF: 2   REF: p. 44   OBJ: TYPE: AP

24. An ad agency representing two companies that compete with one another has an obvious conflict of interest.

    ANS: T   DIF: 2   REF: p. 45   OBJ: TYPE: AP

25. A conflict of interest exists when a person is faced with a decision in which an action will harm one individual or group while benefiting another.

    ANS: T   DIF: 1   REF: p. 45   OBJ: TYPE: KN

26. A real estate agent can represent both the buyer and seller without any conflict of interest.

    ANS: F   DIF: 2   REF: p. 45   OBJ: TYPE: AP

27. The only safe way to handle a potential conflict of interest is to avoid situations in which one might occur.

    ANS: F   DIF: 1   REF: p. 45   OBJ: TYPE: KN

28. Integrity goes beyond truthfulness.

    ANS: T   DIF: 1   REF: p. 45   OBJ: TYPE: KN

29. The personality traits most sought in job applicants are loyalty and truthfulness.

    ANS: F   DIF: 2   REF: p. 45   OBJ: TYPE: KN

30. A CEO tells shareholders that the accounting department intentionally inflated profits for the past five years. However, since she didn't know about the misdeed, she is not responsible. The CEO is showing integrity.

    ANS: F   DIF: 2   REF: p. 45   OBJ: TYPE: AP

31. Employers expect employees to generally act in the best interests of the organization.

    ANS: T   DIF: 2   REF: p. 46   OBJ: TYPE: AP

32. Employees should always be loyal, regardless of the situation.

    ANS: F   DIF: 2   REF: p. 46   OBJ: TYPE: AP

33. An employee "goes public" with evidence of improper actions by his or her employer. This employee is a whistleblower.

    ANS: T   DIF: 2   REF: p. 46   OBJ: TYPE: AP

34. Whistleblowers are always acting out of self-interest.

    ANS: F   DIF: 2   REF: p. 46   OBJ: TYPE: AP

35. Loyal employees are never whistleblowers.

    ANS: F   DIF: 2   REF: p. 46   OBJ: TYPE: AP

36. Most ethical lapses in business reflect the values of the firm's corporate culture.

    ANS: F   DIF: 1   REF: p. 47   OBJ: TYPE: KN

37. Choices made by individuals are strongly influenced by the standards of conduct established within the organizations where people work.

    ANS: T   DIF: 1   REF: p. 47   OBJ: TYPE: KN

38. Development of a corporate culture to support business ethics occurs on the following levels: ethical climate, ethical awareness, ethical reasoning, and ethical action.

    ANS: F   DIF: 1   REF: p. 47   OBJ: TYPE: KN

39. The development of a corporate culture to support business ethics occurs on four levels.

    ANS: T   DIF: 1   REF: p. 47   OBJ: TYPE: KN

40. A code of conduct is an informal proposal that suggests how the organization expects employees to make decisions.

    ANS: F   DIF: 1   REF: p. 48   OBJ: TYPE: KN

41. In addition to codes of conduct and ethical training, firms should provide structures and approaches that allow decisions to be turned into ethical actions.

    ANS: T   DIF: 1   REF: p. 48   OBJ: TYPE: KN

42. One of the first steps in the establishment of sound business ethics is to help employees identify ethical problems when they occur.

    ANS: T   DIF: 1   REF: p. 47   OBJ: TYPE: KN

43. Formally stating that employees must not discriminate on the basis of race, gender or age in their dealings with customers is something that could be found in a company code of conduct.

    ANS: T   DIF: 2   REF: p. 48   OBJ: TYPE: AP

44. A code of conduct rarely goes beyond stating the rules, laws, and regulations employees are expected to follow.

    ANS: F   DIF: 1   REF: p. 48   OBJ: TYPE: KN

45. Many ethical dilemmas involve gray areas that may require individuals to sort through several courses of actions, each with its own set of consequences.

    ANS: T   DIF: 1   REF: p. 48   OBJ: TYPE: KN

46. When it comes to properly resolving ethical dilemmas, most experts believe that there is no substitute for practical experience.

    ANS: T   DIF: 2   REF: p. 48   OBJ: TYPE: AP

47. A manager doubles employee performance goals every quarter. This action will likely increase the amount of ethically questionable actions by employees.

    ANS: T   DIF: 2   REF: p. 49   OBJ: TYPE: AP

48. If managers and supervisors fail to show ethical leadership, it is unrealistic to expect employees to behave ethically.

    ANS: T   DIF: 1   REF: p. 49   OBJ: TYPE: KN

49. Social responsibility is management's acceptance of the obligation to consider societal well-being and consumer satisfaction as being equally important as profit when evaluating the firm's performance.

    ANS: T   DIF: 1   REF: p. 51   OBJ: TYPE: KN

50. A social audit is used to measure a company's social responsibility performance.

    ANS: T   DIF: 1   REF: p. 51   OBJ: TYPE: KN

51. Outside groups often conduct their own evaluations of businesses. Firms typically ignore these reports in favor of internal evaluations.

    ANS: F   DIF: 2   REF: p. 51   OBJ: TYPE: AP

52. Social audits conducted internally are of little value because they are always biased in favor of the company.

    ANS: F   DIF: 2   REF: p. 51   OBJ: TYPE: AP

53. In the past, a firm's social responsibility has usually been evaluated on the basis of its contribution to employment opportunities.

    ANS: T   DIF: 1   REF: p. 51   OBJ: TYPE: KN

54. Some groups organize boycotts of companies they find to be socially irresponsible.

    ANS: T   DIF: 1   REF: p. 51   OBJ: TYPE: KN

55. Alcohol companies have been criticized for targeting teens as well as members of ethnic and racial minorities in their advertising.

    ANS: T   DIF: 1   REF: p. 52   OBJ: TYPE: KN

56. Corporate philanthropy is the notion that businesses should give back to the communities where they earn their profits.

    ANS: T   DIF: 1   REF: p. 56   OBJ: TYPE: KN

57. Helping employees stop smoking is an example of a social responsibility revolving around public health.

ANS: T   DIF: 1   REF: p. 53   OBJ: TYPE: AP

58. Most consumers view alcohol advertising as appropriate, so long as it isn't aimed at teenagers.

ANS: F   DIF: 1   REF: p. 53   OBJ: TYPE: KN

59. Environmental issues are becoming less important concerns of the public.

ANS: F   DIF: 1   REF: p. 53   OBJ: TYPE: KN

60. A number of major employers have come out in favor of preemployment AIDS testing.

ANS: F   DIF: 1   REF: p. 53   OBJ: TYPE: KN

61. Recycling will provide a substantial portion of the materials required in manufacturing businesses.

ANS: T   DIF: 1   REF: p. 54   OBJ: TYPE: KN

62. Pollution is the major ecological problem today.

ANS: T   DIF: 1   REF: p. 53   OBJ: TYPE: KN

63. Consumerism is the concept that business must give consideration to employee wants and needs.

ANS: F   DIF: 1   REF: p. 57   OBJ: TYPE: KN

64. Corporate philanthropy describes the work of not-for-profit organizations in serving the public good.

ANS: F   DIF: 1   REF: p. 56   OBJ: TYPE: KN

65. The area of business responsibilities to company personnel is increasing.

ANS: T   DIF: 1   REF: p. 59   OBJ: TYPE: KN

66. The Equal Employment Opportunity Commission (EEOC) was established to police business compliance with the Civil Rights Act.

ANS: T   DIF: 1   REF: p. 62   OBJ: TYPE: KN

67. The rate of workplace injuries and illnesses has risen in recent years.

ANS: F   DIF: 2   REF: p. 61   OBJ: TYPE: AP

68. Investors are generally unconcerned with whether a company is behaving ethically; instead, they only focus on whether or not it is making a profit.

ANS: F   DIF: 1   REF: p. 64   OBJ: TYPE: KN

69. The principal federal agency responsible for protecting investors from financial misdeeds is the Federal Trade Commission.

ANS: F   DIF: 1   REF: p. 64   OBJ: TYPE: KN

70. Companies who fail to follow high ethical standards often see their stock prices drop.

ANS: T   DIF: 2   REF: p. 64   OBJ: TYPE: AP

71. The percentage of people who say that they admire business executives has dropped sharply in recent years.

ANS: T   DIF: 1   REF: p. 41   OBJ: TYPE: KN

72. Fundamentally, a business is responsible only to its customers and investors.

    ANS: F   DIF: 2   REF: p. 41   OBJ: TYPE: AP

73. The Sarbanes-Oxley Act requires that each member of a firm's accounting department certify the truthfulness of financial statements.

    ANS: F   DIF: 2   REF: p. 42   OBJ: TYPE: KN

74. Even though her company doesn't have a policy prohibiting it, Maria wouldn't make personal long-distance calls at work because it costs the company money. Maria is in the conventional stage of ethical development.

    ANS: T   DIF: 3   REF: p. 44   OBJ: TYPE: AP

75. Individuals at the same stage of ethical development always adopt the same style for resolving ethical dilemmas.

    ANS: F   DIF: 2   REF: p. 44   OBJ: TYPE: KN

76. In the real world of business, loyalty and honesty rarely conflict with one another.

    ANS: F   DIF: 1   REF: p. 46   OBJ: TYPE: KN

77. The first stage in the development of ethical environment is ethical awareness.

    ANS: T   DIF: 1   REF: p. 47   OBJ: TYPE: KN

78. A code of conduct is part of the ethical awareness stage of ethical development.

    ANS: T   DIF: 1   REF: p. 48   OBJ: TYPE: KN

79. Providing employees tools to help them evaluate options and arrive at suitable decisions is part of the ethical action stage of ethical development.

    ANS: F   DIF: 1   REF: p. 48   OBJ: TYPE: KN

80. One of the best measures of ethical leadership is how well a company performs in the long-run.

    ANS: T   DIF: 1   REF: p. 50   OBJ: TYPE: KN

81. The primary social responsibility of a company is to the general public.

    ANS: F   DIF: 1   REF: p. 51   OBJ: TYPE: KN

82. Companies have wide latitude when it comes to the use of environmental terms in advertising and marketing.

    ANS: F   DIF: 1   REF: p. 54   OBJ: TYPE: KN

83. Experience shows that consumers are willing to pay higher prices for so-called green products.

    ANS: F   DIF: 2   REF: p. 54   OBJ: TYPE: KN

84. The U.S. is currently in a trade dispute with the European Union over genetically engineered food products.

    ANS: T   DIF: 1   REF: p. 55   OBJ: TYPE: KN

85. Paying taxes is an example of corporate philanthropy.

    ANS: F   DIF: 2   REF: p. 56   OBJ: TYPE: AP

86. In developed economies like that of the U.S., most new jobs require college degrees and/or advanced technical training.

    ANS: T   DIF: 1   REF: p. 56   OBJ: TYPE: KN

87. The gap between what workers with college degrees earn and what those with high school degrees earn has gotten smaller in recent years.

    ANS: F   DIF: 1   REF: p. 56   OBJ: TYPE: KN

88. One of the goals of consumerism is for consumers to have access to enough education and production information to make responsible purchase decisions.

    ANS: T   DIF: 1   REF: p. 57   OBJ: TYPE: KN